This edition published 2004 by Jeremy Satherley, Myrtle
23 The Tenters, Holbeach, Lincolnshire PE12 7A

Printed by Welland Print Limited, West Marsh Road, Spaldir

ISBN 0-9548731-0-6

--------o0o--------

To my wife, Barbara.

Also to members of the late Mr Eric Lane's family: Mrs Alice Angell Everard,
Mrs Judith Angell Lane Gregory, and Mr Thomas Ernest Lane, whose close interest in this work
throughout was an enormous encouragement.

- **Front cover shows the sign designed and painted for Holbeach by Crispin Taylor in 1984.**

Introduction

'A neat little town' was how William Cobbett described Holbeach when he passed through it on his *Rural Rides* of 1830, and happily it continues to give that first impression to a newcomer today.

On a pleasant summer evening in Church Street, work has finished for the day. As the All Saints tower clock finishes striking the hour, Tiggy the rotund, mottled cat has just been turned out of the Library until morning, and the hedgerow of flowering currant nearby gives off its heady aroma. A remaining shopper, ice cream from Laddies in hand, sits on a churchyard bench and looks up appreciatively at the flower baskets provided by the 'Pride in Holbeach' project, burgeoning with petunias and other summer flowers, and swaying gently from iron posts and shop fronts.

Around the corner in High Street, Heavy Metal music can be heard. The younger generation are beginning to appear, drawing up at the kerbside in customised Novas and Escorts thumping with parcel-shelf bass notes, to sample the wares of the kebab houses before planning their night out.

A mixture of old and new, not unfamiliar to countless market towns around Britain. But Holbeach has its own unique story to tell. Of how it originated from unsuitable surroundings to become important enough for a sizable parish church and market, early on in its history. Of how it bred some remarkable characters of academic, political and sporting persuasion, some of national importance, several of world-class ability. And how it has formed the setting for pranks and plots large and small, sacrilegious and anti-political.

All this has endowed the town with a special character, one that its traditional layout and historic buildings help us to appreciate as we turn each corner. I hope therefore that the following pages —an attempt to capture a fuller history between two covers— will help to put a perspective on that character.

Jeremy Satherley
The Tenters, Holbeach
2004.

Contents

Chapter 1	**Beginnings** –the unusual landscape, Roman and Saxon to Medieval, and early land reclamation.	**3**
Chapter 2	**All Saints Church** –origins, building, architectural features, customs, tithes, its 'Daughter Churches'.	**10**
Chapter 3	**The Living Past** –features of Holbeach past and present, including the Holbeach River, well-known houses, inns and monuments.	**21**
Chapter 4	**Other Churches** –Methodist, Baptist, Congregationalist, Roman Catholic.	**43**
Chapter 5	**Agricultural Development** –from 16th century to the present, a struggle for survival leading to successful specialisation.	**49**
Chapter 6	**Life in the 19th Century** –living conditions, transport services, local events and royal celebrations.	**62**
Chapter 7	**A Bottle of Gin for a Railway Share** –the coming of the railway, description of station life and eventual decline.	**71**
Chapter 8	**Wartime Holbeach** –town life in WW1 and WW2.	**79**
Chapter 9	**Educating Holbeach** –from the origins of The George Farmer Free School to the William Stukeley Church of England Primary and The George Farmer Technology College.	**97**
Chapter 10	**Notables and Characters** –describing some of the famous or well-known people from Holbeach.	**112**
Chapter 11	**Shops and Services: Then and Now** –the many establishments that have served Holbeach over the last two centuries.	**139**
Chapter 12	**Observations on Industry** –milling, ironfounding, rope-making, ketchup manufacture, agricultural implements and other light industry.	**166**
Chapter 13	**Sporting Holbeach** –teams, clubs and special individuals who have put Holbeach on the map.	**175**
Chapter 14	**It Happened Like This** –Holbeach tales of which to be proud, ashamed or amused.	**192**
Chapter 15	**Still Making History** –housing, Holbeach Hospital, the Conservation Area, facilities.	**205**

Acknowledgements

I am most grateful to the following for their willing help and co-operation:

Mr Mike Almond, Head Teacher, Holbeach Cty Primary School.
Mr David and Mrs Val Arnold
Mr David Baker
Mr J W Belsham
Mr J Biggadike, Conservation Officer, South Holland District Cl.
Mrs Elizabeth Boardman, St Hilda's College, Oxford
Mr Frank and the late Mrs Dorothy Bradley
Mrs Patricia Bryant
Mr Kevin Broughton
Mr Tim Burges
Mr Joe Cade
Mr Geoff Capes
Mrs Beryl Clay
Mr John and Mrs Freda Coley
Mr Derick and Mrs Norma Cook
Mr Derek Coward
Mrs Ivy Coward
Mr Peter Coupland
Mrs Sue Crowden, The George Farmer Technology College.
Mrs Ruth Crowson
Mr Peter Cunnington
Mrs E Dixon-Spain
Mr John Elms
Mrs Alice Angell Everard
The late Mrs Ena Fensom
The late Mr Leslie and Mrs Jean Fensom
Mr Cliff Foster
Mr Bruce French
Mr David Gray
Mrs Ann Green
Mrs Judith Angell Lane Gregory
Mr John Hall
Mrs Ivy Hargraves
Mrs Pat Harland
Mr Terry and Mrs Jill Harrington
Mr David Harrisson
Mr Andrew Hawkins
Holbeach Parish Council
Mrs Audrey Holvey
Mr Len Jackson
Mrs Yvette Jacobson
Mr Colin Johnson
Mr David Jones
Mr Tal Jones
Mr Derek and Mrs Nellie Ladbrook
The late Mr Eric Lane
Mr Thomas Ernest Lane
Mr David Lefley
Mr Arthur Leonard
The late Mr Norman Leverett
Mr Patrick Limming
Mr Les Martin
Mr Ronald Matson
Mr Dennis Mashford
Mrs Olive Mitchell
Mrs Mary Mossop
Mr John Onyett
Mr Brian and Mrs Jenny Paul
Mr and Mrs Nick Pogson
Mr and Mrs John Pearl
Mr Roy Pratt
Mrs Sally Reddin
Mr W Rix
Mr Frank Sauntson
Mr Clifford and Mrs Doreen Secker
Mrs Jackie Sheldrake
Mr Peter Shepherd

Mrs Margaret Skelton
Mr Jim and Mrs Ena Sleaford
Mr Bryan Stamp
Mr John D Taylor, CBE
Mr Roger Taylor
Mr Alan Thacker
Mr Richard Thompson
Mr Robin Thorpe
Mr David Tinn
Sister Veronica, Holbeach RC Church
Mr Paul Walker
Mrs Ethel Whitehurst
The late Mrs Anne Woolley
Mr Tony and Mrs Jenny Worth.

Much useful information was also provided by:

The writings of Barbara Hitchings in the 1960s and 70s.

Holbeach & Spalding Libraries

South Holland Planning & Services Department.

The Library of the Spalding Gentleman's Society.

Document entitled: *Archaeological Implications of the reappraisal of Holbeach Conservation Area, Lincolnshire (HCA97).*

History of Holbeach Baptist Church, Arthur J Watkinson, 1976.

Pigot's Directory of Lincolnshire, 1822.

Ancient Laws and Institutes of England, Benjamin Thorpe, 1840.

Guide to the Coasts of Lincolnshire and Yorkshire, Mackenzie E Walcott MA, 1861.

Fenland Notes & Queries, Vol 7 (1907-1909).

Lincolnshire Free Press and Spalding Guardian.

The Lincolnshire Chronicle.

Lecture on the Parish Church of All Saints, Maurice Tennant, 1994

The newsletters of the M & GN Circle.

A Short History of the Midland & Great Northern Railway, Ronald H Clark, 1967.

The Lincolnshire Potato Railways, Stewart Squires, 1987.

Royal Observer Corps: The Story of No 11 Group, Editor Observer J Newton.

United Methodist Ministers and their Circuits, Revd Oliver A Beckerlegge, 1968.

Spalding –The Evolution of a Fenland Town, Bernard A Clark, 1978.

Bulbs in Britain –A Century of Growing, R C Dobbs, 1983.

The Lincolnshire Archives Committee, report No 10, 1ˢᵗ April 1958 – 14ᵗʰ March 1959 (re Harrisson family).

1-Beginnings

'In the middle part of Britain there is a most gloomy fen of immense size, stretching from Cambridge in the south to the sea in the north. This lengthy tract of country consists partly of marshes and partly of bogs, studded with dark mist – haunted pools and wooded islets, and traversed by tortuously-winding streams'. This description of eighth-century Fenland in the monk Felix's biography of St Guthlac, whose hermit's cell originated the site of the Crowland Abbey, lands of which Holbeach was a part, strikes an appropriately mysterious note. For very little is known about our town before the Domesday findings of 1086.

The marshiness and waterlogged nature of the surrounding fenland had been determined by Ice Age deposits, surrounding rivers, and the encroaching sea. While there is evidence of Roman settlement in the South Holland area, conditions at this time prevented practicable habitation. Thus most of the towns and villages were of Anglo-Saxon origin, settled after the sea had retreated sufficiently to create a silt ridge around the Wash, on which Holbeach and neighbouring villages were settled. This explains the name 'Holland', a Saxon word for 'low-lying' or 'sea' land, once covered in previous times by the high tide, and forming part of a large bay extending into neighbouring counties that had been filled both with alluvial deposits from higher lands, and silt and soil washed up by the sea. To William Stukeley, one of the town's most famous figures, it represented a phenomenon that to his imaginative mind would one day –helped by advancing science and natural causes– join the Lincolnshire shores with those of Norway!

The Gwyre arrive
The continuous history of Holbeach probably began in the seventh century, when the Anglo-Saxon people called the *Gwyre* – 'marsh-dwellers'– settled in an area of dry land and named their village 'Holobech', meaning 'deep brook', or 'deep stream'. Certainly, Holbeach is mentioned in a Charter dated AD 833 of Wiglaf, King of

Mercia, to Siward, Abbot of Crowland†. But going back further than the seventh century, we can only speculate on what might have been taking place in the area. In the time of Nero (Emperor, AD 54–68) for instance, there is evidence from discoveries made in 1719 and 1868 to suggest that the Romans may have had a camp on the site of the former railway station. In the eighteenth century, the Holbeach antiquary, William Stukeley, says, 'That the Romans thoroughly inhabited this fertile plain there are many instances to show,' engaged as they were in the construction of banks to hold back the sea in the period around AD 200. In recent years, aerial photographs have shown cropmarks to the south of the town, from which evidence of enclosures and

ROMANO-BRITISH POTTERY. Examples discovered by John Mossop at Holbeach Fen in the late 1930s.
[Courtesy Lincolnshire Heritage.]

droveways has been plotted for the Trust for Lincolnshire Archaeology. And the Revd Grant Macdonald, Holbeach historian in the late nineteenth century, quotes Tacitus as saying that 'the Britons complained that the Romans wore out and consumed their bodies and hands in clearing the woods and embanking the fens'.

Roman discoveries
Further Romano-British (AD 43-410) evidence was unearthed during 1938-39 on land belonging to Joseph and T J Ward at Lamings Bridge, Holbeach Fen by John Mossop, in the form of pottery of all shapes and sizes, pins and buttons, which were believed to have come from a Roman villa. The Samian ware found* could be dated to AD 150-200. In that area and at that time the land level was believed to have been some 15ft higher than it was in the 1930s, but later became submerged, perhaps as part of the subsidence which occurred at the end of the

3

fourth century. The Roman Bank, incidentally, which once ran for miles through Whaplode Parish to Holbeach Bank, passing round by 'Ye Wood House' (hence Woodhouse Lane) mentioned by Macdonald and continuing through to the Hurn and to Fleet, was something of a misnomer, as it is thought to be a mainly thirteenth-century construction. But more certain was the fact that in common with other parts of the country, any Roman advances in civilisation were largely neglected after their departure, resulting in a gradual reversion of the area to its marshy state.

UNDER WATER. Expanse of flooded field beyond Holbeach St Johns gives a good idea of how much of the land looked in Saxon times.

Murky tidal expanses
Holbeach and other neighbouring villages relied on an extensive bank for protection from the sea. Outside this bank (the *fossatum maris*) were expanses of silt and sand that were regularly covered by the tide, an area of intricate watercourses disguised by reeds and frequent blankets of mist, threatening all but the immune and hardy habitants with a form of 'marsh malaria'. It is likely that Guthlac himself suffered from this fever when he hallucinated over the appearance of Crowland's inhabitants, to the extent that he saw them with 'throats vomiting flames' and 'horses' teeth'.

Inhabiting the silt ridge
Generally speaking the land deposits themselves were largely arranged thus: silt on the areas closest to the sea, and loam and clay further inland. The silt area, some two miles wide and bordering on the Wash, was more solid than the rest, thus making it more suitable for settlements such as Holbeach to be established. In all probability houses would have been built of clay mixed with straw, hay or cow dung rather than timber, which was scarce. At some stage a road link was established between Holbeach and Spalding –the latter an important collection and distribution centre for produce– although this thoroughfare, running through Weston, Whaplode and ultimately to Wisbech, would have been little better than a 'track of hoof', and usually impassable in winter.

Communication was also made possible by the Holbeach River, which from a network of channels in the Fen, drained eventually into the Welland. It flowed through the present Church Street, continued out to Holbeach Hurn**, and 'thence to the sea by Holbeach gote', a 'gote' meaning an opening in the sea wall.

Self-reliance in tough conditions
Life in these water-dominant conditions, under constant threat by the sea from one side, and flooding from the other, was harsh to say the least. For some settlers, probably criminals and those with a dubious past, it represented the ideal place to take refuge and assume anonymity. But whatever the personal background, living in and around Holbeach would have required a sense of fearlessness, self-reliance and independence, with day-to-day survival the main priority. Although surrounding water of one sort or another made obtaining food from the rest of the country difficult, the new Holbeachians soon made the most of resources on their own doorstep. There was hay for cattle, wildfowling became a main activity, and streams abounded with pike, tench, carp and eels to hone their fishing skills.

The Anglo-Saxon period coincided with the eventual supremacy of Christianity over paganism, symbolised in this area by the founding of Peterborough on the edge of the Fen in AD 655, the establishment of Ethelreda's nunnery on the Isle of Ely, 673, and Guthlac's abbey at Crowland in 716. Crowland asserted ownership of the lands around Holbeach, but predictably the abbots met with constant resistance from its settlers, and from those of Whaplode and Moulton, over the monastic entitlement to the land and the Abbey's claim on most of the fishing catch.

Danish influence

This period of relative stability was interrupted by the arrival of the Danes in the ninth century. Not surprisingly most of the landings took place in the Wash, which was in a direct line from Jutland and a convenient gateway to the fruitful Midlands. Quickly establishing their presence throughout most of Lincolnshire the Danes attacked Crowland Abbey in AD 870, but chose in the main to raid rather than settle *en masse* in the Fenland. Nevertheless, they assumed complete control over East Anglia in the ensuing century, until Saxon victories and improved sea defences from the mid-900s onwards considerably reduced the Danish presence and influence. The most significant outcome of that presence had been the sub-kingdom of Mercia, of which Holbeach became a part. In Mercia and under Danelaw taxes and laws were imposed, and villages and settlements divided into hundreds, or wapentakes [territorial divisions, derived from the Scandinavian *vapnatak,* when a public assembly confirmed its decisions by the flourishing of weapons]. Holbeach was included in the Wapentake of Elloe, which covered a huge area, with extremities at Crowland, Pinchbeck and Tydd. And as part of the reorganisation, some of this land had been resettled on Crowland Abbey – evidence that the Danes had taken up Christianity in the ninth century.

Adjusting to the Normans

After the Conquest of 1066 the Normans soon found that the inhabitants of Holbeach, in common with those of neighbouring villages who had preserved their Saxon way of life, were a tough group to bring into line. Status, conditions and organisation at peasant level were not changed overnight. This stratum of society had already suffered dislocation, exploitation and precarious security under the Danes, and had grown ever tougher as a result. So emerging as they were on the eve of the Conquest into a state of slowly increasing independence and freedom from servitude, it was many years before some sort of working relationship with their French masters could be achieved. There were disputes over landholding, precedents and a reluctance to accept Norman feudal law, which were interfering with effective tax collection. So in 1085 the Domesday survey was commissioned, to compile a detailed statement of lands held by the king, his tenants and their available resources.

The Domesday report on Holbeach

'In Holebech is soke [district under a particular jurisdiction] of this Manor eight caracutes of land and six oxgangs to be taxed. The King has there twenty-six sokemen and five bordars with eleven ploughs and eighty acres of meadow. This soke is estimated at seventeen pounds, besides the above-mentioned number. In the same Holobech and Copelade [Whaplode] there are five caracutes of land to be taxed, which Earl Alan held; they are now in the King's possession.

'Berewick. In Holobech and Copolade Earl Algar had one caracute of land to be taxed. Land to tax oxen. Berwick in Flee [Fleet] Earl Alan has it, but the King's servants claim it for use of the King. There are three villanes and three oxen in a plough.

'Soke. In the same Earl Algar had thirteen caracutes of land and six oxgangs to be taxed. Land to nine ploughs and two oxen. The soke belongs to Gadeney [Gedney]. Earl Alan has five caracutes of this land. Landric holds it under him. He has there two ploughs and twenty-nine villanes, with five ploughs and eighty acres of meadow. It is worth eight pounds. This is recovered as belonging to the King.

Manor. In Holeben [Holbeach] and Copelade [Whaplode] St Guthlacus had and has one caracute of land to be taxed. Land to six oxen. There is now one plough in the demesne and three villanes with half a plough and twelve acres of meadow. Value in King Edward's time one hundred shillings, now eight pounds. Six caracutes of land which the King's servants claim in Holbeach lay in the King's Manor of Gadenai [Gedney]. Earl Alan now has them of the King's gift for omne Manor.'

The style of expression in this document is itself an interesting study. The Normans brought the use of Latin into official documents, and Anglo-Saxon, when translated into it, made for an unusual mixture. To their credit, the clerks recording the Domesday listings used the simplest possible terminology. But even so, their native Norman-French language made quaint phonetic representations of local words (as in 'Flee' for Fleet, and 'Gadenai'), which grossed up into the Domesday Book as a whole, resulted in conjectures and differing interpretations which have survived to this day.

Some of the words used however are more readily definable. 'Caracute', for instance, from the Latin *caracuta,* crops up several times. It represents the number of ploughs at work on an area of land (the *plougesland* of Anglo-Danish times), and establishes a basis on which the land could be taxed. The 'oxgang', from the Old English word *oxgangen*, was a sub-division of the caracute, and referred to the men who supplied oxen to pull the ploughs. Under the late Saxon taxation system, there had been eight oxgangs to the caracute.

'Villanes' and 'bordars' are a little harder to define and their meaning varies according to the area described, except to say that villane was a convenient term to describe any type of dependent peasant, or one not yet completely absorbed into a manor, with land still at his disposal. The latter had to work hard in return for any land he may have been granted by his feudal lord, and when he died, the lord was entitled to take all. The 'sokeman' (Old English *soknman*) on the other hand had enjoyed royal rights in Saxon times and could sell or grant his land, but only subject to the lord's permission to whom he owed other obligations.

'Berewick' means an 'outlying district'.

At the time of the Conquest, land in Holbeach and Whaplode belonged to St Guthlac's Abbey, Crowland, and Algar, Earl Mercia. After Domesday, the Abbey retained its holdings around Holbeach until the Dissolution of the Monasteries some four centuries later, with the rest being divided between the King and two of his knights who had supported him in battle: Earl Alan Rufus, and Wido de Credon. In all, this shared land amounted to over 100 acres.

Both Rufus and Credon had considerable influence. Rufus, Earl of Brittany and Richmond, was married to King William's daughter, Constance, and had commanded the rearguard at the Battle of Hastings. He possessed no fewer than 442 manors, 101 of them in Lincolnshire, while Wido de Credon had 60 lordships in the same county.

At this period the combined population of Holbeach and Whaplode numbered little more than 40 families, continuing to make their now centuries-old, modest living from traditional farming, fishing and saltmaking. But they represented the foundations of a community that was shortly to prosper.

Medieval prosperity
As already intimated and before land reclamation made any significant progress, the Wash coastline was noticeably different from that of today, with the sea encroaching much further inland.

Salt-making –an important occupation
But even at the time of the Norman Conquest, this did not prevent farming activity from taking place in the area between Hurdletree Bank and the Washway, and the conditions, unfavourable as they seemed, supported long-term local industries of fishing and salt-making. Bushels of salt were produced to a strict regime in Holbeach. Together with similar outputs from Gedney and Fleet, they had to be brought once a year to a 'holy place' outside the sea wall called *le mothow*. There, the bushels were supposed to receive the Lord's sign as a confirmation of their true measure. The work was seasonal, taking place between May and November after the high spring tides had receded, leaving behind a sandy silt. A scooped-shape device called a buyle removed the crucial top inch or two of the deposit, known as *moulde*. Then a separation process took place, with the

resulting brine evaporated in a lead saltpan over a peat fire, the process conducted in a thatched boiling house constructed of mud and timber. Salt-making flourished in Holbeach throughout most of the medieval period, certainly during the twelfth to fifteenth centuries, and evidence remains of salterns at Saracen's Head, Coney Garth and Holbeach Hurn.

Another typical occupation of the early medieval period was the cutting and drying of turf. Not only was it consumed as a heating fuel in the absence of a plentiful wood supply, but it was also used for building dwellings and maintaining embankments.

Pioneering reclamation

With grazing becoming such an important occupation in the Holbeach area by the twelfth century, the more enterprising lords of the manor were concentrating on ways of improving and extending their land.

Here the emphasis was on reclamation, an early example of this taking place around Holbeach Clough between 1142 and 1175. A notable pioneer in this work was Conan, 'Son of Ellis' (1152 – 1218). Described by the historian Kathleen Major as 'the most influential inhabitant of Holbeach in the late twelfth and early thirteenth centuries', he had 'reclaimed' a significant amount of land by 1199, thus making a decisive start to a process which was to transform the usefulness of the land.

An area known as 'Conan's Newland' extended towards the sea, while other drainage was carried out between Saturdaydike and Hassockdike from 1160 onwards. Such gains had involved Conan and other men of influence, such as Thomas de Multon and

RESULTS OF MEDIEVAL EMBANKING. A section of Stukeley's Map of the levels, 1723, shows the progress made with holding back the water, with names like Further Oldgate (which may pre-date 1066) and Saltney Gate, still familiar to us today. Note how the Holbeach River flows Washwards in two directions: originally via the Hurn, but with a diverted channel added later to link up with the Holbeach New River, and ultimately the Whaplode River in the Saracen's Head area.

[Courtesy John Elms.]

7

Richard de Flet (Fleet), in a serious dispute with the Abbot of Crowland, Robert de Reading, over tithes. In 1188, meetings to champion the cause took place alternately at the Prior of Spalding's barn at Weston and Holbeach Church, involving 'all the men of Ellow Wapentake.' It even got to the stage where a 3,000-strong army was assembled to take matters further. But after a confrontation at Load Bank, on the boundary with Crowland Fen, the Abbot sought redress from the King. As a result, the ringleaders, Conan among them, were each fined 20 marks.

But it was the determination of pioneers such as these, whether lords of the manor, their tenants, or 'poor freemen' which resulted in the draining of some 50 square miles of land in the southern fen between 1170 and 1241¶. This was the last significant piece of reclamation made in the medieval period, and was the result of an agreement between the lords and villagers of Holbeach, Whaplode, Fleet, Gedney, Lutton, Sutton and Tydd to divide their common fen. By creating a series of fen banks, it had been possible to increase the arable, pasture and meadowland acreage, allowing farmers to prosper on the profits of cattle, horses and wool.

Such positive developments were reflected in the status of the town, with Thomas de Multon, Lord of the Manor, successful in obtaining a market for Holbeach by a Royal Charter granted by Henry III in 1252. The market was to be held on Thursdays —a tradition that has been followed ever since. Nevertheless, there were times when that prosperity was threatened by a sea that could not always be held back. A Holbeach Extent of 1293, for instance, remarked that there were '240 acres of land lying for pasture, every acre worth by the year 4 pences, and not more because inundated by a sea storm which happened in those parts in the 15th year of the reign [Edward I's], and are flooded at every high tide.'

Macdonald's *Notes* also refer to a meadow overflowed with water in 1321, and to 'a certain piece of Sea (marshland covered by sea from time to time) for the pasture of animals.' In a favourable year, a moderate amount of flooding during the winter was actually beneficial. It created lush conditions for summer, providing not only a good hay harvest but also rich pasture for animals.

Observing or abusing obligations

Even without monastic protest, lesser efforts, such as the digging of new trenches, often disturbed neighbouring tenants, attracting conflicts over fishing rights. In 1396, for example, Guy Bullok of Holbeach was accused at Spalding of narrowing the common river at Holbeach weir 'to the damage of the whole community.' This was followed in 1423 by the tenants of the Bishop of Ely complaining of flooding from neglected sewers at Holbeach, Whaplode and Gedney, and petitioning for a reduction in their annual rents. The inhabitants' obligation also extended to the building and upkeep of roads, causeways and bridges, for which an allotted number of people would be responsible. 'The King's road in Holbeach and Whaplode called Saturdaydike and Goldynge', stipulated the jurors of Elloe, 'ought to be repaired by the said townships.'

At the end of the thirteenth century, the lord of the manor's holding in Holbeach amounted to 298 acres of arable land, and 20 of meadow. It showed that in spite of the difficulties, the effects of improved husbandry were beginning to make their mark on the status of Holbeach.

NAME LIVES ON. Hurdletree Bank, the scene of early land reclamation.

† 'In confirmation and grant of land at Bucknall, Hallington. Gernthorp, Langtoft, Deeping, Baston, Rippingale, Holbeach, Whaplode, Spalding, Drayton, Laythorpe and Kirkby Lincolnshire, and elsewhere.' *Anglo-Saxon Lincolnshire*, Peter Sawyer, 1998.

*More pottery was found, in fragments this time, in a dump during 1966-67 at Aswick Grange, Whaplode Drove, on Richard Grundy's land. John Mossop was again involved in its analysis, the fragments eventually passing to a New Zealand university.

**'A Map of the Levels, described by William Stukeley 1723' shows that at some stage a western diversion was added to the channel so that it merged with the Whaplode River just north of Saracen's Head. The map also shows the existence by this time of the Holbeach New River (today still flowing under Netherfield) which joined the diverted Holbeach River near Saltney Gate.

¶ *Embanking, Draining: The Changing Fens,* Susanna Davis for South Holland District Council

§Rent of ordinary fenland at this time was normally about 6d an acre; better land around Boston, one shilling. [*A History of the Fens of South Lincolnshire, W H Wheeler*].

2 -All Saints Church

THE SOUTH SIDE EXPOSED. 1843 lithograph view contrasts with the tree-shrouded aspect of today.
[Lincolnshire Churches: Division of Holland, 1849.]

The present All Saints dates from the fourteenth century, but an earlier church of the same name stood on part of the site some two centuries previously.

No illustrations of this original church are known to exist, although in the time of Pope Alexander (1159-1181) it is mentioned in a papal bull of 1177 confirming the possessions of Spalding Priory. Fulk d'Oyry, Lord of Gedney and Whaplode, also had rights in the church. These rights and those of Spalding Priory were later bought out by Conan FitzEllis, Lord of the Manor of Holbeach until 1218, as a means of installing his illegitimate son, William, as rector. We already know that the church was used as a meeting place for Conan, Thomas de Multon and Richard de Flet during their dispute over tithes with Crowland Abbey, and Holbeach was reputed to be a wealthy living, stated in

the Taxation of Pope Nicholas IV in 1291 to be worth £120 a year. Architecturally, the style would have been transitional Early English and Norman. Tennant[1] also draws our attention to what he describes as 'the ghost of the original church' showing through the existing building. This reveals itself as subsidence in the north and south walls of the chancel, and in the north aisle the floor is cracked along the approximate line of the original north wall.

Building the present church
The decision to rebuild the church to the present form may have been the result of the Bishop of Lincoln's acquisition of the advowson (the right to a church benefice) of Holbeach in 1332, and his promise in December 1340 to pay for a replacement chancel. This promise also included the provision of vestments, chalices, books, four cartloads of straw per annum for the church, and the building of a house for the vicar on the south side. The cost of the nave, tower and spire was to be met by the parishioners, prominent contributors among whom were the Littlebury family, then lords of the manor. While it might just be possible that as Holbeach landowners, the monks of Crowland Abbey contributed something towards the new nave, the historian Kathleen Major refutes the notion that they were involved in the church's actual reconstruction.

The construction team
Affected by the factors of itinerant work patterns and shorter lifespans, not to mention the effects of the Black Death, construction team manpower would have fluctuated over the long building period. It would have involved a master mason as architect and general overseer, supported by free masons – who, as the term implied, moved around on other work in neighbouring towns and

villages– layers, carpenters and general labourers. A freemason's lodge, the medieval equivalent of a site office, may have been situated in the north-west area of the churchyard (behind the present-day Drydens and the Age Concern café). Here, according to the Holbeach historian, Henry Peet, the raw material –Barnack Stone from the Stamford area– would be delivered by boats from the Welland, sailing via the Wash to unload by the bridge over the Holbeach River. There the cargo was processed by the master mason and his team into dressed stones. Labourers then carried these to the church for the layers to position in regular courses. As a measure of quality control, each mason was required to put his mark on the stones he dressed, and these marks can still be seen round the church today.

Patterns of construction

Beginning with the west end (facing Market Hill) and working eastwards (towards the present Barclays Bank) the rebuilding project took many years, with the bulk of the work accomplished between 1338 and 1352, and culminating in the completion of the spire by 1361. This and the tower measured 180ft. As originally built the tower also featured pinnacles, depicted in Stukeley's 1720s engraving, but these were almost certainly removed by that date. Some recycling of materials went on, for it is believed from the lack of identifying marks that the aisle walls were built with stone from the previous building. And having reached Holbeach by 1350, the Black Death would have had its effects on both the progress and quality of the work, with any surviving artisan's services difficult and expensive to come by. Look at the side walls of the north porch, for instance. Ashlar (regular-cut stone) changes to rubble after a few courses –more obviously on the wall facing Barclays Bank– yet resumes its regular pattern at the top. Was this an example of plague depleting skilled labour?

Be that as it may, the end result was a fine and predominantly pure example of a church in the Decorated style (current from c. 1300-1350) which, with its hint of the succeeding Perpendicular (1400-1500) in the clerestory¶ and tower windows, has survived to this day with very little interference or added-on

afterthought. But ignoring the 1920s attempt at an ecclesiastical boiler house and chimney next to the south porch, there is the odd anomaly: those drum turrets attached to the north porch, for example, have aroused controversy in the past. Were they built simultaneously with the rest of the church, or added later?

The north porch turrets

'Somewhat of an architectural puzzle' that 'contrasts strangely with the rest of the edifice' is how Henry Peet aptly describes them in his *Architectural & Ecclesiastical*

MONGREL MASONRY. Side view of north porch reveals varied quality of stonework halfway up on both sides. A lack of qualified labour, perhaps, during the Black Death?

Notes on Holbeach Church. The reason being, he suggests, that they may have been the building work referred to in Thomas Callow's will dated 1526, to which 'he gives and bequeaths three score pounds.' Romantics have suggested that the turrets came from Moulton Castle, a view echoed by Pevsner, who introduces a further complication by stating that the upper windows of the porch itself 'are certainly c.1700 or early 18th century in style'. But to revert to the turrets, the medieval historian Kathleen Major records a Professor Hamilton's opinion –that they are more likely to be the same period as the rest of the church.

'Too thin' for a castle?

This is borne out by local historian Maurice Tennant, who, while not entirely dismissing the Callow theory, feels that the turrets could not have been salvaged from a castle because they were too thin for defensive work. Not only that, but the close resemblance of the mouldings and courses of stone to those of the adjoining walls indicates that the materials were created on site at Holbeach. As for the motive behind these turrets, the writer offers his own suggestion: that in medieval times, the north sides of churches were often regarded as areas where evil spirits lurked, and the architect may well have felt that something suggestive of protection and defence was called for. The standard of workmanship however is inferior to that of the rest of the church –one reason why both towers have tilted over the years. In the 1890s, hydraulic jacks were used to try and restore the western turret (right hand, as you enter the porch) to the vertical. But this made little impression, almost as if the building has had the final say in the way it wishes to 'settle', for the nave pillars and aisle walls lean outward from the weight of the roof over the centuries, again without hazard.

Importance of the north porch

Its stylistic oddities apart, the north porch was originally more than just a shelter from the weather. Before the Reformation, it was where the 'exorcisms of baptism' were performed before a child was brought into the church, and the first part of the marriage service was conducted there. Until the 1900s the porch featured an upper room, reached by a spiral stone stairway in the western turret. In the eighteenth century, and through to 1811, this served as a schoolroom for the Farmer Free School.

Before and after the Reformation

Pre-Reformation, the discipline exercised in ecclesiastical matters missed nothing. Among other things, a dim view was taken by the Bishop of Lincoln's officials towards Sunday markets outside the church, such as one held in 1423§, when congregations provided a captive audience for trade. In 1523 the authorities commented that, 'The copes and other vestments need repair; the altar cloths are not kept clean,' and continued:

'Thomas Peartree, John Davy, and William Tanson worked on Tuesday in Whitsun week. Christopher Kyd and Nicholas Cooper commonly hold drinking parties during time of divine service.'

Rich decorations, pre-Reformation

The church interior in medieval and pre-Reformation times would have been very colourful and ornate. Walls were painted and hung with tapestries. Candles burned on several altars and saints' effigies abounded.

PRE-REFORMATION SURVIVOR: The 14th-century font.

This is supported by accounts from contemporary records, which reveal that in 1523, Lawrence Delff of Holbeach in his will left 'to the high altar for tithes forgotten 12d, to the altar of the Blessed Mary 16d, to the altar of the Trinity 8d, to the altar of St James 8d, to every other altar in the church 3d, to the light of St Lawrence 1 pound of wax, to the light of the rood loft 6d, and to the reparation of the church 3s 4d.'

But in spite of the implied opulence, All Saints was very much a community centre. It was the meeting place of the four Holbeach trade guilds, including one for masons and another for shepherds. Guilds were a valued element in parochial life. Their activities helped to maintain the church, organise holy day processions and annual feasts, while religious mystery plays were also staged there. The *Three Kings of Cologne*, for

GOOD TRACERY. The original stained glass may be long gone, but the Decorated style is well represented in most of the windows.

instance, one of the *Corpus Christi* cycle of plays usually associated with Lincoln Cathedral, was performed at Holbeach, combining biblical narrative with the vernacular, and irreverent details of medieval social life¶. The plays were supported by a full set of costumes and properties, which were occasionally turned into cash when surplus to requirements, as in 1543, when the churchwardens disposed of 'Harod's coat and all the Apostyls coats and other rags,' for 18/8d.

In 1453, W Enot of Lynn and Henry Nele of Holbeach donated the Saint's Bell, and in 1529, a new organ was installed at a cost of £3 6s 8d. However this was taken down

some 40 years later. Portable organs may have been used after this date, but until the nineteenth century, music for services was to rely largely on a church band, playing wind and stringed instruments in a gallery across the chancel.

Dealing with crime

In times of emergency, or when crucial issues had to be discussed, such as the state of the sea dykes or banks, a bell was rung 'to the intent that the said parishioners hearing the bell should resort thither to commune upon such matters.' One such meeting took place in 1530, when the church was robbed overnight of valuables worth £200 –a huge sum at that time and another indication of the wealth of the Holbeach living. A pair of gloves was found in the vestry, and at the instigation of a local schoolmaster, John Lamkyn, they were sent as clues for the attention of a mystical sleuth named Edmund Nasche, of Cirencester. They led to Nasche incriminating John Partiche of Holbeach, who, ostracised and threatened, sued the churchwardens and appealed to Henry VIII's Star Chamber court for justice.

Effects of the Reformation

The Reformation during the reign of Henry VIII (1509-1547) had far-reaching effects on the history of English religion. Between 1536 and 40 his Act of Parliament closed over 800 monasteries and religious houses, ostensibly completing the King's break with the Church of Rome, and establishing himself as supreme head of the English Church.

The main motive however was financial, for the Act gave the King control over the monasteries' extensive lands. From these he could now either enjoy the income, or reap the proceeds by selling them off to the wealthy rural middle classes. As part of this process, much church property was misappropriated, sold off or destroyed. Crowland Abbey was surrendered to the King on 4th December 1539 and was subjected to a harsher than usual routine of plunder and partial demolition. Its possession, Holbeach, did not escape lightly although ironically, its living, worth £33 6s 8d annually at the time building began on the present church, was worth only £20.13s 4d at the time of the Reformation, and the number of clergy had increased from seven in 1376 to nine in 1526¶. By this time the value of money had also fallen and the vicar was much poorer than his equivalent of a century earlier. Treasures were melted down and walls whitewashed, while some half-dozen richly-appointed altars were destroyed, and their ornaments sold.

Painted glass, some bearing the arms of Scales, Sibsey, Callow, Derby and d'Eyvill apparently escaped the upheaval, only to be destroyed in the main by Cromwellian soldiers during the English Civil War (1642-48), when the Vicar of Holbeach and his opposite number at Fleet were fined for taking up arms for the King (the town itself had opposed raising money for the monarch, and was two years in arrears). A little of the earlier glass survived into the eighteenth century, but neglect and the inherent softness and vulnerability of medieval glazing, with its tendency to micro-cracking, ensured the loss of any significant amount remaining. Now only two small segments are left, incorporated in the window at the end of the north aisle. Most of the stained glass existing today is likely to be Victorian.

SACRED BELL still dominates the east gable.

In spite of the changes, the post-Reformation church in Holbeach remained the focus of community life. The bell of 1623 housed in its cote over the east gable of the nave, and replacing an original from 1453, continued the custom of ringing for sacred purposes. Schoolchildren were taught in the chancel, while the town's fire engine was housed in the nave, operated by the bellringers at a supplement of seven shillings and sixpence a year.

The Littlebury Monument

Sometime between 1634 and 1640; the observations of Colonel Gervase Holles confirm that the Littlebury and Joanna Welby (died 1488) monuments –the families

were connected– were then situated near the chancel. The Littlebury tomb, in spite of its late fourteenth-century style identified by Pevsner, who attributes its work to Bristol craftsmen†, is ascribed to Sir Humphrey Littlebury, who acquired land in Holbeach by marriage to Elizabeth, daughter and heiress of Sir John de Kirton, and possessed a seat at Holbeach Hurn, together with land in Boston and a house at Kirton. There were two Littlebury sisters: Marion, wife of Ralph Pulvertoft of Whaplode, and Isabel, married to Lawrence How, a knight. Sir Humphrey is credited by Macdonald as the possible founder of the present church, and may well have contributed money towards its construction. Macdonald also says that Littlebury was 'living in 1346' although he was believed to have died in 1339 before the work on the church was barely started. Either way, this nullifies the legend that he was killed in the Wars of the Roses (1455-85) in the area of Battlefields Lane* (and in any case, the nearest recorded presence of the Lancastrian army was in 1461, some six miles from Crowland Abbey). Technically, an early Victorian review in Stephen Lewin's *Lincolnshire Churches in the Division of Holland in the County of Lincoln*, describes the Littlebury monument as 'a purfled [decorated border] tomb, on which lies the effigy of a knight in rich armour, with baldrick [warrior's belt], sword, spurs and mail about the neck. In the recesses between the arches are eight shields, alternately two lions passant gardant, and three bars pean. Altogether the monument is worthy of greater care than appears to be bestowed upon it.' A curious but fashionable device associated with monuments of this period is the use of a woman's head-and-shoulders effigy as a head-rest. The fact that the recesses on the right-hand side of the tomb are decorated, while those on the opposite side are plain, suggests that it was originally placed near to a wall where the left-hand side could not be seen. It may also explain why the carved stone of the head is cut away and squared.

The move to its present spot
It is likely that the Littlebury tomb was moved to the north aisle, just to the right of the north door, when box pews were

installed in the eighteenth century. Certainly by July 1833, it is described by W J Monson in Vol. 31 of his *Lincolnshire Church Notes* as situated 'At the west end of the north aisle'. The Joanna Welby monumental brass followed in 1871 when a descendant, Sir Glynne E Welby Gregory, keen that the family names should be reunited, paid for the brasses to be fixed to a new table tomb at the west end of the north aisle, positioned against the north wall. Legend has it, incidentally, that Sir Humphrey Littlebury occasionally haunts the church, but he is probably doing no more than keeping an eye on his investment!

Regular services, disturbing dream

In 1603 –the year James I acceded the throne– the Church was found to be 'in very good repayre and very decently kept', apart from the chancel, which suggested that the Bishop of Lincoln was skimping his responsibilities. A surviving rainhead from 1673 in the clerestory may point to the re-leading of the nave roof at that time, and by the turn of that century, the eastern turret of the north porch had undergone repair.

A visit to the parish by Bishop William Wake in 1705 revealed that All Saints' services were held twice on Sundays and once each weekday. Children were catechized every Sunday, and Communion celebrated monthly and on the three great feasts of the year. This routine suggested that Holbeach was better served than many other Lincolnshire parishes, where Communion could only be held three or four times a year.

All Saints loomed large in a premonition in 1721, when on July 15th, a John Butler told William Stukeley that he had 'dreamed some time before he saw Sam Howet riding down Holbech Steeple; the morning after came news of Howets taken ill, of which sickness he dy'd. Butler was taken ill this day, & I conjectured it would [be] fatal, which prov'd true.' At which point, changing the subject completely, Stukeley records, 'A new weathercock sett upon Holbech Steeple.'

The weathercock itself however was soon to become unstable, to the extent that it fell down in 1751. This happened during a period of 87 years up to 1832 when the church was without a resident vicar, the churchyard had become overgrown, and only essential repairs were being undertaken. However a set of chimes was installed in the clocktower in 1776 by Edward Arnold of St Neots, playing the following tunes delightfully evocative of the period, but mainly obscure to us now: 'Ladies of London', 'Riggadoon', 'Oswall's Air', 'Lovely Nancy', 'Lady Chatham's Jig', 'Seeley's Gavotte', 'Three Generals' Healths', A Minuet by Norris, and the 113th Psalm. In the chamber above, eight bells graced the tower by 1807, the earliest dating from 1648, with four cast in 1770. All but one carry inscriptions, with Stukeley and Captain Edward Northon figuring prominently among the subscribers. A 'dead' or 'passing' bell was rung at funerals, to ward off evil spirits threatening a soul on its way to heaven. In strict discriminatory order, it tolled nine times for a man, seven for a woman, five for a boy, and four for a girl. Campanologists may be interested to know that the ropes are 80ft in 'draught'.

Agistment Tithes, 1760s

The Parish of Holbeach in this period, incidentally, was still entitled to 'Tenths of the Produce of the Earth to the Church'.

This system had its roots in the so-called Laws of Edward the Confessor, which stated: 'If any one have a herd of horses, let him pay the tenth colt...he who has many cows, the tenth calf...and if he make cheese from their milk, the tenth cheese, or the milk of the tenth day', and so on, the principle extending through to 'woods, meadows, waters, mills, parks, warrens, fisheries, thickets, gardens, trade, and from all similar things God has given, let a tenth be returned; and he who refuses, by justice of the King and Holy Church, if it be necessary, shall be forced to pay.' Lapses had been allowed over the years, complicated by farmers moving livestock around to graze in other parishes, so reimposing the arrangement had been difficult. But Cecil Willis, vicar of Holbeach, had braved a 'Torrent of Opposition...from many of the Land Proprietors in this Neighbourhood' to confirm a tariff ratified by the Court of Exchequer in 1768, of a tenth of the value of keeping the following animals, which in the following examples, equated to:

> Store sheep...................5d per month.
> One-year-old horses.........9d per week.
> Two-year-old horses......1s 6d per month.
> Yearling beasts.............4d per week.
> Two-year-old beasts.......6d per week.
> Three-year-old beasts......8d per week.

Many other agistment complexities, on which there is insufficient room here to dwell, were aired, examined and reaffirmed at the time, as a result of which Willis became a recognised authority on the subject for clergy from other parishes. In 1778, to end the chore of answering every query individually, he published his findings as a guide to others, presented in the form of a 'Letter to the Clergy of the Archdeaconry of Norwich' –a wise move, as a demand for 500 copies soon proved. Surprisingly, the problem with the Holbeach landowners appeared to have been amicably conducted, for Willis gave them the credit for 'acquitting themselves like Gentlemen during five Years Litigation, in which a large Sum was expended on both sides.'

Victorian Restoration and Expansion
The arrival of the Revd James Morton heralded a long period of restoration, as part of the county-wide revival of church life in the nineteenth century remarked on by Pevsner. Morton began with a new singing gallery in the tower, equipped with a new organ by Joseph Walker of London at a cost of £225, and manned by a new resident organist, the schoolmaster John Coop, and 12 choirboys to replace the men's orchestral choir. Morton also managed to replace the chancel roof in deal, and although unable to raise funds to restore the nave, was responsible for rebuilding the vicarage with a loan from Queen Anne's Bounty.

The early vicarage
It had been decreed that the vicarage should be positioned on the south side of the Church since 1340. Contents of a survey dated 1606 officially record the vicarage as 'scituate and lyinge betwene the landes of Tristram Coniers, Esq., on the parte of the easte, and a Common Sewer called the Eae [presumably they meant 'Eau' or Holbeach River] on the parte of the weste, and the landes late Mr Hall on the parte of the Southe, and conteyninge by estimacion three acres divided into one garden, one orcharde, one yarde, and a curtilage'. By the standards of the time, this indicated no shortage of amenities, and the premises also included stabling for five horses, henhouses, a pig-sty, a pigeon house and a 'brewhouse'. The kitchen garden alone took up half an acre,

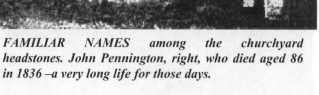

FAMILIAR NAMES among the churchyard headstones. John Pennington, right, who died aged 86 in 1836 –a very long life for those days.

and there were 'two great pitts', one for the house, and another for watering and washing the horses. However, largely untouched since John Stukeley's involvement in the 1680s, the vicarage became long overdue for improvement. In spite of a parlour 15ft by 14ft and *two* similarly-sized kitchens, an 1834 entry in the parish register describes it as 'a very mean building…containing some very narrow and half ruinous chambers of a much older date. ' Most of the east wing was therefore demolished and rebuilt, and a coach house added. The work was finished in 1838, but that June, on the occasion of Queen Victoria's coronation, the house suffered considerable damage at midnight from a mob, apparently rebelling against Morton's refusal to contribute to a fund providing a feast for the poor.

'Calthrope, gent.', disturbs the peace, 1839

The following year, a church official attending to the stoves –at 2.30 a.m. on a Sunday morning, be it noted, as an indication of the devotion to routine duties– had good cause to be alarmed by a sudden crashing noise. The culprit was 'Robert Calthrope, gent.', whose commemorative tablet had detached itself from the north wall after 172 years and tumbled to the ground. So it was fortunate that no congregation was in church at the time.

Fire avoided, 1854

A second incident in Morton's term was fortunately avoided by the prompt action of a passer-by. Scarcely had the New Year of 1854 been ushered in, than the church caught fire. At 5.30 a.m. on 2nd January, a washerwoman on her way to work at the vicarage saw flames coming from seating near the vestry, and raised the alarm. Fortunately the fire was extinguished before it caused any significant damage. It was thought to have been started by smouldering coal left unattended during the night.

Brook's major achievements, 1866-72

Morton's successor, Arthur Brook, intensified the restoration programme. In the six years before he moved on as Vicar of Holy Trinity, Brompton in 1872, he repaired the spire –which had again become dangerous– re-roofed the nave and chancel

in oak, and restored the west entrance, including in this the relocation of the organ to its present position. Although the chancel had only recently received a new roof, Brook shrewdly justified its replacement in a timber to match the nave by spiriting away Morton's roof to the new 'daughter' church at Holbeach Hurn, under construction during 1869-70.

Useful improvements

Other renovations concentrated on interior appointments, including the choir vestry, and reflooring the nave and chancel. Brook personally paid for repairs to the font and the creation of a magnificently-carved pulpit, which survives to this day and was installed in memory of his father at Whitsuntide in 1871. Five hundred chairs were also bought, adding to the impressive state of the Church on Christmas Day that year, when the local

STILL IN FINE CONDITION. The pulpit installed by Brook in 1871.

reporter remarked: 'although in an unfinished state, [the Church] presented a very pretty appearance. The whole of the new seats in the nave were fitted with scarlet and black rug cushions on Christmas Day for the first time.' It was a satisfying achievement for Brook to look back on when he left, proudly bearing his silver model of All Saints

Church, presented to him by grateful parishioners.

The Daughter Churches
Administratively, the Morton-Brook era was a period of important ecclesiastical expansion for Holbeach. For centuries, parishioners from the marsh or surrounding areas had been obliged to walk or ride up to 12 miles to join the congregation at All Saints. But following the initiative begun in outlying districts by the Methodist Church in the 1820s, the establishment of the Daughter Churches brought greater convenience to worship. Beginning with St John's Holbeach Fen in 1839-40, the network was added to in earnest between 1868-70 with St Mark's Holbeach Marsh, St Matthew's, St Luke's Holbeach Hurn and St Polycarp's Holbeach Drove, with the unstoppable Brook overseeing the building programme for each of these later churches. Today Holbeach Marsh, Holbeach Fen and Holbeach Drove are separate ecclesiastical districts, and there are now seven Anglican churches within the old parish of Holbeach.

Restorations with Hemmans, 1880s and 90s
Although an extra demand on funds for the new Daughter Churches had put a strain on available finance for All Saints, the 1880s saw further restoration work under the Revd Fielder Hemmans, beginning with the replacement of the north and south aisle roofs, which was less successful. The former tie-beams were omitted, causing the aisles to lean, and the roofing had to be replaced. The organ was renewed in 1885, and the church must have been a fine sight on the actual day of Queen Victoria's Golden Jubilee in 1887, when flags and streamers flew from the steeple, 180 feet above worshippers attending a special service at 11 a.m., followed by a dinner served in the High Street an hour later for 2,500 people.

Patronising the lady fundraisers
Coinciding with the Diamond Jubilee 10 years later, the north porch was restored, with attempts to underpin and correct the lean of the turrets. Patronisingly, it was suggested that the funds for this work could be raised by a committee of lady bicyclists, with the rider that 'It would be work for the ladies...and the summer evenings could not be better employed than in collecting subscriptions. The ladies would have somewhere to go, and not, as is too often the case, a mere aimless ride out. They would also be accompanied by some of their male friends, who would also get interested in the work.'

A night-time eve-of-burial service
At a quarter to ten in the evening on 20th March, 1884, a congregation of 200 stood by as the body of Captain Barker, a leading Holbeachian, was brought into the church. It is hard to imagine that the town streets were then more active at this time of night than they are now, for the 'spring weekly mart with flaring lights and harsh voices' was still in session. However on the coffin's arrival in a carriage, all proper respect was paid, and a service consisting of a psalm, a hymn and a few prayers was conducted, according to Macdonald, along lines similar to the late Earl Grosvenor's at Eccleston church in London on the evening before. Captain Barker was buried the next day near his parents in Holbeach Cemetery.

Twentieth-century incidents, additions and modifications
In February 1906, the local press carried melodramatic reports of a 'Fire Ball' striking the spire, causing £200-worth of damage. Lightning struck a few feet from the vane, scattering masonry as far as Albert Street, where it shattered one of Mr Waller's windows. However, repairs were soon put in hand, drawing on the very best of steeplejack expertise –a Mr Larkin from Bow, London, who only the previous year had been entrusted with 'decorating' Nelson's Column, and obviously had the right head for heights.

No reserved seats under Hutchinson, 1912
Renovations, alterations and additions to the church over the last century have been less extensive. They have included the widening of the main altar and the installation of a reredos, together with the addition of an altar in the north aisle, in memory of Canon Hemmans in 1912, which coincided with the arrival of Canon Frederick Hutchinson. Five hundred people attended his first sermon, but not everyone liked his new methods, particularly those who had hitherto paid a

yearly subscription for their favourite seats, and found that their name cards had been removed in a bold initiative to make the church free to everyone. Perhaps this was Hutchinson's way of dealing with stand-offishness. 'The first six weeks in Holbeach', he recorded, 'were of blue sky and sunshine. This made up considerably for the lack of public welcome to myself and my family. There was no social meeting to greet us, nor wish us happiness in our new home…Lincolnshire folk do not rush in at a new comer, but as soon as they find he can be trusted, they are loyal to the backbone.' True enough! Loyalty obviously followed in due course, for Hutchinson was to stay until 1936, and by February 1931 he had baptised 1,000 children.

HUTCHINSON'S SWANSONG. A bell dating from 1807 which he had recast in 1936, his last year at Holbeach.

Ongoing maintenance 1920-1996
Enhancements continued with the installation of a rood beam as a memorial to those who fell in 1914-18 War, the boiler room of 1920 in memory of Frank Caudwell Carter, the re-hanging of the bells in 1921 and 1936, and the choir organ of 1950 commemorating Dorothy Carter, which was rebuilt in the early 1980s and slightly reduced in size by Groves of Nottingham. The steeple had been cause for concern again

in 1923, when it was found to be 18 inches out of perpendicular, so the Holbeach Urban Council was happy to accept an estimate of £76 to rectify it from John Thompson of Peterborough, who happened to be building Lloyds Bank across the road at the time. Money for ongoing maintenance was always difficult to come by, relying heavily on church fêtes and bazaars, held as annual events in the gardens of Red Roofs on Fleet Road, when it was owned by A B Bass, or the grounds of Serpentine House, the home of Mr and Mrs E A Lane in Barrington Gate. Both Frederick Kilham Bass (1891-1968) and his sister Mary (1893-1971), who lived at Nutten Stoven in Boston Road, were generous benefactors to All Saints and other Parish churches of Holbeach. It was Bass money which allowed the renewal of the Church wall in the 1980s, and the Mary Bass Room at the west door provided refreshment, kitchen, toilet and meeting room facilities from 1996. This was the year when the replacement of the weathercock atop the steeple presented something of a crowd-puller, with Canon Hill personally climbing the steeple in June to fix the emblem in position, a nerves-of-steel gesture which raised £700 in sponsorship money towards church funds.

Losing a tombstone, gaining a noticeboard, 2000-2001
While the gales of autumn 2000 claimed two trees, one of which fell on and destroyed a table tombstone on the High Street side, the churchyard gained a very tasteful noticeboard –dedicated to the late Joyce Tingle– at its north gate a year later, beautifully fashioned in high-quality timber by Mark Fowler, of Halstead & Fowler in Park Road. It was cemented in place by 'Parky' Walker, so called because he is also responsible for maintenance at Carter's Park and the Cemetery.

As for the church itself, the occasional connoisseur and purist may regret the disappearance of the medieval furniture, comment upon the 'crowded ' tombs at the west end, the 'unremarkable' replacement woodwork and painted glass, or the incidental damage caused by later re-flooring: in short, 'the misguided zeal of both reformers and restorers' commented on by another perfectionist, Kathleen Major. But when spring sunshine plays upon its largely original form, surrounded by a peaceful, wooded churchyard dappled with purple crocus, dwarf tulips, daffodil and celandine, there are few finer examples of a county market town church than All Saints.

♣ ♣ ♣ ♣ ♣ ♣

[1] *Lecture on the Parish Church of All Saints*, Maurice Tennant, 1994.

¶' Fourteen in number .'Still decorated in style' remarks Nikolaus Pevsner in *The Buildings of England -Lincolnshire*, 'which is worth recording.'
'Ambitious and consistent,' is his overall impression of All Saints.

§ *Church & Society in Medieval Lncolnshire*, Dorothy M Owen, 1971.

¶ *Church & Society in Medieval Lncolnshire*, Dorothy M Owen, 1971.

† Pevsner offers the tomb of Lord Berkeley (died 1368) in Bristol Cathedral for comparison.

* 'Battlefields' is likely to be a corruption of 'Baddle Fields' – land once owned by the Baddle family in that area. The name appears as a sixteenth-century entry in the Lincoln Record Society Volume of Wills, held at Spalding Library. 'Battlefields Farm' still appeared on a Holbeach map of 1888, just beyond the Cemetery Lodge.

3 – The Living Past

The development of Holbeach and the positioning of its key buildings was largely determined by the presence of mounds, ridges, accumulating silt, and a river running through its centre, popularly known in later years as 'The Stinker'.

The higher ground still visible in Hall Hill Road is an important starting point in the story. Originally, it was probably a Roman saltworks. But by the eleventh century, it formed a prominent location for a baronial manor or hall and its administrative buildings, hence the name, 'Hallgate'.

Hallgate: the site of an early chapel?
A smaller but similar mound was situated opposite, in the area near what is now the first bend in the road in Hallgate, close to the first junction with the present Hall Hill Road. From a discovery made in 1719 at this spot, when skeletons of men, women and children were found, it was believed to be the site of an early church or chapel, dedicated to St Peter. This was witnessed by the Holbeach antiquarian William Stukeley, who recorded seeing 'many corpses dug up in the yard at making a ditch there. There was also another in the fen side.' A second excavation at the same spot in 1868 revealed a stone which may have been a chapel door sill, but subsequent attempts to preserve the site as a burial ground were abandoned, and the plot sold in 1899 to build the existing St Peter's Villas. The local historian Maurice Tennant, in his lecture on *The Parish Church of All Saints* (1994) believes St Peter's to have been annexed after the Norman Conquest to the baronial manor opposite, and that its construction from basic materials of wattle and daub was responsible for its early decay and disappearance.

After Hallgate becomes Church Street, there is a gradual rise in level up to the crossroads. This is because the High Street runs along the crest of a silt ridge, left in about the fourth century by deposits from the once-encroaching sea line. The silt area went on accumulating, eventually rendering conditions more favourable for further building.

Holbeach River

Another contributory factor to the positioning of the town centre was the Holbeach River, one of a series of drainage streams cutting through the silt from larger rivers, in this case the Welland.

A small Venice
Deep enough to be navigable, it passed right through the middle of town, approximately along the line of the present car parking spaces stretching from the Exchange public house to the Library, and the length of broad pavement running from the west end of the churchyard up to Drydens. At the 'Dryden corner' an essential cross-over point was established, originally spanned by a wooden bridge for the High Street, before the river continued to follow in the direction of Park Road, and eventually –according to Dugdale's map of 1662– flowing into the 'Sea dike' at Holbeach Hurn. Thus Holbeach formed an important bridging point, linking the east-west route between the ports of Lynn and Boston, and the monasteries of Crowland and Spalding –a factor that was responsible for its developing into a town, rather than remaining as a village. The Revd Grant Macdonald, writing in 1884, tells us that a toll at the bridge was said to have been originated by King John while on his march from King's Lynn to Swineshead, shortly before his death in 1216. The toll was still being levied in 1814 on all persons passing over it except the fishermen of Whaplode and Fleet, one fortnight either side of Michaelmas.

The Hallgate manor house and Guildhall
Around the bridge –replaced in the medieval period by a stone structure– and its approaches, important buildings went up from the eleventh century onwards. These included the manor house and its administrative annexes in Hallgate, and the first All Saints Church. Nearby, the Guildhall of Our Lady was another medieval creation, situated approximately where the present pair of bungalows faces the southern side of the churchyard. Meanwhile, the depth of the river and its proximity to adjacent premises always had to be taken into account. In an engraving made by Stukeley in 1724, he shows fencing running along the west side of the church grounds,

from which the vicar then enjoyed grazing rights. This boundary was to prevent sheep falling into the river, and it was not until 1853 that the channel, foul and stinking, was covered over to the relief of all concerned.

Hospital of All Saints
During the building of the present All Saints Church, the Hospital of All Saints was founded in 1351 on the site of what is now the Chequers Hotel, by John de Kirton under a licence granted by Edward III, and providing for a warden chaplain and 15 'poor people'. However, it had ceased to exist as a hospital by 1545 and was taken down by the father of William Stukeley. William himself recalled 'the old stone work and arched windows with mullions [vertical dividers]', which suggests it was a substantial building. Some of this carved stone went into the construction of another house 'built near the bridge'.

Wattle and daub... or just plain mud
Apart from All Saints Church, however, nothing on the surface has survived from the medieval period. This can be attributed to two factors. First, in the period 600-1500, the better building skills were lavished on castles and religious institutions. Secondly, building in stone was the preserve of the rich or well endowed, as it was the only readily available, durable material at the time. The alternatives were timber framing, with walls made of wattle (a basketwork weave) and daub (an appetising mixture of clay, dung and horsehair), or just plain turf, clay or mud– the latter practice of which only disappeared with the last of the mud-hut cottages at Lutton in 1951. Neither of the last two methods was conducive to long life if neglected, a reason why the simple St Peter's church mentioned earlier had in all probability disappeared by the sixteenth century.

Secondly, the very fact that Holbeach soon became a town bred folk with an eye to progress and constant renewal or redevelopment. This was more apparent after the Black Death from the mid-fourteenth century onwards, when work patterns changed. Specialist labour became more expensive, and serfdom was superseded by tradesmen setting up in their own right, giving rise to conditions of greater prosperity. An example of this new status is seen in a transaction of 1541, when some of the Abbot of Crowland's land was sold to a group of 'seven salters, a plumber, a cordwainer, a girdler, a brewer and a poulterer'.

SECOND-GENERATION MARKET CROSS. As rebuilt by John Stukeley, and illustrated by his son William in 1722.
[Courtesy John Elms.]

The Market Cross
Spalding had enjoyed a monopoly in the early medieval period as the only market town in the immediate area, but this was to change. The importance of trade in Holbeach was first recognised with the establishment of a market in 1252, with permission for a fair, held jointly with Fleet, obtained from Henry III by Thomas de Multon, Lord Egremont. Initially the fair was to be held on Thursday, and lasting two days, 'on the Eve and the day of St Michael' –28th and 29th September. The Saturday market, meanwhile, owes its origins to a fair first held on 1st-2nd July 1284, under a charter granted to Peter of Goxhill.

Barnack stone
Until it disappeared sometime in the Victorian era, a market cross stood near the bridge, possibly on the site of the former Lloyds Bank, now Albion Chambers. As early as 1273, the Cross is mentioned in the

'Hundred Rolls', with reference to the Prior of Spalding's entitlement to a fishing toll along the river bank 'as far as the Cross at Holbeach', but R S Pimperton, writing in the 1960s, states that this original version was knocked down during the building of the present church in the fourteenth century, and rebuilt in the same Barnack stone. If so, it lasted in this form until renewed by William Stukeley's father in 1683.

Attracts a local crusader

William Stukeley's illustration of the cross in 1722 reveals it as an impressive piece of street furniture, mounted on a substantial base four steps up, and in its canopied construction resembling the skeleton of a Perpendicular-style church tower. A typical excerpt from a nineteenth-century local press article waxes lyrically of this sturdy monument. Drawing on the fact that the cross was originally built during the time of the Crusades, when 'chivalrous lords' were returning from the Holy Land, the article romances on the stones 'being worn by the knees of that nameless crusader who founded Saracen's Head about two miles away', and the fact that, 'It formed a fitting companion to the venerable Norman Church which then existed. It stood a silent witness to its fall; it saw the consecration of the first stone of the new church; it watched all through that busy period, until finally it beheld the noble parish church much as we see it today.' One Holbeach crusader of this period, incidentally, who is not nameless, appears in the records of the Dean and Chapter of Canterbury as 'William the diker, a young man and unmarried, but very poor '.

Stukeley House and Stukeley Hall

In the grounds of William Stukeley School there once stood what was possibly the most important house in Holbeach: Stukeley House, or as it later became, Stukeley Hall, the name by which it disappeared under the demolition hammer amid great controversy in 1993.

From the Fletes...

In the sixteenth century the site on which the house was originally built belonged to the Flete, or Fleet, family, who are likely to have lived there in a wooden building, also serving as the administrative point for their estates. Later on that century, the Stukeleys made their first recorded appearance in Holbeach, marrying into the Flete family and thus inheriting these estates. Sometime in the 1670s William Stukeley's uncle, Adlard, set up his legal practice in the grounds, and it is he who may have rebuilt the former Flete house in brick, so creating an identity for the property that was to last over 300 years.

...To the Clarkes

In 1706 the house was inherited by Adlard Squire Stukeley (1698-1768), but at some point later in the century, it passed to the Palmer family. In the early 1800s however it was in the hands of the Sturtons, and by that time it is likely, looking at pre-1923 photographs of Stukeley House, that it

AS IT APPEARED BEFORE THE REBUILDING. Stukeley House in 1923.

underwent remodelling in a pleasant, late-Georgian style. After Thomas Sturton was declared bankrupt in the 1850s, the property passed first to William Thomas and then Jane Harrison, who died in 1901. It was purchased two years later by Thomas Clarke, a self-made man who had achieved a good living as a coal merchant, delivering fuel to homes on the marsh and returning with produce to sell on the market.

Clarke was a devout Congregationalist, playing the organ at the Holbeach chapel for 49 years before collapsing and dying at a Sunday service in 1921. In May that year the house was sold at auction for £4,200, when the sale particulars revealed that it had a mere nine bedrooms and five store rooms on the two upper floors, while downstairs the rooms assumed sizable proportions. The dining room measured 24ft 6in by 15ft 3in, a panelled drawing room 17ft by 15ft, breakfast room 15ft 4in by 15ft, and a library, 14ft 6in by 11ft 2in. Even the butler's pantry was 16ft by 8ft 9in, the hallway suggested bowling alley dimensions of 42ft by 10ft 3in, and there were two kitchens each over 16ft by 14ft. Outbuildings were comprehensive, taking the form of a summer house, tool, potting, boot, coal, copper and furnace houses, and a three-stall stable, harness room, two loose boxes, carriage house or garage, granary and trap house.

Carter buys the property
The purchaser of all this magnificence was the wealthy entrepreneurial farmer and benefactor Herbert Parkinson Carter, who lived just across the road at Abbots Manor. But he was intent on making his own mark, and this he did in 1923 by substantially altering the house's appearance to a contemporary style, following the design of architect E Norman Webster. Carter's commissioning of bricks and mortar must have been a preoccupation at this time, for the following year he had Red Roofs (later known as Holbeach Manor) built for his daughter Dorothy on the Fleet Road, another grand affair built of fine materials in a mock-Tudor style, and if anything more pleasing to the eye than the facelift Carter applied to his own Stukeley House.

Requisitioned by the Council
After Carter's retirement from public life to South Africa and his subsequent death in 1944, Stukeley Hall, as it was now known, remained in Mrs Frances Carter's name, but was requisitioned in September that year as 'a home for the sick and aged', followed by a compulsory purchase order for the same purpose by Holland County Council,

CARTER'S CASTLE. The extensive Stukeley Hall, when still in use as a retirement home.

[Photo Brenda Putterill.]

completed in March 1946. Having brought the house under its control, the Council maximised its investment by also adapting part of the building as a fire station from 1954 until 1980, when a purpose-built station replaced it in Fen Road. By the 1980s the pattern of old-age care was changing, the model having been determined locally by Patchett Lodge, situated just behind Stukeley Hall, and designed from the start in 1960 as a retirement home. In 1984 Stukeley was declared outdated as a care centre for the elderly. Its quota of beds was reduced from 37 to 34 to satisfy fire regulations, but its lift was still inadequate for most of the residents, who had to negotiate the stairs with some difficulty. From then on, talk of closure was rife until finally, with the building declared unsafe for senior citizens, Stukeley Hall was closed for good in April 1988.

The following month, Lincolnshire County Council salvaged statues from the grounds to sell at auction. One, a helmeted figure of the Greek goddess Athena, a copy of a Roman copy, made £7,500. The total proceeds of £13,800 went 'towards maximising the income of the County Council', but it was the last easy sale the Council would make, for years of wrangling over Stukeley Hall's future were about to begin. As time went on and the building remained empty, the County Council was even accused of deliberate neglect to encourage demolition.

Deciding its fate
Local opinion on the Chamber of Trade favoured its retention as a hotel and leisure facility, rather than the site for 33 executive homes which the County Council had envisaged. Meanwhile East Midlands businessman Steven Rigby, keen to see it

adapted as a health spa, had his offer of £125,000 above the official valuation refused, as not being in the interests of obtaining the best price. In 1990 boards went up over the large windows, and the Council persisted with the plan for executive homes, which this time specified 27 instead of 33 dwellings. The following year however, the Secretary of State for the Environment, who had been aware of the problem for some time, declared that in the absence of any more satisfactory proposals, the building should be reprieved.

TIME RUNNING OUT. The Stukeley Hall clock in its last few years over the ambulance station block. It survived the demolition and now stands in the grounds of William Stukeley School. [Photo Brenda Putterill.]

The proposal that did come up –one that had been considered by the Parish Council as early as 1989– was possibly the only one in which a reasonable compromise could have been reached: that of creating a second primary school –a need which no one could deny or ignore. At first demolition was not necessarily part of this plan, but shortly afterwards, in October 1991, it was apparent that knocking down Stukeley Hall seemed the only satisfactory way of proceeding with the school development. As a prelude, three trees, a horse chestnut, Turkey oak and English oak, were felled for safety reasons in December 1992, and demolition of the hall itself took place the following year.

The Old Rectory

If, before January 2002, you had ambled across Laddie's yard and approached the farmyard-style gate in the wall, you would have discovered a surprisingly rural scene concealed in the town centre. From a distance distinguished in appearance, in its peaceful setting of undulating greensward featuring a pond, old oaks and grazing sheep, the Old Rectory stood on land owned by the Ladbrook family. The original structure was believed to date from the seventeenth century, with later additions, while a tree was planted in the grounds to commemorate one of Queen Victoria's

AWAITING THE END, but still peculiarly appealing. The Old Rectory behind Laddies in 2000.

Jubilees. From 1895 it was inhabited by Tom Savage and his sister Anne Elizabeth Savage, grandchildren of Thomas Savage, a farmer from Holbeach Marsh, who had been one of the founding fathers of the Holbeach Railway back in the 1850s. Miss Savage, born one year after the railway opened, lived at the Old Rectory for 65 years, some of that time in the company of her niece, Gertrude Dobson, and died in September 1960 aged nearly 101. The property was to remain empty for the rest of its existence after Miss Dobson herself died. Unfairly referred to by yesterday's children –who kicked balls over the school wall into her garden– as 'Dirty Gertie', she made an upright and imposing figure, although her house had no mains electricity nor running water, and the state of the flooring was so dubious in places that a grandfather clock was found nailed to the wall. A curiosity was the outline of two windows painted on an exterior chimney wall.

Early surviving properties and streets

Progressive demolition, or an individual's lack of means to build properties of durable materials, has resulted in few Holbeach properties surviving beyond 350 years. Of seventeenth-century buildings, however, Holbeach offers three likely examples: the Red Lion, the Crown, and the High Street's Mansion House, birthplace of Sir Norman Angell.

The Mansion House

It is even a surprise to its owners that the Mansion House could have been built as

17th-CENTURY GRACE, 19th-CENTURY FAME. The Mansion House situated between East Lea Furnishings and Lisa's shop was built in the 1680s, but is better remembered as the birthplace of Sir Norman Angell in 1872 and the family home of his father, department store owner Thomas Angell Lane, in Victorian times.

early as 1681, since it more typically follows the symmetrically-fronted style of a Queen Anne (1702-14) residence. The earliest owners of the house are not known, although a pawnbroker was reputed to have lived there during the eighteenth century. But after 1802 it was owned by the brothers Thomas and Seth Holliday, sons of a wealthy family in Whaplode, who may well have acquired it with the generous proceeds of their father's will –approximately £10,000 to each son– although these sums were modest compared to other largesse the family had distributed. According to the writings of local journalist Joseph Wilson in 1907, the Hollidays 'flourished in the days when corn made £5 a quarter', and were reputed to have left sums of £70,000 and £40,000 to members of the Savage family, who once occupied Leadenhall Farm in the Marsh. Thomas and Seth Holliday died within a year of each other in 1845-6 and their graves, in the form of imposing table tombs (although Seth's is in

bad shape, braced with cables and patched with cement and brick), can be distinguished at the eastern end of All Saints' churchyard, opposite Talbot Villa.

Musical hauntings

That Thomas Angell Lane's family resided in the Mansion House in the latter half of the nineteenth century is fairly well known, but during the twentieth century it alternated between periods of private and commercial use. In 1980, for instance, it became a small hotel, run first by Bill and Edna Davidson and later by a four-man business consortium. By this time the building had been adapted to include a cellar restaurant with bar, two ground-floor dining areas and four guest bedrooms. The consortium, eventually finding the venture too time-consuming, then offered a prize of £200 for the best future entrepreneurial suggestion for the property. However, the last commercial occupants to date, Janet Clarke and Martin Thacker, continued the Mansion House's use as a restaurant until the

WEALTHY OWNER. On the Church Walk side of All Saints churchyard, the tomb of Thomas Holliday, once joint owner with his brother Seth of the Mansion House from the early 1800s.

succeeding owner applied for planning consent to return it to a private residence. During its time as a hotel, rumours abounded of friendly hauntings, wafting currents of air around bewildered observers on the stairs or in the hallway. And rather reminiscent of those Cole Porter lyrics referring to 'that tinkling piano in the next apartment', locals could remember hearing such an instrument being played in the Mansion House when it was supposed to be unoccupied in the 1950s!

Above and below stairs

From the rear, the house's sturdy triple grouping of chimneys can clearly be seen at the entrance to Wright's Mews in Park Road, to which area the grounds at the back would have once actually extended. Even now, a good-sized 'secret' garden remains at the rear of the property, measuring some 100 by 35ft. As befitted the affluence of the Hollidays and other occupants, the house interior was designed to create a dignified first impression. The hallway and the two front rooms leading off it at either side are panelled, but an archway at a mid-point in its length marks the boundary into a non-panelled section of the house and this treatment is repeated in the rooms upstairs, consisting of four bedrooms on the first floor and two more –originally part of the servants' quarters, at attic level. The upper rooms on both levels can be reached by the main staircase, but there is a separate stairway from the kitchen leading directly to the attic, so that the servants could not be seen coming and going in front of select company.

Stone steps from the ground floor opposite the kitchen lead down to the cellar mentioned in Sir Norman Angell's memoirs, divided into sections. The front portion, extending to the full width of the house, may have been the original kitchen, as it featured a large open fireplace that once included a bread oven. There are two cellar rooms at the rear, one probably designated for wine or coal storage, but both featuring vaulted brick ceilings. The two-storey outbuildings at the rear, attractive in their own right, complement and complete this example of a beautifully preserved period dwelling, and the tone of the High Street owes much to the presence of this house, probably more than is generally realised.

Around the streets

Church Street has seen much change, but eighteenth-century properties are there if you look for them, despite the architectural historian Pevsner's disparagement that 'Only the Victorian Church Hall in robust Tudor Gothic deserves notice', and that the buildings opposite are a 'disjointed jumble of diminutive fronts'!

CHURCH ST. 18th-century houses near the Exchange.

No.31 is one example of an early building, while a date of 1773 is attributed to the properties next door at Nos. 33 and 35.

Across the road and opposite the church grounds, one or two cottages, converted long ago to two storeys and currently signed Holbeach Angling and Cat Rescue, survive from a terrace of late eighteenth-century single-storey dwellings. Next door but one, the fitness centre and undertakers on the corner of Back Lane stand on the site of wool merchant Thomas Everson's fine mansion house. From an 1804 illustration it looks not dissimilar to Thomas Angell Lane's house in the High Street, but it was built much later in 1788, and was demolished several decades ago after its demotion to trade premises.

Dating other properties

Opposite the former Congregationalist chapel, closed for worship since 1963 and now selling furniture and antiques in Park Road, there is a pair of cottages, dated with a plaque at one end, inscribed 'J N A 1827', thus making them nearly as old as the Public Hall that once stood next door to them. In Fleet Street, early buildings include a pair of cottages next to the Black Bull dated 1819, together with a terrace of former almshouses from 1845, while in the High Street, the exterior of Calthrop, Leopold and Harvey, Solicitors, survives largely unmodified from its building date of 1785 –two years after balloon flight was pioneered by the Montgolfier Brothers in Paris. Only the outline of the black night safe drawer betrays its existence for a time as the Midland Bank (now HSBC) until 1971.

Across the road and in various guises, lengths of early nineteenth-century shop terraces survive.

REGENCY STYLE. A shopfront opposite Somerfield.

Opposite Somerfield the pair of dainty shops at nos.14 and 16 Fleet Street –credited in Pevsner and Harris's *Buildings of England* with Regency bowed shopfronts– are a valuable indication of how other neighbouring shops would have looked in their heyday. The 1813 tablet above 'To the Point' is clear enough, but few realise that BKK Thai Restaurant was built as early as 1823, or that, a few doors along, The Hollys gift shop dates from the early 1800s, although once inside, its great age reveals itself in the low ceilings and floor levels several inches below the present road surface outside.

Plentiful nineteenth-century examples
Albert Street, as the name implies, is part of a grid of small streets of terraced houses most probably laid out after the marriage of Queen Victoria to Prince Albert in 1840. Its mid-nineteenth century identity is still very obvious, both from the largely unaltered appearance of the terraced houses, several of which still carry patriotic flagstaff holders from the grand days of Queen and Empire (No.9 has provision for no less than 12 flags to be displayed) and the presence of the Baptist Chapel, built in 1845. Barrington Gate also has its gems from a slightly earlier period. On the way down from the town centre, just before the Sorting Office, there is a pair of Regency houses, one dated 1834 and the former residence and surgery of Doctor Gerald Walker, (whose father, Dr Frederick, first acquired the property in 1908). Then near the bottom of the road on the opposite side stands Serpentine House, built 1831 by Alfred Harrisson. This also

attracts Pevsner's appreciation for its 'nicely detailed rusticated stone steps curving up one side' to the entrance, while Barrington

UNUSUAL ELEGANCE. The gracefully-curving steps of Serpentine House in Barrington Gate, built 1831, for many years the home of Eric and Nora Lane.

House next door, 'also latest Georgian', is noted for its 'five bay front' and parapets curving down at each side, which are described as 'ramped wing walls'.

The Cemetery
Around 1849 a petition organised by some of the townspeople resulted in an official visit by William Lee, a civil engineer and 'superintending inspector', to report on the situation arising over the Church burial ground. From this it was agreed that 'The present Burial ground is objectionable on account of its being in the centre of the Town, as well as on account of the great number of internments.' Over the preceding 20 years, these had averaged some 95 annually, and conditions had reached the point where the closing of the churchyard to further burials was recommended.

So a six-acre site just outside the town centre, and bordered today by Park Road, Park Lane and Edinburgh Walk, was developed at a total cost of £4,896. Of this, £795 was spent on land, £2,457 on the chapel, and the remainder on laying out.

Nearly 1900 burials in the first 20 years

The first keeper of the Cemetery was Charles May (1802-1875), who looked after the grounds for over 20 years. Originally a member of Fleet Baptist Church from 1823, he was described on his death as 'the last survivor of a small band of Christian men who commenced the first Sunday School in Holbeach, sometimes teaching in a wooden building, at others in a cellar.' In his time, 1,889 burials took place in the Cemetery, and May's own gravestone

GENEROUS ACCOMMODATION. The former keeper's house in Park Lane.

can still be seen a few yards to the right, just inside the Edinburgh Walk entrance. The original keeper's house, incidentally, exists opposite the north fence of the Cemetery, at the corner of Battlefields Lane South.

The Chapel of Rest

Situated in the centre of the Cemetery, the chapel's design, with an arch through the centre dividing it into two equal parts, has everything to do with the original formalities.

'DISSENTER'S' EYE VIEW (north side) of the Chapel of Rest.

The southern part of the grounds, backing onto The Tenters –together with the appropriate section of the chapel standing on that side– was consecrated by the Bishop of Lincoln on November 23rd 1855, while the northern part (on the Park Lane side) and accompanying chapel building, was left unconsecrated for 'dissenters'. In appearance the building imitates the Decorated style, crowned by what Pevsner terms 'a very peculiar spire over an archway', although it is still pleasing in the dramatic way it rises out of the avenue of mature evergreens. In a sense we are lucky that both sections of this building still exist, for the north wing was closed as a chapel in 1952 after its roof was found to be 'beyond economic repair', having allowed rainwater to pour in over the years.

EARLY GRAVE. Elizabeth Graves' headstone, 1855.

Decay

Pigeons and their debris had also made their mark, and with only a limited budget for repairs the intention was to remove the good wood from the

BEFORE FLOWERING CURRANT BLOSSOMS. Henry Clarke's memorial (he died in 1883).

north chapel, and use it to improve the south equivalent. It was 'disgusting', said Mr E S Martin, 'that the chapel should have been allowed to get in that state.' While this was true, Victorian building methods were partly to blame for omitting a damp course, and masking the walls with asbestos sheeting seemed to be the only solution.

The spire, too, was causing concern to the likes of Councillor the Revd C V Browne-

Wilkinson, as it had developed a list 'towards the town'.

2½ tons of droppings
But, reassured Mr Hopkins after an inspection, it would still 'be here 50 years from now', and so it has proved. During September 1954, the spire was given the benefit of some maintenance, when 2½ tons of pigeon droppings, 40 dead pigeons, and a two-foot layer of sticks and twigs were removed from its inner heights, while the top windows that had been open to the elements were wired over to prevent more birds getting in.

As to the burial arrangements followed at the Cemetery, Holbeach Parish Council notified all local undertakers in January 1953 that no funerals should take place after 3 p.m. in the winter months, to avoid gravediggers having to use a lantern!

Carter's Park
Carter's Park takes its name from Herbert Carter, JP, a local landowner and benefactor who gave the grounds to the town in October 1929. Previously when in the ownership of George Hix, the land had seen varied use from the turn of the nineteenth century. In the 1880s a map shows a considerable part of it as a cricket pitch, but flax was grown on it during the First World War, after which the field supported grazing cattle, when not in use by travelling circuses and magic lantern shows. A serious fire occurred at this time, with stacks ablaze near the area of the present Park Road surgery, but the presence of a nearby waterpit, and neighbouring house frontages draped with wet cloths, helped to prevent its spread.

Used by schools and speedway
A foretaste of future use came in the early 1920s, with the construction of a pavilion and the laying out of a bowling green and football pitch, of which the Boys School and Church of England Girls School soon took advantage for their soccer, hockey and netball games. When ownership passed to Herbert Carter, regular improvements followed, including the planting of many trees. Beautification was not the only aim, however. A banked cinder track for speedway racing had also been installed: not just for the town's pleasure, but with an eye to social conscience, as it had been laid by unemployed Northumberland miners under a governmental grant-aid scheme. Largely responsible for the layout was Mr E Carr, surveyor to the old Holbeach Urban Council, in its last years of existence before reorganisation in 1932.

Playgrounds and putting greens
A bungalow for the park keeper was built in 1929, to house Ralph Emmitt who was to tend the grounds for many years afterwards, assisted by George Twaite, who worked well into his 70s. Ralph's hours were officially 8 a.m. to 5 p.m. in winter, extended to 6 p.m. in summer. While a children's play area had been created with two swings, a wooden see-saw and a large slide, many youngsters preferred to play on the old First World War cannon which had been moved to the park from the crossroad triangle at Fleet Road and Foxes Low Road.

Unfortunately this was not to be its final resting place, as it was requisitioned for scrap metal during the Second War. For the adults, a putting green proved less popular, unlike the two quoit rinks, which echoed constantly to the once-familiar metallic clang of players aiming their rings at the steel posts.

Children made thirsty by various play activities had fallen into the habit, during 1933, of asking the caretaker for a drink of water, and Coun. John Patchett 'desired [that] a different arrangement be made.' Also making arrangements that year, to play in the park, was the newly-formed Holbeach Cricket Club, while the Spalding & District Motor Club were allowed to race motorbikes on their cinder track, on the understanding that they indemnified the Parish Council from all risks.

Holbeach United Football Club was also to be responsible for its own turf, as it discovered when it requested the Parish Council to pay £17 for 10 cwt of pitch-conserving manure in 1954, and was politely told to pay its own way. It was either that, replied John Mossop, or the children went without their new play equipment for another year.

Bandstand attractions and the Jubilee Shelter

The 30s were also memorable for that quintessentially tranquil British park attraction, the Sunday evening band concert. Bands from Holbeach, Parson Drove,

OLD LANDSCAPING. Traces of attractive features from the inter-war years were still to be seen in the centre of the park in 2003.

Sleaford, Kirton and elsewhere often attracted hundreds of people, enjoying both the music and the heady scent of roses from the sunken garden, planted with bushes donated by Mr Baker of Whaplode in 1932. Further contributions of this kind were to follow. From Mr A E Farrow of Holbeach St Marks, for instance, came a catalpa tree to commemorate the coronation of George VI in May 1937, while Jacques Amand obliged 15 years later with 250 rose trees, free of charge. Back in 1935, the Silver Jubilee of the late King George V had been marked by the appearance of a substantial shelter, opened by Mr S S Mossop and funded by public subscription. This survives, devoid of any embellishment whatsoever, unless one counts the sad proliferation of graffiti, its brickwork painted a clinical light grey.

The last substantial tributes to royalty were the park gates to celebrate Queen Elizabeth II's coronation in 1953, but these were not actually installed and officially opened until the following year. Not that the town had been backward in trying to keep up appearances for the Coronation itself. Eight months before the event, Mr J Franks, Chairman of the Parks Committee, was expressing the hope that the Army Cadet Corps would refrain from leaving ashes outside their hut, and that the Tennis Club would paint their pavilion to match the standard of the other park buildings already

spruced up for the big day. The royal event had provided the impetus to turn over a new leaf, for despite the efforts of Emmitt and Twaite, the Park had reached a low ebb by 1951. It was described as looking 'like a man wanting a shave' and needed £200 to return it to good condition. But, said J L Bayston, it was like 'getting blood out of a stone to get the people of Holbeach to subscribe.'

Bandstand spirit lives on

His disappointment was understandable, for 1951 was Festival of Britain year. Hardly anyone had contributed towards the Festival clock, and nor did anyone seem to care about its intended resting place at the top of the bandstand. The latter was by now in a bad state, and in view of the fact that it was now only used two or three times a year, Councillor Arthur White felt it was a waste

GRACIOUS GATES commemorate the 1953 Coronation, and have stood the years well.

of resources. Nevertheless, the floorboards were repaired that October, although this legacy of more gracious days and behaviour was now on borrowed time. Happily however, while the town no longer has a proper bandstand, it can still boast a band of its own which in summer months continues to play in the Park on certain Sundays. Holbeach Community Band (renamed Holbeach Town Band in 2000) was formed in 1971 by Brian Long and Colin Coupland. Alan Ellis took over the baton from Brian in 1988, and the musical director is now Mel Hopkin. The Band has always attracted players of all ages and when it is not out on its many engagements, its melodies can be heard wafting from its base in Back Lane on Wednesday night practice sessions. In the

1970s an LP record was made, sponsored by local businesses, with stirring renderings of 'Sons of the Brave', 'Y Viva Espana', and 'The Floral Dance'.

In the 50s, as now, some teenagers persisted in using playground equipment intended for much younger children. In 1954, a 14-year-old boy trapped his feet under the rocking horse and brought park-keeper Ralph Emmitt hurrying out with his First Aid box. 'These big lads always want to make it stand on its hind legs,' commented Parks Committee Chairman Mr Franks.

Everyone's park, past and present
With 10 acres at its disposal, Carter's Park was the venue for large agricultural shows and fêtes in aid of the Red Cross during the Second World War years, and since 1945 has accommodated at various times the demands of athletics, cricket, tennis with both hard and grass courts, bowls, Holbeach United FC and initially the Vintage Rally until it moved to King's Field in 1998. In recent decades various benches were donated here and there around the park, labelled in memory of local people. One such was dedicated to J S R Tingle, JP, who did much to further the Park's cause.

WORN OUT. The 1935 Jubilee shelter had seen better days by 2002.

Another bench commemorates Mrs Norah (Nip) Gough, 1924-1995. On the side opposite the stands, display boards advertising many names from Holbeach trade and industry now line the west side of the football pitch which has been bordered in recent times by orange concrete posts and an iron rail. As for the Tigers' clubhouse itself, it looks fit to withstand a siege, with iron bars fronting each window.

By the late 1990s and early 2000s the Park was showing the effects of a lack of investment, particularly where dealing with vandalism and catering for teenagers were concerned, so in 2003 a start was made by creating a skateboard and BMX area as part of a comprehensive plan co-ordinated by Conservation Officer Jonathan Biggadike of South Holland District Council, with input from Lincolnshire County Council. The plans are to include a redesigned play area for younger children, upgraded tennis courts and revised planting and fencing layouts to improve safety and visibility. A kiosk was also being considered as a sales point for refreshments and hiring out games equipment.

SIGN OF THINGS TO COME. A skateboard course takes shape on the east side of the park in May 2003, while the old Jubilee Shelter, its fate in the balance, looks on.

The Public Hall, Park Road

The Public Hall, later to become the former Youth Club, stood on a site now occupied by modern houses, opposite Halstead and Fowlers cabinet makers. It was built around 1825 with public subscription shares, worth £40 each in 1833.

Many uses
After the First World War it saw a variety of uses, first of all as a cinema, where audiences would have seen silent films starring Charlie Chaplin, Buster Keaton and Rudolph Valentino among many others. In this period it became known as 'Rammies', after its proprietor, Harry Ramsdale. But when the talkies arrived in the late 1920s, the cost of converting the cinema to sound proved uneconomic, especially since the Hippodrome, which was equipped for the new medium, was soon to open around the corner. So the hall was reconverted to its original layout to become a dance hall. During the Second World War it was used by the military, before housing the Holbeach Youth Club from 1945.

The Youth Club survived a critical initiation, for in the early 50s it was troubled by poor support and even bankruptcy. A contributory factor was the rumour that Spalding Grammar School and High School pupils were being actively discouraged from joining, and in March 1952, Eric Lane, one of the trustees, suggested that the Club be closed in its existing form, and reopened on Saturdays under closer supervision.

But even without the Youth Club, the Public Hall still played a valuable role in offering extra room for classes of the by now overcrowded Holbeach schools. The pupils' Christmas parties were held there, while a letter to Holbeach County Primary Junior School (and recorded by the head, William Tingle) from the warden in 1953 defines the Youth Centre's use as follows:

'The Schools have a legal right to be on the premises for their various classes in physical education between the hours of 9 a.m. and 3.30 p.m. each day, except Saturdays and Sundays, and in future nothing must be done to interfere with this arrangement.

'Sales are to be held in the large room upstairs...or sales to commence at 3.45 p.m. if the large hall is used.

'The large hall is available to the Magistrates for their monthly court on the third Thursday of every month...occasional special courts to be held in the rooms upstairs at other times.' Varied are the memories maturer Holbeachians have of this place. To Freda Coley, the building had an eerie, haunted air. For Councillor Martin Howard, it was where, in his youth, he fell through the upper floor while in the company of a young lady. But the warden's official definition of use in 1953 continues:
'On days when the Hall is booked for this purpose (Caryl Jenner Mobile Theatre)...may not have access to the hall until after 3.30 p.m. but may use the dressing room and stage, providing there is no interference with such classes.' The Caryl Jenner Theatre was styled after a lady of that name who put on regular performances in Holbeach, some of which were quite thought-provoking as well as entertaining.

One such production in 1952 was *Tomorrow's Child*, a John Coates play which, to a packed audience, interpreted life in England in 1975. One wonders how accurate they were at anticipating the hideous and laughable fashions, colours and hairstyles!

Demolition, 1980s
When the Holbeach County Primary School opened in 1982, thus vacating the old school premises in Boston Road opposite the present Co-op and Tesco, the County Council offered the Youth Club the opportunity to move into something more permanent –a very timely gesture, as by the late 1970s, the Public Hall was in a bad way, with expensive roof repairs looming, and a ceiling that was in danger of collapse. It was sold for building development into semi-detached houses, and the Youth Club, now maintained by a £4,000 per annum grant from the County Council, ceased to be a voluntary organisation and moved into the old school premises in November 1983.

NOW A WAREHOUSE. Park Hall as it is today (top) and below, an interior view showing the former upstairs projection room.

33

Park Hall

Situated next door to Halstead & Fowler cabinet makers, Park Hall is almost a lone survivor of the buildings that served as the traditional entertainment centres of Holbeach, although it has seen varied use over the past century, not only as a live theatre, cinema, and dance hall, but also an auction room, wartime soup kitchen, boxing ring, and Jacques Amand's bulb packing warehouse. It is now owned by Limmings for storage purposes.

Variety shows

Travelling variety shows performed here in the 1920s. There were many such troupes at this time, all dependent on what little they could share from the takings to scratch a living, and, like their equivalents fictionalised in J B Priestley's *Good Companions*, were sometimes stranded in the town through lack of funds. Backstage facilities were primitive, with no heating in the changing rooms with their cold, concrete floors.

Films and dancing

For a time the theatre was managed by the dapper Jack Budd, a trapeze artist by profession, who performed at agricultural and sporting events during the summer. By this time however, variety shows were losing out to the silver screen. For a time, the hall became a cinema in the late 20s, showing silent films as a rival operation to the Public Hall's across the road. But the Public Hall's proprietor, Harry Ramsdale, brought a stop to this by taking over the Park Hall as well, after which it was turned into a dance hall. Lessons for such occasions were also arranged under the same roof, conducted by Mrs Ivy Harradence and Mr Spencer Drinkwater's dancing classes, instructing in the art of the Hesitation Change, the Double Reverse Spin and the Impetus Turn.

Store room of memories

The Girls' Club met there for its socials and whist drives arranged by Mrs Major and one of her daughters, and weekly dances and fancy dress balls became a regular feature in the early 1930s. It was here that Len Hall, part-time bandleader, performed his 12-hour piano-playing marathon in January 1931.

Difficult to date, but probably of the late nineteenth century, Park Hall still dominates the upper reaches of Park Road in a blank-faced manner. Externally, there is evidence of many bricked-up windows, including those of the dank cellar (dampened by the Holbeach River, perhaps?), once used by Mr Pape's fruiterers shop for overnight storage of produce. This shop was tacked onto the Hall's façade near the long-porched entrance, and was later taken down by subsequent owners Limmings, who attempted to run the little shop as a sideline, but found it unprofitable. Inside Park Hall's lofty expanse, PVC rainwater butts, garden furniture and fertiliser sacks are stacked on floorboards once tripped by foxtrotting feet. At the Halstead & Fowler end, a wooden stairway, its worn treads sloping downwards, leads to the projectionist's room, which survives as a dominating inner structure on slim pillars. Round the back, brick toilet edifices remain, but other outbuildings in the yard shared with Halstead & Fowler were due to be pulled down in October 2001.

Limmings took over the property from the Electricity Board, who had used it for storage over several years. As for the earlier occupant, Jacques Amand's business is no longer in the area, his Washway HQ now owned by Angloflora, although his son is understood to be still trading from company offices in Beethoven Street, London. However, there is a link between Park Hall's occupants past and present, as Jack Limming (Patrick's father) was Jacques Amand's manager before going into business on his own.

The Reading Room, or Church Hall, and the Library, Church Street,

This building, in its mildly mock-Tudor style, is situated next to the present Library and was built in 1870, originally intended for use as a small private school.

THE READING ROOM of 1870.

In 1901 it was given

to the town by the trust deed of William Snarey, a reputable Holbeach ironmonger of many years' standing and a keen Methodist, as a male-only reading room in an attempt to lure the young men of Holbeach away from the evils of public houses. Upstairs, under the substantial exposed beams, a billiards room was created and over the years many matches were played there against neighbouring towns and villages. To quote an example, a typical match in January 1931 saw Holbeach Reading Room victorious by 102 points over Lutton Institute, with scores of W Franks 106, R H Bellairs 125, H Griggs 125, and S Tingle 117. The billiard tables remained upstairs until around 1980, although the popularity of these matches had declined after 1939, and by the late 1950s any indications of its original usage had petered out.

Public library services
By then, of course, Holbeach's public library had been a fixture since 1949 in what has now become the Pop-In café, behind the Market House. But it was fitting that when the Library needed larger premises, it re-opened on a site acquired from the Church in April 1973, right next door to the old Reading Room. Branch Librarian Andrew Hemsley now had much more room in which to operate, and Eric Martin, the contractor, presented a showcase of items which had been unearthed during the building work, including a bronze plaque, old bottles and a filigree incense burner. This can still be seen, set into the front of the reception counter. An impressive embellishment was to follow in January 1992 with the installation of a fine stained glass window by the artist Nick Jones, which depicted the traditional Holbeach trades and occupations of milling, bulb-growing and drainage, with the Stukeley Hall clock as the central symbol. No longer a place to be entered in hushed reverence, the Library has become a very busy place in recent years.

The Reading Room refurbished, 2002
As for the old Reading Room, in more recent years the building was administered by All Saints Church, with the intention of funding maintenance costs from hiring fees. But though there were plenty of regular bookings, the cost of renovation work required was clearly going to outstrip income –among other pressing items, the orginal slate roof needed total replacement. With £150,000 worth of restoration required, closure threatened in 1999, but the old-established William Snarey Trust, administered by Roy Staples and Chris Penney, came to the rescue, raising the money by donations and a substantial Lottery grant, and after a seven-month re-fit was re-opened in May 2002 by Vice-Lord Lieutenant Tony Worth.

The Crescent, Spalding Road

BUILT FOR C R THOMPSON'S EMPLOYEES. The Crescent, Spalding Road.

This interesting group of houses at the far end of Spalding Road was built by Charles Richard Thompson, brother of John Thompson, the butcher. 'C R' was the proprietor of a drapery business in the High Street in between Vincents ironmongers and the old Talbot Hotel, on the site later occupied by Countryman outfitters, from the 1900s to the 1930s, where customers wishing to join their thrift club were issued with a special tinplate money box. Charles's sister Carrie lived in one of the houses for a time, although the story goes that they were primarily built for his employees. They were constructed in 1913, reputedly during a slump when building labour and material costs were favourable, in a style reflected more elaborately in Thompson's own house, Highworth, situated farther into town at 56 Spalding Road. A later owner of No. 56 was Lawrence Bayston, whose butchers shop eventually became Swepstone's. On Thompson's retirement, the business was acquired by the Isaacs family, owners of Oldrid's department store in Boston, who continued to trade under the Thompson name for a time.

The Meridian Millstone

TOEING THE GREENWICH LINE. Millstone laid 1959 marks the spot on the Spalding Road corner of Wignal's Gate.

The Millstone positioned at the entrance to Wignal's Gate in Spalding Road represents the point where the Meridian Line crosses Holbeach. It then runs through the rest of the County at Frampton, Louth and Cleethorpes, before passing out to sea at Withernsea.

The Meridian is an imaginary line, running North to South from pole to pole. The need for an agreed line for nautical purposes was first suggested in the eighteenth century, but it was not until 1884 that the Greenwich Meridian was established by international agreement, as a means of measuring longitude, calculated in so many degrees east or west of Greenwich in London. The official centenary was commemorated in 1984 by Holbeach schoolchildren linking hands along the imaginary line, but the actual spot at Wignal's Gate had been marked by the positioning of the Millstone on 6th June 1959, at a ceremony conducted by Councillor Mrs Alison Hunter.

Hotels and Inns

There are currently nine public houses and hotels in Holbeach –an impressive figure, but amounting to less than half of those existing over a century ago, when H A Merry's *Compendium* of 1890 revealed a total of 22, not counting the so-called 'beer houses' run by individuals as a sideline activity.

In 1900, names well known to us all today, such as the Chequers, the Bell, the Horse & Groom, the String of Horses, the Crown, the Red Lion, the Ram, the Exchange, the Station and the Black Bull, were already in existence, and the first seven of those mentioned above had been around for some considerable time before that, listed as they are in Pigot's *Directory of Lincolnshire* for 1822, alongside the now little-known names of the Bull & Dog, and the Highland Laddy.

The Railway Tavern on the Barley Pit

But to revert to 1900, we also had the Talbot Hotel, the Elephant and Castle and the Railway Tavern in the High Street. Other than a quest for topicality after the railway came to Holbeach in 1858, it was difficult to imagine why the Railway Tavern was so named, as it was nowhere near the station. But as a low and rambling cottage-like affair, positioned on the corner of St John Street and High Street (where the Y-Beauty shop is now) it occupied an interesting site nevertheless: one that included in its deeds 'All that messuage including the Barley Pit'. So in addition to the pits that existed in Fishpond Lane, here was another.

The Barley Pit was included in a map drawn of the area by William Stukeley in 1703, who also offered the theory that it was once the meeting place of Corpus Christi, one of the Holbeach medieval guilds. It could hardly have been ignored by the

SOME DISTANCE FROM THE RAILWAY. But as good a name as any. The old Railway Tavern, on the site of the Barley Pit in the High Street. [Courtesy John Elms.]

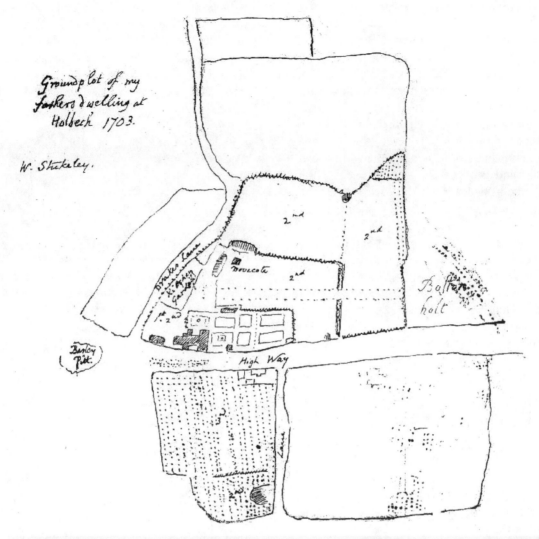

'GROUNDPLOT OF MY FATHER'S DWELLING'. William Stukeley's 1703 sketch shows the Barley Pit to the far left, on the corner of what is now St John Street and High Street. Note that the road in front of his father's house (a site depicted by a series of rectangles and now approximately occupied by the Georgian house now converted into flats) is referred to as 'High Way' instead of Barrington Gate, with Fishpond Lane then known as Drakes Lane.

[Courtesy Mr J W Belsham.]

Stukeley household, as the smell must have been very apparent over at their home just around the corner in Barrington Gate. For into it drained not only the by-products of a neighbouring brewery, but the drainage from two nearby cottages as well. It is not certain whether John Hardy Carter's brewery across the road made use of this pit; at least Carter was self-sufficient in his water supply, drawing this from a pond (long since filled in) at the rear of the present Somerfield site. Other old brewers' names connected with Holbeach are Ridlingtons, the Old Foundry Brewery in Barrington Gate, and Thomas Annison, Penny Hill Brewery.

To continue this pub roll-call of 1900, there were the Waggon and Horses in Boston Road, the Eight Ringers in Barrington Gate, the Retreat in Fleet Street –then newly owned by Morgans Brewers who had paid £480 for it– and no fewer than *three* licensed premises in Back Lane: the Carpenters Arms, the Brewers Arms and the Rose (the latter was owned by Mills of Wisbech, and closed in October 1912 after 28 years}.

St John Street meanwhile had the Lord Nelson, Park Road –or Cemetery Road as it was called in those days– the Oddfellows Arms, and in Station Street, the Railway Inn.

37

Billy and Biddy's Railway Inn

The Railway Inn was subsequently renamed the Station Inn. Bateman's Brewery paid £2,000 to acquire it in 1925 from Lenny Septimus Harrisson, a local solicitor, who because of his family links with the Carter brewing family, had held various licensed property interests. It remained in Bateman's hands for 53 years, tenanted during that time by John Campion* and then the well-known Billy and Biddy Best, who arrived in 1940 after retiring from the theatrical profession. Mrs Best carried on until she was 76, handing over to the Gilberts in 1971. Seven years later, Batemans sold the Station Inn as a free house to Gail and Rodney Fulford.

Holbeach's last thatched building

The Oddfellows Arms, standing at the junction of what is now Park Road and the High Street, was believed to be the last thatched building in Holbeach. Most of it survives as a video hire shop, and served formerly as a toy and cycle business. A feature of the original building was a passageway at the side reaching from front to rear into Boston Road. As a refuge for troublesome or under-age drinkers, however, it was short-lived, thanks to the tactics of Sergeant Lown and an accompanying constable in positioning themselves at either end of the passage!

The Nelson, the Elephant, and the Retreat

The Lord Nelson in St John Street was once a Soames Brewery house, run by Leonard Kilbon. After closure it became a coal merchant's office, and is now identified as the house opposite the Indian restaurant, which follows the curve of the street as it joins Barrington Gate. A reminder of earlier

BREWERY HOUSE AND HARDWARE SHOP. The Elephant (on the present Boots site) finally called 'Time' in 1914.
[Courtesy John Elms.]

* John Campion began a building business there, which later became Campion and Penney, and eventually, Langwith Builders.

days is the tall gate let into the façade, with room enough to admit a horse-drawn dray into its yard. Just around the corner, opposite the present kitchen and aquarium shops, the Retreat, once promoting 'lunches teas and snacks', closed in 1964. It

PUB IN RETREAT. From beer to central heating. The former Retreat in Fleet Street, while serving as Power Motors in the 1970s. *[Peter Coupland.]*

later served as a car showroom and is now the premises of Holbeach Heating. A similar fate had attended The Elephant in the High Street when it closed in 1914 to be leased by J C Harrisson to Mr E Blackburn for his motor and cycle business, while the Exchange in Church Street and the Black Bull were both rebuilt to a contemporary style in the mid-1930s. The first-generation Exchange once had a quoits team, who played in Thompson's Field opposite. This field later became the green for the present-day United Services bowls club.

The Talbot

The Talbot Hotel, like the Nelson formerly under Soames Brewery's ownership, was one of the last to go, ending its days as a long-term blot on the townscape. It was situated next door to Elsoms and C R Thompsons drapers on the High Street's south side, now occupied by Caprice and The Card Gallery, and was once one of the best hotels in Holbeach. Believed to date back three centuries, the coaching age and the era of the horse fairs provided its real *raison d'être*. In the nineteenth century it was a calling place for mounted troops, clattering over the cobbles outside as they arrived in town. As at the Chequers almost opposite, long-distance coach-and-fours stopped there to rest or change the horses and pick up passengers, and in the 1820s a sociable (or open four-wheeled carriage) once departed from its front doors for Boston every Tuesday, Thursday and Saturday mornings at 9 a.m., or to Wisbech every Monday, Wednesday and Friday at 1 p.m. The Talbot was well placed, too, for the Horse Fair trade, the bars crowded with farmers and dealers whose animals filled the spacious yard at the rear. In the mid-nineteenth century it was owned by a James Capp, on whose death the hotel, and an adjoining house and shop occupied by Mr Martin, a cabinet maker, were acquired at auction by Mr Mossop for £1,180 in 1870. Sadly, the establishment suffered a lingering death, for after closure in 1969, demolition did not follow for another five years. Rumours that Brierleys Supermarkets of Peterborough had bought the site came to nothing, and it took until the late 80s before redevelopment into shops and flats by King's Quality Homes was completed.

The Ram

A more recent departure from the Holbeach licensed trade was the Ram, closed in 2001 to become the new premises for Flower Basket florists. It still boasts the large yard at the rear that accommodated much of the visiting traffic attracted by the market's busier days, or which after the war, allowed parking for coach parties welcomed by proprietor Grimwood. From 1901, when it was bought for £1,390, it was owned for some years by Holes Brewery of Newark. At the Bell Hotel, too, which once boasted of 'Interior Sprung Matresses', evidence remains of the horse age, with a small enclosed yard leading off the High Street to receive arriving guests.

The Horse & Groom

In Victorian times and the early twentieth century, the Horse & Groom, purchased by Morgans Brewers in 1899 for £1,500, provided a home in its yard in off-duty hours to the fire brigade horses, the actual fire engine itself being kept just across the road behind what is now Dervensure insurance brokers. To digress for a moment, fire services were not always provided free. A scale of charges existed in the mid-nineteenth century, ranging from five shillings for each of the seven firemen on the team, through seven shillings each for the brigade manager and policeman in

attendance, to £2 each for the use of the two engines if the fire was outside Holbeach. This tariff excluded the fee for the horses. Beyond eight hours' attendance an additional charge of 6d per man was levied. Even in the 1920s, the firemen still received only five shillings each, although their overtime rate had at least increased to 2/6, and they were by then based at Market Hill where the present toilets are situated.

The oldest inns

The Red Lion and the Chequers can claim long histories. It is unfortunate, therefore, that available details are somewhat patchy. Renovations in 1997 at the Red Lion revealed an inglenook fireplace after five tons of rubble were removed, suggesting origins of 400 years or more. It was believed to have been blocked up for at least a century.

Both the Crown and the Chequers are associated with John Stukeley, who built the former and rebuilt the latter in the late seventeenth century, but otherwise the earliest tangible record for the Crown hostelry is an indenture, stating that it was sold as the 'Rose & Crown Inn, Brewhouse, in 1760.

The Chequers

Happily, the Chequers' story is more complete. An inn may well have existed there since the mid-sixteenth century, for after the Dissolution of the Monasteries in Henry VIII's reign, the preceding building on its site, the Hospital of All Saints, which originally had ecclesiastical links with the Church opposite, was not recorded among those suppressed, indicating a timely change of use.

Between 1685 and 1700 the Hospital premises were demolished by John Stukeley, who, to use his son William's words, 'new built the Chequer Inn and fine vaults of brick'. In 1699 the freehold was recorded as being held by Sir George Humble (in whose family it was to remain for over a century). But one gathers that an early tenant in the new premises soon proved a disappointment, for John Stukeley wrote in April 1704: 'Thomas Smith at the Chequer is gone off nearly £300 in debt and all his goods sold. I think I hear of another tenant.'

A family hotel with an under-age barmaid
The next significant event is the second rebuilding of the Chequers to the external appearance we recognise today. This took place in 1783 and a little later on, details become more complete. In the 1840s the freehold was owned by Sir Joseph Hawley, who had purchased it from Joseph Humble. Thomas Showler was landlord throughout the 1820s to 1835, when he was succeeded by David Jackson, the first of two tenants who, as farmers of some substance, saw inn-keeping as a profitable sideline. Jackson farmed 200 acres in Horncastle and employed 18 labourers. During his 16-year tenancy the Chequers was described variously as a commercial, posting and family hotel and excise office. It changed hands twice in the late 1850s before Edward Ulyatt, another farmer with 240 acres, took over. Although Ulyatt's occupation was short, it did coincide with the 1861 Census, which told us something about the staff. Ulyatt and his wife, in their early thirties with a son and daughter both aged 6, employed a workforce of nine. Most of them were well under 30, apart from William Cox, 62, from Newton, who acted as brewer's labourer. By today's standards it seemed hardly appropriate for the youngest member of the team, Alice Brewster, to be the barmaid at only 16, but perhaps she was blessed with a prettiness considered good for trade. Elizabeth Mellor, already a widow at 26, was the cook, assisted by Jemima Jackson (19), kitchen maid, and Sarah Haresign (20), waitress. The rooms were cleaned by chambermaid Mary Wilkinson (20) from Friskney, while James Jarratt (23) from Buythorp brushed up the guests' boots. Edward Mashford, 21, of Moulton, was described as 'bus driver', indicating that the Chequers had its own horse-drawn courtesy vehicle with which to meet guests from the

recently-opened railway station. This hint of the Hotel's self-sufficiency is reinforced by

LITTLE CHANGED EXTERNALLY. The Chequers while run by Copeland between 1896 and 1904. [Photo source unknown.]

William Mears' tenancy from 1863 to 1871, when the establishment was described as including a stables, brewery, coach-houses and yard, gardens, farm buildings, a stackyard and a pasture, the latter probably maintained for milk and meat-producing livestock.

First lady tenant
Harriet Micklethwaite, a 29-year-old widow from Ely, was in charge by 1871, only one of two women in the Chequers' recorded history to hold the sole tenancy. In spite of the family effort, with her widowed father and younger brother as 'assistant inn-keepers', she remained barely a year. But again, the Census obliged with more interesting details, notably the position of Arthur Wotton, 19, as a 'billiard marker' – did this constitute a full-time job? The cook was a mature 50-year-old woman this time – Rebecca Stodthard– and the ostler was 18-year-old George Maxlow.

'Meeting all trains'
A more settled period of tenancies followed, those of William Hargrave (1872-1889). Henry Dawkes (1889-1896), and Charles Copeland from 1896 to 1904. Copeland extended the publicity a little, promoting 'Wines, Spirits and Cigars of Finest Qualities', and a 'Bus to meet all Trains', but

40

failing health obliged him to sell the hotel to Peatlings, the Wisbech wine merchants. Then Morris Turner and William Stuart were successively in charge from the late Edwardian period to beyond the First World War, after which the last lady tenant, Mrs Laurina Longthorp, ran the Chequers from 1922 to 1926.

By this time the establishment was on the phone –no. 47– and Longthorp's successor, John Sample, allowed an individual named Davis to operate a bus service from the hotel yard. During Bert Rayment's reign in the 1930s, the hotel was the venue for many dinner dances. A limited company, Paten & Co of Peterborough, took over from 1937.

Chequers Bowling Club

It is also worth recording that the Chequers ran a thriving bowling club during this period. It had been established in 1909, with Messrs M Turner and F Fletcher as president and vice-president, and J S R Tingle as its captain. The size of the green was soon doubled, attracting many proficient players who went on tour with matches at Peterborough, King's Lynn and Boston.

Wrights Roofing and Holbeach Asphalt now occupy what was the green, which would have been accessed from the puddle-strewn pathway that leads round to Park Road. In its later years the green was ably cared for by Mr English, and until it folded in 1965, the Club was the oldest of its kind in Holbeach.

Post-war rates

After the war, the Chequers was listed as a two-star hotel, with 24 bedrooms, three bathrooms and central heating. According to the 1960 *RAC Guide & Handbook*, the telephone number had now lengthened from 47 to 3247, and bed and breakfast ranged from 20/- to 23/- (£1.00 to £1.15) with weekly terms of 10 to 10½ guineas (£10.50 - £10.75).

Room prices had almost doubled since 1950, but the hotel remained competitive with other local two-star establishments, such as Spalding's White Hart, except that the Chequers did not have the increasingly-important TV room at the time.

Best intentions lead to neglect

With the insensitive 1970s came a cycle of disuse and desolation that seemed to plague the high streets of several local towns and villages all at once. Holbeach was no exception, the Talbot having already succumbed, followed by the Chequers after the Unwins had attempted a renovation of the dining room and uncovered a fireplace believed to have dated back to at least 1783, and speculatively even, to the former Hospital. In 1978, the hotel was described as a sad sight, 'neglected and forlorn', after standing empty for over a year. Its aspect made former glories, such as Alfred, Duke of Edinburgh's patronage when he dined there on his visit to Holbeach in the late nineteenth century, difficult to imagine.

Fate in the balance

Nor were the 1980s a very encouraging prospect for the Chequers. Large, old buildings designed in a previous era of cheaper heating fuel and servant labour, and swallowing large amounts of cash for maintenance, cannot be guaranteed to provide a lucrative income in the meantime. With Arthur Green's departure after four years in 1988, redevelopment by a Peterborough company into flats above and shops below seemed a certainty, had not the Civic Society and Parish Council opposed the plan. Salvation arrived with the McDermott brothers, who bought the property in 1990 and reopened it the following year after spending an alleged £500,000, a fair amount of this devoted to making the bedrooms en suite and restoring the ballroom, which had not seen any regular use for 30 years. The room could once more accommodate conferences and Christmas parties and, reassured the publicity in 1995, 'Neither convenience nor style have been compromised, so that, once you have visited the Chequers, you will want to return again and again.'

Bull Dog to the rescue

Early the following year however, despite the charm of its four-poster beds in which guests dozed off to the muted church bells opposite, return proved impossible, for the hotel was closed down for a further nine months until the Bull Dog Pub Company came to the rescue. Since then the Chequers has kept busy, helped by sundry relaunchings of image which featured Barny's restaurant, where for a while diners enjoyed an American-style menu under a ceiling paraphernalia of old ironing boards, shovels and suitcases. One hundred years on would Alfred, Duke of Edinburgh have approved of a 'Fat Man's Misery Hot Chocolate Fudge Cake'? No matter. Such novelties have helped Holbeach's famous hotel to live again after –dare one say it– such a chequered past.

INNOCENT-LOOKING REMNANT OF AN ODOROUS PAST. The remains of the Holbeach River as it trickles out past Barry Disdel's works near Penny Hill Road.

Origins stay close to the surface

In the last 40 years of the twentieth century, many parts of Holbeach changed almost out of all recognition, with the appearance of housing developments, supermarkets, an industrial estate and rebuilt shops and businesses. Spiritually, the demolition of imposing properties such as Mattimore House, Stukeley Hall, and the flowering creeper-bedecked Cedar House of the Searby and later Golden families in Boston Road symbolised the end of the old world and its more genteel lifestyle. One might even include the removal of Miss Bingham's little shack in Barrington Gate in this category, for it represented, in its meadowed, daffodiled setting, an unobtrusive modesty independent of modern materialism. But in spite of all this, the town's origins are still close to the surface. Houses at the first Hall Hill Road turning sit high on the former saltwork mound. And all the time, under the vehicles parked in Church Street and the provision stalls selling eggs, petfoods, garden shrubs, clothing, cut-price biscuits and marmalade, the Holbeach River trickles on. On beneath its long-buried medieval bridge, and into Park Road past Halstead & Fowler, to break cover in the dyke opposite the George Farmer playing fields, as a living vein of Holbeach past.

4 —Other Churches

The Methodist Churches

The Methodist Church in Albert Street is the newest in Holbeach and was the first church of that denomination to be built in Lincolnshire for 17 years. Yet Methodism's first bricks and mortar in the town were by courtesy of the wealthy Holliday family as early as 1808, when Elizabeth, widow of Francis Holliday, laid the foundation stone of a chapel on 40 square feet of land bought for £35 11s. It was located in Chapel Street, where Hawkins' yard is now situated.

By 1837 the Wesleyan Methodists' church was proving too small for the increasing number of worshippers, so it was replaced by a second building and extended to include a schoolroom at the back, this room being accessed by 'a dark inside passage'. The *Methodist Times* of October 1908 puts the date of this rebuilding at 1842, but it soon proved inadequate, for it was later converted into two vestries and in 1868, land was purchased for a bigger schoolroom in Barrington Gate, later extended in 1886 to include additional classrooms. Meanwhile, a manse, Epworth House, was built next door.

It was with this infrastructure that the Wesleyan Methodists celebrated the centenary of Methodism in Holbeach, before which the original 'horse-box' seats of their Chapel Street church were replaced by new seating, together with new windows and doors.

A respectable membership of over 200 in the 1870s declined steadily thereafter, but the Wesleyan Methodists were able to pay their minister a reasonable £120 per annum, and remained very much in tune with how the outside world fared. In October 1879 for instance, they set aside a Friday as a day of humiliation and prayer, 'having special reference to our National Sins and the present distress in the country relating to Agriculture and Commerce', the arrangement applying to Holbeach only.

The 'Liquor traffic' of the 1890s also caused them much concern, and moved them to send a petition to Westminster in July 1893, supporting the Government's proposals for dealing with the problem.

The horseless carriage, had it arrived earlier, would certainly have benefited the Victorian preachers. From 1874 Holbeach stood alone as a Methodist circuit, with the furthest country chapel at Moulton Washway some six miles away. Other chapels on the circuit were Whaplode, Moulton, Whaplode Washway, Holbeach

MORE LIKE A HOUSE. *The Wesleyan Methodist Chapel once occupied the area of Hawkins' yard.*

Marsh, Holbeach Hurn and Holbeach St Johns. It was considered one of the more compact circuits, perhaps by those preachers fortunate enough to have bicycles.

But just around the corner at the newer Wesleyan Reform Chapel, as Edwin Askew, Minister from 1859 to 1861 remembered, his circuit could take him away from Saturday evening until the following Saturday morning, having conducted 14 services in the circuit villages. His duties could also involve as much as a 22-mile walk in a single day. It had been known for him to walk to Spalding and conduct a morning service there, walk on to Weston Hills in the afternoon, return to Spalding for an evening service, then trudge back to Holbeach at night. Many of the roads, said Mr Askew, such as that between Holbeach and Whaplode St Catherines, 'were silt and like sponge, after a heavy rain.'

Askew's church, first opened in Albert Street in February 1854, was an imposing building, with a façade dominated by a brick pediment above arched windows. At street level there was a wide, pillared porch fronted by iron railings below, later glazed in. At the first meeting of the trustees, chaired by James Longbottom on

OPENED 1854, DEMOLISHED 1985. The pleasing façade of the original Albert St Methodist Church.

3rd February 1854, it was resolved that the building be insured for £300, that Mr Nelson Congreve be chapel steward, and that Mrs Coleman as chapel cleaner should be provided with soap and brushes and be paid 18/- quarterly.

Under a new deed of November 1875, the establishment was renamed the United Methodist Free Church, later simplified to United Methodist Church in a revised deed of May 1916. The minute book for this last revision revealed the many walks of local life from which the trustees were drawn: Robert Merry of Fleet, gentleman; Robert Isaiah Bingham, Damgate Road, smallholder; Charles Robert Thompson, Spalding Road, draper; John Burton, Holbeach, signalman; Henry Horry, Holbeach, baker; Louis Rivaz Neaves, Holbeach, accountant; David Vellam, Moulton, labourer, and Percy Crane Sharp, Holbeach, tailor, to name just a few. A visiting preacher to the Church in the 1850s had been the young William Booth, at that time a Methodist revivalist based at Spalding. Inspired by his experience of poverty and deprivation while once apprenticed to a pawnbroker, he went on to found his own movement in 1861 which was to become the Salvation Army. But Booth retained his links with

Holbeach, visiting the town to address a vast open-air meeting on Market Hill in September 1905. Half a century earlier, he had arrived in a horse-driven farmer's cart at Mr Congreve's door. This time, by now the patriarch with flowing beard, he travelled by new-fangled motorcade, with members of the local fire brigade acting as his guard of honour.

Back in Chapel Street, Methodism continued until 1959-60, when the building closed for worship and the congregation merged with that of Albert Street. The Barrington Gate Schoolroom was

RADIO ORGANIST IN HOLBEACH. Reginald Foort, who played at the Wesleyan Methodist Chapel in September 1951.

absorbed under the same arrangement. But after the new church was built, the Schoolroom made way for housing in the mid-1980s. It was not the only church closure that decade, for the Congregational Church in Park Road had incurred debts of £200, and required a further £1,500 for essential building work on its Victorian fabric. With only a handful of the congregation below pensionable age, the Revd Gordon Bellamy, supervising minister from Long Sutton, saw little hope for its future and closure soon followed in 1963. The building survives, however, as an antique and secondhand furniture centre, the arched mouldings high up on the façade tracing the pattern of the mock-Norman-style windows, now bricked in, while the doorways at each end once had arched entrances in the same style.

Money-raising, of course, can be a problem for churches at any time. But it went without saying that any money raised for the benefit of the Methodist Church had to be obtained by the most scrupulous means. In November 1912, the Revd John Jay stated that no more funds should be raised by holding guessing competitions.

Some might be disappointed, he argued, but now that these competitions had been declared illegal, it was the Church's duty to set an example by following the law.

70 years later however, it became increasingly obvious that no manner of fundraising could save the old building. Even after an extensive renovation in 1963, running costs and the demand for repairs, aggravated by dry rot, multiplied. So in the spring of 1983 proposals were discussed to build a completely new church on the Albert Street/Albert Walk site. This was logical both from the viewpoint of saving £1,500 in annual running costs, and the need to consolidate Holbeach Methodist activities under one roof, although initially South Holland District Council's architect did not agree that the old church was a lost cause, and described the proposed style (later modified) as more appropriate to a modern housing estate than a conservation area. However, permission to build was granted the following month, although it was to be March 1985 before demolition and redevelopment began, during which time it was service as usual, for to quote from D Plevey's poem:

'We shall worship for awhile,
In another street.
Barrington Gate will be our home,
Till the new Church is built.
So –come along and join us there
Till we resume in Albert Street'.

This resumption took place on Saturday 20th April 1986, when the building, designed by Michael Glauser of Status Design and constructed by Langwith Builders, was officially opened by Revd Alan J Davies, chairman of the Methodist district, before a congregation of 350 people.

DIGNIFIED MODERNITY. The current Methodist Church in Albert Street.

The Primitive Methodist Chapel, Edinburgh Walk

Until demolition in the 1980s to make way for modern housing, this building stood at the Fleet Street end of Edinburgh Walk, near the entrance to The Tenters. It was built in 1866 and certified for worship the following year, run in conjunction with a sister church at Roman Bank. Services were held on Sundays at 10.30 a.m. and 6.30 p.m., with a midweek service at 7.30 p.m. In 1900 the minister was the Revd Charles Collins, and by 1930 it had become part of the Spalding and Holbeach Circuit under the Revd Fred Clulow. But its use as a full-time church ended in 1934 and it was sold to the Loyal Albion Lodge of Oddfellows in November 1935. Thereafter it was used as a meeting hall for various different groups and associations, including the British Legion and on odd occasions, the Roman Catholic Church before it had a place of its own. Eadie Reddin was caretaker for a time.

The Baptist Church, Albert Street

Although this Listed building is dated 1845, the Baptist movement in Holbeach

COST £380, STILL WITH US TODAY. The Baptist Church in Albert Street, built 1845 and a dominant period piece in this essentially Victorian street.

goes back much further, having survived a long and occasionally difficult history involving imprisonment, persecution, short incumbencies, lack of adequate premises and internal differences over administration.

Incredible as it may seem, the movement in Holbeach struggled for two centuries before settling in a permanent home. It originated shortly after the establishment of a Baptist church in Spalding in 1646, when one of the new church's members, a tradesman named John Marham, began to hold services in his Holbeach house, conducted by itinerant preachers. This did not go down well with the rest of the town, but Marham continued his meetings, shrugging off arrest and a heavy fine, until he was eventually imprisoned, which broke his health and forced him to leave the area; however, a Samuel Phillips took over his work.

Opposition and persecution continued, so to avoid further trouble, the 30 or so members formed a church at Fleet in 1690 under the ministry of Robert Vellam, a deacon from Spalding. Of the 36 members known in 1740, eight came from Holbeach, but while the Fleet movement flourished, it was to be another 74 years before attempts to re-establish in Holbeach were successful enough to result in the opening of a 'preaching station' in the town. Even then the venture was short-lived, through lack of pastoral and lay leadership. But by the 1840s, things were looking up. Not only had preaching at Holbeach begun anew, thanks to the efforts of the assistant preacher from Fleet, but a new chapel was built in 1845 on land given by Mr William Kime of Grazeley, who laid the foundation stone on May 25th. The building cost £380, over a third of which was raised by a bazaar, collections and subscriptions. The first co-pastors were the Revd Farmer Chamberlain of Fleet and Mr Kenney, followed by Mr Barrass and then the first full-time pastor, Mr Cotten.

An unsettled period began in the 1870s with disagreement between the Holbeach and Fleet churches over open membership. In Fleet's opinion, this violated the terms of the trust deed, and while the Baptist's Lincolnshire Conference appeared to favour the Holbeach request, Fleet would go no further than allowing an open communion table. As a result, the Revd E Moore and his followers removed books, harmonium and communion plate, and joined the Congregational Church. A Revd Hacket followed, at an income of £60 p.a. which he earned for barely two years before leaving for Derbyshire, while two students, who had formally accepted to run the incumbency between them, failed to turn up. By 1874 the church had reverted

to being run by pastors who also shared their duties with Fleet; but this practice ended three years later when Fleet decided it could no longer support Holbeach, to the extent of making their Revd Robinson redundant.

Undaunted, the Holbeach members armed themselves with an interest-free loan of £250 from the Metropolitan Tabernacle Building Fund, and purchased the Albert Street building from Fleet for £270. Relaunched in 1879 under the order of the Metropolitan Tabernacle and with a new pastor in Montague Mather, the Baptists established a more extensive weekly routine to include bible classes for young men and women, a Sunday school and a Band of Hope, while the Church also assumed responsibility for the mission at Holbeach Bank.

This promising turn of a new leaf was short-lived after Mather upset the congregation at the first Sunday service in 1881, by scorning members for coming in late. They did not like the suggestion that their unpunctuality should lead them to worship elsewhere, and said so, to which Mr Mather replied that he would adopt a softer approach in future; but if this did not work, he would resign. Also unpopular was Mather's insistence on using the Revised Version of the New Testament. It was all part of a difficult period for the Church which included inadequate finance, the resignation of the secretary over how the premises should be used, and declining attendances. But it was not the last time that members would vote with their feet; this recurred in 1913 when there were objections to the positioning of the organ in the gallery. The overseeing pastor, Mr Cawdron, refused to consider its return to a corner of the church, so the choir —and reputedly the organist, too— resigned.

Cassidy Travers' ministry from 1887 injected some new life into the Church with more weekly prayer meetings, a stronger interest in the Sunday school, complemented by training classes for the teachers, and the introduction of pew rents. The forming of a drum and fife band was welcomed by some and suffered by others, mainly Albert Street residents who put up both with noise of their practice sessions in the neighbouring schoolroom, and the bad behaviour of the boys in the street afterwards. But ill-health cut short Travers' ministry, thus beginning another period when none of the immediate successors was to stay long, discouraged no doubt by the persistent lack of funds, which prevented any hope of an adequate income for the pastor, and low attendances. For a while, the Church even resorted to the ad hoc engagement of local preachers willing to take a service for 2/6 (13p). Building maintenance might well have been a problem, too, had not 'a lady residing in the south' contributed £21 for renovations in 1897.

Despite these circumstances, the Baptist Church still managed to make its presence felt, as under Mr Crawford's pastorship (1899-1902), when open air meetings were held on Market Hill featuring hymns, solos and recitations, and supplemented by fund-raising garden fêtes, at which the Holbeach Saxhorn Brass Band would provide the music for a fee of one guinea (£1.05). There were Sunday school outings too, some as far as Skegness, as in 1913, when a picnic tea was held on the beach and the total rail fare came to £2.12s.3d (£2.62). Then in 1921 a benevolent fund was set up in 1921 for the sick and elderly, funded by the communion service collections.

When Cawdron left in 1924 for Coningsby, the church was again divided, with some members seriously considering a union with the Holbeach Congregationalists. Although the motion was defeated by seven votes to five, the church was still at a low ebb and after several crucial meetings, Holbeach joined with Sutton St James under the Revd Gordon Fletcher, before becoming part of the East Elloe Group of the South Lincolnshire Fellowship of Baptist Churches in 1940.

The Roman Catholic Church

It could be said that Roman Catholicism is both the newest and the oldest faith to be practised in Holbeach.

Initially, Catholics had of course worshipped at All Saints Church in the Middle Ages, but the Dissolution of the Monasteries in the mid-sixteenth century began a void that was not filled until February 1951, when the Catholic Travelling Mission celebrated Mass at Holbeach Youth Club on Park Road, attended by 40 people. A new beginning indeed after 400 years, but without a proper base, a rather tenuous one, as services were held wherever they could be arranged: a building in Long Sutton was one such place; another was a disused chapel next door to Kildea's Chemist in Sutton Bridge, while the Oddfellows Hall in Edinburgh Walk, Holbeach (formerly the Primitive Methodist Chapel) also provided a temporary home.

A more permanent identity was promised with the arrival of Father Patrick George Mulligan as Assistant Priest at St Dymphnas, as the Sutton Bridge place of

A HOME AT LAST. The Holy Trinity Roman Catholic Church, built in 1966, ended years of makeshift worshipping arrangements.

worship came to be called, in 1955. For after just over a year in that capacity, Mulligan was appointed Priest of a new parish based in Holbeach. The inauguration of this parish by the Bishop of Nottingham followed in 1960, by which time Father Mulligan had settled in Holbeach. But even then the premises question had still not been resolved, as he was celebrating Mass in places as miscellaneous as the Chequers games room, the front room of his house in The Tenters, and later on in the Anglican Church hall.

Eventually however, a church dedicated to the Holy Trinity was built for him at the junction of Fleet Road and Foxes Low

Road, on land formerly owned by farmer Freddy Bass, and it was opened in October 1966. Later on, an adjoining priest's house was built, into which Father Mulligan moved in 1971.

Holbeach has not been ignored by interesting personalities of the Catholic Church. In 1968, Father Ruigrok, who worked for the Franciscan Missionary in New Guinea and whose brother lived in Holbeach Bank, deputised for Father Mulligan while he was on holiday. Then there was Father Mulligan himself. A former Army chaplain with a distinguished war record who had prepared for the priesthood in Ireland and Belgium, Father Mulligan served in Manchester and at Storrington Priory before transfer to the Nottingham Diocese brought him to Spalding. He saw his 50th year in the priesthood while at Holbeach in August 1992, but his retirement a year later to live with his sister in Newry, Northern Ireland, was unfortunately cut short when he died in October 1994.

The Parish is currently served by St Norberts in Spalding, with the day-to-day affairs of the church looked after by Sisters Veronica and Theresa Anne, during whose time the £90,000 Walsingham Hall –partly funded by a Lottery contribution– has been opened by the Revd James McGuiness, Bishop Nottingham, as the Church's own function room in May 2000. Fortified at last by fine modern premises, the Roman Catholic Church looks forward to its second half century of return to the ecclesiastical life of Holbeach.

♣ ♣ ♣ ♣ ♣ ♣

5 –Agricultural Development

By the mid-sixteenth century the population of Holbeach had grown to 147 families, at a time when Spalding had 154, Stamford 213, and Grantham only 132¶. As the town developed, with its market, church, hospital and trade guilds, so too did the management of its greatest asset, the fertile surrounding land, become a matter of increasing importance.

Earlier achievements with drainage and reclamation, as in the twelfth century by Conan FitzEllis and his contemporaries, were not a once-and-for-all operation. This fact made itself painfully clear in the fifteenth and sixteenth centuries.

To begin with, the Black Death had depleted available labour for the maintenance of banks and drainage. Then, with the dissolution of Spalding Priory and Crowland Abbey between 1536 and 1539, centuries of good land management were sacrificed to succeeding layman landowners, many of whom had much to learn about the unconventional demands of fen and marsh.

Thirdly, the threat of flooding was ever-present, and the implications disastrous. R Holinshed in his *Historie of England* recorded the events of October 1570: 'A terrible tempest of wind and raine…the sea brake in betwixt Wisbich and Walsocken, and at the crosse keis drowning Tilnei, and old Lin, saint Marie Teding, saint Marie Tid, saint Johns Wauple, Walton and Walsocken, Emnie, Jarmans, and Stowbridge, all being the space of ten miles.' Elsewhere, 'a ship was driven upon an house', corn, cattle and salt-pans were flooded 'to the utter undoing of manie a man,' and 'Holland, Leuerington, Newton chapell in the sea, long Sutton and Holbich were overflowne', many sheep and cattle being lost in the chaos. Violent tides also affected Holbeach and Whaplode in 1611, covering the saltmarsh with up to three feet of water.

In areas like Holbeach, efforts concentrated on riding out and making the best of prevailing conditions, rather than fighting them. When the higher spring tides had drained off the marshes, farmers waited for rain to flush away sand and salt, after which the remaining properties in the ground not only provided quality pastureland for sheep, but protected the animals from foot rot. Meanwhile shepherds had learned to anticipate high tides, keeping watch in shelters positioned at strategic points on the saltmarsh.

But with the sort of typically-recurring problem described by the jurors of Gedney in 1607, that 'there wilbe some tymes a hundrethe acres of marsh ground: and within three howers space best of it wilbe overflowed with the sea above six foote deep', it was clear that outside professional help would have to be enlisted if land was not to be totally ruined.

17th-CENTURY DRAINAGE MILL.
An illustration from the display boards in All Saints Church.

Even well before the Gedney juror's observation, there had been much discussion in Privy Council proceedings over the Fenland problem. Some action had actually been taken in the dredging of the river at Wisbech, and in 1584 a group of Frenchmen became interested in furthering the project. But overall, a state of confusion, dispute and delay continued, which only encouraged individuals to take matters into their own hands. The 'Ingen' or drainage mill at Saturday Bridge for example, installed by

Mr Carlton, solved his problems at the expense of the surrounding area. It threw out 'so much water from his owne grounde into the river of Holbiche', that further flooding occurred elsewhere. This so incensed a certain William Toyes that he called a meeting of the local dyke keepers at All Saints Church. He scorned them for allowing such mills to be set up, and continued his abuse of Carlton in front of a crowd at the town bridge, 'exclaiminge in foul words and tearmes'. One of the mills was subsequently sabotaged, a load-bearing beam all but sawn through, so that the structure collapsed around a mill-hand when he climbed up inside to oil the works.

Meanwhile, those holding common rights in Deeping Fen had petitioned Queen Elizabeth I, describing the 'lost condition of these fens'. They suggested that a Commission of Sewers should review the matter, and that a suitable expert should undertake the draining. The Drainage Act of 1600 acknowledged the problem, but meeting the cost through local taxation proved unpopular. Already, the way was open for wealthy contractors to carry out the work at their own expense, and claim a proportion of the newly-drained land in return. This happened with the Deeping Fen project conducted by Thomas Lovell between Bourne and Crowland in the south, and extending east and west to Spalding and Thurlby fens. Although the project proved unsuccessful, drainage schemes continued to attract other rich speculators and investors with their eye on newly-reclaimed land and its potential for highly-priced corn.

Royal designs on Reclamation

Under the first two Stuart kings –James I and Charles I– the policy on reclaimed land took a new turn and the outcome affected almost the whole of the Lincolnshire fenland. Until Elizabeth I's reign, no monarch had asserted a royal claim to land left by the sea. But now it was recognised as growing in importance and value. The Elizabethan lawyer, Thomas Digges' *Proofs of the Queen's Interest in Lands left by the Sea and the Salt Shores thereof*, drafted in 1568-1569, had done much to further this new awareness. 'If the prince's land be amplified by the withdrawal of the sea,' he suggested, 'the prince is to receive the benefit thereof, and the subject that entereth thereon intrudeth.' In other words, those who grazed animals on the salt shore –regardless of how long they had done so– had no rights against the sovereign, who could claim saltmarsh throughout the kingdom as part of the royal prerogative. King James I, ever short of finance, made much of this prerogative to assume ownership of local coastal marshland, disposing of some of it in a series of lucrative grants to individuals. While these were to include local inhabitants, only those in Long Sutton and Moulton took up the offer: a shrewd move on Moulton's part, for the 724 acres they bought for £105 2s 4d in 1613 had swelled by natural accumulation of silt to 900 acres by 1634. But those who did not take up their option found their land granted to outsiders. Thus in Holbeach and the marshlands of Wigtoft, Moulton, Whaplode and Tydd St Mary, the Earl of Argyll was granted – through his nominees Charles Glenmond and John Walcott of London– extensive reclaimed land in 1615, which was then drained at the Earl's expense. Nevertheless, one-fifth of this was still to be reserved for the King. Some Holbeach land, however, together with areas in Whaplode, Moulton, Fleet and Gedney, were not subject to drainage operations. These so-called 'wet grounds' were in fact relatively dry and could be let as pasture, for in a survey of 1640, all but a small part was set aside as common land, and represented some 10,985 acres in Holbeach, Whaplode and Moulton.

Some progress, then, had been made. But it is not surprising to observe H C Darby's comment in his *Draining of the Fens* that, 'Differences had arisen over the work before 1634', and, 'In many localities there was much talk and negotiating, but little accomplished.' This could not have been truer than in Holbeach, where as late as 1638, the Earl of Argyll had still not managed to embank the land granted to him 23 years earlier because of the 'disturbances of intruders and pretenders against whom proceedings have been had.'

Some wrangles over common land persisted for many years, with neither king nor inhabitants prepared to give way. But the local people often held the trump card of being on the spot to take advantage of natural developments, before absentee royal grantees could take stock of the situation. During the first half of the seventeenth century, a golden opportunity was provided by the increasing accumulation of silt along the South Holland coast, making it worth risking dispossession by the king. In Holbeach, a survey of 1633 revealed that no less than 1,070 acres had been reclaimed there since the early 1580s.

Nevertheless, the Crown's 'hawking' of land had also provided opportunities for the country gentry, who bought and enclosed during the 1620s and 1630s while the time was right. In addition to some 508 acres in Gedney, Sir William Welby owned two marshes in Holbeach, and John Hudson 270½ acres of embanked and 163½ acres of unembanked marsh. Welby later sold 580 acres of his Holbeach marsh for £3,000, while rents could yield as much as 16 to 18 shillings per acre, depending on the quality of the land. Some owners leased land in large amounts to tenants and sub-tenants. A typical Holbeach leaseholding in Charles I's reign, for example, was Henry Pratt's 400 acres.

17th-CENTURY NETWORKING. The drainage system in existence around Holbeach at the time.
[Drawn by John Elms and based on Dugdale's map of 1662.]

Acreages were naturally much more modest among the poorer or middling peasants. Their holdings remained at between two to eight acres throughout the seventeenth century. At this level, the fen peasant frequently boosted his income by catching fish and wildfowl, both of which found a ready market in London. But the ownership of five acres or more began to define him as a man of substance.

Early benefits of drainage

The effects of the drainage operations were seen in the changing quantity and character of the crops grown. Four hundred acres of wheat, oats and barley were grown on the Holbeach marshes in 1640, although barley acreage declined from 54 per cent of sown area during the sixteenth century to 15 per cent in the seventeenth, and none at all in some areas by 1690. There was more emphasis instead on fodder crops to cater for greater sheep flocks. Also on the increase were peas and beans, averaging over 40 per cent of sown land in the seventeenth century, and oats, which like cole-seed, were particularly suited to newly-drained fen conditions. With less threat of flooding, land devoted to wheat increased from the 11 per cent of sixteenth-century levels to about a third. Other crops suited to fen soils were onions –grown at Holbeach Drove– and hemp, a politically-motivated commodity for rope and sail-making for warships.

Fertility and ague

A contemporary description of our agricultural area in the late seventeenth century confirms the fertility of the pasture belt, where 'about Holbeach…great marshes have lately been taken in from the sea. They supported a great number of fat oxen and sheep which Weekly are sent to London in Droves.' Samphire was observed in the saltmarshes, but so were 'very troublesome midges,' which explained why people were wearing 'nets some made of silk to secure them from being bitten'. Small wonder that 'ague' was 'very rife, few strangers escaping without a seasoning.'

The ague, however, was no deterrent to the increasing population attracted to this new abundance of land and what it could offer. In 1563, the entire Wapentake of Elloe accounted for only 1,473 families. But by 1723 this figure had almost doubled to 2,696, of which Holbeach was responsible for an additional 269.

Alternate farming explored

New land, the result of both silt accumulation and drainage of fen previously under water all year round, had brought in more tenants and more labourers. Coinciding with this influx was a trend towards alternate farming. On Holbeach Marsh for instance, John Cook of Whaplode was granted a 13-year lease of an 80-acre pasture from 1726, on which he was to build a barn and divide the land into two equal portions. One section was to be ploughed and cultivated for five years before being laid to grass, after which the other section would be cultivated for the next five years, and so on.

An earlier decline in horse stocks was reversed as the Fen improved to the point where it became a noted breeding ground. Cattle and some varieties of sheep were also brought to the Holbeach area from other counties to be fattened. The journalist and novelist Daniel Defoe (1660 – 1731), author of *Robinson Crusoe*, wrote of his travels through southern Lincolnshire in 1724: 'The country round this place is all fen and marsh grounds, the land very rich, and which feeds prodigious numbers of large sheep and also oxen of the largest size, the overplus and best of which goes all to the London market.'

It would be wrong to assume however, that such descriptions represented a state of perfection. Back in 1662, W Dugdale's belief that we enjoyed a superior drainage system to that of the Dutch, helped by our 'divers large rivers and streams' and grounds with a natural descent to the sea, was both naïve and short-lived. Neither the Ouse, the Nene or the Welland had sufficient 'fall', or natural gradient, to ensure a rapid flow of water. This resulted in sluggish currents on wide and shallow river beds which, when combined with large amounts of water pouring into the river in wet weather from the upland, only resulted in further flooding. Even the devious Sir Cornelius Vermuyden, the engineer of Dutch origin engaged by King James I to assist with the drainage of the fens, feared that 'in the processe of time, the outfalls of Wisbich and Welland will utterly decay.' Another unforeseen phenomenon beyond the silt area was the lowering of the Fens' peat surface, allowing drains to sink below the level of the channels they were supposed to be feeding.

Further difficult years

Flooding therefore, was still a force to be reckoned with, and the need to embank and drain was an ongoing task. An Act of 1792 provided for the processing of a further 5,339 acres of saltmarshes and lowlands in Holbeach, Gedney, Whaplode and Spalding. This was quickly followed by the South Holland Drainage Act of 1793, for the benefit of lands 'much annoyed in the winter season with water for want of a drainage and out fall to the sea.' The 'want' at this juncture was met by the creation of a new watercourse, the South Holland Main Drain, which followed a west-east course to join the Nene at Petterspoint near Sutton Bridge. This benefited Holbeach and other fenland lying south of the Raven Bank in the parishes of Spalding, Weston, Cowbit, Moulton, Whaplode, Fleet, Gedney and Sutton.

The 1790s also saw a trust formed to deal with one of the last major enclosures of saltmarsh, hitherto 'overflowed by the sea at every spring tide' and formerly of 'little value', involving some 4,600 acres of land in the parishes of Holbeach, Whaplode, Moulton, Gedney and Spalding. Holbeach's share in this gain was substantial, amounting to over 2,000 acres and consolidated by further authorised enclosures in 1812 and 1835. With so much reclamation now achieved, the banks built and maintained by each parish were usually able to cope with all but the highest tides: between 1770 and 1850, for instance, serious flooding occurred only once, in 1811.

Over March and April 1830, the political essayist, reformer and former soldier, William Cobbett (1763 - 1835), travelled through 'rich fen land', researching for his *Rural Rides*. He almost overstated the case for what he saw in the expanse between Lynn and Holbeach:

'Holbeach lies in the midst of some of the richest land in the world. I defy tongue or pen to make the description adequate to the matter: to know what the thing is, you must see it. The same land continues all the way on to Boston: endless grass and endless fat sheep: not a stone, not a weed.'

DIGGING FOR DRAINAGE.
The traditional tools for the job.
[Courtesy Roy Pratt.]

'A neat little town'

Cobbett, finding Holbeach a 'neat little town', had soon made assumptions about the prosperity of the area by the style of its churches, and was obviously impressed by All Saints. It had, he said, a most beautiful spire, like that of ' the man of Ross pointing to the skies…It is curious,' he went on, 'that the moment you get out of the rich land, the churches become smaller, mean, and with scarcely anything in the way of tower or steeple.'

Cobbett's enthusiasm for the subject could be traced to his poor farming background and a deep concern for rural affairs in a newly-industrialised society. As a man with a conscience, who had been forced to flee to America in 1792 after denouncing injustices observed in the British army, one would have expected him to speak more frankly of what he saw, for Lincolnshire at this time was surely showing effects of the national distress. Between 1815 and 1852, levels of taxation increased during the Napoleonic wars were carried over into peacetime. The 1820s and 30s were periods of lower wages, and unemployment aggravated by the introduction of new machinery. Conditions were ripe for crime, and sheep stealing led to the Holbeach magistrates providing for a watch to be set up in 1827. Meanwhile wheat prices had fallen considerably, aggravated by the fact that even as late as 1850, huge imports of the same commodity were continuing to arrive. If we are to believe a Special Assistant Poor Law Commissioner's report that 'The Labourers are generally better fixed in Lincolnshire than in any county in England' –a fact not necessarily reflected in contemporary local press reports–then their subsistence must have owed much to the proliferation in the 1840s of allotments in Holbeach, Spalding, Boston, Spilsby and Grantham. It is true that farmers encouraged employees to keep allotments as a means of self-help, and some even loaned equipment to their more reliable men to help them cultivate corn and potatoes, although certain employers preferred to supervise the cultivation themselves, suspicious of the labourer spending too much time on the allotment!

In some places, it seemed that the progress made in earlier years, up to say, 1838, was under threat. Land that had only recently been reclaimed was allowed to revert to gorse or warren, while a number of landlords found themselves unable to let their farms. Lord Castlereagh, for instance, who had a large estate near Holbeach, could not find tenants, and it was the same near Boston, where it was observed that eight farms were all unlet within a few miles of the town, a situation not helped by the collapse of three local banks. Agents resorted to tactics employed by a Holbeach landlord in the 1770s, when wool prices were low, splitting up large farms into small units to make them a more attractive proposition.

'TIP AND SLASH.' Familiar tools once used by many in the pre-mechanised and labour-intensive era of pea-harvesting.
[Courtesy Roy Pratt.]

Contemporary weather conditions
Impressions recorded by William Burges, tenant of Hurdletree Farm, give us an idea of some of the conditions coped with by local farmers in the mid-nineteenth century:

'May 30 1855: a very cold north wind for several days now. Meadow land lay'd in and this Day are carting Straw out on the Grass Land for the beast to eat and lay upon.

'June 7 1855: a delightful rain and warm and grass growing and poor Cattle sett at Liberty.

'July 26 1850: began to reap ready riggs wheat in good cutting order and a fine day.

'August 26th: Finished harvest and have had fine weather.

'1863: A very dry Summer and Great Scarcity of water, the Beast roving about for water...a very fine harvest and Corn very good, fine open weather at Christmas...have to carry water from the Home ground pit to water the Beast in the Straw yard and hovels.

'1864: A much dryer Summer than last the dikes all dry and the stock more troble [sic] than last year and much less grass, no water in the Dyke untill after Christmas have to Cart water from Mr Halifax's pit for Straw Yards and hovels untill the end of January 1865.'

Diversification to survive the problems

For local agriculture, one way out of the problems besetting traditional cultivations lay in specialised crops, a trend that was already taking shape from the early 1850s onwards. Woad remained locally important in the production of fade-free dyes –at least until it was superseded by indigo at the end of the century– but flax and hemp had disappeared from Holbeach, to be replaced by chicory. On the marshes, mustard seed became widely grown. But the most important development at this time was the intensification of potato-growing. Within 25 years, it was to occupy one-tenth of the arable land in the Holland area of Lincolnshire, and helped local agriculture to ride out the depression years that had been dominated by wet seasons, from 1875 through to the 1880s. 'We have not had so much excitement here as on the high lands', commented A W Fox thankfully, in a Royal Commission on Agriculture's Report of 1895. Nevertheless, some wealthy growers had been slow to share any new-found success with their workers. In 1872, employees on Holbeach Marsh farms may have received a one shilling a week rise in their wages to 16 shillings. But where there was so much wealth among employers, argued Revd J E Moore of the Union Church in a lecture at the Market Hall, there ought not to be so much poverty. A further meeting at the Market House that year echoed this view, during which 40 labourers, insisting that wages should be increased, formed a society for mutual protection.

The rise of the smallholder
In this quest for survival, one occupation gaining considerably in popularity during the second half of the nineteenth century was that of smallholding. These family-run, modest but efficient acreages diversified to make the most of available soil, helping them to survive the 1875-80 period better than many larger farms. Typically, they concentrated on cows for dairy produce, poultry, cabbages, celery, wheat and potatoes, with Holbeach Market, like others in the vicinity, providing the natural outlet for produce.

10 % deposit and 4% interest
Any labourer of good character who could raise the ten per cent deposit on the holding's purchase price could borrow the remaining finance from a lawyer at four per cent interest. Not that it was an easy way to make a living in Holbeach. As Fox's report of 1895 noted, 'The small men work like slaves; sometimes, in the summer, from 3 a.m. to 9 p.m.', and, 'The sons and daughters of many of them are working simply for their food and clothes.' Education suffered accordingly during the harvest in Holbeach, as on 20th September 1876. Local schools were forced to declare a half-day's holiday because so many pupils were out helping in the fields†, the men scything the corn while the women and children followed to bind the sheaves. Some holders claimed they were worse off than normal labourers, but the status of owning one's own land more usually made up for the disadvantages.

Smallholding acreages varied. 'Early potato men' got by on three acres, while near the town, on soil suitable for vegetables and fruit, it was possible to live on five to ten acres. But at that time, it was considered that 'where the ordinary course of farming is followed, the least average on which a living can be made is from 30 to 50 acres'‡.

Those who could make such a living profited from meeting demand with just the right variety: of vegetables, fruit and flowers grown for the northern and London markets; early potatoes and cabbages, horseradish, carrots, celery, and rhubarb; asparagus, turnips, mangold and mustard seed; beans, peas, black and red currants; gooseberries, apples, pears, plums; greengages, cherries; and, as a sign of things to come, bulbs of narcissus, daffodils, lilies, crocuses and snowdrops. †

A new age dawns
At the other extreme, those farmers with the means could take advantage of the services offered by the likes of James and Edwin Hallifax, as 'threshing machine owners', who from the 1880s onwards were hastening the gradual mechanisation of agriculture. Their self-propelled traction engine and its threshing equipment –and machines like them owned by other far-sighted operators– were about to enter a heyday that would last from the 1890s to the 1920s, earning their keep on hire to local farms in a threshing routine that could last from late September into the winter time.

Preoccupations with draining certainly did not end with the nineteenth century and remain a constant source of review, with further reclamations completed in 1949-50 and 1956 at the Holbeach and Lawyers Sluices, while in the neighbouring vicinity a further 40 acres were reclaimed by the Mossop family in 1978. There were pumping improvements, too, during the late 60s and 70s into the South Holland Main Drain, and a new pumping station for Holbeach Marsh in 1983 (at Manor Farm on Worth's land), at Holbeach Bank on the Sluice Road, in 1992, while the Lawyers Outfall installation was scheduled for completion in 2003.

But to revert to the 1890s, the stage had now been set, after centuries of struggle, engineering expertise, personal courage and local assertiveness, for a new era of agriculture which, after initial difficulties, was to adopt a specialisation that was to tide Holbeach and its surrounding area into the twentieth century and beyond.

New age, new dimensions –and bulbs

With the natural gift of centuries of silt deposits and a favourable water table as a foundation, local specialisation aided by the facilities of the industrial age took on a new dimension from 1900 onwards. The tentative diversification of a few years earlier by smallholders into the cultivation of aconites, snowdrops and finally daffodils was of great significance, for the beginning of the new century was to witness rapid development in the local commercial bulb industry, as London markets responded favourably. Growers and specialists from Holland, relating to soil and drainage conditions similar to their own, came to settle in the area and add their expertise.

Of the 'locals', George Dickinson of Whaplode was an early pioneer, but nearer town F H Bowser and O A Taylor had joined the ranks by the inter-war period, when not a few smallholders in the district, undaunted by the roaming pheasant's appetite for tulip bulbs, also extended into flowers to see them through the depression years –

TULIP HEADING AT TAYLORS, in the 1950s.
[Photo courtesy John D Taylor.]

a situation that brought occasional gluts of production and low prices at times, but nevertheless sustained a healthy expansion through into 1939.

The new industry formed its own association in 1916, originally titled the Spalding and District Bulb Growers' and Market Gardeners' Association, but after becoming part of the National Farmers Union in 1945,

it became the South Holland Horticultural Association. F H Bowser was its Chairman over 1949-50, while O A Taylor chaired it for an extended period –1954-57– while the Suez Crisis was on.

Taylors- Crown Colony to Royal Warrant
Taylors Bulbs represents a significant component in the successful story of bulb growing. Gassed and invalided out of the First World War, Otto Augustus Taylor, a former Royal Horse Artillery sergeant and pharmacist's employee from London, applied for one of the Crown Colony Holdings allotted for ex-servicemen at Holbeach in the Sluice Road. With his 10 acres of tenanted land, he decided to join the new wave of interest in flower and bulb growing. Living on the job, as it were, such holdings were ideal for family involvement in the enterprise, and by the time Otto's sons Stanley and Percy had joined him in the business in 1938, their acreage had increased by over six-fold. It was to double in less than a decade with the purchase of Washway House Farm in 1946, and with the formation of O A Taylor & Sons Bulbs Ltd in 1970, the company became a recognised supplier to nurseries and garden centres.

By the time Taylors had proudly reached Royal Warrant status in 1985 as Bulb Growers to HM the Queen, their acreage amounted to 600, enhanced during the 1990s by regular investments in packing, bagging, grading and conditioning technology, and additions of new premises. A significant development in 1992 was the incorporation of the Johnny Walkers specialist bulb division, while the company has won many national awards for its products, including a gold medal at the Chelsea Flower Show every year since 1994. Taylors is very active in charitable support, and in 1999 earned Tesco's Nature's Choice standard for potato production. Today, the company remains very much a family concern, with the brothers John§, Roger and Brian Taylor overseeing an enterprise of some 1,700 acres –all from ten humble acres of Crown Colony!

Meanwhile, what of traditional farming methods with the advent of the twentieth century? It did not signal an end to livestock farming, cattle, pigs and sheep remaining a significant factor until the 1960s; indeed George Thompson is still, in the twenty-first century, a noted cattle breeder. But where the pioneering larger farmers such as Arthur Hovenden Worth were concerned, intensive arable farming became the order of the day. In the first half of the twentieth century, mustard was one such crop. It was grown on a large scale by the Worth and Lane farms for Colmans in Norwich, the client's assessment responding rather like a school report, with remarks like 'Satisfactory' or 'Could do better'. Sugar beet and root seed crops also typified the inter-war output, gathering momentum with the development of nearby canning factories from the 1930s onwards.

FOR HIRE, 4 A.M. TO 9 P.M.: Traction engine and living van, 1900s.
[Courtesy R L Thorpe.]

Potatoes to the fore

But having been cultivated with increasing application by growers large and small in the latter half of the nineteenth century, it was the potato that became the

RUSTING IN PEACE. A surviving example of the Bettinson potato lifter, once the product of an ambitious local firm.

number one crop with pioneering farms such as the Worth estate. Grassland that had provided the earlier generation of wealth – supporting the sheep that had provided the wool– was ploughed up to accommodate a new source of prosperity that became the barometer for local agriculture –to the extent that a bad potato year had a ripple effect on all farming activity over the season.

Initial concerns that these were mineral soils low in organic matter were alleviated by generous recyclings of farmyard manure. Soon, A H Worth was sending 50 % of his potatoes directly to London markets. An infrastructure was tailored around this traffic, consisting of a purpose-built, light railway, operated from 1910 onwards on a narrow, 2ft-gauge track linking the estate with Fleet railway station, where Worth's train ran onto a special loading dock, some 6ft above the full-size railway, and where the 1-cwt hessian sackloads were transferred to mainline goods trains.

All the components for this railway were bought new, unlike later local light railways assembled out of First World War surplus. Horses provided the motive power initially, but as each animal's weight limit was restricted to five tons, they were replaced from 1923 onwards with two petrol and then one diesel locomotive which could pull up to 20 tons at a time. Worth defrayed running costs by allowing neighbouring growers, such as J H Thompson at Dawsmere, to share the use of the railway in return for a fee, and to ensure minimum interference to the smooth running of his transport system, Worth also bought up land at certain strategic points on the line, such as its crossing point with the road to Long Sutton. There was the odd incidence of a road vehicle colliding with the train at this point, on which occasion, if a court case resulted, Worth as a magistrate could not sit on the bench, as he was an interested party! The light railway was run until 1955. But although long dismantled, 'Waste not, want not', has been the motto, with traces of its ironwork reappearing everywhere, mainly as roof trusses for farm buildings.

Following the earlier years of specialisation mechanical developments were stirring in the background. The post-World War One period saw the gradual supremacy of the tractor over the traction engine, with the obvious advantages it offered in reduced manpower, running costs, operating time, greater manoeuvrability and its potential for harnessing to labour-saving devices. It took quite a while however, for old practices to die out, with traction engines still used for threshing into the 1960s. The Cade family's machine was just such an example: bought second hand from Bowsers at Somersham near Louth, it was worked for several years, then sold. But the old friend was bought back again, to be operated until 1966.

As with the previous war, the 1939-45 conflict forced an advance in agricultural practices, particularly where the introduction of new American-inspired machinery was concerned, this time bringing in more sophisticated tractors and the combine harvester. But the Holbeach firm of P B Bettinson came up with a first of its own, the fully-elevated potato lifter. Up until then, potato lifters merely removed the crop from the ground, to be picked up by gangs of manual labour. But thanks to its conveyor belt system, the Bettinson machine not only scooped the potatoes, but dropped them into a trailer running alongside as well. The sales

potential for the machine would have been considerable.

SPRAYING FROM ABOVE. A 1949 advertisement for helicopter spraying from Pest Control, one of two local firms so equipped for the job.

But large-scale production was not proceeded with, and it was left to larger manufacturers to profit from similar designs. It was believed that perhaps half a dozen or so 'Bettinsons' were made. If so, most of them have disappeared. But the original example survives, in a semi-derelict but towable state on Pennington's farmland, a unique example of Holbeach ingenuity which would benefit from being in a museum. Such machines performed well unless bogged down by wet

STILL DOING IT THE OLD WAY. The Cades' engine and crew in action off Foxes Low Road, 1962.
[Photo: Lincolnshire Free Press.]

conditions –one reason why Worth's first potato harvester in 1955 was only used on the lightest soil.

Advent of pesticides

Rape seed and peas were to become increasingly important crops in post-war years, while on the back of streamlined harvesting methods came the tentative use of pesticides. Before their introduction, farmers such as Eric Lane were reluctant to grow bulbs because of the eelworm threat –with nothing more sophisticated than a hot-water treatment to counter it– and the need to keep land 'clean' for other crops. Paraffin however proved effective for carrot spraying, a typical 100 gallons an acre dispensed with abandon, safe in the knowledge that the carrot leaf would not absorb it. Soon after the 1939-45 War, Eric Lane enlisted the expertise of Doktor Ripper from Austria to advise on crop spraying. Ripper's specifications helped yields, but in those early days, the formulae arrived at were less selective, and killed not only the target pest, but beneficial insects as well.

Nevertheless, the process was here to stay, pioneered locally by such firms as G & S G Neal and Pest Control Ltd. Established in the late 1940s, both firms offered helicopter spraying services, Pest Control's publicity material featuring the machine in silhouette form above a globe logo. 'Book Early!' commanded their March 1952 press advertisement. 'Early booking ensures that Pest Control Limited contract spraying service will do the job at the best time. Proved PHENOXYLENE 30 will best clean the weeds in your corn and linseed when applied by skilled operators under experienced supervision.' A Neal or Pest Control-attended field, therefore, was clearly not the place for an illicit picnic!

Eventually however, helicopter spraying was discontinued for environmental reasons, when it was found that rotor turbulence was exposing the underside of the plant leaf. By the 1960s Neals were trading from Fishpond Lane and advertising other exotic products such as Thimet Disyston for aphis in potato and sugar beet, Carbyne for wild oats, and Preeglone Extra Camparol, to control weeds among potatoes.

Long before helicopters took to the air however, Worths had devised their own more leisurely methods for dispensing

TRACTORCADE AT TINSLEYS. An open day in the 1960s shows off a fleet of David Browns.
[Courtesy R L Thorpe]

fungicide, patented by 'A H' himself and built by Gratton. Drawn by a horse, the machine relied on a chain drive which drew the 'Bordeaux' mixture from a hopper into a fan chamber, from where the powder was

FARMERS FOR HIRE. Contractors Ernie and Moss Brooks of Fishpond Lane, sometime in the 1950s.
[Courtesy R L Thorpe.]

blown out through a series of tubes. In season this was a job for the early riser, as the mixture was best applied at 4 a.m. when the foliage was still wet with dew, and therefore offered optimum clinging properties.

Salt versus weeds

With the emphasis so much on chemicals in the post-war period, it is interesting to note a method of weed control by natural resources, tried with some success during the 1960s in the Lord's Drain and all tributaries of the Holbeach River. Salt water was admitted through sluice doors from the Welland and the Wash and left to concentrate in drains for three to four weeks. This prevented the weed growth which normally started in March and April –an idea employed by the South Holland Drainage Board in 1966, after an experiment conducted two years earlier.

Cut flowers from tall greenhouses
Another interesting post-war development was the cultivation of cut-flower roses under seven acres of glass by Eric Lane's son, Thomas, at his Penny Hill nurseries. It reflected a practice followed elsewhere by rosegrowers Pollards in West Sussex, and Geests in Spalding, who employed this method to grow tomatoes, although Lane's glasshouses were among the tallest of their kind and remain an imposing sight in Penny Hill Road.

Changing practices
The 1950s were to be the last decade in which man and beast were to be employed in any number on Holbeach farms. In this period, Worth's complement numbered at least 100 men, supplemented by 30 women, –two of whom were Land Army girls, legacies from the war who left as late as 1952– and reinforced at haymaking, potato-planting and picking time by Irish labourers.

The Worth estate, embracing three farms, could almost be considered a sealed-off colony. Self-sufficient except for telephones and electricity –although the workshop had its own generator– it had its own blacksmith, carpenter's shop, and provided accommodation for many of the workers and their families in over 30 cottages and houses, serviced by 10 miles of cindered roads and 12½ miles of railway.

Fed on the job at harvest time by a substantial diet of hot suet pudding served singly with gravy, followed by home-cured fat bacon cooked in milk and rounded off with steamed pudding and custard, the farmworkers –afforded the luxury of only one week's paid holiday a year by the Agricultural Wages Board– toiled their way through a gruelling twelvemonth that took in, among many other duties, digging twitch with a handfork and planting seed potatoes

early in the year, harrowing potato ridges, planting celery and sugar-beet hoeing in May, crop-spraying in June, haymaking and pea harvesting in July, cutting the corn crop in August, thatching corn stacks after the September's main harvest, potato-picking in October, hand-lifting November's sugar beet, and wheat-drilling in December, often not finishing until darkness had fallen on Christmas Eve.

Softening the blow –with peppermint
But the need to take advantage of new technology and machinery to remain competitive and profitable led inevitably to a reduction in the workforce. As a paternalistic institution, Worths softened the redundancy blow for affected employees for as long as possible by introducing labour-intensive crops, such as spinach, brassica, celery, and on a more exotic note, poppies – a 'dual-crop' grown for both opium and oil seed for the paint industry– and peppermint for the Seymours' Distillery Farm (situated near the present junction of the A151 with the A17, hence the name, 'Peppermint Junction').

The peppermint, which required planting and cutting by hand, was afterwards loaded into wagons for transporting to Distillery Farm, where secret rituals were followed to refine the brew. Reminiscent of traditional vineyard practice, the crop was trampled in copper receptacles and steam blown through the resulting mash to obtain the essence, a hard-won effort yielding only two gallons per acre. Modest the output may have been, but it was very potent nonetheless and any attempt to taste the oil at this stage could result in a blistered tongue! In those days, all the peppermint oil went to the confectionery industry, but the advent of cheaper Third World costs put an end to peppermint-growing as a Holbeach-grown project.

Changes in distribution
Soon the day was coming when it would require more labour to merchandise the potato crop than to grow it. A H Worth had died in 1955, and the Queen Anne-style Hovenden House –built 1911– was transferred to new owners, the Cheshire Foundation, in 1957. Arthur's son, George

Arthur (Dick) Worth, a distinguished wartime pilot, recognising that better wholesale prices depended on a continuity of supply, consistent quality levels and the handling of greater volumes of potatoes, was instrumental in forming a prototype co-operative, in which neighbouring growers could channel potatoes through a central grading system operated and owned by Worths. Under this arrangement, Worths bought the potatoes from these neighbours and charged them for the distribution and marketing.

Co-operatives

During the 1960s, other crops, such as vining peas, were included in the arrangement, which hastened the need for the groups involved to be formalised in 1969 into the Holbeach Marsh Co-operative –a more democratic situation in which the indoor grading stations were owned by all the growers, who each had a seat on a board of directors. By that time also, the QV title had been created (in 1966) in the interests of applying a brand name to the joint project, the letters standing for 'Quality and Value', and packaging methods switched to 25 kg (4-stone) paper bags.

Catering for the supermarkets

Later on, the popularity of such co-operative movements declined, and the enterprise was formed into a limited company with members becoming shareholders. But more changes were soon to follow in the 1980s, with the decline of wholesale markets and the rise of supermarket chains as the dominant buyers. Worths bought out all the shareholders and reverted to full ownership of the enterprise, tailoring merchandise to suit the buyers' requirements, such as individual meal-size packs of potatoes for Marks & Spencer, Sainsbury and Tesco. A further rationalisation of resources brought QV together with Geest and there are now three separate processing units serving the aforementioned multiple retailers, employing some 350 people.

Excepting casual labour brought in at busy times, it now requires a mere 12 men to look after 4,500 acres, a tribute to a level of technology repeated at relative scales on most local farms. Few people need

reminding that growing, selling, preparing, processing and transporting food in South Holland is big business. Wheat, sugar beet and potatoes are currently the most important crops, followed by field beans, peas, barley, oilseed rape, linseed and horticultural crops: brassica, cauliflower, carrots, parsnips, beetroot, onions, peas and beans. No wonder Holbeach is part of an area that has been referred to variously as the Bread Basket, Vegetable Belt or Pantry of England.

♣ ♣ ♣ ♣ ♣ ♣

¶ *English Peasant Farming*, Joan Thirsk, 1957

‡ *A History of the Fens of South Lincolnshire*, W H Wheeler, 1896

† *Agricultural Revolution in Lincolnshire*, T W Beastall, 1978.

§ John D Taylor, CBE, was also Deputy Chairman of the Conservative Party until 2003.

'2 FAT HEIFERS, £54.' Accounts page from the books of William Burges, tenant of Hurdletree Farm, in late 1847. Other interesting entries include: 'received of Mr Festing the Property Tax, £3.7.6 [£3.37½]'; '1 Comb of Wheat' to Mr Jonathan Darby, £1.5.6 [£1.27½]. A 'comb' measured 32 'dry ' gallon measures of grain.

[Courtesy Tim Burges.]

6 – Life in the 19th Century

The nineteenth century was a significant period for the town in that it was a time of changing fortunes –indifferent at the beginning, but improved at the end– of self-sufficiency in its industries, ecclesiastical expansion, two royal jubilees and the arrival of the machine age, including the railway.

It was also the first full period in which, through the medium of newspapers, we had a more continuous and accessible record of Holbeach life with its joys, sorrows, fairs and celebrations.

In the earlier years of the century, there seemed little to celebrate. Unemployment and low wages during and beyond the 1820s and 1830s led to widespread poverty in the town, where regular work was the exception rather than the rule. Of the 805 dwellings assessed in Holbeach at the time of the 1841 census, 258 tenants were excused from paying rates because they were too poor.

Unenviable conditions

When they were in work, farm labourers faced the prospect, with no transport provided, of rising very early and walking

up to six miles to work, along roads which even in the town were unpaved and transformed by rain into mud. The journey home was no more pleasant, often in drenched clothes, and with no means of drying them overnight for the next day. 'No wonder', wagged the finger of local contemporary journalism, 'that many were disabled by rheumatism and became prematurely old, or were cut off by fever and pneumonic diseases, leaving widows and orphans to be maintained at the expense of the ratepayers.'

Many such people entered a spiral of depression, drowning their sorrows in drink or drugs. Opium-taking was widespread among the poorer women, who had to cope with the wretched conditions of their housing all day long. Most of these dwellings were badly built, of lath and plaster construction and restricted in height, usually no more than six to ten feet from ground to eaves, with the sleeping area reached by a rough ladder through a hole in the ceiling. Several were built along the Roman Bank, where the ditch behind provided the open drainage.

In central Holbeach, the river provided the same facility for sewage, dead animals and all kinds of rubbish: prime conditions for stench and disease, which were always worse in dry weather, particularly during 1826, when many townspeople became seriously ill and some died. Conditions here might have been improved a little by ambitious plans, laid ten years later, for the transformation of the Holbeach channel into a navigable river to the sea, with all the advantages it implied for the town's growth and prosperity. At a meeting held on 26th May 1836 chaired by George Harvey and with the Revd Morton included on the committee, there were serious intentions to form a Holbeach Navigation Company, to be financed by 600 shares of £25 each, with local bankers Gurney, Birkbeck & Peckover acting as treasurers. A month was allowed for 'some competent engineer to make a survey and report', but the outcome is not known and presumably the project foundered on the grounds of expense and non-feasibility.

Worst mortality rate in Lincolnshire

Meanwhile, more suffering was to come. Its population may well have almost doubled in the first half of the nineteenth century, but in the years 1841-1848, Holbeach's mortality rate was not only the worst in Lincolnshire, but above the national average: 25 deaths for every 1,000 people, as against 20 per 1000 elsewhere in England and Wales. It was also a black spot for infant mortality, with the astonishing claim that 'Nearly two-thirds of the population of Holbeach died before reaching maturity.' Even by this time, street drainage had barely progressed. It was in the main little better than enclosed cesspools, with several feet of foul mud underneath; or, in the case of one drain in the High Street, a tub sunk into the road and covered by a grating. To this, every day, the landlord Mr Bellairs had to carry every item of drainage in buckets from the Bell Inn. 'Nothing can be worse,' Mrs Bellairs was quoted as saying. 'My husband takes it up every morning, and yet we can scarcely live. I had a child nearly drowned in it!'

As an aside at this point, it is worth noting that it would take another century or more for the septic tank to become a thing of the past. Even in the 1960s, the council lorry calling to drain off individual house sewers was a regular routine of local life, with the contents discharged ultimately into the ground beneath what is now the scrapyard on Fen Road!

New Health Board brings improvements
Fortunately, worsening conditions were checked by the passing of the Health of Towns Act, which in 1850 enabled the setting up of the Holbeach Local Board of Health. With Edward Ayliff as clerk and Edward Millington as the resident surveyor, it consisted of nine parishioners who issued bye-laws for street cleaning, and embarked on a programme of more efficient drainage and the construction of a proper waterworks. Their first major achievement, in 1853, was the tunnelling over of the Holbeach River where it passed through the town. Their efforts must have made a noticeable difference, for the introduction to Holbeach in *White's Directory of Lincolnshire* for 1856 reads: 'Holbeach is a small but thriving and well-built market town…', whereas the updated 1882 entry had not only dropped the 'small' but had us down as 'a thriving, *clean* and well-built market town…' It was also a relatively well-lit one, with the benefit of 48 public lamps fuelled by gas, a private local industry begun in 1834 with works installed in Boston Road by George Malam. Malam subsequently went bankrupt, and ownership of the works passed jointly to Ashley Maples of Spalding and William Crosskill of Beverley, then to Boston Road ironfounder Henry Ellis before becoming a limited

company with its capital increased in 1869 by 500, £1 shares.

Unfortunately, there was little the Board of Health could do about accommodating the underprivileged. For those who could not afford to stay at the Chequers or neighbouring inns, the ten lodging houses in

BED AND BOARD FOR THE HARD-UP. The aptly-named Dirty Dick's in Fleet Street, long before it ended its days as a store-room for Limmings.
[Courtesy Limmings.]

the town were a decided second best. Bedrooms, located in the roofs, provided no ventilation and as many as 20 people, including tramps and down-and-outs, were crowded into rooms of little more than 60 cubic feet, where the entire floorspace was taken up with bedding, and the fire hazard an unthinkable prospect.

The Workhouse
The only other alternative shelter for those with no means of support was the Workhouse. Earliest references to this institution are made in a 'terrier' (or register) of 1661, describing three acres of land given for the purpose by 'R Davye, Junior, late Ampleford' to 'The poor of Holbeach.' According to Gilbert's Parliamentary Returns, the Workhouse was still near the town centre in 1785, situated against the old drain just beyond the present Cemetery, where Mondemont Close now begins. But in 1837 it reopened on Fleet Road, where it survives today in much modified form,

partly as special-care apartments. It was built at a cost of £5,812 by the Holbeach Union Board, and served 11 local parishes to house 'the destitute of all ages', including unmarried mothers and pregnant women – for whom maternity facilities were provided

SPECIALISED APARTMENTS. The 1837 Workhouse on Fleet Road later provided specialist care accommodation.

and who performed a variety of menial chores in return for a basic standard of food and shelter. The old persons in the workhouse were only allowed out for two hours every day, and prison-like discipline and terminology prevailed. The person in charge –Edgar Luke Lance by 1856– was referred to as the Governor, and a Mrs Hannah Millns was the Matron. Other staff were housed in lodgings across the road: hence the name 'Union Street'.

Although enlarged three times during the Victorian era to cope ultimately with a potential 419 inmates, the Workhouse was never filled to capacity, the highest recorded figure totalling 250 in 1851, declining to 179 20 years later. The year before, in 1870, the Board admitted that its strict management style had been a failure, in response to a letter addressed to it by Mr Shipley, Master of the Caistor Union. In it, Shipley emphasised the effect conditions were having on the children in particular. He deplored the use of barred windows and doors to keep them in, and stressed that the more barriers were created, the more children would be encouraged to run away. In reply, the Holbeach Union promised to consider the provision of open play areas and games fields, and to allow boys into the town on errands. At least all inmates were given a good Christmas party that year,

'regaled' according to the press report, 'with roast beef and plum pudding and ale for dinner on Monday last…Mr T A Lane and another provided them with oranges and nuts.' But it is difficult to ascertain whether conditions were measurably improved after Shipley's intervention, except to say that as late as 1907, there were two incidences of a break-*in* to secure a night's lodging! After 100 years' use in this fashion, the Workhouse was converted into Fleet Road Hospital in 1937, when patients were transferred from Caistor.

Events and amusements
For those able to make more of life, there were regular dubious distractions, such as the long-established cockfighting that took place on public house premises for high-value prizes. An early advertisement dated 1810 promoted 'a match of cocks for a gun valued at eight guineas' on 28th September at the Rose and Crown, followed the next day by another offering a silver cup as a trophy, 'the cocks not exceeding four pounds in weight, and the owner paying one shilling entrance for each cock.' Morbid needs could also be satisfied by further 'bye battles and an ordinary each day.'

More suitable for family consumption was Holbeach Fair. Held over three days in mid-October, it was something of a showman's extravaganza, featuring an occasional Wild Beast Show and supported by marionettes, a waxworks, travelling theatre and various sideshows. A press article written towards the end of the nineteenth century tells us that the Fair was a great loosener of inhibitions. It encouraged everyone to keep open house, lured 'staid householders' out into the night to see the sights, and even those unable to go were given a 'fairing' –a present from the fair– by a reveller. A century away from the breathalyser, getting home after consuming vast quantities of gin and water required great concentration for people to 'sit tight on their horse', or be buckled 'carefully in their gigs to avoid a spill ere they reached their destination.' Then, as now, the homeward trek *en masse* left the occasional pointless trail of damage. The Holbeach Local Board once complained that the row of trees planted from the town to the Cemetery was suffering because, 'Some senseless asses are repeatedly in the habit of breaking off the tops', and offered a £5 reward for information leading to the offenders. One wonders if this would have merited investigation by the fascinatingly-titled 'Inspector of Nuisances', who in 1892 was recorded as living in Church Street under the name of Christopher Marshall...

An even bigger fixture, from the aspect of space occupied, was the Holbeach Horse Fair, held on the 17th of May and September annually. Sometimes hundreds of horses were brought to Holbeach from as far as London, the Midlands, Yorkshire and Lancashire. Trading took place in the main road through the town, with animals often lined up from the Red Lion in Spalding Road to the Workhouse in Fleet. Apart from the farmers and dealers, it was a great favourite among the children, who spent so much time there that Fair days were finally declared school holidays. Bidding began at 7 a.m. and could often go on as late as 10 in the evening, concentrating mainly on trap and heavy carthorses in May, and mares and foals in the autumn. The Fair was continued until 1954, by which time the increasing use of farm machinery had irreversibly affected the horse trade.

Scheduled transport services
Without a horse of one's

own before the coming of the railway, communication with the outside world could be difficult, although transport to and from Holbeach was certainly available for those who could afford it. From 1828, William Feast was running the Spalding and Holbeach Sociable daily from the White Horse and Cross Keys Inns, Spalding, to arrive at the Chequers in time to connect with the Boston coach for Wisbech.

It performed the return journey in the afternoon, 'to convey Passengers and Parcels to Spalding the same Evening by Four o' clock.' Mid-century services from the Chequers included the London mail coach, leaving at 4.30 p.m., and Union coaches to Lynn and Newark at noon and 2 p.m. respectively. By this time, horse omnibuses were also operating between Spalding and Wisbech.

Incoming mail arrived at 9.20 a.m. and 11 p.m., with outgoing deliveries at 3 a.m. and 4 p.m. Goods were catered for by carriers, such as Jane Gibbons' and Robert Black's services to Boston on Wednesday and Saturday, and to Lynn on Monday and Thursday. The ubiquitous Black also managed a freight run to Wisbech on Wednesday and Saturday, not to mention a daily run to Spalding.

Opening of the Market House, 1844
Certain occasions helped to boost the town's self-respect, as well as provide an excuse for mass celebration. The opening of the Market House at the junction of Church Street and High Street in October 1844 –four months after the ceremonial corner stone was laid– was paid for by public subscription organised by local residents. There were 13 local dignitaries on the organising committee, comprised of John Johnson, Alfred Mills, Thomas Sturton, Edward Key, Thomas Holliday, Edward Hoff, David Jackson, Richard Hickson, Thomas West Curtis, Henry Ward, William Thomas and Messrs Thomas Edward and John Pearson Savage.

The House was welcomed by all as a means of restoring the status of the market, which had been observed by 1828 as a mere shadow of its once-flourishing state, and was also used as a court house for the petty sessions. As if anticipating the Holbeach Vintage Rally Parades of 150 years later, a commemorative procession beginning in Spalding Road passed through the town, led by a flag-bearer on horseback and followed by local dignitaries and farm-workers carrying symbolic sheaves of corn and fleeces of wool. Various horsemen, the Holbeach Mail Coach and other decorated carriages and gigs brought up the rear.

After the opening, the content of the charter originally granted in 1252 to the Lord of Holbeach Manor, Thomas de Multon, was read out, and a band played to the crowd. In the evening, a dinner was held in the newly-opened public rooms of the Market House – although the menu was probably well beyond the means of many onlookers, at 2s 6d (12½p) per head including malt beer– followed by a fireworks display.

Holbeach now had a prestigious building, a focal point in which to meet, trade, proclaim or mark special occasions. One of the first of these was the opening of the railway in the town from Spalding in 1858, when barrels of tar were burned outside.

Joseph Wilson, then a young journalist and later to become editor of the *Spalding Free Press*, recalled the court sessions there in the 1850s, when he went in fear and trembling of the 'egotistical and irritable' Richard Aparn, the Registrar.

The poor reporter had to crowd in beside the Registrar at the solicitor's table. 'If I wished to escape to catch a train, I had either to climb over a partition into the jury box, or to creep under the table. To request the austere and autocratic registrar to allow me to pass was more than my position was worth.'

Fortunately for Wilson, the magistrates' sittings, with such personalities as Canon Leigh-Bennett, Capt. Barker, Dr Harper, Ashley Maples, B Fountain and J P Sturton were much kindlier affairs.

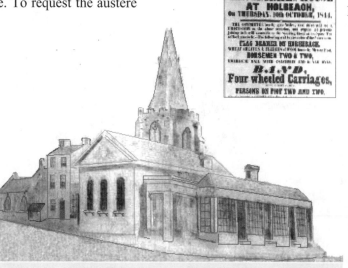

MULTI-PURPOSE. *The Market House complex opened in 1844 provided attractive central premises for trade, court hearings, meetings and concerts. The shops on the Market Hill side disappeared in 1910. [A contemporary illustration by 1 Stennett, of Holbeach Grammar School.]*

Market House relaunched, 1869
In January 1869 the Market House was again the scene for festivities, in celebration

of its acquisition the previous year –together with the integral terrace of shops on the Church Street side– by the Local Board of Health for £925, after a period of failing management.

The Board had furthered its investment with alterations to enhance the building's multiple use as a free market for the sale of butter, eggs and poultry, with adjoining rooms for the County Court, Petty Sessions, public meetings and concerts. Tradespeople of the town immediately put the improved facilities to the test by inviting over 200 'frequenters and supporters of the market to a knife and fork tea.' It also provided an opportunity for locals to show off their talents and set pieces, with John James Harris at the piano, and the 'Spalding quadrille band discoursing sweet music during the evening.' The new chairman, in his 80s, sang a funny song entitled 'Periwig and Hat-band Divo', followed by Mr Bean's rendition of 'Shivery Shakery'. Meanwhile, the response of an old farmer to a particularly popular number called 'My Jolly Old Wife and I', when he jumped up and embraced his wife 'in the presence of the whole company' was widely remarked upon in an era when public displays of affection were supposedly less commonplace!

The several royal occasions in that century were marked with mixed fortunes. A cloud had hung over that of Queen Victoria's coronation, when the vicarage was attacked by a mob. They were objecting to the Revd James Morton's apparent refusal to contribute to a coronation fund for the poor, although the vicar's political sympathies were also thought to have provided a motive, having secured his living through the influence of Earl Gray, a prominent Whig*. Later on, the town's celebration of the Prince of Wales's (later Edward VII) marriage to Princess Alexandra of Denmark in March 1863 began well enough. There were the usual processions, the town was decorated, bells were rung, and at night, 'Mr Snarey, the ironmonger [of West End] had an illumination which made all others pale in comparison.' However, a damper was put on the whole proceedings when an accident occurred in the paddock opposite the cricket field, involving a cannon specially cast for the event by Mr Haslam, a millwright iron and brass founder from Boston Road. His employee, Mr Woods, who had been regularly firing off the cannon in a series of salutes throughout the day, was pressing home another charge when the weapon went off unexpectedly, causing him to lose both an arm and his sight. Others standing nearby were also injured. A collection was raised for the victim, to which even the Prince of Wales himself contributed £10, but sadly Woods was to be seen for many years afterwards, trying to make ends meet by selling oranges on the market.

The wedding of Victoria's 30-year-old second son, Alfred, Duke of Edinburgh, to Grand Duchess Marie Alexandrovna of Russia in 1874 provided an opportunity for more tree-planting, this time in the road stretching from Fleet Street to the Cemetery. A Mr Rhodes of Fleet was responsible both for this new row of oaks, and for suggesting that the road itself be named Duke of Edinburgh's Walk, later abbreviated to Edinburgh Walk.

Victoria's Golden Jubilee, 1887
When Victoria's Golden Jubilee came around, one or two misgivings were experienced during the preparations. All Saints Church bellringers refused to work unpaid, and were frowned upon by the organising committee for demanding 'extortionate' rates for the occasion, instead of volunteering their services like everyone else. But on the whole, the town's celebration, held on Thursday 23rd June 1887, appeared to be a success. The weather

was obviously good enough for a midday dinner to be served outside in the High Street for 2,500 people, who enjoyed main courses of roast beef and plum pudding, and 'the beer, nectar and lemonade gave great satisfaction.' The thoroughfare through town was decorated with floral arches, 'the effect wonderful and beautiful in the extreme', and plenty of activities were planned afterwards, with 'rural sports' from 2 p.m. in Mr Carter's field in Barrington Gate, followed by water sports at the Brick Pits, Fishpond Lane. Anyone with any energy left at this stage could join in the dancing, and at nine-o'-clock lighted tar barrels were carried through Holbeach, as a prelude to lighting a huge bonfire on the sports field.

Measles threaten the Diamond Jubilee, 1897
The Diamond Jubilee ten years later was marred by an outbreak of measles in the town. Schools had to be closed, and official festivities postponed for a month. Many queried whether this was really necessary, and did not appreciate the warped sense of humour responsible for hoisting a black flag inscribed 'Measles', and circulating funeral cards worded, 'In memoriam. June 22nd, 1897. In everlasting memory of the Holbeach Jubilee festivities, killed by a sudden attack of measles…R.I.P.' With the railway now at their disposal, some 200 townsfolk sought their amusement elsewhere, in Lynn, Spalding or Sutton Bridge. But many others, undaunted by the epidemic and instances of street fighting during the day, made the best of the occasion, and still went ahead with decorations, flags and illuminations. Prominent among the streamers stretched across the High Street was the slogan: 'Sixty years, and not out; God bless her'. In the evening, a dinner was held at the Chequers, and even the inmates at the Workhouse were well catered for.

Out of town, on the marshes and other parts of the parish, prominent farming families such as the Worths, Carters, Tinsleys, Crossleys and Pickworths regaled their employees with substantial barn teas, followed by games out in the fields and sweets and nuts for the children to take home. It was compensation for some of those youngsters promised the Holbeach children's tea that had been postponed by measles until July 7th, for several of the women who originally undertook to prepare it had subsequently backed out of the arrangement. This only added to the feeling afterwards that the Holbeach Diamond Jubilee celebration had not been the best handled of events.

The unearthing of the bones, 1868

One of the most significant occurrences in nineteenth-century Holbeach history was the unearthing of a piece of a very different world, of life and custom as it may have been conducted some thousand or more years earlier. In April 1868, an important discovery was made on plots of land near the west end of the Holbeach station yard. Originally bought by the railway company, they remained as undeveloped pastureland and had recently become surplus to requirements. These plots, part of a mound which was almost 5ft higher than the surrounding area, and some 60ft in diameter, had once been attached to Hall Hill Farm, ancient premises then still standing, which had been built on the site of the Lord of the Manor's residence.

'A great quantity of skulls'

A report submitted to a meeting of the Society of Antiquities in December 1887 by W E Foster of Aldershot –a Fellow of the Society who had actually attended the Holbeach excavation– stated that Mr Robb, who had recently bought some of this land, was in the process of levelling out the mound in the area nearest the railway line, when 'he came upon a great quantity of skulls lying close together in a row, about 18 inches below the surface.'

In Foster's view these had been collected and moved to the spot over the previous 100 to 150 years. A contemporary press report also revealed that digging in another area used by Mr Lemon as a garden had brought to light human bones and some 20 skulls, not more than about nine inches from the surface.

Further excavation of Robb's land, more into the mound's centre, revealed a greater concentration of remains. 'These were not laid in order,' commented Foster, 'but had evidently rested there undisturbed for several centuries'. This was the same area in which William Stukeley had described the findings of 1719, when human bones were first encountered during the digging of a ditch. It was obvious that this ditch, now dividing the fields of Messrs Robb and Mashford, had inadvertently cut through the middle of an ancient graveyard. On Mashford's side, even routine ploughing had been enough to surface a complete skeleton and other bones, but the field was promptly sown with mustard seed afterwards, thus halting any further investigation there for the time being. However, the more accessible field revealed up to 130 skeletons of men, women and children. Some of the adult males were powerfully built –as tall as 6ft 5in– and most with distinct, elongated skulls and prominent foreheads, the head itself rising high to the crown. Other skulls shared a square forehead and flat crown.

The skulls found nearest the railway line were described by Foster as possessing good teeth and showing no fractures, whereas the Revd Macdonald's observations of 1884 relate that the adult males found on the east side of the mound showed traces of wounds, 'received probably in battle.' An interesting point, as according to Gooch's *Place Names in Holland,* Wignal's Gate is defined as 'The way to the war mound', from the Anglo-Saxon 'wig', meaning 'war', and 'nol', representing a hillock or hump. But Macdonald went on to suggest that 'They may have been retainers of the Littleburys' in the civil wars…rendered probable by the fact that one of the old halls, belonging to that family, is close to this ancient burial ground.' As an aside, he followed this up with further conjecture that the Littleburys and the Fleets were on opposing sides in the Wars of the Roses.

Remains of St Peter's Chapel?

But reverting to the Hall Hill-Wignal's Gate discoveries, apart from pieces of a strange, red, waxy substance, very few valuables were unearthed. According to Foster, some pottery, charcoal, sand and burned bones were found deeper down in the centre of the mound, but he regrets these were not saved, without giving a reason. Robb did however give a few pieces to Foster which were later forwarded to the Society of Antiquaries.

Nevertheless, the symbolic significance of two relics unearthed nearby, a small clasp knife with its bronze handle fashioned into a fish head, and a much-corroded metal seal with the figure of what resembled a cock for a handle, accorded with Stukeley's theory that this could have been the site of St Peter's Chapel that stood in Wignal's Gate.

Informed opinion admitted a little later that the knife's decoration may have been purely coincidental, while the seal's emblem was not necessarily that distinct. But a section of stone was found complete with a circular recess of four to five inches deep carved into it, which was thought to be a pivotal base for a chapel door.

FINAL RESTING PLACE. The bones unearthed in 1868 now lie in the Cemetery, marked by this headstone.

Other oddments included a few nails, one or two spurs, a silver coin from the reign of Edward I or II ('the Plantagenet being very perfect on one side of the coin' –Macdonald) and various scraps of iron. Yet this was not all. Below the burial ground, but immediately above the silt level, was a significant layer of burnt earth and wood ashes containing evidence of Roman occupation, including urns and other red earthenware typical of a Roman or Roman-British style.

BASE INSCRIPTION. 'The bones that were found were removed with this stone to this place, 1899'.

Possible Anglo-Saxon identity
In a 1,300-word letter to the equally voluble *Stamford Mercury* in May 1868, a Charles Edwards attempted to date the burials by comparing the similarity of the Holbeach discovery to a contemporary find at Kirby

Underdale in Yorkshire's East Riding. Here, corpses were arranged in a similar pattern and the burials had been identified as Anglo-Saxon, 'though the indications are many of their belonging to the Britons or Romanized Britons.' Edwards related that the Romans were known to have had a small camp in the Holbeach area, engaged in the construction of embankments against the sea under the direction of Nero's procurator, Catus Decianus. 'We discover many Roman coins in the town and parish of Holbeach,' affirmed Edwards, 'and if relics of one durable kind be found, why not others equally endurable? For various reasons I think Holbeach would, as compared with other places along the coast, be a very eligible site for a small Roman colony.' In Edwards' opinion, he knew of no other place, except Lutton, that would be likely to attract Roman settlement, and from the artefacts found to date, the soil around the town had offered excellent preservative qualities.

Assuming as he did that the Romans had chosen to occupy this particular area of higher ground in Holbeach as a convenient refuge from the marshland on one side and the spring tides on the other, and allowing for the amount of time required for the deep alluvial and vegetable soil layer to form on top of the silt, Edwards suggested that the mound would have been used as a graveyard 'at the least five or six centuries later' –in other words, the sixth or seventh centuries AD at the earliest.

The remains get a Christian burial
Having disinterred the bones, it remained to be decided what to do with them. At a vestry

69

meeting held in All Saints Church, it was resolved to raise funds by voluntary subscription to excavate the remainder of the burial ground and, 're-inter the bones in a Christian-like manner.'

As to how this should be done was met with a mixed, even 'lukewarm' response. The Revd Brook favoured buying the burial plot for the Church, and Robb was indeed willing to sell for £70. But the Church could not raise that amount, and Brook's subsequent suggestion that he should offer some vicarage land in exchange was opposed by parishioners. Difficulties were foreseen with maintenance, and the potential disturbance to nearby residents from the constant use of vicarage grounds by Robb and his successors. The matter was not settled permanently until June 1899, when it was agreed that the original burial ground should be sold to provide a plot for the building of St Peter's Villas. On 1st July, the bones and commemorative headstone were transferred to the south side of the Cemetery. This stone, with plenty of space still left around it, survives in good condition near to the High family plot. The circular inscription at the top reads: 'Waiting for the Redemption of the Body', while that on the triangular base is inscribed: 'Ancient Burial Ground discovered A.D. 1868. The bones that were found were removed to this place 1899.'

It was not quite the end of the matter. In July 1903, another complete skeleton was unearthed near to the 1868 site while digging the foundations for some more new houses. The specimen this time was reported to be in perfect condition and measured 7ft 2in in length! 'A curious old iron key' was found close by the bones, and added to the museum collection at the Spalding Gentlemen's Society. Then, in October 1950, workmen digging a trench for a cesspool at the rear of St Peter's Villas found a further collection of bones and ten skulls, again in excellent condition –'almost certainly part of a medieval burial ground', reflected the press article. No action was considered necessary by the Coroner, Mr C M Bowser. But even after that, remains kept on appearing. Mr I H Howard, living at 25 Hallgate between 1968 and 1977, discovered more human bone in his garden, for which

the Lincolnshire County Council could find no precedent in that part of the road.

Holbeach, it seemed, had accidentally stumbled on its past, and not quite known what to do with it. But there was little time for self-analysis. The machine age was beckoning, and it was time to move on.

♣ ♣ ♣ ♣ ♣ ♣

*The Whigs were one of the great English political parties of the late seventeenth century onwards –superseded after 1830 by the Liberals– and the term was applied to those who upheld popular rights, and opposed the power of the monarchy.

7 – A Bottle of Gin for a Railway Share

If land reclamation and drainage had represented one successful outcome of struggling with officialdom, rivalries and personalities, the construction of the railway through the town was another. And the Spalding to Holbeach line was a first important link in a route that, almost 30 years later, finally joined the Midlands directly with East Anglia.

Following on the heels of the Industrial and Agricultural Revolutions, railways transformed the means to distribute the output of these new methods. South Lincolnshire, with its flat, wide-open spaces, was well placed between the industrial North, the Midlands and London to form an essential part of the network, while benefiting from the new system to trade its own agricultural produce.

By the 1850s, moves were afoot to develop a line between Spalding and Norwich. Until that period, the only mechanised means of travel between the North, the Midlands and East Anglia was by the tediously roundabout routes of the Great Eastern Railway (GER), who held a monopoly which two other interested companies, the Midland Railway (MR) and Great Northern Railway (GNR) were anxious to break.

The railway becomes a reality

The GNR had a stronghold at Spalding, while the MR offered connections with Peterborough. The next step was to find supportive sponsors, not only to contribute financially and assist with the legalities, but also to establish credibility and help overcome local resistance. Not surprisingly, landowners and tenants were to provide the biggest obstacle. But there were those among them who, together with other influencers from local industry and commerce, were enterprising enough to take the project on board.

Arrangements began with a London solicitor contacting his opposite number in Holbeach, suggesting that a railway could be promoted if 'one or two substantial Holbeach men' could be approached to back it, in which case they would be promised the support of other directors and additional capital from London.

The resulting board of directors was composed of John Chevalier Cobbold, Edward Stillingfleet Cayley, Adderley Howard, Richard Peele, and Holbeach farmer and landowner Thomas Edward Savage, more usually known as 'Old Tom' and considered less of a gentleman than his brother John, but the right man for this project nevertheless. An Act of Parliament was created on 4th August 1853, 'for making a Railway from Spalding to Sutton Bridge and Wisbech.' It was to be called the Norwich & Spalding Railway, with an authorised capital of £170,000 and maximum borrowing powers of £56,000. Beginning at Spalding, where it connected with two existing GN routes, the line was to pass through Weston, Moulton, Whaplode, Holbeach, Fleet, Gedney, Sutton St Nicholas, and Sutton St James. For the time being, it was to 'terminate near Sutton Bridge in the parish of Sutton St Mary', also to be the branching-off point for Wisbech via Tydd St Mary, Tydd St Giles, Newton, Leverington and Wisbech St Peter.

Amid celebrations that included a musical parade, ringing the church bells and burning barrels of tar outside the Market House in Church Street, the line to Holbeach was opened at 4 p.m. on Wednesday 9th August,

1858, and to passenger traffic, after testing that all was well with the line, on Monday 15th November the same year, when there was 'a bountiful distribution of jolly good beer and strong', the linesmen received a 'good dinner', and Mr Curtis, the druggist, provided 'tea and plum cake, etc. for about 250 poor women, widows and wives' –a celebration which continued with dancing until about 3 a.m. There had been a few grumbles, however. The press had spread a rumour that the opening should have taken place on 1st July, and a local newspaper report on the station and its approaches was critical of the 'abominable' fencing and the fact that the platform was too narrow. 'No crinoline must come there,' and 'where abundance of room offers every facility for a beautiful drive to the passenger station, a crouched-up corner is all the present accommodation…In many ways elegance and beauty of design seem an entire stranger to the Holbeach station.'

Despite the adverse comment, the station's small dimensions were no hindrance to the bounty it was now possible to bring to Holbeach –not for a while, anyway. The initial arrival of rolling stock in August 1858 had brought useful commodities for the town. This included a substantial amount of flour, and 50-60 tons of coal, which was immediately sold off at 15/6 a ton, amid much malicious jubilation that Sutton Bridge was no longer the leading place to buy coal. Townspeople were encouraged to cheer the heroes of the project, Adderley Howard and Thomas Savage, and boo Sutton Bridge!

The line had taken longer to reach the town than intended. Engineering difficulties were cited as one reason, cash flow another, and the Crimean War was also reputed to be a

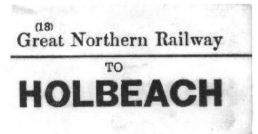

Great Northern Railway labelling dating from pre-1893.

factor, both in hindering the raising of money and the provision of an adequate workforce. Some shareholders had not responded as readily as expected, while the shares themselves were not very highly regarded, even after the line began to pay its way. There was a story circulating that a £20 share, on which only £7 had so far been paid, was sold for a bottle of gin! It was a worrying time for those responsible for raising additional capital, particularly Thomas Savage, who despite his wealth, was rumoured by many in Holbeach to be facing financial ruin from the railway. Nevertheless, the original four daily train services each way were soon proving inadequate, with revenue averaging £40 to £60 a week, and it became obvious that the railway would be a going concern, provided the GN addressed the problem of overcrowding –which had seen passengers packing into the guard's van and even riding on the engine, India-style, during the 25-minute ride to and from Spalding!

Extending the line
Meanwhile, the original Act authorising the construction of the line had expired, and it took nearly a year to obtain a second Act to continue the line beyond Holbeach. Nevertheless, the Holbeach to Sutton Bridge link was completed by July 1862, and the Act of July 1865, under which the GN and MR was to pay the Norwich & Spalding Railway a minimum rent of £7,000 a year for use of the line, placed matters on a surer footing. By this time, too, Holbeach was soon to become part of a network extending from the other side of Bourne at Essendine in one direction (and on the main GN route to King's Cross) to Lynn in the other, complemented by a second link with the London line at Peterborough that connected with Sutton Bridge via Wisbech. To cope with the

additional traffic this implied, alterations were eventually carried out at Holbeach in 1889 to double the track through the station and add another platform on the opposite side, while the original structure was widened to a safer width. Thus the network had now come to fruition. Beginning with an amalgamation with the Midland & Eastern in 1877, what had started out as the Norwich & Spalding Railway became part of the Midland & Great Northern Joint Railway in June 1893.

At long last, holidaymakers from Holbeach could now travel from their doorstep to the Norfolk coast, a facility for which they had waited 29 years. But instead of leaves on the line, the reason for the delay had been a more plausible one of engineering difficulties, local conflict and officialdom. There was every reason to sympathise with and be thankful to the companies and forward-thinking individuals who had been prepared to take risks and show resilience in the face of prejudice, daunting legislation, greed over land sales, and the demands of local physical geography.

Inevitably, there had been certain projects within the overall scheme that never got off the ground. The plan, for instance, to run a loop line from Weston over Moulton Common, through Holbeach St Marks and St Matthews, rejoining the main line at Sutton Bridge. Or an alternative scheme for three dead-end branch lines to the sea bank from Weston, Holbeach and Long Sutton. Both failed through lack of financial support, and the subsequent development of road transport.

Incidents

As a new means of transport, the railway provided a fresh source of incidents. Within the first year of the line's operation, the unskilled status of certain early railway employees was reflected in a misunderstanding of September 1859, when a locomotive bound for Holbeach alarmed the passengers at Moulton with 'the horrible and continued din of the railway whistle and the gradual slackening of the pace of the train.' The cause had been the sight of a red light in the distance, taken as an emergency signal to stop immediately. When the guard

asked the gatehouse keeper the reason for showing red, she replied, 'Why, lawks, it's only the fire in my room at the gatehouse, with the door wide open.' It is not recorded what choice language ensued.

Such amusing incidents apart, the M & GN had a proud safety record, one which could claim never to have killed a passenger throughout its history, although in 1876 a maintenance man named Mitchell was seriously injured at Holbeach when he fell through the roof of a disused engine shed onto a pile of scrap iron, and in the late 1930s, the Vicar of Gedney, whose rectory grounds had been divided by the railway, was knocked down by an LNER Sunday excursion train while using a foot crossing.

Of the one fatality that did occur in the years of the Midland & Great Northern, it was ironic that this should happen at Holbeach, and involve a device intended to prevent

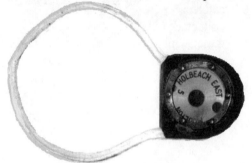

ESSENTIAL TOOL. Handing in the all-important tablet confirmed when a single stretch of line was clear.

accidents. Many stretches of the line from Lincolnshire into Norfolk were single track, and to guard against two trains meeting on the same rails, a tablet system was installed from 1897 onwards. On entering a stretch of single track, the engine or its driver picked up a metal token from the appropriate signal box, and deposited it at the next point where doubled track, usually through a station, began. Once the tablet was given up, the signalman had his confirmation that the single line was clear for traffic in the other direction. Depending on the location or the type of engine in use, tablets were sometimes exchanged by hand, but at Holbeach, Whitaker's Patent Tablet Catchers were featured. These consisted of a primeval-looking metal 'beak' on a pivoted pole, which picked up the tablet from the engine as it passed, and relied on side draught from the train to push the pole down, enabling staff to retrieve the tablet.

On 2nd January 1913, a locomotive pulling a guard's van containing railway inspector Stephen Youngman reached the end of single line working at Holbeach West signal box. The catcher collected the

DANGEROUS OBJECT. **Daily Mirror's** *picture of January 1913 shows the spearhead catcher with a tablet ready for the signalman's collection.*

tablet, but the pole was not deflected downwards sufficiently and Mr Youngman, poised on the van's step ready to get off, was caught up with the mechanism and died of his injuries later that day at the Johnson Hospital.

Freak weather conditions in March 1916 turned a routine journey from Spalding to Sutton Bridge into a 12-hour ordeal, when high winds brought down a telegraph pole just before Holbeach. The pole fell between two coaches of the 3 p.m. from Spalding and could not be dislodged, in spite of eight substantial characters trying their best to lift it. The engine uncoupled and went on ahead to Holbeach to fetch help. Beyond the station, however, the line was strewn with further poles. All the grammar school children aboard the train stayed the night in the town, while a few other passengers walked on to Sutton Bridge, arriving at 3 a.m. The state of the railway was at least an improvement on the road from Holbeach to Spalding, which was completely impassable, with vehicles diverted via Moulton Chapel.

The railway's heyday

On a brighter note, Holbeach station in its earlier M & GN days at the turn of the nineteenth century would have been a busy and colourful place. The locomotives were finished in what was described as 'Golden Gorse', a colour chosen by the chief engineer's wife as representing the gorse growing on Norfolk heathland –through which many of the trains passed before reaching Lincolnshire– and the carriages were painted a grain-effect brown to represent teak, picked out in gold lining. All goods wagons carried a distinctive, brick-red livery, with M & GN lettering in white, and black ironwork. Later on the loco livery changed to dark brown, which was often mistaken for black once it became grimy!

Apart from anything else, the station had to act as an adequate depot for the town's fuel supply in pre-electricity days. White's 1882 Directory reflected new storage and distribution methods taking effect. Coal had been highly publicised as one of the first commodities to reach Holbeach by rail in 1858 and three coal merchants, Thomas Clarke, H Cox and J and W Ridlington had since availed themselves of this newer transport medium by taking space in the railway station yard, as a means of improving stocks and delivery schedules.

A major user was the Holbeach Gas & Coke Company. Its advertisement of June 1894, drafted by Thomas C Willders, invited tenders 'for the supply of 400 tons of gas coal (Railway Weight), to be delivered at Holbeach Railway Station at the following times, namely: 150 tons by the end of July

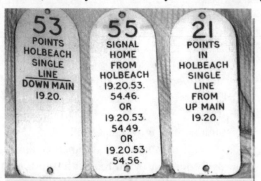

SIGNAL SPEAK. Explanatory tags formerly attached to levers in the signal boxes.

next, 150 tons by the end of September next, and the remainder in January next.'

It was not surprising then, that fairly extensive sidings became necessary to cope with the heavy and varied goods traffic. Certain of these track sections were even named after regular users of the railway's facilities, such as 'Clarke and Grey' (coal merchants), Boston Coal Company, the obscurely-named 'Alice' (capable of holding 22 wagons), or most amusingly, 'Jumbo', a stretch of line into which a visiting circus train would be shunted, to unload the animals and equipment from as many as 18 wagons. Rolling stock was administered with strict instructions that each goods wagon was to be allowed 6½ yards of siding space.

Young cattle were brought in from the Midlands for transitional fattening and return, but above all the station became an important handling centre for locally-grown potatoes, flowers and fruit.

Before the First World War, bulbs had been imported from the Netherlands via Lynn Docks, but as home production increased, special trains were introduced onto the Spalding line and Holbeach achieved record levels for flower loading, especially in the early months of the year. Up to 45 vans a day were filled with daffodils, narcissi, hyacinths and tulips, all part and parcel of

'DUN ROLLIN'. No wheels left on this century-old example berthed in Holbeach Drove, but coaches like it must have passed through Holbeach many times.

a workload which, when combined with other goods handled, involved an average turnaround of 70-80 wagons a day, reaching a peak of 123 wagons on one occasion. May onwards brought the fruit traffic, of gooseberries, strawberries, raspberries, and

red and blackcurrants. Among the 30 or more staff were specifically-named potato porters to unload farm carts into wagons, and three coal handlers. Substantial four-wheeled fruit trolleys, pulled by hand, were used to carry up to 3½ cwt of goods to the loading stage in the yard. All fruit was 'passenger-rated', travelling as part of a carriage train, whereas vegetables carried during the same season, such as new potatoes, were 'goods rated', and made up a goods train also designated to carry lettuces, cabbages, broccoli and particularly green peas. Station equipment on hand included sack barrows with hoists, parcels hand carts and luggage barrows with two, three and four wheels to cope with all descriptions of period baggage from hatboxes to trunks. Horse-drawn vans delivered goods from the railway to the town and beyond, and it would be well into the 1930s before they were superseded by motor lorries.

The long decline

The railway's heyday was from the early 1890s to the 1920s, coinciding approximately with the ascendancy of bulb growing and the resulting flower traffic, and when the rise in annual tonnage handled at Holbeach rose from 40,000 to 110,000 tons. After that time, overall M & GN profits fell away appreciably, from £57,716 in 1928, to a loss of £30,966 in 1932. Although the following year showed a modest surplus of £4,175, and 1934 figures revealed passenger receipts of £94,535, with £489,353 earned for goods carried, the effects of

LIGHTING THE WAY. An old oil lamp from Holbeach Station.

the Depression and the continuous improvement in the road haulage network and lorry design were making themselves felt.

Not that the M & GN had taken the lorry situation lying down. Their own Country Collection scheme, for instance, had made use of hired vehicles to carry goods from farm to goods yard, while the Joint Traffic officials, from the stationmaster upwards, mingled regularly with the farming fraternity to keep an eye on crop progress, thus ensuring enough goods wagons were available when needed. And initially, when the going got tough, the upstart haulage firms themselves would often subcontract to the railway, as for instance, when conditions were foggy.

When Station Foreman Bob Watson first came to Holbeach Station in December 1935 however, it was still business as usual, even if the surroundings seemed unimpressive:

'I was rather taken aback by the unkempt appearance of the buildings and yard. Some sleeper-built huts, rented by potato merchants, were the worst aspect. Some of the brickwork was beginning to powder in places, being merely silt bricks...I thought the station a depressing place —some untidiness one would expect, with large quantities of straw in use inwards and outwards for seed and ware potatoes, and also the mud from the sugar beet loadings; but the nondescript huts and the waste ground between them and Station Street were most unsightly. The latter ground being littered with old prams, a mattress or two, etc.

'The Stationmaster was not infrequently away in the afternoons, going off about 2 p.m. with a golf stick...After the flowers slackened off there were small quantities of fruit, but until July there were no potatoes after late April. And we found time rather hung on our hands.'

Bob Watson also gives an interesting insight into how items were loaded. Pea growers were very particular, insisting on only one layer of bags of peas in a wagon. New potatoes, by contrast, were packed in hundredweight barrels and placed in large cattle wagons carrying up to 10 tons each. Clover hay was another ' regular', which the railway was to refuse if the consignment was mouldy, but rarely did because 'it was difficult to find hay which wasn't mouldy!'

Inwards traffic was relatively light, apart from coal in the winter seasons, occasional wheat deliveries for Tindalls mill, boxwood for a firm making trays, Snettisham gravel for minor road repairs, and consignments of crockery for a wholesaler.

But from September 1936 the London & North Eastern Railway (LNER) took control and began rationalisations. Thirteen locomotives were scrapped, the rest painted black so as not to show the dirt, and the carriages re-coated a dull brown. Long-distance Sunday excursions were discontinued. But such economies did not inspire the LNER to invest in essential modernisation, such as further doubling of the line to ease congestion in peak-season through traffic. This gave rise to the sort of situation once related as happening between Sutton Bridge and Spalding —the exact location is not recorded, but it must have been very near, if not actually at Holbeach. Two excursion trains of 14 coaches each tried to pass each other on doubled track through a station, but neither could resume the single track beyond because the last carriages of each train were

NEW MASTERS FROM 1936. But the LNER had no great ambitions for the line through Holbeach.

still in the way, and all sidings were occupied. Station staff phoned the local headquarters at Austin Street (King's Lynn) for advice, but no-one was available. However one of the drivers, John Cartwright, thought it over, sketched out some manœuvres on the Stop Press column of his newspaper, and handed the diagram to the senior porter. After ten minutes' delay, the day was saved.

Brief revivals

The line came briefly into its own again during the war years on account of its through connection between the Midlands and Great Yarmouth port, and the fact that it served at least 10 airfields along its route.

But afterwards, the back-to-normal situation was short-lived. There were one or two notable events: the passing of the royal train through Holbeach in July 1947 was one, when King George VI and Queen Elizabeth travelled from Sandringham to open the Royal Agricultural Show at Lincoln. Another came in the form of a last gasp, when the Suez Crisis of 1956 and its attendant petrol rationing into the spring of the following year led to a renewed dependence on the railway, in spite of BR's tame attempt at tactical advertising. The funereal ad read:

'PETROL RATIONING: British Railways (Eastern Region) offer their services. We are doing our best to meet emergency requirements and invite your co-operation and support. Write or telephone your local goods agent or stationmaster, who will be pleased to help you.'

But the reality was that the service was under-used, and as early as 1950 it did not take much of an economist to deduce that 11 trains per day, picking up an average of 24 weekday passengers in total from Holbeach was clearly uneconomic.

Even five years after the war, the bus already had the upper hand. Before car ownership proliferated, this form of transport was then at its peak, not only offering greater flexibility in serving isolated villages, but in providing extra vehicles at weekends and on market days.

Closure

First outward signs of doom came in 1953, with the withdrawal of night-time goods trains. Five years later, the truth was finally known. Excepting a few Norfolk routes, all passenger services were to cease after 28th February, 1959.

INDIAN SUMMER OF A RAILWAY. An excursion train for Yarmouth Beach arriving at Holbeach Station on 9th August 1958, pulled by locomotive 0-6-0 4F, No . 44122. Families await a Spalding train on the opposite platform.
[Photo Frank Church c/o Essex Bus Enthusiasts Group.*]*

Naturally, the news was received with shock by the faithful few who actually used the service. What were the young mothers of Holbeach to do, without their 'Pram

77

Specials' to take them shopping to Spalding? In a letter to the Parish Council, British Railways tried to play down the inconvenience, talking casually of 'alternative rail routes within easy reach of Holbeach district', to which John Mossop's response was, 'Try walking to French Drove station!' His feelings were echoed more vehemently by Leslie Roll, Senior Public Health Inspector for Stamford Borough Council. He condemned the closure as 'a deliberate and systematic attempt since 1936 to starve the M & GN Joint Line of every bit of traffic that could possibly be diverted', not to mention the lack of essential improvement to the track system.

Betjeman-like, 'Ayscoughfee Owl's' column in the local press of 27th June, 1958 spoke up cosily for the status quo of train travel. 'For a few bob I can relax…I can glance up from my magazine to contemplate, across the fields, the pile-up of vehicles under a haze of petrol and oil fumes…My luggage is stowed neatly and orderly in the guard's van, not slung in the boot, and a chap shuts the door after me when I get out.'

But the door was about to close in a more abrupt fashion. Authorities were intolerant of protest, and the die was cast. Midnight on Saturday, 28th February 1959 marked the end of passenger services through Holbeach, grimy and familiar Class 2-4-0 MT engines having passed up and down for the last time with 'That's Yer Lot!' posters –from the hand of Sutton Bridge station employee John Barker (later to become a Cross Keys Bridge operator for 40 years until he retired in October 2001) and other backs-to-the-wall messages scrawled in chalk on their smokeboxes. The line was retained to handle goods traffic in fruit, flowers and other produce to Spalding, although the immediate removal of track beyond Sutton Bridge –at a ruthless 8 a.m. the following Monday– severed the Norfolk link for ever, and Holbeach West was one of a number of signal boxes taken out of use, together with those at Sutton Bridge Dock Junction, Gedney and Moulton. Justifiable though the freight service still was, its days were soon numbered, and all activity ceased on April 2nd, 1965. All along the local line, railway landmarks soon sprouted weeds and undergrowth as dereliction took hold. It is some consolation, therefore, to find the main station building and its platform at Holbeach surviving today in reasonable condition.

So a century of that special branch-line atmosphere –one you could almost say was a family railway, with several generations serving the same company– had finally been lost to the town. True, it may not have been cost-effective in its latter years. A somewhat generously-manned work force may well have found moments to spare for the odd card game –as typified by the scene behind the packing cases in the *I'm All Right Jack* film– or been on hand to advise young trainspotters when the next interesting engine was due. But with the disappearance of their M & GN (the 'Muddle & Get Nowhere'), many living in Holbeach could no longer share the thoughts of the poet Siegfried Sassoon when he wrote of a train's familiar sounds:

'That somehow its habitual travelling comforts me,
Making my world seem safer, homelier, sure to be
The same tomorrow: and the same, one hopes, next year.
"There's peacetime in that train." One hears it disappear
With needless warning whistle and rail-resounding wheels.
"That train's quite an old familiar friend," one feels.'

THE LAST POSTS. One of two station yard gateposts still standing at each end of David and Susan Lefley's forecourt in 2004. In the background, the main station building survives. Other railway buildings, or parts of them, were to be found behind the garage.

8 – Wartime Holbeach

1914-1918

On 26th July 1914, the Spalding Company of Territorials left for their annual training under canvas at Bridlington. The routine was not too strenuous for these part-time soldiers: an hour's drill by company officers before breakfast, braced by the seaside air, followed by a march to another training area, until finishing for the day at 2.30 p.m. But they were not to know, in their comradely holiday camp, that within nine days they would be among the hundreds of thousands of men pitched into the bloodiest war of the century.

Finding the men

Once war was declared on 4th August 1914, Holbeach reacted swiftly to the call-up. With Kitchener's initial appeal for 100,000 men –to be followed in September by the PM's plea for a further half million– police were empowered to visit all farms in the district and order any reservist on the workforce to join up at once.

GUN ON THE CORNER. The WW1 cannon at the junction of Foxes Low Road and Fleet Road, later removed to Carter's Park in the 30s and scrapped in World War 2. [Courtesy the late Dorothy Bradley.]

Twenty agricultural workers were found by this method within 24 hours of war being declared, and left Holbeach station for their regiments on 5th August, with a large crowd to cheer them off. They were followed the next day by 21 horses for military use, despatched by rail to Grantham. By then another reservist, local policeman PC Cross, was already into his second day with his old regiment, the 12th Lancers, having set off early by car and mail train to Woolwich. But less than a month later he was among the wounded, shipped back from the front to Southampton.

Mobilisation had also pricked the odd conscience or two. J H Rowett, a chimney sweep living with a wife and six children in Church Street, gave himself up as a deserter from the Navy 16 years previously. He was given the King's pardon, provided he joined a ship at Plymouth immediately.

Meanwhile, the police force PC Cross left behind made up for depleted numbers by asking 'tradesmen and stalwart townsmen' to act as special constables, which met with an overwhelming response, thus providing 'immense moral support to Supt Burton and his men in allaying excitement in the times which lie ahead.' Also reassuring for local security was the formation of gentleman-farmer A H Worth's brigade, a sort of prototype Dad's Army 'preparing themselves for emergency at home' by reporting for drill sessions on Tuesday and Friday evenings– instruction that included practice in taking orders by whistle and arm motion only! Curiously, although well attended, interest in shooting practice was only lukewarm…

Watching for suspicious characters

Inevitably, anybody or anything with German associations was to be treated with the utmost suspicion. Car owners, or garages dealing in or hiring out vehicles, such as Dickens in Chapel Street, were instructed 'not to let out motors to Germans', nor were Germans allowed even to possess a car without the written permission of the local chief of police. With espionage a great talking point, a little too much enthusiasm was sometimes shown in watching the movements of others. The war had scarcely begun when, just down the road at Long Sutton, two men standing on Popbottle Bridge, holding what was claimed to be a large unfolded map, were on the point of being apprehended as German spies when it was discovered that they were J L Proctor of Fleet and his visitor from London holding a newspaper. Nevertheless, it impressed the *Spalding Guardian*. 'Such keenness augurs well for the safety of Popbottle Bridge', was its comment.

Providing for war

The first meeting of the clumsily-titled Holbeach District Sub-Committee of the

War Assistance Committee took place in September 1914, with J W Banks JP, J S R Tingle, JP, A H Worth and T C Willders as principal members. Fund-raising and charitable activities got off to a flying start. One hundred Holbeach ladies under the direction of Mrs C Wass of Wass & Eastaugh chemists (later to become the old Boots shop in the High Street) were already meeting at the Albert Hall in Albert Street on Wednesday and Friday afternoons from 2.30 onwards to make clothing for soldiers and sailors. Then there were fêtes and attractions held in the grounds of the town's grand homes, such as Stukeley House in aid of the local Nursing Association, where the Kirton Prize Band played for the dancers and the printer J C Chamberlin lost by a whisker to Miss Horry in the bowling-for-a-pig competition. His consolation prize was a fowl donated by butcher John Thompson of West End, while Mr J C Cox, having guessed the weight of the pig correctly at 2 stone 7¼ lb, was rewarded with a copper kettle. Similar events were repeated for the benefit of the Prince of Wales's National Relief Fund, with a bowling tournament held on Mr Fletcher's lawn, and a charity football match between Holbeach Town and Holbeach Crocks. An appealing novelty was a Button-Holing Day, arranged by Mrs Walker and featuring 'a bevy of young ladies' selling flowers –so young in fact, that they were excused from the mental arithmetic of giving change. A creditable £30 was raised in this way, the Misses Patterson top scorers with £3. 4s 10d.

Higher food prices; less waste?
One immediate effect of the War was the rise in food costs. Spalding bread prices had escalated to 7d for a 4lb loaf, caused by flour going up from 25/- (£1.25) a sack to 40/6 (£2.03). Characteristically for the time, it was an opportunity to moralise: 'One of the effects will be to prevent much of the waste which has been going on, even in working class homes,' the press rejoiced.

By contrast, Holbeach market prices were praised for staying at a reasonable shilling for 11 (why not a dozen?) eggs and 1/1 for a pound of butter. But then, as now, panic buying took place, and was frowned on by the Church where, at a special service two days after war was declared, announced by

town crier and attended by over 400 people, the Revd Hutchinson spoke out against the better off who were buying up provisions, 'to make themselves secure against any peril'. Later All Saints services provided further opportunities for charitable appeals; a typical request was for 24 blankets, one for each of the latest group of Holbeach recruits. The mood was gloomier over at the Baptist Church in Albert Street, where the Revd Cawdron spoke of the 'terribly dark war cloud hanging over the nation', and looked to 'Divine Guidance' and the Cabinet to bring the war speedily to an end, establishing 'peace with honour'. He went on to remark, in that March of 1915, upon 'the people [who] do not appear either eager or anxious to leave home in the evening part of the day. No lighted streets, and a dread of Zeppelins keep them indoors, and it really seems useless to arrange for anything to take place until the lighter evenings come along.'

Houses for heroes?
But even if peace was to be established with honour, to what sort of living conditions could the soldier expect to return? At an East Elloe Council meeting, a proposal to stop building houses for a year because of the increased cost of building materials was discussed. With many of the younger men away at the war, some argued they would not need housing. Chairman J W Banks differed, and believed existing building projects, such as sites in Fleet Road, should be completed before postponing further developments. 'As soon as the men come home, ' he said, it is only reasonable they will want more creature comforts than they have had at the front, and they will want good homes to go to.' By the middle of the war, however, economies had extended to keeping the roads in a minimum state of repair, cutting the cost by 'treble figures', but not –to local residents' disappointment– with a corresponding reduction in the rates.

Coping with the hazards
As already suggested by the Baptist minister Cawdron, a serious threat to the safety of East Anglian and East Midlands towns was the German's use of Zeppelin airships, produced in series since their introduction in 1900. In spite of the obvious suitability of the local landscape

for providing the minimum 50 acres necessary for aeronautical use, Britain dithered over eligible sites for aerodromes in South Lincolnshire while L1-type Zeppelins cruised over Holbeach and surrounding vulnerable fenland, the flat terrain affording excellent visibility of this and other towns. A notable occasion was the evening of 31st January 1916, where over a period of 9 hours from 6 p.m. onwards, a German naval airship squadron dropped bombs on built-up areas in Lincolnshire, Derbyshire, Leicestershire and Staffordshire. Many bombs fell in open country, causing no real damage. But even so, the attack claimed 54 dead and 67 injured. Holbeach escaped harm, but in Spalding, where the explosions could be heard and counted, 'owing to the absence of railway noise', the offensive was a little too close for comfort, but at least it knocked any remaining complacency on the head. In future Zeppelin raids, Holbeach was urged to follow Spalding's example, cutting off gas supplies as airships approached, and recommending the closure of all shops after 6 p.m. Ringing of church bells on Sunday evenings was discouraged, in case the Zeppelin was hovering above low-lying mist or cloud with the engines stopped, listening for any sign of life. Supt Burton also feared that too much light generally was being shown, stipulating that Saturday market-stallholders should stop using lamps during evening trading. The police had already made an example of a prominent local person causing a lighting offence when, during the 31st January 1916 raid, wealthy farmer Bartholomew Young Banks, of Sutton Bridge, was seen outside the Chequers with his car sidelights on.

'OUR LOVELY OLD LANE'. Malten Lane (now Damgate) is where the lady writing this postcard hopes to meet Aubrey again soon, probably when he next comes home on leave. The side wall of Mattimore House (now bordering Mattimore Close) is visible to the right.

[Courtesy Mr & Mrs D N Cook.]

Special Constable Fowle (normally J F Fowle, High Street chemist) jumped onto the running board, but Banks refused to stop until he reached Fletcher's shop, where two soldiers shouted, 'Put out those lights!' He was fined ten shillings (50p) with costs.

Entertainments

At least some soldiers were enjoying a taste of home life: those who, for a time at least, were fortunate enough to be billeted in Holbeach, enjoying the hospitality of certain townspeople on the Social Committee, who arranged regular functions in their honour.

Suppers were arranged at the United Methodist Schoolroom, followed by table games. These were interspersed with whist drives on Wednesday evenings at the Hall in Albert Street, hosted by Mrs Cooke, Mrs Hill and Mrs Curtis, with generous prizes. On one occasion Lance Corporal Wright won a Morocco leather case, faring better than a Mr Wakefield who made do with a consolation prize of a statue of Charlie Chaplin. Then there were billiard matches held on Tuesdays between officers and men at the Reading Room in Church Street, while Invitation Concerts, organised by Major and Mrs Cook in the Old Girls' School in Albert Street, attracted more creativity. Here on an evening in 1916, 'an array of plants at the foot of the improvised platform gave an artistic touch to the stage'. Mr Fern's animal imitations went down well, and the organisers themselves were not bashful in coming forward, Major and Mrs Cook performing in a duet of 'Pretty, Pretty Maiden', followed by Miss Sturton intoning an ingratiating 'The Army Today Is Alright', and more improbably, 'I Want

To Meet The Kaiser'. Such frivolities could only have been equalled by an evening of 'Military Fun' at the well-used United Methodist Schoolroom, where Mrs Hamilton, probably to not a dry eye in the house, sang 'When You Come Home', a sergeant major, 'I'll Take You Home Again, Kathleen', and Mr R Clark, 'Oh, I Have Never Had A Night Like This'. Presumably this had no bearing on a Chris Green's subsequent rendition of 'Hold Your Hand Out, You Naughty Boy'.

All such events helped to distract attention from the horrors abroad, and the fact that the area was short of men 'to fill up the gaps'. As the succeeding series of innocents began their recruitment training in the town, learning the art of musketry drill under a sergeant's watchful eye on Tuesday evenings at the Old Girls' School, their fellow Holbeachians who were now fully-fledged Tommies were enduring hell around the clock in the trenches, some never to return. Two or three years into the War therefore, it was unusual to find anyone eulogising over their lot as much as Carter Howard, former employee of Chamberlin's Printers, who as a stoker in the Navy, not only found the work satisfying and the food excellent, but liked the officers as well. A much more unfortunate man was Private Ebbage who, with his pass home in his pocket was killed with most of his company the day before returning to Holbeach on leave. His brother survived in a military hospital at the cost of a leg.

Communicating with the Front

For those relatively lucky enough to be captured, it was good to know that the food parcels arranged by the leading ladies of Holbeach were getting through, to the extent that the response could even sound somewhat choosy. 'Received a parcel from Mrs Wass', wrote Private A Sewell of Church Street, a prisoner in Germany by 1916. 'Thank her very much. We have had a passable Christmas. Don't send me bread, as the ladies of the Suffolk Help Society are sending every man of the Regiment two loaves of bread per week. You can keep sending butter'.

Soldiers' letters like these would have been censored for security reasons, a process that involved Private Harold Wise of Spalding Road in quite a coincidence, when he discovered that one of his letters home had been censored by Capt Lawrence Hemmans, son of the late Cannon Hemmans of Holbeach! Those who did manage visits home while their lives were spared, such as Private Harold Pape of Cemetery Road (later Park Road), were given a hero's welcome. But how such men, after the jingoistic optimism had worn off, could face the station gates for the return journey cannot be imagined. In all, some 84 men from the Holbeach area were to lose their lives in the Great War, 65 per cent more than the loss figure for 1939-45.

'LOVE FROM FELIX'. Woven First War postcard addressed to Mr and Mrs Hilliam of 18 Windermere Terrace, Fishpond Lane. [Courtesy Mr & Mrs D N Cook.]

Call-up problems

Naturally there were many who hoped that their occupations or commitments would prevent their call-up. Appeals for Exemption, as they were termed, were heard and considered by the Holbeach Urban Tribunal. The Holbeach Gas Company applied to retain their manager Richard Willey, as they claimed they could not find a replacement who could perform his duties as effectively, even though, as Herbert Carter of the Tribunal observed, demand for gas was reduced because the streets were no longer lit at night. However, the matter was shelved for six months, which bought the Gas Company and Mr Willey a little more time.

More usually the cases involved young men who could not, in their own or their parents' estimation, be spared from the running of the family business. The son of a local miller, for instance, appealed on the grounds of his parents being totally dependent on him, the father ill and unable to climb ladders, and with 10 acres of land, four horses, three cows and some pigs to look after as well as the mill. He had, however, another brother available to help, while the fact that the family already had two other sons serving in the Royal Engineers and Canadian Engineers cut no ice with the Tribunal. 'I should have thought the brother could have worked the mill and this man be serving,' was Major Bell's retort –a view endorsed by the Tribunal chairman who added, 'The fact that a man may be indispensable to private business is not sufficient. The question is: is the business indispensable to the nation?

Saving the married men
In hindsight, it is surprising that any activity relating to food production was not 'indispensable', if not to the nation, at least to Holbeach. But at this mid-point in the War, Kitchener's directive to tribunals was ' to stay their hands in excusing so many young men'.

Also the aim wherever possible was to prevent a situation where married men in essential work were having to be called up because single men were not coming forward. By now, too, the East Elloe Rural District Council had also lent its weight to the situation, S S Mossop, then Junior Clerk, calling the bluff of employers 'who continually state that they would willingly release these single men if married men would take on the job…Hiring day will soon be here and married men will be well advised to apply for any vacant posts…in the list of certified occupations, and masters should endeavour to engage married men in preference to single men'.

Charitable and voluntary support intensifies

As the casualties mounted, charities to support them proliferated. More 'young ladies', presumably older than those who had been unable to calculate the change on Button Holing Day, volunteered to collect for the Holiday Home for Disabled Soldiers at Lowestoft. The surnames involved with this work are still familiar to us today, such as Freda Lane, Marjory Tindall, Mollie Walker, M Wass, Dorothy Carter, Nora and Bertha Thompson and Dot Tinsley.

The older women were busier than ever. Mrs Elvis of Langwith House became organising secretary for French Red Cross Society collections, and Mrs Fletcher applied herself to a national egg collection for the wounded. In the first week of the campaign she and her helpers collected 500 eggs, but it was disappointing to note that the wealthier people of the town were the meanest, 'leaving part of the business to their poorer neighbours'. However, Mrs

TRIBUTE TO THE FALLEN. The First World War memorial tablet in All Saints Church, totalling 84 men.

Fletcher's efforts were appreciated, certainly by the soldier in a French hospital who wrote: ' Thank you for the egg with your name upon it. I am in hospital through having been frostbitten and standing up to the knees in water for four days in a German trench we had captured.' Fascinatingly, seed potatoes also went to France, donated by local farmers and sown 'just behind Verdun' by their French counterparts, whose land had been devastated by the German invasion.

The closing years of the War were dogged by shortages of labour to cultivate local crops. But Land Girls had just been introduced as part of a Government scheme, with certificates issued to all those who had registered for work on the land, followed by the awarding of armlets on completion of two months' service. Their efforts were supported seasonally by senior schoolboys. Then in July 1918, 115 Boy Scouts camped out on F Pennington's fields engaged in work at Whaplode, followed by the arrival at Holbeach station in September of three carriages full of Manchester grammar school boys to help out generally on the land. Meanwhile the Local Volunteer Corps was instructed by Mr J C Harrisson to guard the flax crop by night. 'Any night prowler, enemy or otherwise, might set the whole lot ablaze and it is very necessary in view of the importance of the crop that it should be watched.'

The 1918 harvest was full of uncertainty. The strawberry season had been short and disappointing, and July's heavy rain and wind had laid flat some of the oat and barley fields. Yet the yield was satisfactory, the only problem being one of sufficient manpower on threshing day. But in late September activities were rained to a standstill, much of the corn spoiled.

An epidemic was threatening, too. 13-year-old Ethel Digby of Northons Lane died in early July, the first effect on Holbeach of a national influenza epidemic that hung around for the rest of the year, claiming several others of all ages in Sutton Bridge, Long Sutton and Gedney. In Holbeach it peaked in late October, causing the schools to be closed for a fortnight; but its effects in the town appeared less serious than elsewhere, and by Christmas, a measles outbreak among the children was claiming greater attention.

Prices were still increasing, the benchmark commodities of eggs and butter at Holbeach Market reaching seven for 2/- and 2/2 per lb respectively by February 1918. Holbeach Gas Company prices had to go up by 10d to 6/3 (31p) per 1,000 units, because of dearer coal and its production. It was also in short supply, with an autumn directive to traders to 'Close at six or be short of gas'. Then the Master of the Workhouse ran out of meat and had to advise the Guardians of his decision to kill the two pigs they kept on the premises.

With the cost of living rising so much that even the Inspector of Nuisances was awarded a pay increase of £5 per annum, the Urban Council was prepared that April to consider a petition from 60 men to turn some suitable land into allotments. The petitioners suggested the cricket field, or land on Boston Road, Foxes Low Road and Grammar Lane. This drew a constructive response from Herbert Carter (Later to donate Carter's Park to the town) who, with a specially-formed committee to acquire 16 acres of land near the Workhouse, sold off portions of it to prospective allotment holders able to pay by monthly instalments, giving them the opportunity to use the resulting freehold for house building if they wished.

News of the Great War's end reached Holbeach about noon on Monday 11th November, 1918. The flags soon came out and happy crowds flocked the streets to hear addresses given at the fiveways crossroads by J S R Tingle, Herbert Carter and the vicar, followed by loud singing of the National Anthem.

Gradually the drift back to normal gathered momentum. Muffled peals rang out from All Saints on Sunday 29th November, announcing special services for those who had made 'the great sacrifice' in the war. This did not extend to financial sacrifice, however, as the women potato workers at C Bowsers reminded everyone when they went on strike after being refused a sixpenny rise to 6/- a day. Meanwhile, over a period of many weeks, soldiers returned from their regiments or prison camps abroad, accompanied by older men who had been away on munitions work, such as Mr Bielby and Sid Horry, anxious to be back running their businesses in Church Street.

And after all the town had been through, many must have identified with a poem circulating that Christmas:

In the year Nineteen-nineteen
We hope that margarine
Will drop in price
And be quite nice
And less like vaseline.

In the year that follows this
There are many we shall miss
Who fought and died
And side by side
Are now in realms of bliss.

In the year next on the stocks
The Land Girls now in smocks
Their work all done
(They've had some fun!)
Will perhaps return to frocks.

In the year Nineteen-nineteen
we hope our King and Queen
Will with us see
A Britain free
And world at peace serene.

The Star Supply Co. and William Curtis among others would ensure the quality of the margarine improved. But in 20 years' time, there was nothing any of them could do to save the 'peace serene'.

1939-1945

♫ *[Verse] 'Talk about a bust up, there's been an awful row.*
And though I am a peaceful man, I got me rag out now.
A certain party you know, has overstepped the mark.
He sez the bulldog wouldn't fight, it only knew how to bark.

[Chorus] 'That started it, that started it, that's how the trouble all began.
He sez that I begun it; I sez, "It's 'im wot dun it".
He sez: "I'm right fed up with you,"
I sez, " You know wot you can do",
And that started it, that started it, that's how the trouble all began.' ♫

At the beginning of September 1939, before Alan Breeze warbled those words in Billy Cotton's Band, the only immediate cloud on the local horizon was the prospect of milk going up to 7d a quart. The catalpa tree in All Saints churchyard was once more in bloom, and East Elloe Rural District Council had just approved the redecoration of the public lavatories on Market Hill at a cost of £11 7s. Mona

House, at 5 Church Walk, was due to be sold at auction (later withdrawn at £550 when the housing market became totally uncertain), while just opposite in this pleasant backwater, the vicarage rebuilding programme, following the demolition of the old house that spring, was on schedule for the Vicar and Mrs Boswell to move in again by Christmas. Work was also in progress on the Church chancel, and over at Carter's Park, the bandstand was about to receive a new roof. The weather must have been good, too, for Burtons in St John Street was advertising 'Something good for the hot weather', comprising jellies for 2d, 'tablecreams', blancmanges, and lemonade powders for 8d per pound. Hix & Son had just held a good auction on the Thursday, best cockerels fetching up to 4/-, hens 3/6 and eggs 1/5 a dozen. *Bulldog Drummond's Secret Police* and *The Little Adventuress* were showing at the Hippodrome, or you could have been brushing up your exterior woodwork with Ned Hall's hard-gloss paint at 2/- per pint.

Local people able to afford motoring holidays abroad at the end of August had witnessed the first rumblings. Petrol had been difficult to obtain in Calais amid obvious military preparations, and instead of the usual two vessels each way per day, there were continuous sailings of cross-Channel ferries for home, each ship crammed so full that some owners had to leave their cars behind in France for separate shipment.

Declaration of war and ensuing preparations
When the spell broke at 11.15 a.m. on Sunday 3rd September with the Prime Minister Neville Chamberlain announcing the declaration of war, one of the first events to be cancelled, some three hours after his speech, was the afternoon meeting at Bell End Speedway near Weston Hills (early hopes of 'recommencing shortly' were finally wound up together with the Holbeach and Spalding Motor Cycle and Light Car Club's affairs in January 1941).

Other arrangements long discussed beforehand were now a reality. The Park Road clinic became the First Aid post attended by Doctors Martyn, Walker and Ormsby, watched over by Home Guard regulars such as John Coley. Doctors gave occasional lectures there on how to deal with various different injuries, supported by First Aid practices conducted by Mr Staley and Mrs Bayston.

Blackout paradox

As a town that was largely to escape any enemy action, First Aid knowledge came in more useful for the many accidents suffered in the blackout, when there was no street lighting and vehicle lamps had to be masked off to a minimum. Typical among the incidents was a collision in the gloom between a runaway horse from the Chequers at Weston and a car driven by dairyman and farmer A W Taylor of Whaplode, resulting in a five-shilling fine and 12/6 costs for the Chequers landlord. Such traffic hazards may well have prompted the East Elloe Rural District Council's decision to fit skid chains to the Holbeach, Long Sutton and Auxiliary Fire Service vehicles. But blackout conditions presented a no-win situation. You could be penalised for showing a light in a building at night, PC Coddington ensuring fines for offenders of between ten shillings (Jane Winkworth of Station Street at 12.15 a.m.) and £2 (Sidney Hardy from a shop in Hallgate). Yet riding a bike without lights, if PC Fryer saw you, relieved you of another five bob (25p) and there were many such contradictory offences throughout the war.

Strategic gunpoint

Apart from blackout precautions, other sights and sounds were introduced as the local backdrop to war. Prominent among these was the Lewis machine gun emplacement in the bay window over the International Stores (now the Nationwide), strategically trained over the central crossroads in town. The building was so heavily sandbagged that it caused structural damage. Armament for the Home Guard, however, had not been immediately forthcoming. It took some time for weaponry to arrive from the USA, and when it did, heavy coatings of preservative grease took an age to remove. Open expanses of country on the fringes of town were defended by devices like the gun pit in Plowright's Field on the Fen Road, or the pill box near Holbeach Hospital, near which place a German pilot once baled out and was apprehended by Bill Stannard, Freda Coley's father.

To avoid confusion, any fire alarm was to be announced by the Church bell, the emergency siren itself having been reserved for use in air raids. The siren was positioned on the roof of the fire station, (now the public toilets) on Market Hill. Its wail was familiar enough, but for those living close by, it presented a strange phenomenon: 'You weren't aware of it going, unless you'd heard it start off', was the son of the International's manager, Jim Sleaford's impression.

Military presence in Holbeach

MASTER BAKER READY FOR ACTION: Wally French.
[Photo Bruce French.]

In the early part of the War, with invasion of our accessible coastline and flat terrain a very realistic possibility –reason enough for the Home Guard to patrol the roof of Tindall's Mill as a prime lookout position– the presence of troops could hardly be ignored. Alighting at Holbeach railway station, their arrival announced by military bands, regiments like the Royal Sussex and Queen's Own marched into town, to be billeted *en masse* in any building large enough to accommodate them, such as the Public Hall, Park Hall, the Women's Institute and sundry barns, outbuildings and even washhouses on surrounding farmland. Yet more inhabited the football club grandstand, convenient for training sessions in Carter's Park, which was also the parade ground for the Home Guard. Around the corner in West End, Dormer House (later to house nurses from Boston Road Hospital after the War and now the One Stop Shop) provided lodgings for the Land Army Girls, who filled the labour shortage left by farmworkers responding to the call-up. The girls performed many backbreaking and humdrum tasks in local farms, such as hoeing, weeding and driving horses and carts, and some became so indispensable that they stayed until the early 1950s.

On the eastern side of town, a rifle range was set up off Foxes Low Road, and a field down Damgate served as another training ground. Mattimore House, then on the corner of Fleet Road and Damgate, was the battalion HQ for the 'A' Company of the Home Guard, the 3rd Holland East Elloe Battalion, commanded by George Thompson from Holbeach Hurn, whose officers used Malvern House in Fleet Street, now a hairdressers, as their mess. The Battalion's administration relied on the services of part-time support staff such as Ivy Pollard (later to become Mrs Dowse and now Mrs Hargraves), who was Battalion secretary in the afternoons, after completing her morning shift at John Mawby's farm at Holbeach St Johns. Reporting to Capt McCoy, Ivy's duties included matters relating to clothes issue and typing reports, one of which, she recalled –on the subject of an enemy plane that had crashed at Holbeach St Johns– became an ordeal of several retypes because of her limited wpm skills! Wartime practice, however, obviously made perfect, as Ivy went on to serve as a farm secretary at Penningtons into her late 80s.

Holbeach men in the war

Many of the indigenous male population had lost no time in answering the call. As early as April 1939, 20 men formed 'Dog Two' –No.11 Group Royal Observer Corps– whose regulation-issue hut and canvas wind screen was soon transformed by fenland ingenuity into a more convenient affair with the aid of bullock trays, sheets of corrugated iron and a glass screen.

Before September was out, Gordon Woodman, Bell End Speedway's Clerk of the Course, volunteered for active service and was accepted into the tailor-made role of despatch rider with the Royal Corps of Signals. As early as 1st September, crossroads traffic was left to its own devices as Arthur Hallam, the RAC Scout, was called up for the RAF and posted to the Shetlands. Another person departing early was his RAC colleague at the Bull crossroads in Long Sutton, Charles Rowett, who lived in Park Road. The War meant rapid promotion for Charles's brother, Thomas, who had just spent 4½ years in India. Less than three months after elevation to Sergeant Major in 1939, he was commissioned as a Lieutenant in the Royal Artillery. Meanwhile, 228 men between the ages of 20 and 22 in the Spalding and Holbeach district registered

at the local labour exchange for military service. About 80 favoured the RAF, 30 the Navy, while the rest had no particular preference.

Another to join up early was Jack Stearn, Secretary of Holbeach United Football Club, and now serving in the RAF. While responding to the Club's presentation to him of a clock at the Horse & Groom following his wedding, he hoped he would soon be back to continue his duties in the town. But how soon? Barely a month into the war, news came in of a first casualty. Sergeant Ronald Herd, RAF, who lived in Spalding Road, was part of a raid on shipping over Heligoland when the Hampden bomber he was piloting was one of five destroyed by German fighters. He

UNDER THE COPPER BEECH. A memorial plaque in the Churchyard to Sergeant Ronald Herd, RAF, the first Holbeach casualty of the Second World War.

was buried in a war cemetery at Oldenburg. Today, in season, bluebells encircle his Holbeach memorial, a majestic copper beech tree whose 30-foot stature sighs in the breeze at the Church Street pavement edge of All Saints churchyard. It all represents peace and serenity, and the choice of tree was symbolic, for Ronald was red-haired.

Len Mallett, Boys School headmaster for a short period, left to join the RAF in 1941, already preceded by some of his ex-pupils who were by then experienced soldiers: Private Kenneth Grimwood of Fleet Street, for example, who saw action in raids on the Norwegian coast, was believed in 1942 to be the district's only commando –quite a contrast to his first job as a messenger boy at Holbeach post office. At 17 Wignal's Gate, no fewer than four of the Todd brothers were serving in the Forces, one of whom, George, was safely evacuated from Dunkirk and later discharged in 1942 on account of his wounds. It was also the year the Revd Ross, former Methodist minister at the Albert Street church, was reported as 'safe' while serving as an Army chaplain in Singapore at the time of the capitulation to the Japanese. Not so fortunate was Lieut Maurice English, RNVR, of Fleet Road, killed in action in mid-1943. He was the son of the late Maurice English, head of the Boys School for 10 years, and Mrs D K English, a teacher at Fleet School. Another loss, in December that year, was Osborn Reddin, a young server and Sunday School teacher at All Saints, who was buried at Salerno in Italy. Some years after the War, a plaque to his memory was discovered behind the altar at All Saints Church, and is now displayed in a more prominent position at the end of the north aisle.

On a happier front, Sidney Knipe of The Tenters, with the RAF out in Ceylon, put his talents to good use while a guest presenter on the Ceylon Overseas Service, from where he broadcast a programme of dance tunes, four of which he had composed himself. And shortly before the War ended, Lance Corporal Cassey, also from Holbeach, was awarded the Military Medal for bravery shown when clearing mines under mortar and machine gun fire on the North West Front in August 1944. Thanks to his contribution, armoured vehicles were able to continue with their capture of Ondefontaine.

Raising funds for the troops
Many attractions were staged, usually by the pubs, as a means of showing appreciation for the men and women in uniform. Both The String of Horses and the Station Hotel ran soldiers' cigarette funds, financed by entry fees for darts competitions. A typical prize might be a bag of potatoes, or at the Station, a tankard donated by the licensee, Billy Best. The Station Hotel also maintained a ' Boys and Girls Box' which collected money to be shared out periodically to each local man and woman serving with the forces. In March 1942 this amounted to 32 serving locals, each of whom received seven shillings (35p) by this method.

Countless other events were held in the name of fundraising, providing excellent opportunities for a knees-up. In fact, it could be argued that wartime Holbeach created an atmosphere of camaraderie and sociability that the community has never quite recaptured since. The Public Hall in Park Road was the scene of many whist drives –prizes distributed by Mrs Major– or carnival dances, organised by Frank Holland and W H Swepstone under festoons of balloons and streamers, bristling with novelty numbers and spot prizes to the music of Jack Wilson and his Band.

For an hour or three, it took minds off war, and kept everyone going with a perpetual list of something to look forward to.

The British Red Cross was one of the main beneficiaries from these festivities, supported by its gift shop in the town which earned £600 in the six months to December 1942 alone. The Hippodrome Cinema also played a part, the premises lent periodically by H Bancroft and the Holbeach Amusements directors for Red Cross Grand Variety Concerts, one such featuring impressionist Maudie Edwards, soubrette Margaret Day, boy singer Ralph Fell, an anonymous illusionist and Teddy Franks and his violin all helping to make it a memorable evening. Holbeach also supported the Russian Red Cross on a few occasions, with a darts tournament at the Bull's Neck, for instance, followed by a singalong led by the licensee's wife Mrs Elger at the piano, and an East End Firewatchers whist drive at Tagg's Café. And that genteel association, the Women's Bright Hour, a haven of hymns, prayers, recitals and Mrs Batterham at the piano, also acknowledged Russia with a Linen Appeal for their hospitals in 1942. Thanks to their Mrs Islip, the Soviets received 21 sheets, 40 pillowcases, one towel and a quantity of linen.

Out on the street, the financial progress of more major projects was recorded by a 'barometer' on the wall of what is now Dryden's shop. 'Work harder, spend less, save more in this Wings for Victory Week', exhorted 13-year-old Doreen Horner's prize-winning poster (it won her 2/6), depicting three accurately-drawn fighter planes. The East Elloe RDC Spitfire Fund was an early success, amassing £2,000 by January 1941; worthwhile, too, was East Elloe Warships

Week the following year, when a cinema van containing a model of HMS *Warspite*

PROGRAMME
....

1. Syd Swain   Compere.

2. Teddy Franks and His Violin.

3. Margaret Day   Soubrette.

4. Walter Freeman   Tenor.

5. Frank Dey and His
   Hammond Electric Organ.

6. Maudie Edwards   Impressionist.

7. Walter Freeman   Tenor.

8. Illusionist

9. Ralph Fell   The Boy Singer.

10. Margaret Day   Soubrette.

11. Teddy Franks and His Violin.

12. GRAND FINALE
    Maudie Edwards, Frank Dey etc.

GOD SAVE THE KING.

....

HAPPY HIPPODROME FARE. The cinema gives up its stage for a wartime concert in aid of the Red Cross.

[Courtesy Mr W Rix.]

generated some useful publicity (Women's Bright Hour members donated £140 alone) and doubtless excited a few small boys. Exciting a few older ones, if they were affluent enough, was the opportunity to kiss a Land Army Girl for £5, or take her out to tea for thirty bob (£1.50), the proceeds going to the Red Cross Agricultural Fund.

Another successful venture was the British Restaurant, situated in Church Street at what is now a florists. Converted from Mr C Lawson's workshop and opened in April 1943 by Councillor G A Mitchell, it made over £150 profit in its first five months when it was declared to be self-supporting, unlike its Sutton Bridge equivalent. Less impressive, however, was the Restaurant's performance in the Meat Pie Scheme, Holbeach's sales of 912 pies comparing poorly with Long Sutton's 1,317 and Whaplode's magnificent 7,887 figure. However, the scheme was continued into 1944, its range extended to include jam tarts.

Located behind the Restaurant was the Ministry of Food Office, the workplace of Ena Morriss, later to become Jim Sleaford's wife. As supervisor, her work took her regularly out of the office, either to the Council offices in Spalding Road to take dictation, or as far afield as the prisoner-of-war camp on the Sutton Bridge river bank, to update the cards of the German servicemen held there. Not such a daunting prospect for a young woman as it appeared, for relations with the prisoners became cordial enough for Ena to join in with their choir, although with language as a barrier, she wasn't always sure what she was singing about!

The ladies' contribution
Mention of Ena's varied duties recalls the supporting role played by ladies of all social levels in wartime Holbeach, especially in terms of healthcare, education and nutrition. Medical resources were strengthened by Mrs E Major's making over of a large room in her house, Abbots Manor on Spalding Road (now Mossop & Bowser's offices) for the Nursing Division of the St John Ambulance Brigade. It was used as a hospital supply depot, turning out garments and bed linen at a rate that much impressed Lord and Lady Liverpool on an early official visit. Over at the Women's Institute in Park Road from December 1939, the highly-active WI prepared up to 100 Christmas parcels annually to troops at home and abroad, each package containing a toothbrush, socks, razor, scarf, helmet, shaving soap, cigarettes, sweets, chocolates and a mouth organ. Fully answering the call from the Produce Guild of the Holland Federation of Women's Institutes to help with bottling, canning, jam-making and preserving whatever they could, a Jam Scheme run by the Fruit Preservation Committee was in full swing by 1942, with chief helper Nora

Lane and her team of Mrs A Penney, Mrs Hardy, Mrs Walton and Mrs A Coward using the Institute kitchen and utensils as its production centre, and the Barrington Gate Schoolroom as the sales outlet. Meanwhile Mrs Herbert Carter and Mrs Golden co-ordinated the distribution of clothing and footwear, sent by the Lion Hospital Aid Society of London for the local evacuees. Clothes were also mended and pyjamas and nightdresses made for foster parents of evacuees who could not afford new garments, as part of a programme of sewing classes to cater for the many needy temporary residents.

Evacuees from London

This influx of children was not without problems. As the education chapter shows, it caused the unsatisfactory arrangement of half-day attendance in school, with Holbeach children having to wait until the afternoon to use their classrooms while evacuees occupied them in the morning. With its first-hand experience of evacuees the WI was better informed on this subject than most, and protested to the Director of Education that there were several suitable buildings in town in which to resume a proper routine, and that the half-day arrangement was unfair both to Holbeach parents, and to the fosterers on whom the evacuees were billeted.

With too much time on their hands, the visiting children caused havoc in orchards and gardens during their scrumping raids on fruit trees, trampling on plants and vegetables with 'no idea of the value of fruit in the fields'. Naturally, such clumsy footwork miraculously became more expert when the occasion demanded, the Evacuated Schoolboys beating the Holbeach Bank Council Schoolboys at football by seven goals to nil in October 1939. In the end, it was these more independent, fostered children who adapted to rural life better than those who had come with their mothers. As early as two months into the war, many a more fickle parent-and-child combination had opted to return to the relative danger of London, rather than cope any longer with local life. 'These women', sighed the *Spalding Guardian,* 'who have been accustomed to town life with cinemas, cheap food, shops and other urban attractions are totally unable to adapt themselves to the life in a quiet country town or village. It is difficult, too, for adult women to settle easily in another's home'.

Not that there was limitless room for evacuees in Holbeach and its district, for by 1941 the town's billeting officer, councillor George Campling, complained that his equivalent in Long Sutton, the Revd T W Hunter, had been referring newcomers to Holbeach, and had no right to do this. Chief billeting officer at this time, incidentally, was Cecil Pywell, Clerk to East Elloe Rural District Council, whose wartime duties also extended to evacuation officer, food executive officer and organiser of the auxiliary fire service.

Fortunately, the town could not be accused of inhospitality towards evacuees braving out unfamiliar conditions. The Mothers Union and Women's Bright Hour, led by Mrs P E Boswell and Mrs C R Thompson, held regular evacuee parties for mothers and young children, aided by a grant of 9d (4p) a head from London County Council. Further integration by 1941 was evident at the Boys School in Church Street, where John Thomson, originally the incomer-head of the Vernon Square Infants School near King's Cross, was now headmaster in place of Len Mallett, called up for the RAF. Thomson also helped the ladies with evacuee entertainments, while equivalent events at the Boys School promised much in the way of laughs. Their 1941 Christmas Concert Play was an up-to-the-minute production based on the current *ITMA* ('It's That Man Again') radio show entitled 'The Arrangement of Funf', with Jack Train's famous character played by Denis Watson, Fusspot by Derek Bowell, and Mrs Tickle by Derek Sleight, with Charles Hardy in Tommy Handley's role.

CHARACTERS OF ITMA.
A cartoon by 'Vicky'.

Afterwards, the rather Enid Blytonesque Pitt Memorial Prize for the 'Best Type of Girl in Vernon Square School' was awarded jointly to Rose Hales and Pamela Philp, billeted at Holbeach St Matthews and Holbeach respectively.

Training with Geoff Parker's ATC

Meanwhile Geoff Parker's Air Training Corps 1406 Squadron, based at his garage

EVENING CLASS AIRMEN. The sleeve badge worn on training nights by boy messengers, shop assistants, and apprentices eager for action.
[Courtesy Jenny Paul.]

workshop, provided emerging youth with its first taste of service life. While some of their mothers enjoyed the house to themselves in the evening, listening perhaps to Chick Henderson on the radio singing, 'The Breeze and I', teenage lads born in the mid-to-late-1920s drilled on Fleet Road and learned Morse, semaphore, aircraft recognition, and experienced the bonus of simulated flight in Geoff's special link trainer, activated with the aid of Peg Parker's vacuum cleaner and a pipeline of modified National Dried Milk tins.

There was also some hands-on experience in July 1942, when a German Dornier 217E plane came down at Fleet Fen and the ATC were allowed to examine the wreckage. The crew had surrendered to the local constabulary and was conducted to Fleet police station by PC 'Ted' Holvey, his 12-year-old son Rex listening excitedly to the proceedings at the top of the stairs. (It must have been the most significant event in Fleet since the tragedy of April 1936, when Henry Smith, aged 18, was arrested for shooting and killing his elder sister Dorothy while she was cycling to the Baptist church, and for seriously wounding his father John, a Council roadman who had previously been repairing the pavement in Barrington Gate.)

Most ATC trainees had already tasted responsibility from their first jobs after leaving school: Tom Todd, for instance, of 17 King George V Avenue and nephew of the four brothers in Wignal's Gate now on active service, was a Co-op shop assistant; Roy Speed, 61 Station Road, International Stores Assistant; James Sleaford, Back Lane, porter; Frank Sauntson, 47 Crown Colony, milk roundsman at A Brocklehurst's; R J Freeman, 17 Tolls Lane, greenhouse worker at F H Bowser; Leslie Fensom, Mill Lane, Holbeach Fen, outfitter's assistant at Cheer & Sons; Ronald Wright, Brewers Arms, Back Lane, printer's apprentice at Chamberlins; and Roy Biggadike, Holbeach Clough, boy messenger at Holbeach GPO.

Davenport Benjamin Thomas — Holb. Boys' Sch.
Address: Red Roofs Cottage, Fleet Rd, Holbeach
Employed as: Junior Clerk. At: Mossop's & Bowser's Sols, Holbeach.
Training as: W.op/AG Born: 4th Aug. 1926.
Desires to join: RAF

FROM PEN TO PROPELLOR. The entry for Benjamin Davenport, solicitor's junior clerk at Mossop & Bowser, in Geoff Parker's record book. *[Courtesy Jenny Paul.]*

Occasionally the Corps met at the Boys School, where they might be divided into sections for various activities. One group might hear a lecture from Geoff Parker on 'The Theory of Flight'; another would receive instruction from the Home Guard on handling the Lewis Gun, while a third could draw the short straw of a session of physical drill under the verbal bombardment of a regular army sergeant. The peak of fitness one assumes this produced saw its worth in more agreeable pursuits such as football, when Holbeach ATC beat their opposite numbers from Spalding 6-0 in March 1942. Some lads went into active service soon after joining the ATC. Leslie Daubnie for one, farm labourer at Eric Lane's, or Tom Fletcher for another, accepted by the Aviation Candidates Selection Board at Cardington for pilot training after only one month's pre-entry with Geoff Parker. Others resumed civilian callings such as the meat trade. Like baking, this was a reserved occupation. Wally French, for instance, later to become Holbeach's renowned footballer, was on call to bake bread in Peterborough in the event of a national crisis.

Agricultural changes for War

It was a time to concentrate on essentials if the local population was to be fed satisfactorily, so crop values came under the searching review of the Holland War Agricultural Committee. It was chaired by Alex West, a Holbeach Marsh farmer of some standing, with a keen interest in potatoes. He was also a County Councillor, and Chairman of the Parish Council. Avoiding land wastage was a key issue and an early decision was made to reduce the strawberry acreage, by ploughing up all beds over three years old and not allowing more than 75% of the cleared area to be replanted.

But the measures were to extend beyond strawberries. Others who suddenly found themselves growing the 'wrong' commodity included flower-grower J F Cheesewright, of Marsh Road. There was no compensation for him and fellow growers who had invested their life savings in bulbs. By 1942 plantings had been reduced to 25% of 1939 figures, with surplus stocks destroyed and all rail traffic in flowers halted. Ironically, tulip bulbs had been valuable enough to use as barter for American armaments, but 'I am now compelled,' said Mr Cheesewright in 1943, 'to grow vegetables, which I can sometimes market, and sometimes have to destroy'. Flowers, he argued, had a sentimental value, most of those grown destined either for hospitals or cemeteries, and with both places featuring so strongly in wartime, he certainly had a point. But from now on, it was a case of concentrating on produce such as vegetables, essential fruit, honey, eggs and milk. Even after the War, the rebuilding of the flower industry took longer than expected, hampered by food rationing which persisted until 1953, and the need to regain standards threatened by pirate firms in the post-war seller's market, peddling inferior bulbs by mail order.

Machinery imports

The 'spring offensive on the home front', as it had been called in 1941, saw new farm machinery pouring into the area as part of our share of the 4,000 new tractors imported from America in the first quarter of that year, supplemented by a similar number produced in Britain. In Holbeach, Pearl Taylor from Dormer House drove the first lend-lease tractor, a John Deere, around Carter's Park in her Land Army uniform. Such machines were not allowed to stand idle, and once the farmer had finished work on his own farm, he was expected to hire it out to his neighbour. In prevailing national circumstances, the future of farming was at stake and in April 1942, the Farmers Educational Foundation, chaired by the Revd P E Boswell and with Eric Lane as Governor, agreed to hold an examination for four junior exhibitions: two for boys, and two for girls.

Social life

In other respects, considering the future took second place to living life day by day and hoping for the best. Apart from the dances, whist drives, darts tournaments and kissing Land Army Girls for a fiver, semblances of normal life could be seen in the homely routine of the Carter's Park Bowls Club, captained by Mr Rose, the Rabbit Club (Secretary, Mrs D Papworth) and the fact that the Hippodrome Cinema continued to show films throughout the war almost uninterrupted.

Weddings continued uninterrupted, too. Not necessarily white ones, in deference to austerity and shortages, but their sense of occasion suffered little. Recalling two or three at random as being typical of their kind, Florence Johnson of Wignal'sGate, cashier at the Hippodrome from its first opening, had married railway worker Alfred Ebbs in October 1939. She wore a dark green, two-piece costume with matching hat and a spray of pink carnations and a fern. Then in 1942 there was local footballer Alfred Upson, who married Edna Diss. With the bride resplendent in her brown-and-fawn tweed costume, again set off by pink carnations, the happy couple danced afterwards to the

Spalding Accordeon Serenaders. More unconventional, however, was Ivy Pollard's wedding. Few would choose their workplace as the ideal spot to get married, but to Ivy early in May 1945, Mattimore House was more than suitable, for even a shortage of confetti was circumvented by the quartermaster-sergeant scattering the couple with rose petals plucked from its garden.

Romantic larceny
In 1944 there was even a little crime mixed with romance for added human interest, when a 25-year-old Scottish dress designer got drunk in the Chequers after a tiff with a Free French officer, prompting her to steal a camera from an American master-sergeant and less accountably, an alarm clock from a Florence Wright. One could almost imagine contemporary stars like Patricia Roc, Charles Boyer and Robert Beatty acting this out on film, with an unamused judge, played by Felix Aylmer, pronouncing sentence.

But there were other less romantic realities that could not be ignored. With the number of market stalls falling to less than three on Saturdays, it was costing the Parish Council more in Sunday street cleaning fees than they were collecting from the stallholders. The contractors, Holland County Council, could not perform the task for less than £23 per annum, so it was earnestly hoped that the market would return to prosperity after hostilities. Then there were Councillor Fred Bowd's exhortations, in the last November of the War, to prepare now to vote Labour at the next election –a recommendation that certainly bore fruit nationally, if not locally. Fred's hour had almost come, as a stalwart of the Labour party, a magistrate and a tireless supporter of the Agricultural Workers Union. He

was awarded the OBE, although the loss of a leg in 1950 placed an unfortunate restriction on his activities.

Shirking firewatchers
Bowd was also vociferous in exposing, along with fellow EERDC Councillors Wilson and Bemrose, evidence of shirking among the local firewatchers, whose efforts had degenerated into 'a joke'. Wilson stated that 'Nowhere was anyone doing his bit' when it came to watching and doing his turn. 'People laugh when you walk down the streets because they know what a mess the whole affair is in,' he went on, 'people slacking, giving excuses.' It was unfair on those who did pull their weight, and involved a 'good many who ought to be in the army.' Bowd asked the Clerk, Cecil Pywell, to identify the offenders and take proceedings against them; after all, had it not brought results when similar action was taken against the Home Guard?

Houses unfit for heroes? The ladies intervene
It appeared however, that complacency was not unknown in the EERDC itself, when the question also arose in 1944 of co-opting women onto the post-war housing committee. Unyielding male views, that acceptable building standards were already being achieved without feminine interference when it came to details such as windows, sinks, bathrooms and bedrooms were refuted by a deputation consisting of Mesdames Lane, French, Smalley and Walton. Not only did these ladies have the backing of the Government's view –that women should be consulted on such matters– but Mrs Lane also spoke from experience, having visited the Tolls Lane development. There she found inadequate shelving, pantries facing south, no curtain fittings in the

ARMY ON THE DOORSTEP. The Holbeach Home Guard.
[Courtesy John and Freda Coley.]

bedrooms, dust-collecting door panels, and 'extravagant' cookers using too much fuel and creating unnecessary work. Amid the chauvinism came one or two sympathetic male voices. 'Would it mean,' ventured Councillor Campling, 'if the ladies were elected to the Committee, we could get houses built any quicker? If so, I am sure no one present would object.' But the matter rumbled on into May 1945, by which time Mrs Lane and her colleagues had still not been co-opted, and Councillor Lloyd Thompson was adding his support. He, too, had visited houses and was particularly concerned about inadequate power points, with women ironing from light fittings on unearthed concrete floors, and the hazardous positioning of coppers in bathrooms, where there had been an instance of a child being scalded.

MP: 'Let the Germans build the homes'

The post-war housing question excited other controversial views, not least from the local MP. In April 1945 an 'interesting' plan for the solution to Britain's housing problem appeared in London's *Evening Standard*. Its author, Herbert Butcher, Conservative member for the Holland-with-Boston Division, suggested that as the Germans had destroyed other people's homes, the quarter-million prisoners-of-war currently in Britain should be trained to lay bricks, to the extent that if each prisoner could build 12 houses, thus creating three million new homes, 'they could then go home, having learned a peaceful and useful trade.' This was an unwelcome reflection on those many ordinary German soldiers who could not all be branded with the same malevolence, and it was fortunate that a significant number of ex-prisoners found the South Holland area accommodating enough to want to stay on after the War, make it their home, and contribute to the economic life of the community.

The final war years

Light at the end of the tunnel was suggested by events like the grand extravaganza staged in August 1944 at Carter's Park. 'Spend with an easy conscience,' reassured the publicity, 'at the Agricultural Show and Fête in aid of the Red Cross at Carter's Park.' 'Fête' sounded an understatement, considering that there were not only two bands –the Honley Prize Band and the Band of the 2nd

Kesteven Battalion Home Guard– but that the official opening was also performed by Lord Brownlow, Lord Lieutenant of the County (and the friend who had escorted Mrs Simpson into exile after Edward VIII's abdication in 1936). Top of the bill was Tessie O'Shea, the ample music hall singer 'of BBC and Variety fame', and the programme included a funfair, dancing, baby show, horse show, horse racing, farm machinery demonstration, children's sports, a sale of live and dead stock, and the chance to win £1,000-worth of prizes. This surely, was foretaste of better things to come?

Parting shots

Yet 1945 dawned in disarray. Up until then, the town had escaped any significant mishap while witnessing several potential hazards. Air raid warnings had peaked in 1941, as enemy planes passed over towards Midlands cities. The Observer Corps had certainly experienced frequent near-miss machine gun fire from German aircraft, and on clear nights, had even seen the trails made by V2 rockets as they left their Dutch firing bases. Three of these devices had rasped their way over Holbeach, and although one came uncomfortably low at tree-top height, it kept going (unlike the stricken German bomber on 24th July 1942, of whose crew two baled out and surrendered to S Bayston of 'Dog 2'). Landmines had also fallen at Gedney at one stage, disturbing plaster in Fleet. And had not another German bomber once dumped its remaining load of incendiaries rather near to Kilby's Mill in 1942, as it returned from a raid? It was certainly enough to raise charge nurse Roy Woolley from his bed in Albert Street, and send him on his way to Fleet Road Hospital, concerned in case his patients were in a state of panic. But with the war nearly over, no one expected a target to be as close as Sergeant Lown's bath.

On the afternoon of Friday 29th December, 1944, a cannon shell fell through the police station roof in Edinburgh Walk and landed in the bath of Sergeant Lown's new living quarters upstairs. Fortunately he was out at the time, but he was not the only one to suffer. About a dozen other shells fell across the town, wrecking roofs, ceilings and Mr Franklin's water tank up in the Mansion House roof. People out in the streets were terrified, especially when two of the shells dropped only feet away from a youth in the High Street, and narrowly missed a girl in Albert Street.

It transpired that the ammunition had been discharged accidentally from a British plane. After reviewing the situation, the EERDC advised that the incident could not be assessed as war damage if the plane was on a practice exercise, in which case the townspeople would have to claim compensation directly from the RAF. A policeman's lot was not a happy one that day, and one could imagine the pilots receiving the fabled clip around the ear, had Sergeant Lown encountered them afterwards on his beat!

Anticipatory celebrations
With the town dusted down, it was time for a few more modest festivities. Mrs Field, for 21 years headmistress of the Infants School, celebrated her 91st birthday in January 1945, stating there were few things dearer to her than a hand at whist. At Jubilee Villas, the Public Assistance Committee Home in Fleet Road, it was party time for the children that month, with tea followed by a slide show given by Mrs Lane. Her daughter gave out sweets to the children and after games had been 'played with great zest', Mrs M J Mitchell JP gave out the prizes. As for the two foster-mothers, the Misses Mills and Colclough, they were no doubt very thankful to have at least one day's tumultuous routine taken care of for them.

As spring approached, plans were being laid for the victory celebrations. The Forces Commemoration Fund Committee met at the United Services Club in early April, when it was agreed to have a huge bonfire, and licensing arrangements were modified by a special meeting of the justices in Spalding. Pubs and clubs would be allowed to stay open until midnight, with music, singing and dancing licences extended to the same hour.

I'll be back again after the war, meanwhile —

this month's STORK leaflet is "LIVER, HEART, KIDNEY, TRIPE, etc." THESE delicious non-rationed meats make delightful meals, and can be served in dozens of different ways. Recipes approved by Ministry of Food. Send for your leaflet.

STORK MARGARINE COOKERY SERVICE

Holbeach gets lit up
When War in Europe ended on 8th May 1945, a crowd gathered around the old lamp post at the fiveways crossroads in central Holbeach for some impromptu community singing –rather as they had done in 1918. Two lads walking down Barrington Gate told Mrs Mary Mossop that they were on their way to 'burn Hitler', or rather, set light to an effigy of him, made from remnants they hoped to find in Ladbrook's scrapyard. Whether they succeeded is not known, but a candlelight parade took place in the evening, under the watchful eye of Sergeant Lown who had to apprehend the odd lad or two for letting off fireworks in the crowd.

After the immediate festivities, there was a thanksgiving service on Sunday 13th May, at which the National Anthem was sung. A mass parade filled the streets composed of the Home Guard, Guild of Army Cadets, the ATC, ARP Wardens, Royal Observer Corps, the Ambulance Unit, WVS, British Legion, Boy Scouts, and not forgetting the Wolf Cubs, Girl Guides and Brownies. At the Hippodrome it was time to enjoy George Formby playing a War Reserve policeman in *Spare a Copper* –not exactly the latest release, as it was a 1940 production– and a Roy Rogers 'B' movie.

Evacuees, drains and more extravaganzas
With arrangements completed for the 21 unaccompanied evacuee children left in the Holbeach area to return to London by special train from Peterborough, attention was turned to the drains. The trouble was, a £950 quote from Shelvoke and Drewry for a new cesspool-emptying lorry was sounding rather expensive, so the EERDC decided to buy second-hand instead.

Early in June, another Red Cross extravaganza was held in Carter's Park, this time featuring a Wild West Rodeo. 'Miss Colorado the Canadian Cowgirl' amazed everyone with her display of trick roping and stock whipping, and Buck

Ryan, world champion trick and bronco rider, famous for his bucking performances at Wembley in 1924 and White City in '34, was the star turn, while Carl Dane anticipated Geoff Capes by 30 years with his 'feats of strength'.

But it was also a time to reflect. The Rodeo was opened by RSM Lord, a former prisoner of *Stalag 11B* after capture at Arnhem. At the microphone he praised the work of the Red Cross, and went on to say that no matter how hard people at home had worked, none would have experienced the same trials and perils as those who had served in the forces. Such men deserved the best that could be given them.

One could follow his reasoning. A rodeo may have been an unusual occasion on which to express those words, but he and his comrades had endured a rough ride of their own. Those 29 Holbeachians who did not survive it are remembered with gratitude, on a memorial behind the organ in All Saints Church.

♣ ♣ ♣ ♣ ♣

9 – Educating Holbeach

While it is known that there was once a free grammar school in Holbeach founded by Edward III (reigned 1327-1377) all records of it have since been lost. Similarly, we know little more of a John Lamkyn during the sixteenth century, other than that he was residing in Holbeach, 'there teaching and instructyng children in the sciens of grammar, and having his lyvyng by the same.'

George Farmer and the Holbeach Free School, 1671

The earliest reliable reference to a seat of learning organised on formal lines comes in 1671, with the founding of Holbeach Free School. It was made possible by a legacy from George Farmer, a gentleman of means from St Andrews in Middlesex, who appears to have lived in Holbeach at an early age. Although he was originally from a family of Leicestershire gentry, the Victorian local historian Grant Macdonald says that records referred to Farmer, at the age of 19, as a Prothonotary (clerk or registrar) 'of the Court of Common Pleas of Holbech, Co. Lincoln, Esq.', and that he married Elizabeth Oldfield of Spalding in 1629. Of their four children, Edward, the eldest, was created a baronet in 1660, and was also described as 'being of Holbech'.

Financing and staffing the Free School
George Farmer had died in 1670. Under the foundation arrangement, his will financed the school with endowments of some 56 acres of land in Holbeach and Weston, which were let at £250 per annum, and the establishment was to be run by 'a discreet person, being a master or bachelor of arts, to teach and instruct the children of Holbeach' in a school house specially built for the purpose. The first of these 'discreet persons' to teach at the new school was probably John West (died at Holbeach, 1713). But the reference to 'specially built' premises is something of a mystery, for in William Stukeley's time at the school, during the 1690s under the Master, Edward Kelsall, lessons were taught in the chancel of All Saints Church, later removing to a room

over the Church's north porch for possibly the whole of the eighteenth century, during which seven Masters succeeded, after Kelsall left to head Boston Grammar School: William Smith (1698-1709), Thomas Tipping (1709-1714), John Brittain (1714-1727), William Frankland (1727-1741), Thomas Hunter (1741-1751), Richard Gibson (1751-1783), and Robert Hood (1783-1811).

A SCHOOLROOM UNTIL 1811. The Church's north porch once had an upper floor providing a classroom for 40 pupils.

As for the schoolmaster's income, he was to rely on the rents from the lands paid 'on the four most usual feasts of the year', and was to receive nothing from parents or scholars. Typically he would have had a Church background, as in the case of Thomas Hunter, who served as Master (see dates above), having been previously both a curate at Spalding and a Master of Spalding Grammar School. Masters were watched over by feoffees, or agents, who were empowered to remove them if their performance was unsatisfactory. Richard Fawssett, who appears regularly in the old vestry minute books, was one such agent, who presided over matters in the late eighteenth and early nineteenth centuries. The trust provisions set up by Farmer were enhanced in 1698 with a donation of five cottages worth £440 by John Warsdale, and again in 1719, when a bequest of James Thompson augmented the schoolmaster's salary by £5 per annum to cover the teaching of 12 local children of the poor, to be selected by a panel composed of the Master himself, churchwardens and overseers of the poor of Holbeach. These children were to be instructed free of charge in reading, writing, 'casting accounts' and 'the principles of the true Protestant religion.' For a while this was undertaken by another schoolmaster who kept a day school, although it is not known where. The obligation then reverted to the Free School for an ensuing 50 years before being questioned by the incumbent Master, the Revd Robert Hood, who contended that as his school was of grammar status, it was not his responsibility to teach at an elementary level. In fact, Hood, who had been Master since November 1783, had been criticised at a vestry meeting in 1805 for refusing to teach free of charge any subject except Latin and Greek. However, after legal consultation the Free School was instructed to observe its original arrangement.

Nineteenth-century premises, staff and administration upheavals

 The classroom over the north porch of the church continued to serve the school until 1811. At this time the pupils numbered between 40 and 50, so quite how they fitted comfortably into a room of this size is a source of wonderment. In that year however, the schoolmaster, Robert Hood, died, and lessons were transferred to a new building costing £500 in Church Street, able to hold 200 children and funded by accumulated rents from the Holbeach and Weston lands, plus a public subscription of £60.

A review of school affairs in the local press of 1867 revealed a somewhat chequered history of indifferent headmastership, overcrowding, middling academic achievement and inadequate funding. Mr Richards, Headmaster from 1845, had paid for his own appointment in the interests of reducing school debts. But once in office, he preferred to teach only those boys who paid £1 quarterly for classics and mathematics. As a result, the rest of the school received little better than a primary level of education, which was left in the hands of 'an usher'.

After Richards' resignation in 1856, the usher was left to cope on his own, performing 'with a good deal of tact and energy', and gave 'general satisfaction', which he must have done to preside daily over several classes held simultaneously in one room, containing up to 100 boys, and relying only on monitors for help. In spite of the potential for distraction, discipline was satisfactory, and although dictation skills were below average, spelling classes did reasonably well, and slow progress with subjects such as long division was down to poor attendance more than anything else.

Nevertheless, parents became anxious for the quality of their children's education, and met at the Market House to bring about a Charity Commissioners' enquiry into the situation. From this it was agreed that the Court of Chancery should enforce a scheme of 1845, which stipulated that a headmaster should be employed 'to teach classics and mathematics and other requirements of a first-class school'. Speaking at the meeting, Mr Richard Mossop said that it was of the utmost importance for Holbeach to have a good classical school, and that at the very least an establishment of the 'second grade' was essential. There was even talk of Greek and one or more modern European languages being taught, not to mention the waiving of fees in deserving cases. But such stirring words were followed only by disappointment. Funds were inadequate, and only temporary arrangements for classical instruction could be made.

The Grammar School after the Endowed Schools Act

In 1869 the Endowed Schools Act put an end to Free Schools of the Farmer category, and new arrangements were made for its management. By 1874, the second-grade

The Grammar School building from 1877, providing premises over the years for the girls, infants and now the Small Saints Playgroup.

school mentioned in Mossop's speech had become reality, optimistically adapted to accommodate an estimated 80 boys, including 20 boarders, with provision for a few free places subject to passing an examination. A move from Church Street followed in 1877 to new premises built behind the existing Master's lodge in the High Street, the latter forming part of a stylish terrace of houses incorporating dormitories for the boarders.

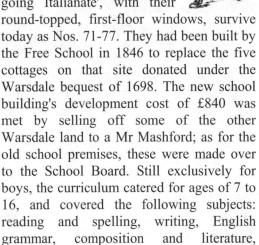

These houses, with an archway passing through their centre, and described in Pevsner's *Buildings of England* as 'still Georgian but going Italianate', with their round-topped, first-floor windows, survive today as Nos. 71-77. They had been built by the Free School in 1846 to replace the five cottages on that site donated under the Warsdale bequest of 1698. The new school building's development cost of £840 was met by selling off some of the other Warsdale land to a Mr Mashford; as for the old school premises, these were made over to the School Board. Still exclusively for boys, the curriculum catered for ages of 7 to 16, and covered the following subjects: reading and spelling, writing, English grammar, composition and literature, history, political and physical geography, arithmetic, the elements of algebra and geometry, mensuration and land surveying(!), natural science, French, Latin, optional German, drawing and 'vocal' music. For this the headmaster received a salary of £100 a year, with a supplement based on the number of boys attending and fixed at not less than £2 a head. A distinguished old boy of this school in the late nineteenth century was Sir Norman Angell, who later paid tribute to his Holbeach headmaster as 'a man of culture, sensitiveness and understanding,' and a welcome change after the head of his previous prep school. One assumes, therefore, that Angell's respect extended to not eating his favourite chocolate creams in the Revd Ram's classes.

TO SCHOOL THROUGH THE ARCH. The High Street terrace, originally built as dormitories and headmaster's accommodation, is a gem in the town's Conservation Area.

Education at the Workhouse

There were those however, to whom 'mensuration and land surveying' could only be a pipe dream, even had they known what the term meant: the boys of the Holbeach Union, or Workhouse children. By the time the Free School was being reconstituted, the Union Board was reaping the results of years of a misguided management that had kept poor children under lock and key. In 1870 this culminated in a juvenile mutiny, with all the boys, not just a few, resisting discipline and persistently running away, no matter what punishment was imposed. The situation was only resolved by their schoolmaster's resignation and, commented the local press sportingly at a time when children were supposed to be seen and not heard, 'it is evident that the mutiny has been the result of mismanagement in some form or other, and the resignation of the schoolmaster at an earlier date would probably have led to a better state of things'.

This 'better state' was a matter the Union Board –presided over by the Revd E L Bennett– took on in earnest, following advice from the Master of the Caistor Union, who felt that surrounding children with walls and iron bars could only be harmful to discipline and self-respect. The gaol-like system was declared a failure and permission was sought to provide playing fields outside the Workhouse, while endorsing Caistor Union's view that 'Those who manage children should be nature's gentlemen.' As for preparing for life after the workhouse, the Master of Caistor, a Mr Shipley, was again forthcoming with sound and impartial wisdom.

IT HAD A FINE MAPLE FLOOR. The Girls' School in Albert Street from 1844 to 1914, now converted into flats.

Menial tasks such as turning handles and picking oakum, he said, were of no use to anyone, and priority should be given to employment in agricultural labour. But Shipley went further: the boys on long winter nights should be taught to knit, darn, and mend so that 'they might in after life render some service in their cottage over an evening pipe,' a view that would still draw applause from wives and partners in the twenty-first century! Whether the Holbeach Union was broadminded enough to take on this suggestion is not recorded. But there was a subsequent improvement in conduct, and the replacement master, Mr Loweth, 'found the boys very willing and tractable to obey him', although conditions could never have been ideal as long as the Workhouse system lasted.

Early girls' schools

But what of the girls? As far back as 1811, a Miss C Goodear announced her intention to open a boarding and day school 'for the instruction of Young Ladies' on Monday 29th December. The Young Ladies however could only have been the daughters of the well-to-do, for board and tuition was advertised at 16 guineas (£16.80) per annum, while there was an entrance fee of 10s 6d (53p) for boarders and 5s (25p) for day pupils. Much later, in the early 1890s, the Girls Boarding and Day School (also Boys Preparatory School) was in existence at Albert Villa under the auspices of the Misses Clark and Juncker, who also held dancing classes in 'the large room' of the Chequers Hotel. The outcome of such ventures is not known, but from 1844 the All Saints National School in Albert Street, expressly built for girls and infants, was in session on the Victoria Street corner (in more recent years, the former Karin's

Studio and now converted into flats). Twelve years later there were 90 children attending the school, and by 1892 numbers had risen to 158. A feature of this building was its fine maple floor.

The Boys' Board School, 1877 onwards, and closure of the Grammar School

BOYS ONLY. *The Board School in Church Street existed from 1877 to 1958, when The George Farmer opened. It is now the United Services Club. [Photo courtesy J W Belsham.] Right: Leslie Fensom's school report from 1939.*
[Courtesy the late Leslie Fensom.]

The boys' alternative to the Grammar School was the first noticeable outcome of the formation of the School Board, referred to earlier as the new owners of the old Free School site. The Board, established in January 1875, was composed of seven members, including John Willders, Clerk, and Thomas Squire, Attendance Officer. By 1877, a new building was ready on the Church Street site, nowadays recognised as the United Services Club, although a small triangular tablet inscribed 'Board School for Boys' can still be seen behind the Club's hanging sign. Built to accommodate 230 children, the Board School's average attendance was 191 by 1892, with John Mottram as the Master. But that same year, the Grammar School, under the headmastership of the Revd Charles William Nelson Lowe, BA, could boast only 12 pupils, and by 1904, it had closed. Under an Order in Council of January 1912, the traditional Farmer endowment, now worth £350 annually from land and investments,

was apportioned to scholarships for eligible children of the parish of Holbeach to attend certain secondary schools or universities.

HOLBEACH BOYS' SCHOOL

Class Teacher *C Challett* **Report** for the *Christmas* Term, 19 *39*.
Name *Fensom Leslie* Age *14* yrs. *0* mths. *1st (6) Class*
Place in Class *2* No. of Boys *8* Average Age *13* yrs. *11* mths.

Subject	Mark obtained	Max. Mark	Av. Mark of Class	% for Term
ENGLISH—				
Reading ...	10	10	9·5	
Literature ...	17	20	15·5	
Composition ...	15	20	16	77·8
Grammar ...	22	30	20·2	
ARITHMETIC ...	44	60	36	
HISTORY ...	✓	✓		
GEOGRAPHY ...	✓	✓		
SCIENCE or NATURE STUDY ...	✓	✓		
ART	25	30	19·7	
HANDWORK ...	27	30	23	

Displays thoroughly sound workmanship in all he does and can be relied upon to do an honest piece of work.

No. of times School opened *87*
" " Absent *nil*
Parent's Signature *J? Fensom*

C Challett Headmaster

The Girls' School, later the Voluntary controlled Infants, off the High Street

Following the closure, the Grammar School building behind the High Street was to have many more years of useful life ahead. First, it was leased to the managers of the Church of England All-Age Girls' Elementary School, who, having spent a lavish £4 13s 3d on gracing the walls with a new clock and framed pictures, occupied it from July 1914 until the pupils were able to attend the new George Farmer School from the late 1950s. At first, facilities were not self-contained: hockey and netball had to be played in the Park, and cookery was taught in the Methodists' Barrington Gate Schoolroom. Later however, mobile classrooms and a playing field were added. After the girls' migration to George Farmer, the old Grammar School was home for the next 36 years to the Voluntary Controlled Infants. In October 1977, its centenary was commemorated with a special thanksgiving service conducted by the Bishop of Lincoln, the Right Revd Simon Phipps.

The new William Stukeley Church of England Primary School temporarily occupied the premises between July 1993 and September 1994 until its new building was ready, during which time –in May 1994– former pupils of the old Girls School held a reunion organised by Olga Pringle, Joan Gregory and others to give their building a good send-off. Over 70 ladies attended, including Aggie White, who had attended the school on its first opening for girls, and the former head mistress, Dorothy Ford, then 93.

The 'school through the arch' now serves as the premises of the Small Saints Playgroup, who, with the support of donations from local businesses, were thankful to move in as leaseholders after 10 years in a makeshift unit.

As for the old boarders' quarters on the High Street, these underwent several internal conversions over the years. During the 1920s for instance, one of the cellars in the terrace was used as a bakery for Miss Flaxman's pastries and cakes. In April 1975, when still leased from the Holbeach Farmer Education Foundation, plans were announced at a Housing Committee meeting to transform the rooms into nine self-contained flats. At that stage their structure was still declared sound following a recent re-roofing, although the outside had suffered some neglect. Fortunately they have survived into the millennium as one of the more worthy architectural features of Holbeach, and their present-day attractiveness as characterful residences was reflected in an asking price of £192,000 when one of the houses went on the market in July 2004.

The nineteenth-century infants, meanwhile, had outgrown Albert Street by 1871, to be only temporarily resettled in premises which are now the Church Hall. Built to the order of the Revd Arthur Brook on land held by him, the hall's layout was adaptable to other uses if the infants' occupation was to be merely temporary, as proved to be the case when for some reason the children were returned to Albert Street in 1876.

A more permanent solution had to be found, and by 1894 five old cottages in the former Cabbage Row had made way for a new Infants School in Boston Road –now the

Youth Club next to Bryan Thompson Windows.

Holbeach Infants and County Primary

NOW THE YOUTH CLUB. The original infants school of 1894 in Boston Road.

The School's original logbook for the Boston Road premises no longer exists, but succeeding logs, kept from 1931 onwards, reflect a selfless smiling-through on the part of the staff in the face of fluctuating attendance levels, freezing classrooms, regular outbreaks of measles, chicken-pox, impetigo, diphtheria, scarlet fever, whooping cough and two sad deaths among the five and seven-year-olds of meningitis.

The longest-serving head teacher was Miss Elsie Ransom, from 1926 to 1953. In September 1931 she and the assistant head, Miss E Burrage, were the only staff to hold a 'Trained Certificate' qualification. The third team member, Miss Broughton, who had been appointed in 1929 (retired 1968), was as yet unqualified, while Connie Love of Holbeach St Johns was 'observing' as an unpaid trainee before proceeding to a more permanent post at Long Sutton.

The School Management Board
The staff were presided over by a very 'hands-on' management board, prominent on which was 'Jack' John Sharp Patchett, nearly always reverentially referred to in Miss Ransom's neat copperplate hand as 'J S Patchett, Esq.' The brother of Charles Patchett, John Sharp Patchett (1874-1955) lived at Fleet Lodge and farmed land off Branches Lane. A prominent Wesleyan and a supporter of the Liberal party, he had been elected Chairman of the Holbeach Urban Council in 1919. He was a regular caller at the School, usually to check and sign the register, but also to deal with any problems, as in April 1945, when the toilets were left in a bad state after the public had been using

them out of school hours. Miss Ransom sent for Mr Patchett, who had locks put on the gates and notified the police so promptly that within six days she was able to report: 'Lavatories are quite in order today.'

Personnel difficulties were also aired in 1945. The caretaker had been unable to light the boiler because of her lumbago, so Mr Walmsley was engaged as a replacement.

Understandably he was not prepared to work for less than £1 a week and refused any extra duties. But 15-year-old Dorothy Lewis filled the breach by washing children's milk bottles and sweeping up after school dinners for 2/6 (15p) a day.

Mr Patchett, meanwhile, distributed oranges and apples to the children at Christmas, and time was sometimes granted for special treats, such as an afternoon at the cinema in November 1931. Other days off were regularly given for royal events, such as the

PRACTISING WITH PEN AND INK. Example of a copy book exercise, benefiting both handwriting and spelling.

King George V's Silver Jubilee and the Duke of Gloucester's wedding in 1935, George V's funeral the following year and no less than three days' Coronation Holiday in May 1937, before which John Sharp Patchett presented a Coronation Medal to each child.

The Managers also allowed the School to be closed for the All Saints Church and Nonconformist Sunday School Festivals in June and July.

Lack of amenities
The School, of course, needed these bright spots in its routine, for working conditions were far from ideal.

A register of 139 children by 1933 was already too great for three teachers to cope with, and a fourth 'young and inexperienced teacher', to quote the school inspector's report, was taken on to help the Head with her class of 50 children. 'The building is a serious handicap,' said another report in February 1938. 'With 48 children in each class, the rooms are too full of desks to allow of much moving about or of any very bulky material for play or handiwork activities.' Not mentioned was the lack of mains electricity and flush lavatories. These were not even considered by the County Architect before 1939, and in the case of toilets, took another six years to carry out, while the School was not connected to the town sewerage system until 1970. No telephone was installed until 1954. Heating was unreliable. Individual stoves were replaced by a central heating system in the late 30s (after which, 'we were missing the cheerful light of a fire on a dull afternoon'), but frequent references were still made to low temperatures for years afterwards. With only 40 degrees (and it had fallen even lower than that previously) recorded inside the School on February 3rd 1947 during one of the worst winters for years, permission was urgently sought from the Managers to buy a Valor oil stove for Miss Yale's classroom – 'always the coldest in the School'.

At other times, classes were often badly depleted by illness, particularly at the turn of the year, with attendance dropping to around 60 per cent or lower on several occasions during the Thirties and Forties. In 1940, the School had to be closed altogether for four days on Dr Booth's advice, when measles struck yet again. Another factor was adverse

103

winter weather, which made it very difficult for children to get to school at a time when very few parents had cars. Sometimes only just over a third of the pupils turned up, making it hardly worth taking the register.

Wartime imposed even more trying conditions on the school. When war was declared the Board of Education delayed the school's reopening after the holidays for eight days, after which, to accommodate the Vernon Square Infants School evacuees from the King's Cross area of London, an awkward shift system was put in place by which the Londoners were to have use of the building in the morning, while the Holbeach children resumed classes in the afternoons. After two months of this unsatisfactory routine, the United Methodist Schoolroom became available and provided the Vernon Square Infants' temporary home until October 1940, by which time most of them, including their teacher, had returned to London and the remaining 11 children were absorbed into the Boston Road premises. By the end of that year, school hours had to be changed to 9.30 a.m. to 12 noon and 1.30 to 3.30 p.m., as part of the Government's 'Continuation of Summer Time', in force until February 1941. Bigger changes to the timetable were to follow, with the Board of Education's request to stagger the summer holidays, closing the school from 1st to 18th August 1941, reopening until 10th September, and then continuing the holiday into mid-October.

STAPLE DIET. The ⅓-pint milk bottles of earlier schooldays, almost straight-sided and sealed with cardboard tops.

[Courtesy Roy Pratt.]

Other interruptions to the routine came in the form of air raid alerts, usually in the late morning and afternoon, which kept staff and children in the shelters anywhere from 25 minutes to over 4 hours. These warnings peaked in 1941–the year of the Spalding blitz–with 13 alerts. Some children actually enjoyed the experience, and if the alert coincided with lunchtime, meals and cocoa were served underground. But where longer sessions in the shelter were likely to continue beyond the end of the school day, and if no aircraft could be heard overhead, the staff had to decide whether or not to risk sending the children home. 1941 and 1942 brought more problems –not just with Josephine Overson who managed to wedge a piece of chalk up her nose and had to be taken to Dr Walker's in Barrington Gate, the *Luftwaffe* permitting – but with shortages of school milk in May and June 1941. The Co-op manager explained that this was caused by a scarcity of bottle tops, but was willing to compromise by supplying milk in churns, if the school could measure out the quantities and retain and wash the bottles on the premises.

Staggering the holidays was one thing; ensuring the teachers had sufficient time off was another. In 1942, the Board of Education suggested that the school should be opened during the longer part of the summer vacation for any children or parents wishing it. Twenty-one pupils turned up, each allowed a generous two-thirds of a pint of milk daily, and some of the time was passed taking the children for long walks. But after four weeks, the staff succeeded in getting a much-needed week off for themselves with the Managers' permission.

Lunchtime supervision was becoming unreasonably hard work. By December 1943, Miss Ransom was appealing to the School Managers for additional help from the caretaker, to relieve the staff from lunchtime chores. Over 80 children were staying for school dinners, each to be provided with hot cocoa, following which the teachers had to wipe down the desks and move them so that the floor could be swept before lessons. The wish was granted, but it was never easy to keep caretakers as they were paid so little, and even then only quarterly. Officialdom also needed watching that September, when the Council wanted the School railings for salvage, thus removing any protection from the main road. This Miss Ransom vigorously protested to County Architect level.

William Tingle: new Head, new methods
Retiring in the summer term of 1953, Miss Ransom was presented with a wireless set from the children and a Goblin Teasmade from the Managers, two of whom, Eric Lane and John S Patchett, appeared in the presentation photo, Patchett formally dressed in a wing collar for the occasion. Miss Ransom was succeeded by William Tingle, who was to remain in charge for the next 18 years. His time at the helm symbolised the beginning of a working relationship with the new George Farmer School from the late 50s onwards, representing as it did the educational destination for most of the Year 6 pupils. Out of 48 children leaving the Junior School in 1968, for instance, 29 went on to George Farmer and with one boy leaving the district altogether, the remaining 6 boys and 12 girls were accepted by the Spalding Grammar and High Schools respectively.

Tingle's era also reflected explorations into new methods. He co-operated with the Education Officer's experiment in 1966 of substituting parental choice for the written selection examination, while a new approach to teaching mathematics and a six-week teaching practice secondment of three students from Stoke Rochford College of Education presented new experiences for his staff. Tingle and the School Managers were also invited to outline discussions on

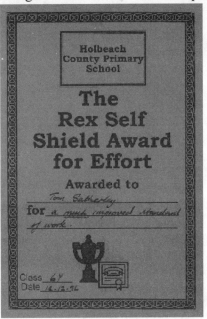

HIS NAME LIVES ON. *The Rex Self Award, presented for good work at Holbeach County Primary School.*

reorganisation for implementing Comprehensive education in 1967. Had this been introduced unmodified, it would have put a very different face on the way Holbeach was schooled. There was general agreement, for example, that it would be best to have only one school in Holbeach for the five to nine-year age group, and that the school should be a new one situated on the south-east corner of the George Farmer site. The George Farmer School itself would have become a Middle School for 9 to 13-year-olds, with older children channelled to the Peel School at Long Sutton.

One observed, too, a broadening outlook in the way children were encouraged in outside interests. There were police films at the local cinema on road safety, talks from the RSPCA on pet care, a Commonwealth Institute lecture on journeying around the world and a demonstration for the girls by the Singer Sewing Machine company. No less an expert than Henry Mossop addressed the top class in 1966 on old coins and other interesting archaeological finds from the Stone, Bronze and Iron Ages. Known to some from his distinguished war record as 'The Flying Farmer' and a younger brother of John Mossop, Henry Mossop was an acknowledged authority in his field, and was reputed to hold the largest collection of British Celtic coins in the country.

After William Tingle retired in 1971, he was succeeded by Rex Self from Boston, whose career was cut tragically short when he died suddenly six years later. His name lives on, however, in the form of the Rex Self Award, a shield presented to pupils who have made a special effort in their work.

New identity and struggling expansion, 1948-82
From December 1948, Holbeach Infants was officially re-named Holbeach County Primary School. To ease the situation

slightly, boys living in Fleet territory at Jubilee Villas –built 1935 and now the workers' hostel backing on to Fleet Road Industrial Estate– were transferred to Fleet Wood Lane School. This was easier said than done, for initially it involved an even longer walk for the boys until transport was provided. Even so, numbers at Boston Road had risen from 80 children in 1926 to 364 by 1953.

This was why the opening of The George Farmer School five years later was so timely. It absorbed the pupils of the old Church of England Girls School, and allowed the infants to be transferred from Boston Road to the girls' newly-vacated buildings off the High Street. The latter were then redesignated Holbeach Voluntary Controlled Infants, with Miss Harrison as the first head teacher, while Boston Road's title was modified to Holbeach County Primary Junior School.

DUAL ANSWER TO A PROBLEM. The new Holbeach County Primary School from 1982 (top) and William Stukeley Church of England School (below) from 1994 eased the overcrowding which had dogged the town's junior schooling for years.

However, the fact could not be disguised that by the 1970s an 80-year-old building could no longer cope with ever-increasing numbers. End-of-term assemblies and Christmas parties had to be held in the Women's Institute Hall, and no less than nine temporary rooms had been added to a site of less than an acre since the late 1940s, causing local MP Richard Body to comment in October 1976 that 'It is like trying to force a gallon into a pint jar.' Discussions about a new site had begun as early as 1968, but it was to be another 14

years before the new £340,000 premises at the A17 end of Boston Road took shape, into which the School moved in February 1982 under the headship of Mr Atkins.

There had been some controversy over whether the new school hall was too small to accommodate the intended 320 intake. As always, it was a question of available budgets, although helped by the opening of the William Stukeley School, Holbeach County Primary managed to survive structurally unmodified until the early 2000s, by which time room was made for two extra teaching areas, a new information/communication technology suite-with-library and further office accomodation. As at April 2001, there were 307 children on the roll, looked after by Head Teacher Mike Almond and his team of 11 teachers, 5 ancillaries, 9 lunchtime staff, and two special needs teachers attending on certain occasions each week. Holbeach Primary is not a church school, but supports Christian principles through its links with the local church and community. The Parent Teacher Association has also played its part in developing and maintaining an environmental site, featuring wooden tables and a grassed 'quiet area' where children can sit and chat or play board games. All factors that make children more complete individuals and help achieve the aim, to quote Mike Almond, 'of all pupils achieving their maximum potential and leaving school as numerate and literate future citizens of the 21st century.'

William Stukeley School

After a delay caused by a fire in 1992, William Stukeley Primary School began its existence from July 1993 in the old girls' school buildings off the High Street, until its purpose-built premises were ready for the new term in September the following year. These took the place of Stukeley Hall – latterly an old people's home and fire and ambulance depot, and finally authorised for demolition by Environment Secretary Michael Howard after it had been decided that the Grade II Listed building was 'of no particular architectural or historic merit'. That August, in 1994, David Church of Langwith Builders handed over the keys of the £853,000 building to Headteacher Jackie Sheldrake, who before her appointment had been on the staff at Holbeach County Primary School.

ATTRACTIVE TIMEPIECE. The former Stukeley Hall clock –once Herbert Carter's pride and joy– now graces the grounds of the William Stukeley School.

As school grounds go, the approach to William Stukeley School presents a pleasing aspect. The main entrance opposite Northons Lane is still graced by the substantial and elegantly-curving brick wall and gateposts of the former Stukeley Hall, leading you in through tranquil grounds intersected with public footpaths that wind through massive, established pines, heavy in season with cones and rustling with the movements of grey squirrels. It might not have been so, had the County Council's original plans to develop the site for executive homes not been defeated by a public enquiry. Not that it was plain sailing from there on. The County Council's subsequent offer to sell the 2½-acre site to South Holland District Council for £1 sounded attractive enough, until South Holland realised that it would have to pay for the upkeep.

Gracious grounds and a Princess Diana memorial

The situation was later resolved, so that both public and school can now share enjoyment of the grounds, although a further legacy of Stukeley Hall, the clock tower, remains as an occasional source of discussion. The Holbeach & District Civic Society felt that this timepiece, a last remnant of the old Hall and the pride and joy of former owner Herbert Carter, should be moved for greater visibility when the school buildings were extended from eight to ten classrooms in 2000. But again, the County Council referred on the question of cost and maintenance charges, this time to the Parish Council. Elsewhere in the surrounding parkland, however, the town has been happy to add some extra touches of its own, such as the memorial tablet to Princess Diana in 2000, or the nearby seat, donated by Ashwood Homes, surrounding the base of a tree.

Stimulating environment

Such a setting surely contributes to the 'stimulating environment ' of the School's mission statement, 'within which all children are valued, encouraged to care for others, and strive for excellence in all they do.' With Church of England associations, a strong Christian ethos is practised. The children are also encouraged to care for the environment with an annual involvement in National Spring Clean Day, picking up litter in the company of South Holland District Council's Civic Pride Officer. Although not an Aided school –where financial considerations and the appointment of most of the governing body are in the hands of the Church– its Controlled status supports collective worship, encourages Christian acts and is accessible to other denominations. The School opened to 198 children, rising to over 251 by 2000, and was presented with the Investor in People award in May 2002 by the Diocesan Director for Education, the Revd John Bailey. On this high note, Mrs Sheldrake handed over to her successor David Flynn when she retired before the new school year began.

The George Farmer Technology College

' We weren't prepared for the size. I'd been for a term to the old Holbeach Boys School, an old Victorian building, very cramped. So it was a bit of a change for us. For one thing we weren't used to going to school with girls.'

So said David Hatton, a former fruiterer in Church Street and one of the first pupils of Holbeach's biggest educational advance since the 17th century.

No languages were taught in his time and the woodwork bench was more familiar to him than the cookery, needlework and crafts practised by his son 25 years later. But with the opening of The George Farmer School on 22nd April 1958 –six months

ahead of schedule– education in the town took on a new dimension.

The new school had no constitutional links with the original George Farmer bequest of 1671. But in view of the long-term significance of this name to schooling in the town, the new governors, headmaster-elect and education officials meeting in February 1958 at the East Elloe Council Offices, Mattimore House, agreed that the new establishment should be called 'The George Farmer County Secondary School'. Its identity was further established by a specially-devised insignia that combined the herons from the arms of Holland County Council, and an adaptation of the Farmer family crest, taken from the armorial bearings of Sir Edward Farmer, George Farmer's son. The School motto chosen was *'Altiora Petamus'* –'We Seek Higher Things'.

JUNIOR ATHLETICS AND LONG-HAIRED WOODWORK.
Two scenes of George Farmer life from the mid-1970s.
[Photos: Lincolnshire Free Press.]

The choice of site succeeded despite early objections following the County Council's compulsory purchase order of 13¾ acres in 1954. Those against talked of its nearness to an open sewer ('The drain ought to have been filled in years ago', said Mr R Clay), that it prevented expansion of both the Cemetery grounds and recreational facilities in Carter's Park, and that it would be better positioned behind Stukeley Hall. But the

108

Council won through. At a time when the Holbeach street scene was still distinctly Georgian, Victorian, or pre-war, the architecture was revolutionary. It was unusual in this part of the world to see big-city expanses of glass descending to ground level in pressed-steel frames, alternating with coloured panels to form a whole that is still largely unchanged today.

Personalities over the years

George Farmer's first Head was John Fathers, supported by Miss D P Ford from the superseded Girls School as Deputy Head. Senior Master was R G ('Dick') Kent-Woolsey and Senior Mistress, Mrs G I Clay. Veronica Gale was the original Head Girl, and James Ashton, Head Boy.

The official opening of the £160,000 building by Sir Herbert Shiner, Chairman of the Executive Council of the County Councils Association, took place on 22nd April 1959, exactly a year after pupils had first walked through the doors. Since John Fathers left in 1971, head teachers to date have been Robert Side (1971-76), Anthony Barker (1976-84) Pat Glenn (1984-96), Tal Jones (1996-2001), and Steve Baragwanath, assisted by Gill Graper. Each has represented a chapter in a rapidly changing era in school life, beginning with the traditional discipline applied by Mr Fathers, through the more flexible approach to school uniform in the 70s, to the more self-expressive and technologically-informed pupil of today.

Additional facilities and opportunities at 'The Georgie', as generations of pupils have called it, followed in a form never witnessed before in the town's schools. 1963 saw the installation of an outdoor swimming pool, and in

WHEN GIRLS WORE DRESSES. The pattern used for their summer uniform in the 70s and 80s.

1972 the strict uniform rules that had characterised John Fathers' era were relaxed when trouser suits for the girls in navy blue Crimplene and modelled at a preview by Rosemary Starr and Mandy Descamps, were introduced. The pupils' verdict: ' Smashin' '. The following year, the first exchange visit took place with pupils from Sézanne, one of Holbeach's twin towns in France.

A computer arrives, 1983...

Back home, go-karts were to be found buzzing around the school field on an open evening in 1975 –tangible evidence of the arrival that year of David Hollings from Bradford, to supervise school motor mechanic courses. His technical expertise was in demand in a different sphere when, with the early Eighties, came the unobtrusive delivery of a solitary appliance that was to determine the eventual status of George Farmer as a Technology College –a computer. The County Council was aiming to supply one to every school in 1983 and it fell to Mr Hollings to explain its mysteries to the rest of the staff. With the advent of greater sexual equality and a growing number of boys showing an interest in cooking and food preparation, times were also changing in the domestic science department, with £50,000 expended on new home economics facilities in the late 80s.

Industry Day with local businesses

Keen to be recognised as community-conscious, George Farmer has for several years established links with a dozen or so local businesses to stage an industry day. The idea behind this was to familiarise students with the skills expected of them after school before they had decided on their choice of GCSE subjects, and the scheme, arranged in co-operation with Holbeach household names such as Lefleys Garage, Greens structural designers of Whaplode, and Lingardens of Weston has been conducted successfully for several years now.

Sporting achievements

When it comes to sports, George Farmer has long been famous for educating Geoff Capes. Geoff, who went on to gain the title of World's Strongest Man in a career spanning two decades in active sport, and an even longer one as a celebrity involved in many charitable and business ventures, freely admits he was not a model pupil when he attended The George Farmer in the Sixties. Nevertheless, it was clear from the way he represented the school in just about every sport, from basketball and soccer to cross-country running and gymnastics, that his was a talent just waiting to happen. And when he was selected, at the age of 11, to put the shot victoriously against a young hulk from Donington –not because he had any previous experience, but because he was the biggest boy available to take on the opposition– his 'job for life', as he put it, was assured.

Dick Kent-Woolsey, the Senior Master in Geoff's time, once remarked that 'If that boy ever represents England, I'll eat my hat.' Had he been there in November 1998, he would surely have been prepared to nibble just a little on his headgear when Geoff returned to present The George Farmer School with the bronze bust of himself that was struck in 1974 to commemorate his successes, and which had previously been on display at the Crystal Palace sports arena. Also presented for the first time that year was the Geoff Capes Award for Sporting Achievement, received by Sarah Mayes.

It was a time, too, for other triumphs. The wide range of lunchtime and after-school sports developed in the 80s and 90s formed the foundation that bred further talent to County level in athletics, basketball and hockey with names like Louis Evling-Jones, Ben Coupland, William Jones, Glenn Martin and Joanne Hall. It led to the Sportsmark Award of 1998 for

GCE BECOMES GCSE. Art teacher Paddy Palgrave's artwork on a booklet cover reviewing the changes, 1988-89. [Courtesy The George Farmer Technology College.]

raising the profile of PE in schools, and there was more to come in '99 when George Farmer's female under-15s won the Lincolnshire Girls' Football Grand Prix for the first time.

NEW SYMBOL. Technology status meant a new logo.

New status from 2000

School numbers –up from 412 in 1992 to 540 in 1998– had increased as dramatically as the demands of employers during that decade, now universally dependent on the computer and the Internet. The observation at the time in an OFSTED report, that the School could have better technology facilities, and the official approval of George Farmer as an affiliate of the Technology Colleges Trust in January 1999, were the first signs that an important new upgraded identity was in the offing for George Farmer. This was confirmed the following year by the announcement that from September 2000, the School was to be redesignated The George Farmer Technology College. This move took into account the changing face of careers by placing a greater emphasis on subjects like maths, science and design technology. 'The aim', said Headteacher Tal Jones, 'is to raise achievement at the School and I believe that we will be able to do that. The other subjects will still be there, but extra emphasis will be given to technology subjects.' The move has placed George Farmer at a strategic roundabout on the local Information Technology highway, acting as the feeding-in point for children

110

familiarised with computers at Holbeach County Primary and William Stukeley Schools, and directing them on routes to the Lincolnshire business community, Boston College and beyond.

Higher technology arrives, 2000
At a cost of £180,000, a figure exceeding that of the original building itself, construction work began in July 2000 as concrete evidence of the School's new status. Thirty new computers were ordered to add to the 30 already installed, and the transformations included refitting the redundant motor vehicle workshop and adding new graphics, computer-aided design and design-and-technology classrooms to a complex that had already been enhanced five years earlier by an impressive new library, with plans already in the pipeline for a second information and communication technology suite. The library, it should be noted for future historians, is built over a device tailor-made for archaeologists in the form of a time capsule, containing national and local newspapers, contemporary coins and stamps, school development plans and prospectus, examples of pupils' work and class lists, all from 1995.

Today, Steve Baragwanath heads a teaching team of 38, supervising 580 students on the roll. It equates to a pupil-to-staff ratio of fifteen to one –a factor Miss Ransom around the corner would have welcomed 70 years earlier, with 50 children to a class, only one other qualified member of staff, a floor to sweep herself after school dinners and no mains drainage or electricity. With the College thus equipped to meet the twenty-first century, one wonders what George Farmer, Gentleman of Middlesex, would make of it all were his ghost to stand outside the grounds, the exposed length of the Holbeach River on Park Road the only familiar strand with his past. He might be buffeted by Nike-bagged youth, fresh from Broadband surfing in Holbeach Clough, swooping up from the A17 underpass on chunky mountain bikes. His ghostly ears are likely to be assailed by non-harpsichordal music fizzing from the Walkmans of passing girls wearing not smocks, but dark trousers. Perplexing, too, to his seventeenth-century eyes, the presence of schoolteachers'

horseless carriages parked alongside the playground. But with over ten times the number of children that his endowment originally educated in the choir of All Saints Church, all receiving the latest form of instruction in the three 'Rs' regardless of means or station in life, he would surely approve.

♣ ♣ ♣ ♣ ♣ ♣

10 —Notables & Characters

Sir Norman Angell

1872-1967

[Photo Mrs A A Everard.]

Had he been a father, the claim that, 'My father knew Lloyd George' could have been surpassed many times over by Sir Norman Angell. For he knew not only Lloyd George, but worked closely with a later Prime Minister, Ramsay Macdonald, offered advice to U S President Woodrow Wilson, and counted George Bernard Shaw, Jerome K Jerome, J Maynard Keynes, Bertrand Russell, Arnold Bennett, G M Trevelyan, Harold Nicolson, Lord Northcliffe, John Buchan, Winston Churchill and many others among his acquaintances, not forgetting the Gestapo, on whose hit-list he prominently featured. His was a remarkable career that began with precocious self-sufficiency and went on to devote itself unswervingly to the principles of rational and international peace, expressed through the medium of countless newspaper articles, lectures and over 40 books, one of which, *The Great Illusion*, earned him the Nobel Peace Prize in 1933.

Family background in Holbeach

Angell, who modified his name thus by deed poll, initially to keep his journalist and author's identities separate, was born Ralph Norman Angell Lane in 1872 at the Mansion House family home in Holbeach High Street. His father, Thomas Angell Lane (1832-1900), was an unusual man in himself: entrepreneurial as the owner of a chain of small department stores –one of

which stood next door to the house on a site now recognised today as East Lea Furnishings– yet an enthusiast of French literature and accepted sufficiently by the local Victorian upper middle class to become a magistrate, Holbeach Grammar School governor, and chairman of various local governing bodies. This was in spite of himself, for Lane Senior was no social climber and often defied convention, in contrast to Mrs Lane. She was best defined, according to her son Sir Norman, as a good Victorian woman, very conscious of class distinction and 'with not much regard for intellectual attainments unless they could be translated into material and social advantage.'

As a man whose adult working life kept him largely abroad or in London and the South East of England, Sir Norman's Holbeach recollections were mainly those of his extreme youth. In his writings he makes the odd reference to the town in an unconsciously tantalising way, leaving you hoping for more. Fascinating, for instance, was his childhood encounter with an old man breaking stones for road repairs, who told him that he had 'fought with the Duke at Quarter Brass.' This, Norman's father explained to him later, would have been *Quatre Bras*, a rallying point of the Duke of Wellington's army at the Battle of Waterloo in 1815. In which case, this made the old stone-breaker an even older campaigner than 94-year-old Holbeach resident, William Slator, who was reported in December 1892 to be living with his wife 'on a small dole' from the Parish, having served under Sir Edward Codrington on the warship *Holbein* –74 guns– during the Greek War of Independence against the Turkish-Egyptian fleet in 1827.

Angell recalls, too, certain details of the Mansion House, its cellar floors laid with 'great stone flags, each a yard or two square', which he supposed must have been brought some distance, given the lack of locally available stone –as was the case with All Saints Church. In the largest of the cellars, he describes the existence of an eighteenth-century mangle, 'of strange and elaborate construction; an enormous box like an enlarged coffin, eight or ten feet long, two or three feet deep, filled with stones; under this box, a dozen wooden rollers, which could be removed.'

Memories of his Holbeach schooling revolve chiefly around the impression made upon him by the Revd Ralph Adye Ram, MA, Headmaster of the Grammar School a few doors down from the Lane's house in the High Street. Norman had been transferred there from an unnamed preparatory school, where he had suffered being sent to Coventry for a month at the head's instigation, following a relatively minor offence. After such a traumatic experience, Ralph Ram's sensitivity and understanding provided a welcome contrast. But while it led the young Norman to 'respect' the Victorian Church of England for fostering such humanity, he stopped short at some of the dogma it preached and the effect it had on faithful adherents. He could not understand Mrs Ram, for instance, scolding some of the Grammar School boys for gathering conkers on the Sabbath –at odds, in his youthful opinion, with Christ's biblical exchanges with the Pharisees on a not dissimilar subject– while Norman's own mother would not allow skating on a Sunday.

Life at the Mansion House must have followed a highly-principled but generally comfortable and agreeable course. His father, probably with Mrs Lane's encouragement, retired early to an income of about £500 a year, but this still allowed for a lifestyle that included several servants and a horse and carriage. Tom Lane, the eldest brother, was prominent in amateur dramatics and whenever a touring company was in town performing at the Assembly Rooms, he would invite them all to a convivial supper at the Mansion House.

A precocious childhood
Five of the six children, given their solid start in life, fulfilled acceptable and comprehensible expectations. Tom, the eldest, and the father of Eric Lane (owner of Serpentine House until 2003), went into farming and seed production. Harry took up

medicine; Alec: engineering; Will: land agency and auctioneering, while their sister, Caroline, married a schoolmaster. Only the youngest, Norman, dismayed and possibly disappointed. Not by his idleness, but as a result of his insatiable appetite for reading, among other works, Voltaire, Tom Paine, Kingsley, Morris, Carlyle, Walt Whitman and notably John Stuart Mill's *Essay on Liberty,* which had helped him shape revolutionary views on economics, politics and religion at a very early age.

The frequent airing of these views at the family dinner table tended to distress his mother and try the patience of the rest of the family. In fact, eldest bother Tom was once goaded to say: 'One more quotation from John Stuart Mill, Herbert Spencer or Darwin, and in the interest of family peace I'm going to give you a first-class hiding.'

In a sense, the parents had only themselves to blame for planning their youngest child's education in such a way as to encourage this train of thought. After the Grammar School in Holbeach, his next school was to be a French *lycée* in St Omer, an almost incredible change for a boy barely into his teens since, not only was Sir Norman left to travel there on his own, but he was for a time the only English child in the whole school. Ironically, it was there that he came across a copy of Mill's *Essay on Liberty,* which he read while convalescing after a leg injury. Attempts to discuss the book with his teachers were dismissed with the warning that he should learn solid facts before dabbling in speculation, advice which fell on stony ground. At the end of his time at St Omer, the *professeurs* must have been relieved to see the back of this lad who queried everything he was taught, instead of dutifully learning it by heart like his classmates.

But deserving of a hiding from his brother or not, the youngest Lane's airy discoursing was the natural adjunct of a highly-developed literary sense that had already earned him a reporter's job at the age of 15½ on a Weymouth newspaper, and the editorship of an expatriate periodical in

Geneva, where he soon forged links with the university and some of its radical and revolutionary students. Run-of-the-mill newspapers however were not ideal platforms for avant-garde views, and he was soon back in England reporting for a paper in Ipswich, a position which ended when he dared to criticise the apparently extravagant travel arrangements of General Booth of the Salvation Army!

A fresh start

Temporarily back in Holbeach at the ripe old age of 17, lying out under the trees of the Mansion House garden and chewing chocolate creams, it was time to reconsider his future. After a period of self-pity alternating with taking stock, emigration appeared the only means to a fresh start, and with his father's encouragement, which included £50 to help him on his way, he sailed for America with the West Coast as his goal.

As with the *lycée*, this was to provide another complete contrast to his previous existence. His new life was one of hard graft, rubbing shoulders with hardened Americans, Mexicans, Portuguese and Germans engaged in vine-planting, creating irrigation banks, and shifting cattle hundreds of saddle-sore miles from one place to another. He transformed himself, to use his own words, from 'the introspective and somewhat morbid youngster coming from the sheltered life of a Victorian middle-class home', into 'a man of too much action, desiring to do many things a once.' As part of his aim to become a successful part of Western life, he progressed to setting up his own ranch. But the six years of hardship, debt and struggling with the elements that ensued –and even this he positively described as 'a rest from intellectual effort'– drew him back to newspapers again, first in San Francisco and then in France.

French journalism and time for thought

Angell's arrival in the Paris of 1898 at the characterful English-language *Daily Messenger*, with its quaintly outdated production methods and bilingual French staff proficient in Cockney expletives, offered the unlikely conditions for Angell's resettlement into his chosen career. The dingy newspaper office at *Rue Croix des Petits Champs* was no Impressionist painting. But in a country whose politics had been split by the Dreyfus affair against an international background of brooding for eventual war, with Germany intent on naval and colonial expansion, it was the springboard to an intellectual involvement in world affairs that was to shape the rest of his life. During his editorship there, he found time to write *Patriotism Under Three Flags*, the first of his 42 works. This advanced the theory that feelings of patriotism and nationalism were born of nothing more than high emotion and predominating opinion, leading to irrational decisions and an inability to live in peaceful co-operation. Commercial failure though this publication was, it formed the prototype of many of his subsequent treatises.

When after a few years the *Messenger*'s owners proposed to wind up the paper as unprofitable (partly through an unwillingness to modernise) Angell attempted a rescue sale by approaching Lord Northcliffe at the *Daily Mail*. Northcliffe refused, but offered Angell the editorship of the Paris *Daily Mail*. This paradoxical working relationship of the intellectual and the popular-press baron worked surprisingly well, for Northcliffe, prepared to ignore prevailing opinion that Angell was cranky and 'too literary and viewy to make a good businessman', was impressed by his quick grasp of a subject and understanding of people. He allowed his employee a reasonable freedom in which to express his views. So much so, in fact, that it led to the publication of Angell's most important work to date in 1909: *The Great Illusion*. In it, he stated, no modern war could make a profit for the victors. The main objective should be peaceful defence, coupled with a need to examine and discuss differences beforehand. War was always the outcome of human failing and while it might not be possible to change human nature, Angell argued, we could certainly change human behaviour, otherwise 'we should still be fighting duels, torturing witnesses in our courts of law, burning nonconformists at the stake.' In taking this stance, Angell was not a pacifist in the accepted sense, a popular misconception at the time, even among those who should have known better, such as Hilaire Belloc. In fact, as Angell himself said: 'Non-resistance is no remedy…If reason, impartial judgement is to prevail, the victim of lawless violence must be defended by society.'

At first, the book was no best-seller. In fact, no publisher at the time would touch so unfashionable a subject as Peace. Fellow journalists warned him to steer clear of 'that stuff, or you will be classed with cranks and faddists, with devotees of Higher Thought who go about in sandals and long beards, [and] live on nuts.'

Success with an 'Optical Illusion'

Undaunted, Angell's tactic was to condense the message into 28,000 words and 100 pages, call it *Europe's Optical Illusion* and have it published at his own expense for distributing to two to three hundred 'public men' connected with politics in Britain, France and Germany.

After a few months' inertia the work began to be discussed in diplomatic circles, which the press construed as 'something bound to be very important', and an ensuing two-page review in the *Nation* pushed the book well on its way. 'Even King Edward VII read it', recorded the historian D C Somervell, 'and he seldom read anything that was neither official nor amusing.'

BIRTHPLACE OF A NOBEL PRIZE WINNER. *The blue heritage plaque attached in 1976 to the front of the Mansion House in the High Street.*

Thus relaunched, *Illusion* within 18 months had been translated into over 20 languages and over the years and several editions, sales ran into millions.

As a commercial venture, therefore, the book had become against all odds an unqualified success. But if, as Angell said, it could be judged a failure in not preventing the two world wars that followed its publication, the moral was there for all to see: to disregard bitter experience is to risk repeating it.

In an ideal world of rational people, there would still have been time, between 1909 and 1914, for national temperaments to be influenced by Angell's doctrine, even in Germany. Over 1912-1913, and in support of an advertising campaign promoting the German translation of *Illusion*, the American Carnegie Foundation arranged a lecture tour for him, taking in the major German universities. Even in Holbeach, people began to take notice, for preaching on Peace Sunday at the United Methodist Church in December 1913, the Revd J Jay drew a comparison between Angell and the apostle Paul. The German tour, meanwhile, proved most revealing. Although the meetings were often stormy, animosity tended to brew between factions of the audience rather than direct itself at the speaker. Angell came away convinced that if he and his supporters could have had another five years to work among the younger Germans, 'We could have diluted Prussianism sufficiently to have rendered it much less dangerous, helping to prepare Germany for that "Western" role if Western Civilization is to defend itself against the East.'

Return to England

By now, Angell's extra-curricular commitments had led him to resign his position on the *Mail*. He returned to England where he had become involved with the Garton Foundation, a trust set up by wealthy industrialist, Sir Richard Garton, 'to promote and develop the science of international polity as indicated in the published writings of Norman Angell.' Administered from Angell's flat in King's Bench Walk, London, the Foundation's activities were just getting into their stride when war was declared in 1914.

Then 42 and anxious to contribute, Angell enlisted early on as a stretcher-bearer at Dunkirk. But he was so appalled at the bureaucratic incompetence and delays over care for the wounded, that he decided his priorities were elsewhere in the interests of securing a workable peace. Back in London, he met up with Ramsay Macdonald –who was to become Prime Minister in 1929– Charles Trevelyan, Arthur Ponsonby, Philip Snowden and E D Morel to form the Union of Democratic Control. Although its object was a British foreign policy supporting an alliance of powers all acting with equal strength in the common cause of defence, this development alienated him from the Garton group, who felt he was becoming too politically involved.

To the USA once more

Nineteen-fifteen saw Angell on his way to the USA to further the cause, his ship sailing through the grim wreckage of the *Lusitania*, torpedoed only the week before off the west coast of Ireland. Initially he was Director of Studies at the Cornell University Summer School of International Relations, but it was his editorial involvement with the *New Republic* paper, then an unofficial mouthpiece of the White House, which provided Angell with a line of communication to President Wilson.

Originally Angell was concerned that America's neutrality could only be harmful to the Allied cause. But during Wilson's second term of office in 1917, the USA declared war on Germany. A further encouraging note was struck the following year, when the President issued his Fourteen Points for a League of Nations, a well-intentioned but ultimately flawed scheme for the peaceful settlement of international conflicts. It was indeed a step in the right direction, but given Wilson's character, Angell observed the danger signs all too clearly.

The Presidency during the War was in Angell's view, 'a dictatorship without human contact'. Wilson was inflexible on the subject of the League and failed to keep others around him informed of his actions. Nor was Wilson 'forceful and insistent just where he should have been'.

Angell's judgement was accurate, for Wilson did nothing to check the wave of dangerous jingoism that took hold on America after it had entered the war and which went on to demand a punitive peace from Germany. The French, under Clemenceau, driven by a political unity Wilson lacked, were in a similar frame of mind. Worst of all, the League of Nations was not ratified by Congress. So the USA could therefore not join the League and the compromises demanded by Britain, France, Italy and other Allies ensured that the Treaty of Versailles was far from what Wilson hoped, imposing conditions on Germany that were eventually to lead to the Second World War. It was equally disappointing to Angell, who for six months in 1918 had been a leading light in the League of Free Nations Association.

British politics –and a reluctant knighthood

In 1920, 'N A ', as he was known to his friends, joined the Labour party. Not for any political grandeur, but because he felt it provided a sympathetic outlet for his views on industrialised economy and internationalism. During his electioneering campaigns he had the support of socialist intellectuals and leading writers such as G Bernard Shaw and Jerome K Jerome, but it took defeats at Rushcliffe, Nottingham and Rossendale, Lancashire to achieve final election as Bradford North's MP in 1929.

On entering the Commons, disillusionment soon set in. Members of the House he considered to be too many in number, of 'bad intellectual quality', and practising the absurdity of voting on bills they knew little or nothing about. Meanwhile, the economic and monetary chaos he had always predicted as war's aftermath was gripping the country, and he was dismayed to find Labour responding to the situation by waging war on class and capitalism. The economic question having divided the cabinet and rendered socialist legislation impossible, the Prime Minister, Ramsay Macdonald, invited Angell to join his Coalition government, hinting at a peerage 'if it were not practicable to work from the House of Commons'. But Angell refused, mainly from his lack of confidence in Macdonald's approach to foreign affairs, and the Premier's frequently aloof indifference to advice.

Leaves Parliament

Angell resigned from Parliament in 1931, the year he received a knighthood. At the time, he was not in the mood to be honoured. Macdonald had apparently ignored his ideas for a marketing organisation to relieve unemployment, and he fully intended to reject the PM's offer of a knighthood as little more than a 'bauble'. But close friends wisely persuaded him that a title would help his credibility, especially with those who had been sceptical or cautious of his views.

The Nobel Prize, 1933

Of far greater importance to Sir Norman than a knighthood, however, was the Nobel Peace Prize, awarded to him in 1933 for the principles expressed in *The Great Illusion*. A new edition of this title had appeared that year as a restatement of the original work of 1909 to 1930s conditions. Of the many tributes received on this occasion from intellectual friends, one from Philip Noël-Baker stood out: 'It is of course twenty years overdue…If peace comes it will be more your doing than that of any other man alive. Other people have battered on the walls of hell, but you have undermined the foundations, and the man who does that is the man who breaks them down.' Another friend, Gilbert Murray, added: 'I think the Nobel Committee have done themselves credit, in selecting a real peace-worker who is not a cabinet minister or a general or a head of a State.'

Not that this was a cue for 'N A', now 61, to rest on his laurels. Leaving Parliament enabled him to concentrate on his work with the League of Nations Union, the Royal Institute of International Affairs, and lecturing tours of the USA, France, Holland and Scandinavia. During the fateful 1930s, several other works expressing the Angell doctrine followed *The Great Illusion*, some aimed specifically at the American public in the days before Pearl Harbor. Audiences, reluctant to see another war, were now more receptive to his ideas than they had been 15 or 20 years earlier.

Wartime lecturing

When war did come, Angell left for America in 1940 with the blessing of the Foreign Office and Ministry of Information, to continue his lectures and writings promoting the British cause. If Whitehall, in not providing any briefing or financial support for the tour had presumed that a self-starter like Sir Norman would soon generate a mission of his own, this was indeed the case. For it developed into a routine that was to take up half of every year well beyond 1945,

when Russia and Communism replaced the Third Reich as world preoccupations. Once again, a favoured Angell theory was acting itself out: the failure of allied nations to present a united front to the aggressor. 'We know', said Sir Norman, 'from experience again and again repeated, that Russia will make no accommodation, no concession, if the evidence seems to point to the fact that the West is incapable of unity in resistance to her domination.'

ALL HIS OWN WORK. Like Churchill, Angell could turn his hand to building work, a practical legacy of his time as a rancher in the Mid-West. He fashioned this superstructure on Northey from tree trunks and old barge timbers. *[Photo Mrs A A Everard.]*

At home on Northey

Leisure time must have been at a premium in Angell's life, but his long-term enjoyment of sailing led to the discovery of Northey Island, on the Blackwater Estuary off Maldon in Essex. For a man disposed to 'craving solitude as a drunkard craves gin', the island offered the ideal retreat, and he acquired it around 1920 from a military eccentric, Vere de Crespigny, who had hitherto preserved his privacy with an uninhibited shotgun from a mobile shed. Northey's 300 acres boasted only one farm cottage as accommodation, but Angell, fascinated by the process of bricklaying and putting his ranching experience to good use, built a house of his own design next to the cottage. Supported by stout timbers fashioned from trees and a derelict sailing barge, the house survives to this day, now maintained by the National Trust, although it might well have been otherwise.

The strategic importance of the Blackwater was not lost on the Germans, while Angell's name was alphabetically high on their liquidation blacklist in the event of an invasion. So it is almost no surprise to learn that the farm cottage received a direct hit from *Luftwaffe* bombs in 1940. Fortunately, Angell was not in residence at the time, but lost many of his papers stored next door.

It would be easy to assume that so serious-minded a man as Angell had little time for frivolities, but flashes of humour appear frequently in his writings. As in his Parisian newspaper days, for instance, when after prolonged spells of working late, he would be disturbed by *femmes de ménage,* whose 8 a.m. carpet-beatings on neighbouring balconies resounded like cannons. 'It was so maddening,' he related, 'that I would go out at times onto my own balcony, and imagine myself the possessor of a rifle, shooting these noisy creatures as I once shot deer in California.' (Rather akin to modern Holbeach, where a fair proportion of traditional early risers inflict strimmers, power saws, hover mowers and chattering diesel engines on the less practical still asleep!)

His response to eccentric critics, of whom he must have attracted many, is also worth recording. To the American poet Ezra Pound's several abusive letters, bristling with irrationalities and misspellings such as 'bastid' and addressed care of 'The Bank of England, Needle and Thread Street', he retorted neatly: 'It is perhaps a commentary on a certain prevailing worship of incomprehensibility that a committee of American and English poets should have awarded Pound…a Congressional prize.' What would he have made of today's award ceremonies?

Finally, there was the telegram mix-up, which caused raised eyebrows with the local post office when 'N A', a confirmed bachelor, was sent a telegram out of the blue proclaiming: 'Can sleep with you after the theatre Friday night. Love Rosalinde.' On further investigation with the lady concerned, it transpired that the original message should have read 'sup', as in 'dine'. Angell, then still in Parliament and living on Northey, half-jokingly threatened his colleague, the Postmaster-General: 'I could do with a few thousand [damages] just now

for the development of my farm.' Control of the island farm, incidentally, passed to Sir Norman's Holbeach nephew, Eric Lane, after 1945. It contrasted strongly with fenland farming conditions, as Cecil Pywell Avenue residents John and Freda Coley found when they worked there for a few months in the 1960s. Mains services were not a *fait accompli* and more than once, after a day's work, they had to row back to the mainland with only tractor headlights to guide their way!

'Satisfaction from an interest pursued'
It was unlikely, both before and after the Second World War, that Norman Angell's busy schedule allowed him much time to revisit Holbeach, although he did address a Holbeach Literary Society meeting in 1937, chaired by Canon P E Boswell, on the subject 'From Holbeach to Geneva.' In the 15 years immediately following his death, however, his name placed Holbeach in the limelight on two auspicious occasions, beginning with the attachment in his honour of a blue Heritage plaque to the Mansion House façade in November 1976. This was followed by the auction of his Nobel Peace Prize gold medal in February 1983, by one of his former secretaries to whom he had bequeathed the decoration. At a sale which made the columns of the national press, it was bought for £8,000 by Sir Norman's nephew, Eric Lane, of Serpentine House, Holbeach, 'purely out of sentiment' and for the enjoyment of his family. Mr Lane and his daughter, Mrs Alice Angell Everard, subsequently presented the medal to the Imperial War Museum on indefinite loan.

Sir Norman was still conducting lecture tours at the age of 90; proof enough, when he died four years later at Croydon in 1967, that the lifelong task he had set himself was one of immense proportions. In old age he related that it was typical of someone to ask him, given that his doctrine had failed to prevent two world wars, if he would not have been better off concentrating on say, being a good newspaper editor and thereafter enjoying golf and sailing with his friends, as a prelude to dying in peace. But it was even more typical of him to reply: 'Only a small minority can find the adequate satisfaction of life in mere physical comfort.

Satisfaction comes from an interest pursued, even at the cost of great physical discomfort.

'The end I chose –elimination of war– I would, without any hesitation whatsoever, choose again.'

♣ ♣ ♣ ♣ ♣ ♣

William Stukeley , 1687-1765

BREAKFAST SKETCH. Isaac Whood depicts Stukeley lightheartedly as a Roman dignitary (in hindsight of somewhat Tarbuckian appearance) on 10th May 1727, while they were breakfasting with the Duke of Bedford at Grantham.

[Courtesy Mr J W Belsham.]

'A learned and honest man, but a strange compound of simplicity, drollery, absurdity, ingenuity, superstition and antiquarianism.' That was how Bishop Warburton of Gloucester described his old friend, William Stukeley .

In considering this assessment, it is fascinating to note that in the historical life of a small market town such as Holbeach, there has been room for more than one formidable character capable of academic versatility.

In this respect, Stukeley immediately invites comparison to Sir Norman Angell. Both were born in Holbeach and attended the same school founded by the Farmer bequest. Both developed a taste in literature at an early age. And both went on, with their restless, questioning natures, to depart from careers in which they could have remained comfortable and successful for the rest of their working lives.

Those of us who may have wondered, when speeding down the A14 to the M11, if a sign pointing to 'The Stukeleys' has any connection with Holbeach, can be assured that this is where the story begins. For William's father once told him that 'those towns [Great and Little Stukeley] were the place whence our Name and Family came, and where our Ancestors formerly lived.' In fact, contemporary employees of the family firm humorously referred to these places as 'Adlard' and 'John' Stukeley, after the names of William's uncle and father.

The family establishes itself in Holbeach
Beginning with marriage to an heiress of the Flete family, the Stukeleys secured property in the Holbeach area –'almost all the land for a mile round Holbech Church'– and appear regularly in the Holbeach Register from the late sixteenth century onwards. William's grandfather, John Stukeley, born in Holbeach in 1623, lived the life of a country gentleman with a small estate at Uffington, near Stamford. But as William Stukeley was to observe, his grandfather's rubbing shoulders with local nobility cost him dearly, 'keeping them Company at their Sports & Diversions, Raceing, Hunting, Gameing & the like.' As a result, a significant part of the family estate, including 'the 10 acres now in the possession of Mr Ball wherein is the Mill' and other land in 'Battell fields, Damgate, & the farm between the Vicarage house & Barringtons gate', had to be sold. Grandfather John died insolvent in 1675, which probably explained why his elder son, Adlard, took up law as a means of income.

Adlard Stukeley, who lived at Stukeley House where the Church of England primary school is now situated, ran the practice from this house in conjunction with his younger brother, John. At 29, John married Frances, the 17-year-old daughter of Robert Bullen, of St Lamberts Farm near the sea bank at Weston, and settled in a house on a site very close to the present Littlebury House in

Barrington Gate. Their son, William, was born on 7th November 1687.

As befitted an antiquarian's eye for detail, William is appropriately specific about his own first appearance in the world. We learn from his diaries that the birth took place between '7 and 8 at night…in my Fathers (more probably in my Uncle Stukeleys) house in Holbech, in the chamber the south east corner of the house next the Garden (as I suppose) called the Blue Chamber.' After this, 'I suckt of my Mother about a week and then was brought up by the spoon.' His christening by the vicar, William Pimlow, followed on 21st November. And at the age of 12 months, William assures us, he could walk on his own.

He described his mother as 'the fondest parent in the world, yet she had that peculiarity that she could not show in the common feminine tenderness, so that she scarce in her life ever kisst any of her children, and I remember perfectly well that even at the age of 16 I was a perfect stranger to giving a common salute to a woman.'

From this it can be gathered that William's father was the more inspirational parent, a detail inviting digression at this point. In addition to being a lawyer, John Stukeley was a man of many projects and at the time, few individuals could have imposed their stamp on a town more strongly.

Beginning with his own house and grounds, considerable additions and landscaping were effected to include stables, garden walls, a 'back house', 'Quick' hedges, the planting of ash, oak, elm and walnut and a 'Fine Avenue' leading into the churchyard after the style of a walk created by his father at Uffington near Stamford, not to mention the

raising in level of all his approach roads, involving 'many thousand cartloads of earth'. But John Stukeley's thirst for environmental improvement extended well beyond his own doorstep and also benefited Holbeach at a rate that makes a mockery of today's bureaucratic delays. He built wells in the town –'a great benefit to the Country so scarce of water in summer time'– erected a 'large Mercat Cross' –thus replacing the medieval version he was alleged to have pulled down in 1683– attracted the butter trade to the market and organised a postal service from Spalding.

He was responsible for reviving or bringing into existence two hostelries that are still with us, rebuilding 'the Checquer Inn' – making 'fine vaults of brick'– and building the Rose & Crown. From Sir George Humble he bought some old shops near the bridge and market place, redeveloping the site for five new houses 'at vast expence' with stone from Lincoln, 'fine oak timber from Tumby Wood' and roofing them in a tile or slate not previously seen in the area. To All Saints Church he donated a new reading desk, pulpit and seats, and rebuilt the churchyard wall on the High Street, while organising a collection for rebuilding the vicarage.

Outside the town, he was very active in land reclamation and drainage, obtaining permission from the Spalding Commissioners to install water engines, but his death soon after interrupted the worthwhile progress made. The fruits of his great efforts at tree planting, however, 'vast plantations of young trees', sown from acorns and 'other plants' on the borders of his fields, lived on for long afterwards,

YOUNG WILLIAM STUKELEY'S HOME. John and Frances Stukeley's house in what is now Barrington Gate, approximately on the site of the present Littlebury House. [Courtesy Mr J W Belsham.]

many of them transplanted by William 'to sett in distant places'.

The solitary boy in Whaplode wood

William Stukeley's education began at about the age of three, learning 'the first Rudiments of letters of Mrs Collingwood, an old decayed Gentlewoman of Holbeach, who taught all the Children in the Parish.' He progressed to the Farmer's Free School in 1692, then still conducted in the choir of All Saints Church and with Edward Kelsal as Master. There he was taught to write by Mr Coleman, whose 'mighty knack' with the pen fired William's natural talent for drawing. He attended Mr Butler for dancing practice, and found flute lessons good exercise for his lungs, reputed to be vulnerable in childhood to consumption. Later on, gout, a hereditary complaint, was to trouble him at frequent intervals.

As a bright child, he tended to be a loner. While other boys of his age hunted for birds' nests, William would often disappear into woods near Whaplode to read a good book, studying shrubs and plants, or 'cutting my Name on the bark of trees with the date.' He resumed the company of his classmates when it suited him however, conducting a lucrative trade 'at a reasonable rate' in supplying summaries of the previous Sunday's church sermon to meet the lazier pupils' homework deadlines. William even played truant for three days, 'but was catched by my Father on horseback at an unreasonable hour and place and sent captive to school.'

Living under the roof of a materially successful parent was not without its fears for the teenage Stukeley. At the age of 15 he claimed to have had a dream, for four or five nights running, that the house was being robbed, causing him to wake up with a start.

On the one night he did sleep soundly, he was roused by the maid knocking on his door to say that the house had been 'plundered' by two or three horsemen seen in the yard and garden. John Stukeley's desk in the study had been broken open, money and plate taken, and to William's greatest regret, 'a silver-edged hat –the first and only one I ever had', was also stolen.

On leaving school at the top of his class, William began employment with the family law firm at the age of 13. But the routine soon began to pall, enlivened only by the surreptitious reading of schoolbooks smuggled into the office, and visits on business to London, where he was able to clamber around the scaffolding of the new St Paul's Cathedral, then still several years from completion. By the time he was 16, a greater interest in medicine had won the day, so his younger brother John took his place in the office at Holbeach and with his father's agreement, William entered Corpus Christi College, Cambridge in November 1703.

University dissections 1703-1708

The value of dissection and chemical experiments were just beginning to be recognised and at Cambridge a laboratory was created from an old lumber-house in Trinity, supervised by the learned but alchoholic Italian Professor Vigani. So intense was Stukeley's interest in botany and anatomy during his studies that he resorted to stealing dogs for dissection, a practice perfected just before graduating, when he visited Holbeach and dissected 'Old Hoyes', a local character who had been buried at the roadside after hanging himself. By the standards of the time Stukeley's action was not as outrageous as it sounds, for in London it had already become accepted practice, after hangings at Tyburn, to pass on the corpses, often over the shoulders of the crowd, for transporting away and dissection by surgeons. In any event, Holbeach vagrancy had never been so honoured, for, following the dissection, Stukeley had Hoyes' bones mounted in a specially-inscribed glass case as a bizarre gesture of gratitude.

Mixing medicine and antiquities

Leaving Cambridge in 1708 and rapidly building a reputation that afforded him an early Fellowship of the Royal College of Physicians, William Stukeley practised medicine in Boston and London between 1710 and 1726. With one of his acquaintances, Sir Isaac Newton, he became an early member of the Spalding Gentlemen's Society, founded in 1710 and where his letters to the founder, Maurice Johnson, survive. During this period, having built so much on the youthful interest first promoted by his father in studying inscriptions in Gedney and Holbeach churches, he was a prime mover in establishing the Society of Antiquaries of London, acting as its secretary for several years from 1717.

The Society aimed to cater for those interested in both Greek and Roman civilisation and the ancient history of Britain, moralising that 'the History of a man's own Country is (or should be) dearer to him than that of Foreign Regions.' Here Stukeley led by example, describing in his first antiquarian work his visit to the famous Arthur's Oven in Scotland. Then with his friend, George Gale, he rode the whole length of Hadrian's Wall, recording the experience with detailed notes and drawings. Geological opinion is colourfully evident, too, on his journey to Edmondthorpe (between Stamford and Melton Mowbray) in Leicestershire, where he saw 'some huge and perfect scallop-shells, antidiluvian [sic], in the stone. I know Leicestershire consists of a red stone, brimful of the petrified shells of the old world, especially all round the bottom of the great cliff, which generally bounds Lincolnshire and that county.'

First to interpret the crop ring?

Stukeley is also credited with being the first person to observe the significance of a crop ring, at Great Chesterford, Essex, in 1719, and all without the benefit of today's aerial reconnaissance. 'I summoned some of the country people', recalled Stukeley, 'and over a pot and a pipe, fished out what I could from their discourse, as we sat surveying the corn growing on the spot...The most charming sight that can be imagined in the perfect vestigia of a [Roman] temple, as easily discernible in the corn as upon paper...'

Further archaeology, Roman Knights and speculation

This and other accounts of Stukeley's antiquarian travels all over England appear in his *Itinerarium Curiosum,* published in two parts in 1724 and posthumously, 1776. This second edition is known as the *Centuria,* and recognised since Victorian times as the more collectable. While his

interest in British archaeology was wide-ranging, from prehistoric to medieval periods, Stukeley and some of his friends were keen to promote a greater interest in Roman matters to the extent of founding another club, the intriguing but short-lived Society of Roman Knights. Its members assumed Celtic names associated with the Roman conquest, Stukeley's wife Frances being known as Cartismandua.

With the wane of the Roman Knights, Stukeley devoted much energy between 1722–1724 to visiting and recording archaeological findings at Stonehenge and Avebury, an involvement in the subject

IN THE STYLE OF THE TIME. *Stukeley's artwork for a map in 1723 adhered faithfully to the eighteenth-century romantic-decorative.*

which earned him the nickname of 'Arch-Druid'. He was the first to investigate the burial mounds of that neighbourhood, and his engravings and restoration work at Stonehenge were regarded as valuable.

But his two essays on the subject bordered on airy speculation, a tendency which attracted criticism at this and other stages in his life, as when his *Account of the Medallic History of Marcus Aurelius Valerius Carausius, Emperor of Britain* was published in 1758. It later prompted the eighteenth-century historian Edward Gibbon, author of *The History of the Decline and Fall of the Roman Empire* (six volumes, 1776-88) to say: 'I have used his materials and rejected most of his fanciful conjectures.' Horace Walpole (1717-97), politician and distinguished man of letters, was similarly sceptical when it came to Stukeley's views on earthquakes: 'One Stukeley…has accounted for it, and I think prettily, by electricity –but that is the fashionable cause, and everything is resolved into electrical appearances.' However, without Stukeley's observations, occasionally flawed though they may have been, much valuable matter would have gone unrecorded for ever. What should not be forgotten is that he and his like-minded contemporaries represented a movement that resolved to go out into the field and find out for itself, and apply as intelligent a construction as possible to those findings, rather than accept the lore handed down over centuries.

A change of direction, 1729

After moving to Grantham in 1726 to continue his medical practice, Stukeley felt obliged to take stock of his position. For one thing, his work on the Druids had inspired him to study Christian principles in some depth, and increasingly, he was 'becominge enamoured therewith'. For another, he may also have felt, after a mixed reception in Grantham, that it was time to move on. Environmentally, the town had suited him very well, the 'great cascade' of the River Witham providing a soothing aural background, and in season 'all the roads round us …so thick with violets that you can scarce bear the fragrancy.' His garden, too, was a mixture of the romantic and the practical, a woodland Druid temple, 'stations of dyals, urns and statues ' providing the unlikely setting for 'vegetable experiments' and 'inoculating mistletoe.' But naturalists were still treated with suspicion in the eighteenth century, of which the horned owl incident was a sober reminder. The Duchess of Ancaster had presented Stukeley with such a bird, but when it died and he buried it in his garden, the Grantham gentry displayed righteous indignation and encouraged a mob to hurl abuse at him. 'The truth was they were glad of so trifling a handle to show their envy and malice', he remarked afterwards. And so, encouraged

by Archbishop Wake, he entered the clergy in 1729.

After ordination at Croydon, he was soon back in Lincolnshire, this time at All Saints, Stamford, and appropriately accommodated, for a man of his antiquarian leanings, atop Barn Hill in a house where King Charles I had slept his last night as free man. As a continuation of his landscaping indulgences at Grantham, Stukeley spent his 18 years' residence in Stamford beautifying his home and grounds in equal priority to his involvement in the town's public life, social and musical societies. Obviously proud of occupying a house with such a famous royal connection, he enhanced the top of an arched gateway, through which Charles had entered incognito a century earlier, with a battlement carrying the Stukeley coat of arms and the year in which he completed this work –1746– 'In the victorious year of Culloden', the battle which ended the Stuarts' claim to the throne.

Small wonder then that with such a taste for beautifying and embellishment, Stukeley should be so appalled to visit Holbeach the following year and find alterations inflicted on his parents' old home by a new occupant. One of the first things new houseowners often seem to do is chop down trees, and it was just the same in 1747. 'I saw with the greatest indignation,' wrote Stukeley, ' the fine grove planted by my father, and called the Walk…cutt down. The whole beautiful plantation is not only cutt down, but the very roots dug up, and the town robbed of this elegant ornament, which was the common Mall of the place. It was done by the present owner –Cleypon, of Spalding, a stupid penurious wretch.'

Final years

Stukeley had married in 1728 at the age of 41 to Frances Williamson, who bore him three daughters. But Frances died nine years later in Stamford and he remarried in 1739, to Elizabeth Gale, daughter of the Dean of York. His Stamford incumbency, coinciding with national recognition as an authority on antiquities, ended with his being offered the Rectory of St George the Martyr, in Queen's Square, London. He had obtained this living from the Duke of Montague, whom he had met some years earlier as a fellow founder of the Egyptian Society. An obvious admirer of the Duke, Stukeley flattered himself that he had a fair amount in common with him, once writing in his 'Common Place Book':

'I have often observed a strange similitude of disposition between the Duke and Myself – the same desire of being in Company of those that know more than oneself – the same Philosophic disposition – the same natural modesty and regard for the fair sex – thinking there is generally somewhat divine in them'. From this point on, however, the comparisons become so virtuous and faultless that those who did not know him well could have been excused for considering him totally immodest!

Stukeley was to remain in the capital from 1748 for the rest of his life. As a younger man he had sought, soon after graduation, a country life in which 'To better my fortunes and at the same time indulge' in its simplicity.

But passing years had modified this view considerably, to the extent of condemning the country dwellers' traditional attitude to people and matters they did not understand. 'After 20 years' experience', he wrote, 'I find the insufficiency of the Country life to answer the purpose of one of my turn and taste. Though no one could relish it better, yet, for want of proper relief and variety, in good company and ingenious conversation, the faculties of the mind sink and flag, and at best such an one can be but said to live a dead life there…Nay, the people in the Country are so far from endeavouring to make themselves agreeable to one of that sort of genius, that they shun and avoyd you; and will by no means herd with you in a familiar way, as conscious of their inability to please.'

As if to support Stukeley's argument, a letter from his friend George Arnet in 1734 read: 'I hear sometimes from Holbeach, and I hear it is a declining town. Thank God I have left it, and set my feet upon a rock. I was, before I left Holland, up to the neck in quagmires, and I should, before now, have been over head.'

London, therefore, suited Stukeley's final needs: 'I love solitude in London, and the beauty of living there is, that we can mix in company in solitude in just proportion; whilst in the country we have nothing else but solitude.' His routine became less concentrated, and he developed the habit of retiring every evening at six-o'-clock with 'his contemplative pipe'.

William Stukeley died of a stroke on 3rd March 1765 at the age of 77 and was buried in the churchyard at East Ham, in a grave unmarked at his request. For such a multi-faceted character, whose fascination with life ranged from antediluvian scallop shells and the velocity of gun charges, to the artificial hatching of eggs and his interrupting of a church service to allow his congregation to view an eclipse, it was indeed a modest end.

♣ ♣ ♣ ♣ ♣ ♣

Henry Peet, 1856-1938

Besides William Stukeley, Holbeach's other antiquarian was Henry Peet, born on 16th April 1856, the son of Mr Major Flintham Peet, a High Street merchant. He was descended on his mother's side from the Huguenot De Vantier family, who had settled in Thorney.

Educated at Gosberton Hall School and Westminster, he moved to Liverpool as a young man and set up as a chemist. As a reputable businessman, he soon involved himself in public life, becoming a churchwarden of Liverpool Parish and from 1894, a Justice of the Peace. As a member of the city's judiciary, he was involved in administrating the Lunacy Act of 1890, and was chairman of the Warwick Charitable Trustees.

In his leisure time, Peet, like Stukeley, enjoyed travel, antiquities and archaeology, following William's footsteps into Fellowship of the Society of Antiquaries of London. Also a member of the Huguenot

Society, he wrote articles on a variety of historical subjects, acknowledged his roots with a book on *The Architectural History of Holbeach Church* (1890), and contributed to the content of *Lincolnshire Notes and Queries*, an informative series of volumes published from the 1890s onwards. This was followed by his *History of the Huguenot Family of De Vantier* (1902), and the *Register of the French Church of Thorney Abbey with a History of the Huguenot Settlement There*. Another contribution to Lincolnshire local history were his observations on the parish registers of Horbling, presented to Lincoln Public Library in 1903.

Peet married Charlotte Tinsley, who died in 1902 at the age of only 46. He outlived her by 36 years, ending his days at Birkenhead, although he was buried with his wife in Holbeach Cemetery. A memorial tablet to him can be found at the west end of the nave, on the wall near the entrance to the Mary Bass Room.

♣ ♣ ♣ ♣ ♣ ♣

Susannah Centlivre

1667-1723

An exotic name for a mere Holbeachian, and a ground-breaker in her field. Like many other ladies of Holbeach past and present, she was a woman in a man's world, except that instead of, say, working on the land, her recognition came as an actress and dramatist at a time of change in the English theatre.

Described as a mannish-looking woman who delighted in playing men's parts, she was baptised at Whaplode in 1669 and is said to have been the daughter of a well-to-do William Freeman of Holbeach, while her mother, Anne, née Marham or Markham, came from an equally prosperous background in King's Lynn. After Charles II's Restoration in 1660, however, the Freeman's unsympathetic religious and political convictions forced them to flee to Ireland, following which, accounts of Susannah's early life history become

conflicting and vague. Nevertheless, it makes a good improbable story, rather akin to Margaret Lockwood's role in the old Gainsborough film of *The Wicked Lady*. One account has her running away from home, dressing as a boy and living in Cambridge, where she came under the guardianship of Anthony Hammond, later to become Commissioner for the Navy. Another talks of a relationship and possible marriage with the nephew of Sir Stephen Fox, and a similar liaison a little later with an officer named Carroll, who died in a duel. If some of this is approximately true, then it gives credence to the view expressed in Boyers' *Political State* that after various colourful adventures she had 'so improved her natural genius by reading and good conversation, as to attempt to write for the stage, in which she had as good success of any of her sex before her'.

'Ingenious and sprightly'

In the late seventeenth and early eighteenth centuries, a woman featuring in English theatricals was still a novelty. Until an unknown actress played Desdemona in *Othello* in December 1660, no women had been seen on a London stage. But after the Cromwellian years of prohibited performances the theatre enjoyed a revival at the Restoration, from which it never looked back.

By the early Queen Anne period, Susannah was at her most prolific, delivering productions audiences most wanted to see – comedies of manners and social or political satires. A foppish high society that drank champagne from ladies' shoes or fried them in batter as a delicacy was up for ridicule, and playwrights like Susannah could combine these situations with an astute political awareness to produce plays that, while they were not always original, were in the main successful and acknowledged as 'ingenious and sprightly'. Of the 19 plays she wrote, 15 were performed, mainly in the provinces. Her best productions were *The Busie Body* (1709) –although 'so coldly regarded by the actors that Wilks is said to have thrown down his part as Sir George Airy', *The Wonder, a Woman Keeps a Secret* (1714), in which David Garrick, one of the most famous actors of the mid-eighteenth century, noted for speaking his lines in a natural instead of declamatory style, later played Don Felix, and *A Bold stroke for a Wife* (1718).

In 1706 she married Joseph Centlivre, cook to Queen Anne at Windsor, and settled in Buckingham Court, Spring Gardens, London, where she died in 1723 at the age of 56. She left a lot of valuables presented to her by the royalty and aristocracy, to whom she dedicated many of her plays.

♣♣♣♣♣♣

William Rippin, the blind watchmaker

1815 - 1857

William Rippin was a man with time on his hands in a different way. He knew exactly how to apply the right touch to the innards of a clock or watch to make it work again – yet he was blind for most of his working life.

Born in Spalding, and following the family tradition, he began a watchmaker's business in his early twenties in Holbeach High Street. But at the age of 28, he contracted an infection that defeated the efforts of leading oculists of the day, resulting in amaurosis, a form of blindness which, ironically, left the outward appearance of the eye unaffected.

Rippin, however, was made of sterner stuff than many who would have quite naturally despaired of the situation and relied on the parish to support them. After much perseverance he developed his sense of touch to such a degree that he was able to clean timepieces –and work on musical instruments, too– as well as, if not better than, before. The only procedure with which he needed help was the pinning and unpinning of a hair-spring, which he had trained his wife to perform. The customers meanwhile had every confidence in him, his daughter estimating his average workload at 100 watches in the shop at any one time, some brought from as far away as 200 miles for his expert attention.

Five feet ten inches in height and described as of 'splendid physique' and 'possessed [of] very intelligent and handsome features', Rippin was certainly known of nationally, for he was mentioned in the *Illustrated London News* of 23rd August 1851, when it was stated: 'Some years previously, Rippin was robbed and the property taken from him consisted of watch wheels, hair-springs and other tiny things belonging to the trade. The thief was traced and convicted at Spalding Sessions, the blind man having sworn to his property by feeling'.

His expertise did not end there, for in his leisure time he could play cards, dominoes, bagatelle and was able to carry on both as a musician, leading the Holbeach Brass Band, and a cricketer, winning two single wicket matches. After his early death at the age of 42 on 12th October 1857 –resulting, it was claimed, from 'the severe treatment' he had undergone in attempts to restore his sight, members of the family continued two watchmaking businesses in the High Street: that of James Rippin, also listed as landlord of the Horse & Groom in 1882, and Mrs Ann Rippin, who in the same year was trading from the Old Market House, and who lived on to the age of 83 in 1893. In All Saints Church, a stained glass window was installed (the last one in the north aisle, on your

RIPPIN'S WINDOW. Donated by daughter Anne and situated in the Church's north aisle.

left, as you enter by the north door) during the 1890s, to the memory of William and Ann Rippin –a gift from their daughter, Anne.

♣♣♣♣♣♣

Henry Rands

Henry Rands was born in Holbeach and began his ecclesiastical career as a monk at Crowland Abbey. He was both a Bachelor of Divinity and a Doctor of Divinity, but the name of the Cambridge college where he qualified is not known. He was however, Prior of Buckingham College, a Benedictine house at Cambridge. Subsequently he became Prior of Worcester, then Suffragen Bishop of Bristol, rising further to First Dean of Worcester and King's Almoner. Ultimately Bishop of Lincoln, he assumed the title of Henry Holbeach, dying in 1551. By then he was somewhat discredited, having profited from selling Church property to the Crown. But Rands' worthier achievements included a joint compilation of the Liturgy (church service) and the creation of a Hebrew lexicon which, it was maintained by a John Pitts, was plagiarised by Robert Wakefield, the first Hebrew professor at Cambridge.

♣ ♣ ♣ ♣ ♣ ♣

Bartholomew, Edward and John Northon

The Northon name appears frequently in deeds and documents relating to Holbeach, notably in the eighteenth and nineteenth centuries. Under the tower in All Saints Church, Bartholomew Northon, a well-to-do merchant, is recorded as having died at the age of 42 in April 1763.

Meanwhile, Captain Edward Northon, who lived through the same period, was a local public figure of some importance. His name was recorded on the first and seventh church bells, towards the cost of which he contributed, and he was also an agent of Farmer's Free School. It is likely that Northons Lane was named after him and a tablet in his memory was placed in the south aisle of the church after he died in April 1797, aged 60.

Close by, buried under the floor of the south aisle, is a more recent member of the family, the Revd John Northon, who was Curate of Gedney Church for over 40 years, and died at the age of 68 in 1814.

The Revd Grant Macdonald

1846-1923

It is fitting that 'Holbeach's only authentic historian', as he has been described, should find a place in this book.

Born in India into a large family, he was related to Flora Macdonald, who had helped Charles Edward Stuart, the Young Pretender, escape to Skye after the Battle of Culloden on 1746. He was educated at Cheltenham College and St Mary Hall, Oxford after which he was ordained, aged 25, at Grantham in 1871.

Curate at Holbeach between 1871 and 1879, Macdonald began collecting information on Holbeach clergy from the 1225 period onwards, and after researches which led him not only to parish registers, but to manuscripts at Lincoln Cathedral, the British Museum and the Public Record Office, this blossomed into a much larger project, culminating after 11 years into *Historical Notices of the Parish of Holbeach in the County of Lincoln, with Memorials of its Clergy from 1225 AD to the Present Time*. By this time he was Vicar of Holbeach St Marks (1879-1897), from where he went on to St Johns Spalding until 1913. He married Louisa Edith Benn-Russell in 1872, and there were ten children by the marriage.

♣ ♣ ♣ ♣ ♣ ♣

The Harrisson Family

The Harrissons and the Carters go back several centuries as major property and landowners, both in Holbeach, and within a ten-mile radius to the west and southern sides of the town, including Spalding, Weston, Moulton, Whaplode, Sutton St Edmund, Sutton St James, Tydd St Giles and Tydd St Mary.

It was thought that the Harrissons' presence in Holbeach originated from the late eighteenth century when Joseph (1769-1809) and Robert Harrisson (1771-1804) from Tydd St Mary married Charlotte and Margaret, daughters of Thomas and Sarah Everson (née Sturton) of Stukeley House. A map of 1828 also shows a large area marked 'Harrisson's Farm', off Hallgate.

JOINT MEMORIAL. The Harrisson and Carter plot in Holbeach Cemetery.

The Harrissons' connections with the Carters began during the lifetime of John Carter, a brewer of 1 Fleet Street, who from the 1840s extended the family's empire by buying further land and local properties, investing brewery profits in a large network of public houses. Subsequently, this infrastructure provided valuable settlements in the 1870s, which were divided between his son and daughter, John Hardy and Emma Jane Carter.

Milling interests
Over 1867 and 1868 both Emma Jane and John Hardy Carter married into the Harrisson family, who had substantial farming interests, thus forging an even stronger commercial alliance. The Harrissons were also involved in milling, the business at Barrington Gate begun by Frederick Adolphus Harrisson in 1828, but appearing solely in Mrs Louisa Harrisson's name in trade directories from the 1850s to the 1880s. During this time Louisa lived in the elegant Georgian house next door to the

mill. Continuing the farming and milling tradition, Frederick Augustus Harrisson (1833-1890) and his new wife Emma Jane lived at Mattimore House. Mattimore was inherited by their son John Christopher, and on his death in 1928, it was bought by Florence Gertrude Wright, mother-in-law of C J Harrisson (son of Christopher Charles), who occupied it until the war years. Later on Mattimore House became the East Elloe Rural District Council offices, before its demolition in 1980.

Meanwhile John Hardy Carter, who had married Frances Charlotte, daughter of Alfred Harrisson, followed in his father's footsteps as an acquisitive brewer. He lived in Barrington Gate, carrying on his main business where High Street becomes Fleet Street (on the present Somerfield site), and was listed in Kelly's Directory of 1889 as one of the main landowners in Holbeach.

Septimus the solicitor
Emma Jane Harrisson died in 1916. There were 11 pregnancies, but only seven children survived. She had five sons, one of whom carried on farming –Christopher Charles, at Holbeach Hurn– while the four others went into the professions. Alfred Everson –who once delivered quads at St Neots– and Ernest Henry took up medicine, while Lenny Septimus –so named because he was the seventh child, later known in the family as 'Uncle Sep'– and John Carter Harrisson became solicitors. The latter had offices in the High Street (later acquired by Mossop & Bowser circa 1955-60), while 'Uncle Sep's' practice survives to this day in Woodbridge, Suffolk as Cooper & Harrisson.

In addition to their legal duties. Lenny and John served the town as clerks to various local bodies, and from 1911 both brothers acted as Vestry Clerk, John succeeding Lenny in the post in 1920. John was also Clerk to the Governors of Holbeach Grammar School and Clerk to the Farmer Education Foundation, thus providing him with an ability that was to suit him admirably during the Great War as keeper of the letter book to the 1st Battalion Lincolnshire Volunteer Regiment between 1917 and 1920, in which he served as a

Second Lieutenant. It may have been in this period that he lost a leg, as there exists a letter written to him in the 1920s, apologising for having previously invited JCH to participate in some sporting activity, unaware of his 'disability'.

Sporting prowess

Earlier on however, John Carter Harrison seemed to have had the midas touch in several other directions. After education at Wisbech Grammar School, this eldest son of the family achieved a first class honours degree at Magdalen College Oxford and distinguished himself in various sports, notably cricket and football. The family were very sport-minded, and had even formed their own team against Holbeach Rangers on occasion in the 1890s, captained by Alfred Harrisson (a football 'Blue' at Cambridge University) and 'composed of picked men' from Wisbech St Augustine, Holbeach, Spalding and Boston.

When part of the Holbeach Rangers team in the Nineties, John Harrisson played in goal, with his father, 'F A', on the wing. One or two of these matches generated a certain amount of controversy. It was common to see in contemporary press match reports phrases like, 'Complaints were loudly indulged in by the spectators', but in early 1893 it was the team's turn to complain: about the match they had lost 2-0 against Horncastle Town Gridirons. Holbeach claimed that one of the Horncastle team should have been barred from the field because he had played during the closed season. The case was serious enough to be heard by the Lincolnshire Football Association at Lincoln, but the protest was not upheld. Instead, it was agreed that the two teams should bury the hatchet in a friendly match that April. This proved something of a travelling marathon for Holbeach, for non-existent train services forced them to rely on horse transport after Spalding, setting out at 11 a.m., and not returning home until the same hour that evening. They lost the match, but at least Horncastle had paid Rangers' £3 expenses as part of the arrangement!

'J C' also played golf, as did his brothers Christopher and Lenny. But it was in cricket that one sees him constantly mentioned in late-nineteenth and early-twentieth century reports. In 1891, for instance, as captain, he was described as 'instrumental in giving a stimulus to cricket in Holbeach'. Although bowled by Godefroy for 11 in the Married v Single match in May 1895, he scored the most runs of his side and helped to win the match for the Singles. His finest hour must have come in May 1906, when he scored a century against Holbeach Hurn.

♣ ♣ ♣ ♣ ♣

Herbert Carter, OBE, JP

1862-1944

Carter's Park owes its name to a self-made agriculturalist who became one of the town's greatest benefactors: Herbert Parkinson Carter, who was born in Spilsby in 1862.

PORTRAIT OF A BENEFACTOR. Carter's picture watches over the Tuesday tea dancers in the Women's Institute.

Educated at Burgh training college and Lindum House, Lincoln, he came to Holbeach at the age of 23 with very little capital and in the middle of an agricultural slump, to take up farming at Holbeach Marsh and the Hurn. He married twice: to Annie Caudwell of Old Leake in 1886, and secondly to Frances Ethel Orr, a South African who involved herself equally in Holbeach life. As Founder-President of the Women's Institute in Park Road, Ethel largely funded its building costs herself, and was also Founder-President of the Holbeach Amateur Dramatic and Operatic Society, and chairperson of the local Conservative Association.

Early success

Herbert Carter's first farm at Holbeach Hurn was the springboard to further acquisitions of land, to the extent that he soon owned 2,000 acres locally and was joint owner and tenant of an additional 1,500 acres with

Arthur Hovenden Worth at Eastville and Wainfleet. Like Worth, Carter pioneered large-scale methods of potato-growing and as early as World War One was ahead of his time in believing that farmers and growers should form co-operatives to weather the difficult times ahead. From the very beginning, he possessed the ability to 'think in Continents', and as an arch-delegator, could boast of farming the whole of Lincolnshire with just 'a telephone and a motor car'. Indeed, so confident was he of his success that he was even quoted as saying that he did not mind coming across employees 'playing' in the fields instead of working, 'as long as I am making a profit'. Other sweeping statements of his, when aimed at the farming community at large, did not always find favour. In 1913, for instance, the normally reserved John Sharp Patchett Junior, who farmed at Fleet, took issue with him over Carter's generalisation that land preserved for game was chiefly poor soil and unsuitable for cultivation.

Welfare and community involvement

The paternalistic side to Carter inspired him seriously to consider forming an agrarian party to look after farmers' and workers' interests, but this did not materialise, largely due to the land-workers' traditional preference for the Labour party to champion their cause. However in 1918, as an immediate sequel to his ubiqitous presence on local war and war agricultural committees between 1914-18, Carter became the first Chairman of the Holland branch of the National Farmers' Union, a position he held until 1934. He was also at various times a member of the General Purposes Committee, a Governor of Holbeach Grammar School and a churchwarden at Holbeach St Lukes.

Trappings of success

His leisure pursuits included those of shooting, cricket, motoring and croquet, and predictably he did not do things by halves when it came to private residences. His first home in Holbeach was Abbots Manor in Spalding Road (now Mossop & Bowser's offices). But his eye for architectural aesthetics may not quite have matched his business acumen, for he later moved across the road to Stukeley House, renamed it Stukeley Hall and considerably altered its appearance in the early 1920s to a contemporary style, which the historian Nikolaus Pevsner described as 'muddled magpie', although he was gracious enough to admire the stable block's 'dinky lantern'.

Despite Carter's changes to its appearance, he ensured that Stukeley Hall continued to stand in meticulously-tended and landscaped grounds. It was requisitioned during the war as a retirement home, and in its latter years was also adapted as the fire and ambulance station, finally to be demolished in 1993 to make way for the new William Stukeley school.

Donates Carter's Park, 1929

Carter's lasting memorial to the town, however, was Carter's Park, land that had been used variously for sports and grazing into the early 1920s, but not adapted in any specific shape or form. He bought the land for £2,000, oversaw its development, and paid off any additional expenses incurred before presenting the park to the Holbeach Urban Council in 1929.

It was about this time that hard work was beginning to take its toll, and with health problems threatening, Carter was forced to resign from much of his committee work. Meanwhile, both his children had died: Frank during the First World War, and Dorothy Carter, a spinster who lived at Red Roofs in Fleet Road (now renamed Holbeach Manor) in July 1936.

Dorothy was a philanthropist in her own right. Under arrangements which became operative after her father's death, she left £5,000 and £500 to All Saints and Holbeach Hurn Churches respectively, and £10,000 towards the building of a maternity hospital in Holbeach (now the hospital in Boston Road). Her chauffeur, Stanley Goate, who lived opposite in Alpha Cottages (in later years Mrs Dorothy Crawford's house) inherited her small car.

For Herbert it seemed time for a change of scene in retirement. Shortly before the second war, he returned with his wife to her native South Africa, where they settled in Johannesburg. Florence was to outlive him by 22 years, for this 'prince among men', as an obituary styled him, died in July 1944.

♣ ♣ ♣ ♣ ♣ ♣

Kathleen Major
1906-2000

'In the Kingdom of Thy grace
Give this little girl a place.'

An average child would have recited those lines countless times without once considering their meaning. But for a certain small girl, returning from All Saints Church Sunday School sometime in 1910, this wasn't enough.

'Why does that little girl always ask for a place? Why does she never ask for haddock?' she asked her nurse.

Early intelligence
Even at four years old, her mind was showing signs of logic and great intelligence. For Kathleen Major's career as a distinguished medieval historian, college principal and an accomplished and fair administrator place her on a podium with Sir Norman Angell and William Stukeley when it comes to Holbeach's most outstanding academics.

In this she was entirely self-made. Her father, George Major, was one of three brothers who sought their fortune in London, first with a stall, and then a shop, selling agricultural produce in Covent Garden. The venture was successful enough to enable the brothers to buy land in the Holbeach district, Whaplode Marsh and Newton to grow their own potatoes, and until the 1970s Major Bros kept a warehouse in Barrington Gate, behind what is now the Secondhand Land shop.

The family home was at Abbots Manor on Spalding Road, formerly the residence of Herbert Carter and a large house that her mother was to adapt as a hospital supply depot during the second world war. After the Majors moved out, it became a hotel, then the Milroy Country Club during the 60s and 70s and ultimately, Mossop & Bowser's offices. Educated at Wilton House School,

Reading, Kathleen went up to Oxford in 1925 to read history, thus beginning a 40-year association with St Hilda's College as undergraduate, graduate, Librarian, Fellow and Principal, before leaving to take up the vice-chancellorship of Nottingham University.

Dedicated interest in medieval history develops
Kathleen's taste for medieval history was inspired by the teaching of Agnes Leys and Sir Maurice Powicke. The first daunting challenge she set herself, with the support of Sir Frank Stenton, was to collect and edit details of all the charters issued to churches around the country by Stephen Langton, Archbishop of Canterbury between 1207 and 1228. This was easier said than done, for it involved an exhaustive tour of cathedral archives all over England.

The analysis of medieval documents is not an over-subscribed subject among students of history, but Katheen Major's grounding in the essentials of Diplomatic, a curiously-named subject to do with the study and purpose of official records, equipped her with the right approach to make that difficult first step which, once negotiated, brought her into direct contact with the minds and intentions of the persons who had drafted those manuscripts so many centuries ago – an aspect which brought her the greatest sense of fulfilment, alongside dealing with 'eccentric canons and curmudgeonly clerks': personalities little different, in fact, from their ancestral office-holders, and perpetuating a largely unaltered ecclesiastical system.

Published works
Her work on the Langton project brought her to the Lincoln diocese, and to the notice of Canon C W Foster. Since 1916 he had been committed to a marathon of his own entitled the *Registrum Antiquissimum*, which was to involve the editing and publishing of 3,000 documents from 1072 to the mid-thirteenth century, all relating to Lincoln Cathedral and its extensive medieval diocese, which at one time stretched from the Humber to the source of the Thames. Impressed by the young Miss Major's track record, Foster enlisted her help as assistant

editor of the *Registrum*. Unfortunately he died in 1935 with only three volumes published, but Kathleen Major took over and triumphantly completed the task, six volumes and 38 years later. It had been a labour of love, requiring many returns to Lincoln over the years, compared with which, her university careers at Oxford and Nottingham –dedicated as she was to them– intervened almost as interruptions. So it was fitting that the Langton and Lincoln works eventually won her the recognition she deserved as a Fellow of the British Academy in 1977. But Major published several other specialist works, such as *A Handlist of the Records of the Bishop of Lincoln* (1953), *The Office of Chapter Clerk at Lincoln in the Middle Ages* (1950), *The Finances of the Dean and Chapter of Lincoln from the 12th to 15th Century; a Preliminary Survey* (1954), *Blyborough Charters, a Medieval Miscellany* (1960), *The Teaching and Study of Diplomatic in England* (1968), *Minster Yard* (1974), *The D'Oyrys of S Lincolnshire, Norfolk and Holderness, 1130-1275* (1984), and in conjunction with S R Jones and J Varley, *A Survey of the Ancient Houses of Lincoln* (1984-90).

Holbeach however was not neglected, for she also wrote *The Story of All Saints' Church, Holbeach,* and researched the history of Conan, son of Ellis, whom she identified as the most influential inhabitant of Holbeach in the late twelfth and early thirteenth centuries.

Personality
Major's disciplined approach to study and research, combined with a competence in financial management probably inherited from her father, stood her in good stead after her appointment as Principal of St Hilda's in 1955. Up until that time Oxford's only all-female College had not been entirely self-governing: a situation that Kathleen Major with her democratic outlook set out to change, by introducing a more workable administrative system and ensuring that junior fellows had as much say as their senior equivalents. And when in 1965 the beneficial effects of a comprehensive College rebuilding programme –including the new Wolfson residential block to house all its own undergraduates– were threatened by the City's plans for a dual carriageway, her protest that, 'The ruin of this college, for the sake of some motorists to make a slightly more convenient journey, would stand as a monument to the false values of our age', resulted in the scheme being abandoned.

St Hilda's, which in recent years has included the Labour MP Helen Jackson and TV journalist Zeinab Badawi among its alumni, is still run on broadly the same lines as those established by Major in the 1950s and 60s, an achievement she managed against a background of trying to look after her ailing mother, once a staunch contributor to the Holbeach war effort, but by then living in Nottingham and expecting the full attention of both Kathleen and her younger sister.

In appearance perhaps the stereotype of the spinster academic, many found Kathleen Major's lofty presence rather awesome, with her formal manners and intolerance of those who failed to think a problem through. Yet she was basically a shy person and paradoxically, it was troublesome or problem students who experienced her most human side. On these occasions she was always prepared to give someone a second chance and even offer them financial help.

'Retirement' in Lincoln
After her retirement from Nottingham University in 1971, Kathleen Major took an active part in the establishment of county record offices, of which Lincoln's in particular is a testimony to her work in this sphere. This city, which had been the nucleus of her personal studies for so long, had already become her home, thanks to a father who, enlightened enough before the age of equality to believe that even single women should be independent, arranged to have a house built for her in Queensway many years previously.

She continued to be a loyal and generous friend, especially to those who shared her historical interests, and after her death in December 2000 it was appropriate to recall the tribute paid to her almost 30 years earlier by Nottingham University: 'All who have worked with her, as pupils or colleagues, have learnt to respect the extent and depth of her knowledge, her sound judgement, and her unshakable scholarly integrity'.

Burges
–one of the oldest names in Holbeach
Cast your eye over most of the substantial fencing to be found in and around Holbeach, and it is very likely that much of it will have been created and put up by Tim Burges, of Spalding Road. What may not be generally realised however, is that his is one of the oldest family names in Holbeach, which can be traced back at least as far as a 1619 entry in the Parish Register to Bridget, daughter of Benjamin and Elizabeth Burges.

Furthermore, while other familiar local names may have been modified since that time, such as 'Curtice' to 'Curtis', or 'Croson' to 'Crowson', 'Burges' has retained its original spelling and not assumed an additional 's'. Some say the name is of Flemish extraction –'Bruges'– while others have suggested a Spanish origin, as in 'Burgos'.

Either way, there has been no sitting on the fence where the deeds of the Burges ancestors were concerned. William Burges was a tenant of the Duke of Somerset at Hurdletree Farm for some 50 years during the nineteenth century, and retired to a house he had built in Fleet Road, which still exists, called Ravendale, after his wife's maiden name. He was a direct descendant of the Revd Octavius Burges, who as Chaplain in Ordinary to Charles I, was appointed by the King to be the 'arbitrator of religious controversies' and was a special preacher at St Paul's Cathedral until the King's death, after which he removed to Ireland.

In 1832 William himself was the subject of religious controversy when he left the Church of England after it refused to recognise him as a lay preacher, but he rejoined the fold when the Duke of Somerset threatened him with the loss of his farm if he did not re-occupy his appointed pew in church.

Other Burges men fought battles of a different kind. Richard Rundle Burges, 45-year-old Captain of HMS *Ardent*, died a hero fighting the Dutch near Camperdown

on 11th October 1797, when he was 'cut in two by a chain shot'. His ship, disadvantaged by having one of the smallest crews in Admiral Duncan's fleet, got in among the enemy closer than instructed to ensure every shot went home, and continued in action until it was reduced to a total wreck with 98

'I ALWAYS HOPE FOR THE BEST'.
The Burges family crest.
[Courtesy Tim Burges.]

cannon balls embedded in it, at a cost of 148 men killed and wounded. A monument to Burges was installed in the nave of St Paul's Cathedral, where, it was recorded, 'His skill, coolness and intrepidity immensely contributed to a victory equally advantageous and glorious to his country.'

Some 50 years earlier, it transpired that branches of the family had actually fought on opposing sides. This was by reason of the later Hume connection, when Dr George Burges married Anne Hume of Gedney. The Humes had supported the pretender Bonnie Prince Charlie at Culloden in 1745, but his defeat resulted in the beheading of Alexander Hume at Carlisle the following year. Meanwhile, who should have captured the standard of Prince Charlie's bodyguard but a Captain George Burges!

With such a glorious past, it is fitting that a Burges coat of arms exists, bearing the motto: *Semper Meliore Spero*, or, 'I always

133

hope for the best'. Prospective fencing customers are assured, however, of a more confident attitude when Tim is putting up fencing, as the end result is always sturdy and long-lasting!

♣ ♣ ♣ ♣ ♣ ♣

Geoff Parker, 1902-1985

[Photo: Lincolnshire Free Press & Spalding Guardian.]

Although strictly 'just beyond the pale,' so to speak, as a resident of Fleet, no account of Holbeach would be complete without reference to Geoff Parker, since he involved himself so much in the town's life. Rather like Superman and Clark Kent, he is remembered as much for his alter ego, Santa Claus, as for the creative and multi-talented man he was for the rest of the year.

As a child, his father once told him: 'If you want anything, you've got to make it yourself'.' Geoff was true to this motto for the rest of his life, even if it almost took precedence over running his own business! Before arriving in Holbeach from Boston he had already made a name for himself, during an apprenticeship in Lincoln, by designing and building his own motor bike, featured in the *Motor Cycle* of 20th August, 1925. 'Mr Parker even made the patterns for the castings', enthused the editorial, 'and about the only parts he did not make himself are the timing gear wheels. He considers that the

machine, in production form, would cost £70.' Designed with the emphasis on a low riding position, good handling and performance at a modest cost, it was unfortunate that no more versions of this 640cc, single-cylinder bike were made.

Motorbikes to Flying Bedsteads
Moving to Holbeach in the mid-1920s, Geoff began a motorbike and cycle repair business in a group of wooden shops in Church Street, while lodging at Miss Thompson's around the corner in Millfield Terrace. However his activities soon shifted to opening a garage business on Fleet Road at the corner of Branches Lane –a site that was also to become his home when he completed the distinctive L-shaped house next door in 1930. He was thus a reassuring prospect for Muriel, known to everyone as 'Peg',(a teacher at Holbeach Junior School from 1948 to 1962) whom he married in 1930 and honeymooned in the 'Flying Bedstead', a rakish vintage car with a sharply-pointed tail like a Brooklands racer which, family photo albums reveal, actually made it to the Forth Bridge.

Electric novelty
Initially Geoff's new garage business was named the Electric Filling Station, indeed a novelty at a time when not only were most rural petrol pumps –where they existed– manually actuated, but Holbeach as yet had no mains electricity. The establishment had its own Heath Robinson generator which, whenever it expired with a bang, was revived by a bell-push control from the house. With the delightful timbered embellishments added by Geoff over the years, guarded over by the famous fifteenth-century knight, the garage became a well-known focal point and is described elsewhere in this book under 'Shops and Services'. Geoff handed over the business to his daughter and son-in-law in 1961, but this could hardly be called retirement, as his involvement in the social life of Holbeach could be termed a career in itself.

Wartime activities
Over the War years, with restrictions in car use, the garage business was closed for normal trading and Geoff worked at Bettinson's foundry in Boston Road. But

after hours he was active in the local Home Guard, for whom he converted his Morris Cowley to a gun carrier. The Germans may have had their eight-cylinder Horch *Schützenpanzerwagen*, but had they appeared in the Fens, would they have dared to trifle with this Holbeach secret weapon? We shall never know its strategic potential, for as far as is known, it never fired a shot in anger…

However, Geoff was chiefly recognised for his command of the town's Air Training Corps. In the regulation-issue Flying Officer's uniform, he conducted training sessions at the garage workshop, where up in the gallery Holbeach youths, newly out of school as junior agricultural workers or shop assistants, practised Morse, semaphore and aircraft recognition, or were drilled outside on Fleet Road, untroubled by passing traffic which had more or less ceased for the duration. Corps travel to camps like Waddington and Digby, accomplished with a fleet of bikes and an Austin Seven to carry the main equipment, was a model exercise in rotational fair play. One member of the group rode for a while as a passenger in the Austin, changing over with someone on a bike after a certain distance, until every cyclist had received his turn in the car.

Although discouraged by a father who told him there was no future in it, Geoff had nurtured ambitions to enter the aircraft industry, ever since he had seen the first aircraft land in Boston as a boy. That the potential was there was amply demonstrated by the Link trainer he made for his Corps, equipped with junked instruments from RAF Sutton Bridge, all of which, characteristically, he made to work. Movement and turbulence were simulated with the aid of an ingenious connection to Peg's vacuum cleaner! Happily this trainer survives in the air museum at Tattershall Thorpe.

Mobilising Father Christmas

After the War, further diverse activities lay in store. With Geoff's ingenuity, the Morris Cowley was now to provide the motive power for Santa Claus, combining the elements of sledge, cottage-like grotto and mechanical reindeer all in one. Like the monster dragons engineered in the 1920s German film studios, it required men hidden inside the structure to operate it: one to do the driving –typically Frank Bradley– and another to manipulate the shafts to the reindeers' legs. There were seasonal sound effects, too, provided by a wind-up gramophone.

The part of Father Christmas was played by Geoff himself, a role he was to continue, to the delight of Yuletide Holbeach, until 1974. Peg, Geoff's wife, was senior mistress at Holbeach County Primary for 14 years, so naturally the School became an important part of a busy itinerary at Christmas. 'Today Santa arrived in his fantastic sledge', wrote Miss Ransom on 23rd December 1949, 'and escorted all the Junior children to the Youth Centre Hall, where Santa amused the children and distributed presents –apples and sweets– to all. A very happy time was spent.' An undertaking like this took a great deal of preparation. The garage would be closed for a week while all staff were diverted onto converting the Morris to Christmas mode. Meanwhile, entrusted with a small budget from the school, there were all the presents to buy and wrap. Jenny Paul, Geoff's daughter, recalls buying books for the purpose at Fields stationers in Boston Road and everyone seated around the kitchen table afterwards, wrapping scores of gifts at a hectic pace.

It was typical of course of Geoff's generosity and the time he was prepared to give for others. He set up Arthur Morris, invalided out of the war with TB, in a taxi business, providing him with a Vauxhall car free in return for certain considerations, while he was constantly performing favours for people who wanted odd items made, charging them nothing for his time. He even successfully fettled a friend's artificial leg to make it more comfortable!

Coach horns, organs and model railways

Mechanically-minded as he was, Geoff had a soft spot for horse-drawn traffic and possessed among many other artefacts a coaching horn with which, quite by chance, he once responded, 'blind', to a trumpeting coach and four on the other side of

135

Holbeach, doubtless to the astonishment of the coachman! Not that this was the limit of Geoff's musical repertoire, for he built an organ for the new Roman Catholic Church in 1966 and played it himself, although a devout Church of England man. Meanwhile his love affair with steam engines led him to install an impressive model layout, large enough to ride on in his garden and in later years, devise his own bedroom equivalent –probably a more reliable one– of Railtrack.

Geoff died in 1985, truly deserving of the familiar accolade, 'they broke the mould when they made him.' As a candidate for *Desert Island Discs*, explaining how he would survive alone on a tropical beach, he would have been ideal. But as it would have benefited no one but himself, he would have preferred to be closer to home, exercising that resourcefulness for others.

♣ ♣ ♣ ♣ ♣ ♣

The town crier, the 'witch', and the dog enthusiast

Any time up to the early post-war years, when strolling into Carter's Park and approaching the bowling green, you would have encountered a white-haired man in a pinstripe jacket and grey trousers, sitting in the park shelter and regaling his friends, or anyone else who made up a captive audience, with his many reminiscences.

EASY RIDER. Transport for deserving dog in Church Street.

John Rowatt may have been self-appointed as a town crier, but he was admirably qualified for the role with his deep, resonant voice, announcing forthcoming sales, fêtes, seasonal vacancies for pea pickers at the Market Hill crossroads, each announcement preceded by a peal of his small, highly-polished bell. John lived at No. 4 Back Lane long before the street was

redeveloped to its present form. Father of a huge family himself –eight boys and eight girls– he was born in 1878 and ran away to sea when he was 16, sailing the world with the marines. Then he worked in the mines before becoming a local chimney sweep, and moved to Holbeach from Gosberton in the early 1930s.

Another familiar figure to be seen around the Park Road-Park Lane area up to the 50s and 60s was Ivy Perry, whose constant companion was a jackdaw which, when the fancy took it, would alight on somebody's shoes and peck their laces undone. Some unkind locals called her a witch, although her permanently unwashed hair was gathered up inside a beret rather than a pointed hat, her hissing pet geese supplied the terror, and she relied on matchsticks rather than magic to mend broken flower stalks. The town would be the poorer without a continuation of such characters, represented in more recent years by a lady whose dogs, by means of a succession of old prams, are kindly excused from walking.

♣ ♣ ♣ ♣ ♣ ♣

Anne Woolley, 1916-2004

Assembling a chapter of this kind presents certain difficulties. With historical figures, the choice of persons to include is more straightforward. But when it comes to those relatively unsung heroes of the present-day, who have regularly put more into the community than they have drawn out, the potential list is a long one, making the process of fair selection virtually impossible. The only way around this dilemma, it seemed to the writer, was to decide upon Anne Woolley as the representative of all those sterling people he has just described.

From hospital visiting to British Legion
Born on February 12th 1916, Anne was a native of Barrow-upon-Humber, and settled in Holbeach from 1940 in the Albert Street corner house she occupied until 2003, after marrying Roy Woolley, a charge nurse at the then recently-created Fleet Road Hospital. From that point on, she became a familiar figure, seen every day in central Holbeach.

Right from the start, Anne had always wanted to make herself useful. As a younger woman she worked at the Park Road clinic, in the days when mothers arrived to collect their appetising entitlement of cod liver oil and National Dried Milk, and lit the fire every day in the old girls' school room opposite her house, when it was used as a church hall ('It had a lovely parquet floor in there…').

She soon undertook flag day collections for the lifeboats, the blind and cancer relief, extending to hospital visiting and involvements which were to last for decades with the Holbeach Hospital League of Friends, Mothers Union and the Women's Section of the Royal British Legion, formed in 1947. The Legion in particular benefited from her input –from 1949 in fact– and her late 80s saw her still serving as Chairman of Holbeach Women's Section, and representing it at the annual Presentation of the Purse. Anne was standard bearer for 17 years, occasionally before royalty, and sold poppies every year for half a century. But her contribution didn't end there.

Visiting war graves for the benefit of others
Anne's father, a policeman, had been one of a family of 17. He was long affected by the loss of two of his brothers in the Dardanelles and the Battle of Loos during the First World War, and Anne was determined to do all she could to preserve and honour the memory of those millions who had given their lives in two world wars.

Greatly inspired by the poem of the Canadian doctor, Colonel John McCrae ('In Flanders' fields the poppies blow…'), who died of wounds received in 1915, Anne visited his grave in Wimereux, France. It prompted many more visits to war cemeteries in Belgium, France, Germany, Poland, Burma and Israel, bringing back valuable information on burial locations to surviving relatives, supported by her photographs and slides –all taken on behalf of others. Travelling conditions brought their tribulations, but to her they were always worth the effort, as on one occasion when she visited the Middle East to find the grave of a Legion colleague's father near the Mount of Olives.

'The heat nearly killed me,' recalled Anne. 'I got on a coach, then a taxi, and had to walk 1½ miles up a lane, but I found it and took the photograph.' Other journeys took her to India, China, Iceland and America as part of her zest for life, and as a Christian believer, to marvel at what God had created. It was an experience she was able to share when she once met US astronaut James Irwin, one of the first men to land on the moon and himself a practising Christian, when he visited Peterborough Baptist Church.

For someone who had hip replacements to contend with, extensive travelling and pursuing her various voluntary activities around Holbeach could not have been easy. But Anne was one of an unassuming generation who never made a performance of what it had done, and put positive achievement –or working towards that end– before self or any thought of personal discomfort.

Even when things were not going well, such as the changing fortunes of the Holbeach & District Community Vehicle when it was experiencing operational difficulties, Anne was out there

ANNE CUTS THE TAPE, and relaunches the Holbeach & District Community Vehicle service at the Red Lion, West End, in June 2002.

helping to raise funds, manning the stall through alternating sun and rain for hours on end at the Holbeach Vintage Rally and elsewhere, as well as supporting and serving the Community Vehicle committee over many years.

Awards
Fortunately, the community returned the compliment to this lady, who will always be a credit to the town. Honours included the Bowen Courtesy Cup and the Gold Award, 2002, for outstanding services to the Royal British Legion Women's Section, a medallion for selling poppies for over 50 years, the Rotary Club of East Elloe's Paul Harris Fellowship award, and the International Year of the Volunteer 2001 certificate for her commitment to the Holbeach Community Bus.

Meanwhile, back in 2000, she was one of those selected to appear before the Queen at Lincoln Cathedral, to receive a presentation of Maundy Money. It was all part of a long lifetime of local achievement which Anne, accompanied by her music-loving tortoises and seated by the fireplace in her Albert Street back room –filled with mementoes and countless model animals– could reflect on with sheer pride, in the rare moments when she was not out and about in Holbeach.

♣ ♣ ♣ ♣ ♣ ♣

11 –Shops and Services: Then and Now

One hundred and fifty years ago, with Holbeach much smaller than it is today, it is difficult to imagine how so many shops and services accommodated themselves in a town that, as a result, could offer a level of self-sufficiency second to none. Granted this was desirable, in an age of no telephone and limited travel opportunities. Even so, by the 1850s a modest population of 5,000-plus could have its pick of 18 insurance agents, eight bakers, 15 boot and shoemakers, 12 butchers – four of them in the High Street– five confectioners, four druggists, 12 grocers, five milliners, nine tailors, five cabinet makers, and 11 other unclassified shops. And 40 years after the opening of Britain's first photographic portrait studio in London, William Cheffins was well established in 1881 as the town's resident photographer in Tenter's Field, later known as The Tenters.

EARLY PHOTOGRAPHER.
Mr Cheffins at his Tenters studio.
[Courtesy the late Dorothy Bradley.]

The Jack-of-all-Traders

What impresses most in the late Victorian-turn of the century era is not just the range of services on offer, but the sheer versatility of the business community. Amusingly, it seemed accepted practice, according to the trade directories, for a baker to double as an offal dealer, while plumbing was almost synonymous with painting, glazing or paperhanging.

In addition to taverns and inns there were many 'beerhouse' owners who stretched themselves to other activities such as carpentry, shoemaking and renting out machinery and horse traps. One, a Mrs Fields of High Street, was even a tinner and brazier. In fact, it could be said that in the business life of Holbeach there was little time for the frilly crinolines and swooning vapours typified by Cartland novels. Women

featured strongly in trades as varied as farming (Mrs Elizabeth Freeman, Northons Lane), baking, corncake and offal dealing (Judith Lewin Horry) and grocery and provisions (Mrs Presgrave of Cemetery Road –now Park Road).

William Millns must have been a busy man. He was a 'grocer, dealer in mats, rope, twine-sacks, netting, tar, drain pipes, lime, agent to the Markfield Granite Co., Registrar of Marriages, emigration and insurance agent'. But when it came to the definitive Jack-of-all-trades, what price John Blinkhorn Hardy in the High Street? Not only was he an ironmonger, gunsmith, gas fitter and bellhanger, but he was also fire brigade captain and parish clerk. Hardy and his brigade effectively controlled a serious fire in Albert Street in January 1903, when William Reddin's furniture warehouse caught alight before dawn and a strong wind drifted blazing embers down the High Street towards the Grammar School. Hardy ran out 1000 feet of hose to draw water from the pit in Fishpond Lane. At that time the fire appliance would have been ideally situated, in a yard behind the present Dervensure insurance brokers, with the horses kept across the road at the Horse and Groom. Hardy's private house, when he had time to be in it, was in Albert Street.

Curtis for everything

Such versatility was enhanced by the development of the bigger entrepreneurs. Notable among these was Curtis's, on part of the High Street site now occupied by Woolworths (Hardys saddlers and leather goods occupied the corner premises next door). Originally a corn and cattle cake merchant, Curtis had by the end of the nineteenth century extended his activities to chemist and druggist, seed merchant, general commission agent, and agent to the Railway Passengers Assurance Company. One of his lines that stood the test of time was his baking powder, which was still being advertised in the press during the First World War, by then with '20 Years Reputation' at 4d per pound. When James Curtis died in 1915, the business was carried on by his son, Walter Derry Curtis, who expanded it into one of the largest retail and wholesale enterprises in the district. He became prominent in local government and sporting circles, and by 1938 was President of the East Midlands Council of Grocers Association.

French literature. When he died at the age of 68 in April 1900, the floral tributes were reputed to have been 'more numerous and beautiful than has ever been witnessed in Holbeach'.

The market was as busy as ever, although its cross was no more. The base of its predecessor however, taken down by John Stukeley in 1683, was believed by some in 1888 to be still acting as the foundation stone for the lamp post then standing in the centre of the crossroads on the High Street. The road surface in the town centre also underwent some improvement in this period, with new stone blocks, 'specially made in Leicestershire' and of 'a sort much used in London', laid between Mr Curtis's shop and Mr Mashford's during 1893.

'THANK YOU FOR YOUR ESTEEMED ORDER, MADAM'. Lane's shop had become Fletchers after 1900 when this photo was taken, but his name is still visible in the facia area below the lamp fitting.

[Photo source unknown, loaned by Mr A Leonard.]

Long-forgotten names, changing times

In the 1900s, the rapid turnover in some High Street commercial names was as remarkable then as it is today. Writing in November 1908 after revisiting Holbeach, Joseph Wilson commented: 'During the last quarter of a century, I had seen little of the town...The points that struck me as I passed along the highways were –How few of the shop fronts bore the old names, and how rarely I caught a glimpse of anybody I knew in the past.'

Only two years after Wilson's observations, in 1910, several shops –one of them known to be a grocers– disappeared at once when the row built onto the Market Hall on its Church Street side was demolished. They were to join the names of many other shops, a few recalled only by some long-defunct

Thomas Angell Lane

Further down the High Street, where East Lea Furnishings now stands, the premises of Thomas Angell Lane, 'family grocer, draper, silk mercer, tailor, outfitter, general warehouseman and stock valuer' made an impressive sight. It was the flagship of three branches, with the other two situated at Holbeach Hurn and Sutton Bridge. Lane, the father of Sir Norman Angell, the Nobel Peace Prizewinner, was born at North Walsham in Norfolk in 1832. He was a prominent figure in town life and was also a magistrate and Holbeach Grammar School governor, with a keen leisure interest in

photographer's camera, that have passed through the last century against a backdrop few of even the earlier generations would recognise today.

Clocks, merino pants and llamas Tingles the clockmakers for instance, whose shop was once to be found on the Market Hill corner site now occupied by the old Lloyds Bank. At least one example of their timepieces survives, however. This rare and handsome wall clock was still ticking on at Guy Wells in Whaplode before its owner moved away from the area in 2000. Or Sprotberrys, where Laddies now is, begun in 1897-8 and dealing in boots and shoes for many years. And who living now would remember, a little further along Market Hill, J Waller's, 'For Good and Cheap Tailoring', where all manner of suiting could be supplied from 'best west of England' cloth to 'Serge' suits? For the working man there were 'good brown cord' trousers from 7/- to 10/6, and it was the pre-synthetic age of meltons, llamas, vicunas, beavers and bannockburns. All cloths and coverings little heard of today, and where garments could be made to measure on the premises –without travelling to some sophisticated city– for 'Mourning Orders, Dress Suits, Ladies' Jackets and Cycling Breeches', not forgetting 'Merino Pants' for keeping out the fenland winter chill.

WHERE YOU GOT THAT HAT. In the 1890s, at Willertons, High Street. [Courtesy J W Belsham.]

Continuing the list of the long gone, Waller's services were complemented by Willertons, 'Woollen Draper and Hatter' in the High Street opposite the Mansion House, and ladies fashions at Pearson's 'London House',

while a short distance away, next to the present health food shop, the short-sighted were catered for by J F Clark opticians, whose giant spectacle sign above the frontage would have been hard to miss.

Boy's eye view of the 1930s High Street
More within living memory, the sights and sounds of the inter-war Holbeach retail trade are evocatively captured in this excerpt from a poem by the late George Crowson. We join him as he and his boyhood friends are passing the Chequers:

'The Chequers Hotel follows this,
The menu on the wall.
We read and quickly make a wish
That we were rich and tall.
Past the hotel and carriageway
It's Freeman, Hardy Willis.
Boots and slippers lay,
Neatly arranged by Phyllis.

'The smell of freshly baked new bread
Reaches us from Bayston's shop.
The wafting scent goes to our head,
We slow our steps and stop.
A schoolboy's dream now meets our eyes;
Such a glittering array;
Trays of meat and custard pies-
All kinds were on display.'

The aforementioned Thomas Angell Lane's shop –at that time still joined on to the Mansion House– had later become Fletchers before the First World War. But now it was Franklin's name that continued that respectable department store's tradition:

'The Franklin store now follows on
A most imposing sight
Run by Daddy and his son,
Mod fashion at its height.
Ladies' clothes, and crockery,
Boys and menswear, too,
Second hand a mockery

141

Here it was brand new.'

And against a background of dark wood panelling, change machines whizzed across the shop, above:

'Haberdashery of all kinds
Curtains, beddings, sheets,
Material for roller blinds,
Here the nobs all meet.
Melia's, grocers, then Perc Sharp's.
Sweets, fags and bacca too.
Ornaments, some shaped like harps,
Arranged for all to see.'

Continuing on past the Bellevue Garage, the boy would have walked beneath petrol pump pipelines suspended high above the pavement and arranged to hang down by the kerbside. Then, once past the former Midland Bank (now Calthrops) and the Horse & Groom, the junior Crowson introduces us to the delights of:

' "Tulip" Drage's fish shop steaming
"Bogy" Wilding with his broom,
His comb and scissors gleaming.
Wander past the Girls' School Chase
Cis Driffil's plumber's yard.
Get to Ritchie's, slow our pace:
Johnnie Walker stands on guard'.

Ritchie's was a grocers and wine shop in a building of pleasant dark brick which has survived in a series of short leases in recent years, on the immediate left of the Somerfield car park entrance. Now a bed-and-breakfast offshoot of the String of Horses, evidence of its wine shop origins remains in the wrought-iron grape design of its handrail to the front doorstep. At the time of this 1930s poem it stocked Sandeman ports, gin and Jamaica rums, cigars in wooden drums and cider in halves and quarts.

Filling the gap between this shop and the present Somerfield stood the doctor's house. Crowson describes its brass plate 'shining like gold', with the added confidence of a day and night bell on the wall: no concerns then about night-time calls to medical control rooms in another county for home visits!

Personal touch
It was the little niceties offered by shops in this period that really added value to that now much devalued phrase, 'personal service'. Who, for instance, would take the trouble to sort out all the liquorice comfits

Electric Clippers	Hygienic Shaving

Here we are, all of us, ready and willing—
Haircutting Sixpence ; with Shampoo, One Shilling,
So smartly and quickly, yet soothingly done,
That you'll feel out of Eden you've recently come.
L. Parsons and Assistants are waiting to greet you,
So hope they will soon have the pleasure to meet you

— AT —

West End TOILET SALOON,
HOLBEACH

| Soaps | | Creams |

POETIC BARBERS. Lawrence Parsons promised much at his West End salon.
[Courtesy John Hall.]

from a cheap sweet selection, so that a five-year-old child could use them for pretend-lipstick? Miss Triffit did for the late Joyce Tingle's benefit –and all for a halfpenny, too!

CUSTOMER'S EYE VIEW. Early 20th-century banking hall, West End. [Photo The Royal Bank of Scotland Group Communications Dept.]

Banks
Today's financial marketers take pride in how much more proactive they have become with their sales-driven ethic.

But even in the old days, bank managers went out to get the business –even if it did take place in the Chequers more than anywhere else!

Barclays

BARBERS SHOPPE BARCLAYS.
The Bank in its pre-1961 premises, now a hairdressers, on the corner of Albert Street.
[Photo Barclays Bank Group
Archives Dept.]

Lincolnshire Bank partnered by Gurney, Birkbeck, Barclay and Buxton, who had opened a branch in Holbeach as early as 1794.

Together with 20 other private banking firms, this bank merged to form Barclay & Co in 1896, and in 1911 proceeded to take over another bank in the town, the Stamford, Spalding & Boston Banking Company.

Until 1961, when the present premises were opened on the site of Vincents ironmongers, Barclays traded from the existing Barbers Shoppe building at the corner of Albert Street. These premises wore an unbank-like, almost Continental aspect, with their attractive sunshades to the upper floor windows, a glazed-in wrought-iron corner balcony, and cobbles paving the streets below.

When Vincents was being demolished to make way for the new branch, a skeleton was found six feet down by the demolishers, Jellings of Peterborough. It was just outside the boundary of the churchyard, and in the opinion of the Deputy Coroner, John Mossop, the area could well have been part of the original Holbeach cemetery. The absence of a coffin suggested a parish burial, in which case the less well off were taken to the burial spot inside a parish coffin, which was then emptied for the next ceremony. But the circumstances still posed a mystery.

Why, if the area was part of the old cemetery, were there no other neighbouring skeletons? And if it was not cemetery land, was it a suicide case? Suicides were interred in unhallowed ground,

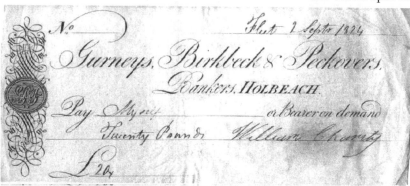

EARLY CHEQUE of 1824, drawn on Gurneys, Birkbeck & Peckovers, an ancestral firm, pre-1896, of the present Barclays Bank PLC.
[Barclays Bank Group Archives Dept.]

By the inter-war years, most of the major banks were represented, such as Barclays, Lloyds, Midland and National Provincial.

Barclays itself can claim to be the oldest bank in the town, as it is a descendant of the private banking firm of the Wisbech and

without coffins. But it was customary to bury them symbolically at a crossroads with a stake through the heart, to prevent evil spirits escaping –as had allegedly been done with Dr Watson, one of the Holbeach Revellers, in 1803. The question remained unanswered, as the District Coroner, Mr C

M Bowser, deemed it to be outside his discretion.

Lloyds
Of the financial houses, the former Lloyds on the corner of Market Hill and West End is the most complete example of traditional

FINE EXAMPLE *of inter-war bank architecture.* **Lloyds' previous branch, built 1922. It is now a solicitors and accountants.** *[Photo Lloyds TSB Group Archives Secretary's Dept.]*

bank architecture. The Bank had originally opened at West End as the Capital and Counties Bank in 1911, and did not become known as Lloyds until 1918. Four years later, the Bank bought the shop premises at 1 West End for £800 and demolished them to put up the present building, completed by builders John Thompson and Sons at a cost of £3,850 –plus £348 for fittings– in March 1922. Despite the later addition of safety screens and other security devices, the small banking hall retained its mellow woodwork and brass trim to the end. As a sequel to the rationalisation that followed Lloyds' 1999 merger with TSB, the building was put on the market in November 2000 and promptly sold on by Hix. In the late afternoon of Wednesday 24th January 2001, its unfrocking process was well under way as the cash machine was removed and a piece of chipboard installed in the resulting gap in the wall. This board was eventually succeeded by a tablet handsomely inscribed 'Albion Chambers' –now the offices of John C Woolley, Solicitor, K Savage & Co, Accountants, and Russell Watchorn Financial Services.

The local savings bank
Having joined forces with TSB, Lloyds now shares the latter's premises next door to the

Bell. The East Midland Trustee Savings Bank, as it was originally known, was a late arrival on the Holbeach banking scene, but a very successful one. First opened May 1951 in the attractive Victorian building now housing Elegance hairdressers just beyond the church wall, it had opened 1,000 accounts worth £125,000 by October 1953 and was run on different lines to its rivals, with local dignitaries sitting as its trustees: John Mossop, for instance, was Chairman of the Trustees, and H C Marris, Chairman of the Management Committee. Its continued success, with the branch assets reaching £½m in 1962, justified the opening of the present premises at 23 High Street two years later, when the local MP, Sir Herbert Butcher, flattered Holbeach in his speech by referring to the town as 'the natural centre for a prosperous, fertile, hardworking community', and in the innocent days before co-habiting, credit cards and 0% finance, went on to say that the trustee savings movement 'offered no better way for the young married couple to save.'

National Westminster

STILL WITH 'BANK' ABOVE THE DOOR. The former Natwest premises in West End. *[Photo The Royal Bank of Scotland Group CommunicationsDept.]*

Across the road in West End, in the tall three-storey house with steps leading up to its front doorway which to this day is still inscribed 'Bank' beneath its pediment, the

National Provincial and Union Bank of England had resumed its Holbeach branch operation from 1919, after an unexplained interruption of many years. In fact, the Bank's roots in the town could be traced back to at least 1838, while the following year it had subscribed £3 towards the paving of Holbeach. But in 1844 this agency was closed. After reopening in 1919, the Bank's name was to change again, simplified to 'National Provincial' in 1923, and becoming 'National Westminster' in 1970 after merging with the Westminster and District Banks. In the early 1970s, the Bank moved into purpose-built premises next door at 20 West End, in the process demolishing Maurice Clarkes ironmongers, purveyors of '1,001 different lines' and 'Established Six Reigns'. Since March 2000, Natwest has been controlled by The Royal Bank of Scotland.

HSBC

MOVING NEXT DOOR. 63 High Street hands over to the ex-Lefley premises at left, in 1971.
[Photo HSBC Group Archives Dept.]

The bank at the other end of the town, HSBC –opposite the junction with Chapel Street– and until recently known as the Midland Bank, established itself in the present Calthrops Solicitors premises in 1909, still under its original private banking title of the Lincoln and Lindsey Banking Company (founded 1833). It became the London City and Midland Bank from 1913, remaining at 63 High Street until September 1971, when the move to new offices next door, purchased two years previously from Edward Lefley, was completed. Old No. 63 was then sold to Spalding solicitors

Hastings, Hall and Folley, for £6,000. Several changes of legal partnership followed over the years, and from 1999 the practice became known as 'Calthrops Solicitors, Incorporating Peter Frost & Co.'

The Garage Trade
In 1900, seedsman and farmer Tom Lane of Serpentine House in Barrington Gate was reputed to be the first owner of a motor car in Holbeach. It was an Argyll, of Glaswegian manufacture with a single-cylinder, quarter-litre engine –a far cry from the Ford Zephyr Estates later run by his son, Eric. Not surprisingly for a make that did not survive much beyond the First War, nationwide dealerships and service facilities were unheard of. The owner, soon finding that few people could cope with the car's vagaries beyond the limited attempts of the local blacksmith, sold the car shortly afterwards.

A few years later, however, Holbeach got itself up to speed with the horseless carriage, with W O Dickens of Chapel Street as one of the earliest motor engineers in the town by 1914. He repaired, sold and hired out cars and cycles, dispensed petrol in containers and charged accumulators for lamps, as the town was not to receive mains electricity until the 1930s. Meanwhile, the First World War accelerated the reliability of, and need for, motor vehicles. On the farm the occasional tractor, in a form still recognisable today and typified by the Fordson of 1917, began to make its appearance.

The Thirties saw a doubling in the numbers of vehicles on the roads nationwide and even in Holbeach, where Sgt Lown had booked a lorry driver for exceeding 12 mph in 1930, the traffic congestion reached the point, five years later, where the Parish Council's decision not to install traffic lights at Market Hill was met with disbelief by those who had to put up with the chaos that ensued at this junction, after the RAC scout went off traffic duty in the evening. So it was not surprising that several young hopefuls, fresh from their apprenticeships or military mechanical experiences, set up garage businesses to cope with the new demand. One such was the Belle Vue Garage.

Belle Vue and Lefleys
When Lefleys departed from 59 High Street, it marked the end of its near half-century's use as garage premises. Belle Vue House, as it was then known, had at one time been a private school. In 1920 it was purchased for £375 from jeweller John Clarke by Nelson Honnor, an auctioneer's clerk from Maidenhead. Its façade was much taller in those days, with two upper storeys and a row of attractively deep and narrow first floor windows. The conveyance document itself makes interesting reading as to its then neighbouring properties, 'abutting upon' the properties of Alfred Curtis, Frank Fletcher, 'on or towards the East upon property of Lenny Septimus Harrisson', and 'including a cinder ash tennis court'. The 1925 RAC Handbook listed the new business as Honnor, Bettger & Clarke, trading as the 'Belle Vue Motor Works'. But Honnor, in debt to the Midland next door, was in difficulties by 1930 and found a buyer in Hugh Harrison, who in turn sold on the garage for £2,000 to Edward Lefley, a Kirton motor engineer, in 1939. During the 1930s, Frederick Powley once recalled, it was possible to hire a car from Belle Vue at 10s (50p) a day, including a full tank of petrol.

Lefley's clientele was not lacking in character. One, a wealthy farmer from Boston Road, had all the badges of his Rover 90 removed so that his choice of car should remain anonymous, while another from Spalding Road, who repeatedly dented his Bentley, embarrassed the panel beater with the instruction to 'just knock it out with a hammer and spray over it, mate'. This vehicle was driven for so long with a slipping clutch that when the mechanism was eventually fixed, the owner was unaccustomed to the immediate response and ended up through the front wall of Barclays Bank's sub-branch in Sutton Bridge. Lefley's also had the mixed blessing of servicing the Council's effluent lorries. Pulling a handle at random on one of these trucks once led to the son and heir of the

business becoming anointed with more than he bargained for!

With most of the railway's elements cleared away by the end of the 1960s, Lefley's new garage premises took shape in the old station yard. For safety reasons alone, this must have been a welcome move on Lefley's part. The old High Street 'jungle vine' petrol pump tubing had on one occasion entangled with a departing customer's bumper, rupturing the pipe and spraying petrol all over the place!

West End Garage
This left one garage business on the main west- to- east thoroughfare through central Holbeach, that of G F Walker & Son, –now West End Garage. George Walker had set up there after the

VINTAGE BIKER. G F Walker at West End Garage.[Photo P Walker.]

Second War in what had previously been Jack Stennett's works, from where Stennett had operated since the 20s repairing motor cycles and light cars. Even before that, these premises had been serving the horsedrawn wheel, as Bellairs wheelwrights and coachbuilders. While preparing this book, I was shown a brass hub fashioned at these former works by Brian and Jenny Paul. It is inscribed 'Sharp'.

A native of Fitton End near Gorefield, George Walker had previously worked for Belle Vue in the 1920s before a spell as a mechanic at Saracen's Head. In the days before extended service intervals, expensive sealed units and diagnostic tuning, he, like many motor engineers of his generation, fettled anything that was thrown at him, whether it was a motor cycle, car or tractor. George became a distinctive local character and was often to be seen at the wheel of one of his vintage Rolls-Royces, a Twenty and a 7½-litre Phantom I, which might also be towing an equally venerable Willerby caravan at weekends in impressive mechanical silence. West End's forecourt was a lot more confined than it is today, with small houses occupying valuable space at each end of it. One, next door to the Sibley Guest House & Restaurant (where was to be found, 'After a pleasant trip around the local Tulip Fields...an excellent

WHEN PETROL WAS FOUR-AND-SIX A GALLON. Evocative Fifties view of West End Garage, with BP and National Benzole pumps, 1949 Ford Prefect at the kerb and a 1937 Vauxhall DX 14 behind the staff. *[Photo Paul Walker.]*

meal' from Mr A T Boyce) served as the garage shop, with accommodation above. Eventually weakened by sewerage trenching underneath, it was pulled down by Paul Walker and his wife in the 1960s and the two BP and National Benzole petrol pumps repositioned away from the pavement into the centre of the forecourt.

Since the mid-1980s, the business has been owned by the brothers John and Paul Beeken. The workshop, built by Walker post-war, strikes a characterful note, with festoons of wheeltrims hanging from the walls, and is still adequate for today's busy throughput of cars, be they Pete Clement's cherished 1935 Austin Ten, or a visiting German *Fräulein*'s Trabant. The two pumps are now under the Q8 logo, although these had to be concealed with sacking during the September 2000 petrol panic, when queues of motorists blocking Spalding Road refused to believe that the Beekens had finally run dry! The other house on the frontage, the

former property of Mrs Bailey which featured an unusual galleried interior, survived until 1995 when it, too, was found to have structural problems and was demolished.

More recent members of the Holbeach garage trade include Holbeach Tyres, in business since March 1969 when they set up in the old laundry in Battlefields Lane – where J T Ward's Joinery Manufacturers is now situated. They soon extended into the adjoining fish and chip shop before further expansion moved them to what is now Bryan Thompson's offices in Boston Road –originally extensions to the Boston Road school. But from 1993 trading took on a new dimension from purpose-built premises nearer the String of Horses, on a site that in the last century had housed a wheelwrights, the Central Drainage Board, Parkers Fireplaces and finally an unsuccessful development company. John Tinn's family business, now run by son David and daughter Suzanne, has an 11-strong team specialising in a drive-in, while-you-wait service for exhausts tyres, MOTs and general servicing, and also goes out to surrounding farms requiring replacement tyres and batteries for agricultural vehicles.

Massey O' Brien and Bettinsons
Just across the road, Massey O' Brien Cars, as it has been known since 1978, began as H B Massey and carried on a Ford dealership that went back to the original occupier of the premises, the ubiquitous Percy Bettinson. Any town's history is so much the richer for its more flamboyant characters and Percy is well remembered by the older generation as someone who had aspirations to become the foremost entrepreneur in Holbeach, touring the district in his chauffeur-driven Rolls-Royce.

With a background in agricultural engineering sales, he first came to prominence as an ambitious employee of Levertons in Spalding, when he was sent to the USA to secure a Caterpillar franchise for the firm. What he actually returned with was a UK-wide contract that was unsuitable for Levertons to handle, and which had to be shared out with Jack Oldings in the South.

This led to Percy parting company with Levertons, but financed by a consortium of

CORTINA AT MASSEYS, 1964, In the former Bettinson garage premises in Boston Road.

→

For Ford Service & Sales

SEE

H. B. MASSEY

FORD DEALER

BOSTON ROAD
HOLBEACH
Telephone 2005

farmers and a solicitor, he came to Holbeach and set up his own foundry and agricultural engineering business in Boston Road. Other business interests included ironmongery and hardware, a building enterprise and a tailors, Fletchers, in Long Sutton. The foundry was kept busy between 1939-45 on war contract work, while another product of this period was the Bettinson potato lifter. Advertising itself in the early post-war years as 'Manufacturers of Quality Farm Equipment and Agents for all Good Farm Machinery and Massey-Harris Distributors and Ford', P B Bettinson & Co staged regular shows of farm machinery featuring the latest innovations.

In February 1953, the firm was offering single front-wheel conversions for both old and new Fordson Major tractors, while two new models of a high-speed rotary cutting machine for potato haulm destruction and topping attracted 'special interest'. The firm nearly sold its service station premises to the East Elloe Rural District Council in 1954, when the latter body, having established its own work force from 1948, was looking for somewhere to keep its service vehicles. While £8,250 was not considered an unreasonable price, the Council opted to centralise operations around Mattimore House, so the deal did not go through. Percy

Bettinson carried on with the Ford dealership at Boston Road until 1960, when H B Massey Ltd took over the garage side.

On two wheels: Gordon Woodman, Watson & Garwood, and Terry Rudd
Motor cycles, too, were catered for locally at a time when the bike, and often the sidecar combination, was still essential transport for those who could not afford a car –especially during the petrol rationing periods of the 1940s and 50s– rather than the sort of mount ridden more for pleasure today. In premises now occupied by Morriss & Haynes undertakers, BSAs and Nortons could once be heard revving up at Gordon Woodman's, who dealt in 14 other makes of famous British names now long lost to the Japanese, such as AJS, Ariel, Douglas, Francis Barnett, James, Matchless and Watsonian, with up to 18 months of 'easy' payments available. Woodman was a genuine enthusiast himself, having been Clerk of the Course at Bell End Speedway in the Thirties and Secretary of the Holbeach & Spalding Motor Cycle and Light Car Club. It was all quite a contrast to his beginnings as a newspaper roundsman, when one family at Star Cross nicknamed him 'Rupert', after the famous bear featured in the copies of the *Daily Express* he delivered. His other line, right at the forefront of technology in 1953, was TV sales, with an exhortation to 'Instal for Coronation Year', although with prices starting at £50.8.0. (£50.40) for a Bush nine-inch table model, you had to be a wealthy royalist to do so, and expect to have several eager neighbours hovering for an invitation to watch your set.

After Gordon Woodman's death, two of his employees, Messrs Watson and Garwood, set up their own motor cycle business, initially at the back of Geoff Parker's garage but later moving into the former Wesleyan chapel in Chapel Street for a while, in the days before Hawkins' expansion. 'Wally' Garwood, incidentally, had been a prisoner-of-war under the Japanese, an ordeal from which he never fully recovered.

Spiritual successor to these businesses, just outside the town on Fen Road, is Terry Rudd Motorcycles, established 1981 as Honda agents from the start, and developed in the grounds of the detached house that stands on one of the last sweeping bends into Holbeach. It is now the longest-established business of its kind in the town, even if Terry Rudd has had to rush off occasionally in the middle of dealing with a customer, during his 20-year spell as a retained fireman –a risky secondary occupation for which he was well fitted, after a decade of road racing with sidecars! The Rudd competitive spirit lives on in Terry's sons' love of motocross racing, while just across the forecourt, Lee Rudd's popular L R Signs & Designs service has been in existence since 1997.

Geoff Parker and the Electric Filling Station

Soon after coming to Holbeach in the 1920s to repair motor cycles and bicycles, Geoff Parker switched his attention to four wheels on Fleet Road.

His new garage was the first electric filling station in the area, at a time when petrol in rural districts was more usually bought in cans, or at best dispensed from pumps worked by hand. Scarcely had Geoff begun operations when talk of a Holbeach by-pass raised fears of diverted traffic and lost trade. So he opened a second Electric Filling Station on the A17 in the Washway, later managed by his parents during the war years. By the early 1950s however, the family link had ended, for the garage was advertised as H Pooley (Holbeach) Limited, agents for Hillman cars. This building survives, as an intact example of 1930s commercial architecture.

As it happened, the by-pass plans were not to materialise for several decades and the garage on Fleet Road became a fascinating local landmark, with a proliferating Tudor theme that eventually enveloped the whole forecourt. First evidence of this, at the beginning of the war, was the ornate

KERBSIDE MEDIEVAL. Geoff Parker with the famous knight in his turret at the corner of Branches Lane, 1974.
[Photo Lincs Free Press/Spalding Guardian.]

workshop, built without foundations around an earlier one which was then pulled down from the inside. This creation, in spite of its utilitarian intentions, was a thing of beauty, especially the interior, and later served as the venue for Mr and Mrs Charles Ingamells Patchett's golden wedding celebrations in June 1946. For many years afterwards, their commemorative gold horseshoe, left behind after the party and still with a ribbon attached, remained nailed to one of the beams above the room, where it had kept company with the inevitable reindeer's head.

With a restriction on car use during the war, Geoff temporarily closed the business and went to work for Bettinsons in between his Air Training Corps and Home Guard duties. But on opening up again, more rustic embellishments appeared over 1948–50. A sturdy wooden canopy, both ornamental and practical and reminiscent of the Arts and Crafts style, was added over the pumps. This was also the era when the familiar knight statue made its appearance. Happily this distinctive effigy lives on in careful storage in Fleet, as a respected family heirloom.

Complementing the forecourt's ambience, a Rolls-Royce Silver Ghost breakdown truck stood at the ready. Before its demotion to a towing vehicle, this had travelled London's Park Lane many times in the 1920s as the property of a titled owner. In Geoff's hands it was worked hard for many years, pulling boxy Austins, Morrises and other errant vehicles out of dykes. On one occasion it delivered a huge iron fuel tank, dangling precariously from the hook at the rear, to the bus depot (where the Factory Shop now is), and after business hours, transported redundant millstones from Whaplode and Kilby's Mill to serve as Geoff's garden ornaments. It was disposed of in the Sixties to an enthusiast in the North East.

Geoff continued with the garage business until 1961 when, eager to be released to his many creative pursuits, he handed everything on to his daughter and son-in-law, Jenny and Brian Paul.

A new venture at this time was the acquisition of the Fir Cottage site on the opposite side of the Branches Lane junction, to include a showroom for the Wolseley, Singer and the French Simca agencies. Popular with local car buyers in the 60s were the Wolseley 1500, Singer Gazelle –an upmarket version of the Hillman Minx– and the Simca 1301 and 1501. A stray cat adopted the Pauls on the day the first Wolseley Hornet version of the Mini arrived in the showroom, so Jenny named the animal 'Hornet' in commemoration! Another novelty at the garage, to the dismay of the competition, was the introduction of Jet low-price petrol (four gallons for £1).

However when sewerage transformations took place, closing the road for long periods and affecting trade, Brian and Jenny decided enough was enough. They kept the Elizabethan-style machine shop next to the house, but sold the rest of the concern to Burmah Petroleum, who installed Georgie Baines as manager. The business passed through several hands, including those of Mr Laws of Sycamore Farm, Mr Wing and Mr Turner. Fleet Road Garage, as it is now known, specialised in Skodas from the mid-1980s on: the reason why many Holbeach motorists drive Felicias, Fabias and Octavias.

Pete Coupland Autos

Quite a few others drove Mazdas, as a result of the franchise held on the Fen Road by Peter Coupland from 1976 until he retired in 2000. Peter's original intention was to be a car body repair specialist, but with so many people asking him to find them 'a good car',

he felt obliged to offer vehicle sales as well, eventually extending into the paddock where, in his later years, Eric Bowser used to visit his pet cows. The planning department's resistance to his business developments, on the grounds that they could not take place amidst a residential area, was mollified when Peter showed them photos of a general dealer's next door ('Stop –Look Around– Good used Clothing, Furniture & Ornaments Bought & Sold'), C E Storey's Motorist's Shop in Barrington Gate (later Roy's, now demolished), Ernie Johnson's ex-slaughterhouse yard in Park Lane full of A40s, Minors and Renault Dauphines (in a life before Mondemont Close), Power Motors in Fleet Street (the old Retreat, then featuring sash windows upstairs with false shutters, and now Holbeach Heating), H J Doktor's Texaco garage on Church Street (now Lynas Vokes) and Turners Motors in Barrington Gate in the present Secondhand Land premises. But

LIFE BEFORE MONDEMONT CLOSE. Yard containing Renault Dauphine, Minor and Rover 2000 at Ernie Taylor's motor business in Park Lane. [Photo: Peter Coupland.]

the ensuing neat and tidy appearance of the Coupland premises showed that the planners need never have worried. Nowadays Peter pursues a busy retirement, which includes his continued fund-raising activities and long-term treasurership of the Holbeach and East Elloe Hospital Trust*.

N E Gray & Sons

A few doors away from Peter Coupland on the Fen Road, Norman Gray opened his garage business just before the Coronation, on 1st June 1953, as a sequel to his original partnership with haulier Ted Coward on the same site. Norman and his wife occupied the house next door (clearly dated 1952 on its frontage) for some years, and from 1959 to

*See pages 207-209.

1971 the firm dealt in Rootes Group cars – Hillman, Humber, Singer and Sunbeam– but after an interval of used cars only, took on its longest-running agency to date after 1978, selling and servicing Mitsubishi vehicles with a proficiency that earned N E Gray & Sons the Dealer of the Year title in 1996, and Southern Dealer of the Year in 2002. Aided by agricultural rationalisation, long gone are the many typical farmers of the 50s and 60s who bought Super Snipes and Gazelles, replaced by a specific customer preference for four-wheel drive models, particularly the extended-cab pick-up. But beneath it all, and with David Gray currently at the helm, assisted by his wife and son, N E Gray & Sons remains very much the family business it started out as in 1953 –even down to the steel framework of the original garage, hidden in the structure of the smart showroom!

Holbeach Motor Auctions
At one time, car sales were not just confined to garages. The alternative was provided by Holbeach Motor Auctions, conducted by Franks & English, who once a fortnight held sales of venerable vehicles outside the Exchange Inn. In 1952, with estimated prices of a 1932 Rover Ten at £60, a 1938 Morris Eight for £300, or a 1937 Vauxhall 14 at £250 as part of a typical Saturday line-up, one hoped in those pre-MOT days that the bargain would at least get you home to Gedney Drove End before expiring in a steam cloud, or careering brakeless into a dyke.

Branches and Chain Stores
George Crowson's reference to Freeman Hardy Willis is a reminder that the inter-war period witnessed the introduction of chain stores to Holbeach, the parent companies recognising that a town significant enough to hold two market days a week was worth closer attention. The Star Supply Co of West End, where the Nationwide Building Society now stands, was an early example of this network. It became the International Stores in 1931, with manager Mr Sleaford and his family living above the shop. His staff consisted of an assistant manager, three girls in the grocery section, two apprentices, one roundsman and a cat, which always occupied one of the two customers' chairs, to

discourage vermin and dogs. Even in its final years, self-service never invaded the routine here. At the completion of a transaction, the counter assistant presented you with a docket to take to the girl in the cash desk. Mr Sleaford went on to other branches of the International, including his native Skegness for a while, but appropriately, returned to Holbeach for his last tour of duty, having received his long-service watch from the company in 1965. The shop stood empty for a couple of years until occupied by a toy business, and is now the Nationwide Building Society.

A shopworker's day in the 1930s
A few doors down, next to the Rose & Crown, Currys had been trading since 1917, selling cycles and electrical goods such as radios, mangles and new-fangled washing machines. Much of this hardware had to be lifted out bodily for display outside the shop frontage, especially on Saturdays, while weekly pay packets were still heavy in workers' pockets and wives could steer them away from the pub. Frank Sauntson, then a young teenager, remembers his Saturday job there in 1937. For this, Currys paid him 10/-, which sounds quite generous for the 1930s, until one realises that his hours were 8 a.m. to 10 p.m.! In fact, as Ivy Hargraves (formerly Mrs Dowse) of Fishpond Lane reminds us, it was normal in those days for many Holbeach shops to be open until at least 9 p.m. Ivy's pay as a young assistant at Rossington tailors in Park Road was only 7/6 a week, but she managed to save enough to buy her first new motorbike, a Coventry Eagle registered JL 17, at the age of 20 in 1932.

Frank Sauntson's responsibilities were varied, to say the least: 'It would be a good day for trade. My day started by sweeping the footpath and the roadside gutter for the full length of the front of the shop, then putting out the goods for sale. There would be rows of new and secondhand cycles placed at an angle on the footpath in front of the display windows, together with new washing machines, hand-operated and electric, old-type mangles –cast-iron with wooden rollers– and modern stands with rubber roller wringers. This was if the weather was fine. If not, you had to look out for a brighter period to get them all out, or be ready to get them all in again if it rained.

'The rest of the day I would help in the shop selling torches, batteries, bulbs, tins of calcium carbide, lampshades, tyres, tubes, toys, mend punctures, fix acetylene lamps, and radios. Old crystal wireless sets were giving way to valve equivalents, and I also charged lead acid accumulators on a weekly basis, as the Boston Electric Company had only recently brought mains electricity to Holbeach.'

There then followed a rather harrowing routine ride to Moulton Seas End –as yet still deprived of mains electricity– delivering some two dozen acid accumulators in a sidecar attached to a pushbike, when the all-up weight tended to steer the bike rather more than Frank could! This was second only to the fright he got

*CURRY'S DELIVERY SERVICE. **Their Morris 8 van in the mid- 1930s.*** *[Photo source unknown.]*

one dark night in the wartime blackout, when riding home to the Marsh with no lights. Having just passed the Bull's Neck, he realised that he had somehow come face to face with the hot breath of the real thing in Lane's paddock opposite, bovine eyes fiercely glaring.

But a shock of a more embarrassing kind awaited Frank when he delivered a repaired radio set to Cedar Lodge, which stood in the grounds now occupied by the Tesco and Co-op sites. The set belonged to the young lady of the house, Miss Golden, and her father (presumably the then manager of the National Provincial Bank) asked Frank to

take it up to her room, only to find Miss Golden still in bed!

Before leaving these pleasant reminiscences, it should be noted that Frank was still serving the community many years later in retirement when, despite indifferent health, he has devoted most of his spare time tirelessly to raising thousands of pounds for the Royal Air Forces Association at the Anglia Motel and other local venues such as the exit doors at Somerfield, not to mention door-to-door collections, in a routine that would have exhausted the tenacity of many younger individuals. He, his wife and fellow collectors have made a superb effort that has furthered the good name of the RAFA Holbeach Branch, and earned it several trophies for exceeding targets.

The post-war scene

The post-war period saw little reduction in the number of shops and businesses, most of them family-run, that made up the wide choice available to the Holbeach public. An early casualty however was the British Restaurant. A greater success than its Sutton Bridge equivalent, it seemed for a while like a going concern, for even as late as Christmas 1947, it was advertising for a kitchen assistant at £1 19s 4d (£1.97) a week. But less than a year later, it was making a loss which could only be met by the ratepayers, so the Rural District Council closed it in September 1948. For a while, into the Fifties, it was to live again under the ownership of Holland County Council, providing low-cost meals for schoolchildren and the general public.

Curtis retires

Another famous High Street business came to an end in 1948, with the retirement of Walter Derry Curtis, retail and wholesale grocer, who sold his premises to P B Bettinson & Co in what was described as 'one of the biggest changes in property ownership in South Lincolnshire in recent years.' Curtis's retirement, to his home in Park Road, was unfortunately short, for he died in 1951, aged 70.

Lenny Curtis

Another Curtis still around at this time offered expertise of a different kind –that of taxidermy. Leonard Marshall Curtis had run an Aladdin 's Cave of a shop, where Morriss & Haynes is now situated, since the 1930s. A sign over his bungalow, named Red Gables in Park Road, proclaimed, 'L M Curtis for any old thing', which probably understated the case quite appreciably. His speciality was stuffed animals of all kinds, particularly fish which, Lenny informed us, should be stuffed with sawdust and packed down tightly to avoid shrinkage, having been accurately sketched by him on arrival so that the correct contours could be followed. The largest fish he dealt with in this way was a 20lb pike, of the species which could only be found locally in the River Glen.

But it wasn't the largest fish of its kind to be displayed in Holbeach. This honour fell to the 35lb specimen staring blankly from its glass case in the Mossop family home, Elloe Lodge, in Barrington Gate. It had been landed by Samuel Septimus Mossop at Lough Conn, Ireland in May 1898. Nevertheless, Lenny would have been quite capable of creating his own monster had he been so inclined, for he did not necessarily need the original creature as a basis. His likeness of a huge salmon, for instance, was just such a masterpiece, improvised largely from an old gaberdine raincoat, but so lifelike that it was used as a prop in the Whaplode Occasional's production of *A Quiet Weekend.* This man should have trodden the boards himself, for character oozed out of him, or rather from his seasoned trilby, pullover and ever-smouldering pipe.

'I like making things,' he said once. 'When I go to bed at night, I usually think of something, and the next day I make it.'

And so it proved. Models of common British fish, some only 1½ inches long, carved from balsa wood with celluloid fins, 'swimming' in their glass cases through facsimile weeds and river plants. A self-ejecting cigarette case, with a lighter incorporated in its handle, or walking sticks of all designs –but no ordinary sticks, naturally. They were made of holly wood, their handles decorated with illustrations of animals and birds, or in another example, fashioned from a shark's backbone. As a more orthodox part of his routine, he repaired fishing rods for people from all over, or made them new ones from greenhart wood. It was the sort of expertise that had won him the craftsmanship category in a national newspaper competition some years previously, and one could visualise him appearing solo in an edition of Channel 4's *Scrapyard Challenge* and treating the whole project, whatever it might be, with contemptuous ease!

As a master improviser, Lenny possessed the sort of calculating eye that gave an almost magical meaning to 'Waste Not, Want Not' : even his pet hedgehog enjoyed an after-life as a clothes brush. But who would have seen a further, entirely unconnected use for old paint daubings? Lenny did. From a joiner's workshop he took away an old door on which the men had been cleaning their paintbrushes for 30 years, carefully removed the thick paint skin, and after much delicate fettling, planing and smoothing, made it into an attractively mottled clock case. And had you wondered what to do with an old crab carcass, say, picked up from the tidal creeks at Sutton Bridge, here was one Lenny had finished earlier: an effigy of Will Hay.

Furniture, prams and own-fed beef

Reverting to window shopping, Mays sold chintzy furniture in West End –also the 'House for Perambulators', be it noted, when infants, swaddled in A Tingle's best babywear, could ride gracefully on large, well-sprung Silver Cross wheels instead of today's rattling trolley castors. In certain places, two shops existed where there is only one on the same site now. Martins newsagents is just such an example, once Elsoms, and Smiths the butchers. Other butchers were Rowells, George Adams and Ivor Dowse, all successive occupants of today's Cyprus Kebab takeaway, itself a door or two away from Swepstone's butchers, once the empire of Bayston pursuing the same trade. Meat sales also continued around the corner in Albert Street, where Tubbs boasted of 'Own-Fed' Beef that had won Champion and Silver Bowl Awards in the Thirties.

Sheds and coffins

Thirty-two Fishpond Lane looked after you from the garden to the grave with a greenhouse, packing shed or coffin from builders and undertakers Knipe & Johnston, while florists C A Gray at No.32 provided the wreath. Not to be outdone, Spalding Co-operative Society's 'No.1 Branch' at Church Street could also have been of assistance in this area, and intriguingly, promoted a Painting and Decorating Department as well.

Printing, photos and betting

From 31 High Street you walked tall in North's 'Dryfoot' shoes, possibly in a Daks Town and Country suit from Hector David, while your old suit could be advertised for you in the local press by J W Chamberlin & Son's, newsagents and stationers, taking down the details with one of their latest Biro ball point pens.

Later occupied by Forbuoys, older shoppers will remember the sound of Chamberlin's printing machinery as it thudded away upstairs, turning out, among many other items, local sports clubs' programmes and fixture lists, the ceiling reinforced to bear the weight.

Holiday snaps, typically those small black and white prints taken blurringly at waist level with Brownie box cameras, could be developed by Swepstone's of 60-62 High Street (the business was begun by Bill Swepstone, not to be confused with today's butchers of the same name, which was originated by a relative, Eric) who interestingly, stocked a 'Full range of Peter Scott Reproductions'. Scott was still recognised as a local artist at that time, having lived in the East Lighthouse at Sutton Bridge from 1933 to 1939. Ray Wiseman, Swepstone's later proprietor, eventually retired to a modern house behind the shop, where in later years he watched the comings and goings of St John Street from the comfort of his summer house.

In Barrington Gate, you risked your shirt on a 'Bet with Bert' at Gilders, or drowned your sorrows in a cup of tea afterwards at Elizabeth's Snack Bar or Taylor's Café.

Woolworths arrives

Woolworths arrived in 1955, after it had taken over the hardware shop originally built earlier in the decade by Bettinson. The ground-floor Park Road windows were bricked over in the process. Little changed externally today, apart from a mild facelift in the mid-90s to discard its traditional 'W' monograms, and sport a rather abrupt automatic doorway to become 'Woolworth Local', this is with Boots –who occupied the old Wass & Eastaugh chemist shop for 52 years until moving to new premises a few doors down in March 2000– the last of the older-generation national High Street names to remain in Holbeach. Currys, for instance, was to close in January 1963, relying instead on its Spalding branch. For most of its existence the Holbeach shop had been managed by Len Kirkham, who in 1956, together with his wife and sister-in-law, received three gold watches from the firm in recognition of their combined 100 years' service. The shop was sold to the brewers Steward & Patteson, whereupon it was eventually demolished and the resulting space used as the Crown car park.

Pigs and bread

On the way home, it would have been fish and chips from Nellie Parsons (an unlikely-looking chippie proprietor who lived in respectable Edinburgh Walk) in Church Street, Cyril Tabor's against The Ram, J W Thorogood's at 67 High Street, or even battered scallops from Reddins at the top of Spalding Road, not forgetting a crusty loaf to pick at from bakers French & Hargraves, up whose steps one now ascends for a Kan-Ton takeaway. In fact, out of the names just mentioned, French & Hargraves, where pigs once snuffled in the back yard, survived a little longer than most. Wally French, renowned centre forward for the local football team, left the business in 1965 and his son Bruce went into the garage trade at Lefleys and later Sutton St James. But Frank Hargraves, who lived above the shop, carried on until the mid-1970s. At one stage he had 11 employees, each one of whom received an annual Christmas cake and mince pies from the boss. After Frank retired, the building served as a pizza takeaway before graduating to oriental dishes.

Devotion to duty

Meanwhile, nothing short of Armageddon stopped the newspapers being delivered to your door, at least as far as George Steele was concerned. As the loyal employee of Annie Robb's and later Claude Chapman's High Street newsagency, with only two days off sick in George V's reign, one wonders how many miles he must have covered on his bike between 1924 and 1975, not just slotting the news through the letterboxes of Holbeach and surrounding villages, but performing the neighbourhood a multitude of favours, posting its letters, putting out its dustbins and collecting prescriptions. In short, a selflessness that has become a rare commodity nowadays.

The 1970s –more closures

Advertisements in the Seventies reveal a list of names now disappeared.   'While the

TOO THRILLING FOR WORDS! Howard Hughes' lavish production, starring Ben Lyon and Jean Harlow, reached Holbeach Hippodrome in 1931.   [Courtesy John Hall.]

Winter Months away with a Thomas transistor organ' was the advice of Holbeach Music Supplies in Chapel Street, for instance, who once published a regular list of top ten tunes: in January 1972, their No.1 was 'I'd Like to Teach the World to Sing', by the New Seekers. Such pop-consciousness was entirely appropriate for a town that had educated Raymond Burrell, alias 'Boz' of King Crimson, who had attended The George Farmer. Then there were Halls D-I-Y (to become Hooks), in whose forecourt cattle drinking troughs, made by Hardys in Albert Street, were once displayed, Dickersons butchers, Denspares motor factors, Chapmans china, Burtons bakers, and The Pot Shop, to name but a few. After 1975 Franklins department store had become Coleys, who continued trading in groceries, but no longer made use of the upper floor. By then there was a small butcher's shop attached to it, in which a young Ivor Dowse started trading before moving across the street. As already mentioned, the International Stores became a nationwide casualty of the 1970s, as supermarket shopping began to get the better of the old, unhurried atmosphere of sighing bacon slicers, half-pounds of New Zealand butter, and corned beef in greaseproof paper.

Not even entertainment was safe from the all-conquering supermarket, when in August 1970, the Hippodrome cinema closed for the last time under Mr Denny's managership. Saturday and Wednesday matinées (but no pictures on Sundays, of course) with long queues waiting to get in, were now a thing of the past, a way of life that had begun forty years earlier, when six usherettes and a liveried commissionaire had welcomed excited crowds to the first local showing of the 1929 talkie, *Sunny Side Up*, with Janet Gaynor and Charles Farrell. The words of the title song must have been on everyone's lips for days afterwards –'When you have nine sons in a row, baseball teams are lucky, you know…', and so on.

But the cinema's own luck had now run out and speculation and rumour abounded. Would it now become a swimming pool, a bingo hall, or a supermarket?

Two years later self-service had won the day: it may have changed its identity a few times, with names such as Vivo's, Gateway, and eventually, Somerfield, but it was here to stay –a development that was also to signal the end for the former residence of Dr and Mrs Alison Hunter, to make way for the store's car park entrance.

Dr Hunter, incidentally, was one of the last of the patrician breed of doctors from the pre-NHS era, driven on his rounds by chauffeur Tegardine in an immaculate Ford V8 Pilot. By this time he had retired to Fen Road. But it was still sad to see his house, in its final form a combination of flats and Fox's antique shop, give way to the bulldozer. Another link with the medical world had also disappeared by this time: Midwife Nurse Doolan's cottage, which used to stand where Somerfield's car park is now.

So for better or worse, the 1970s began a long period of redevelopment, the inevitable outcome of progress in a practically-minded town.

In Church Street, just across from the second-generation Exchange public house – built in 1939 behind the site of its predecessor– old wooden shops from the First World War period, where Mr Court had his shoe repairing business and Geoff Parker had begun trading, were replaced by a short row of modern equivalents, one of which provided Holbeach with a launderette for the first time.

Limmings –'Everything from Mars Bars to Rat Poison'

***SHOP PREMISES AT LEFT , DIRTY DICKS NEXT DOOR FOR STORAGE.** Limmings original premises took the unusual form of a shop (now The Carousel card shop) and an old lodging house.*
[From Limmings 40th Birthday leaflet.]

More changes were to follow in the 1980s. Following the development of the supermarket site, there were other transformations to come in the form of a better customer environment and working conditions for Limmings, whose business had hitherto persevered by storing its wares in the decaying Georgian remains of 19-21 Fleet Street.

This house, once known as Dirty Dick's, was where tramps and ex-servicemen from the First World War seeking casual work would stay the night, presided over by the proprietor's wife, who smoked a clay pipe.

Jack and Anne Limming had made do with this arrangement since beginning their garden, pet supplies and horticultural sundries business in February 1960 in the adjoining shop premises at 17 Fleet Street– also their living quarters– that in more recent years has served as Fleet Cards, now renamed the Carousel. In those early days, the shop was open from 7 a.m. to 7 p.m. during the week.

Unfortunately Jack died in 1977 before his aim of a purpose-built shop could be realised, but in a planning permission marathon lasting four years, his son Patrick carried on the battle against all odds, which

***MILLENNIUM CHANGEOVER.** Limmings made the most of the occasion in town with this bold display.*

included questions being asked in Parliament over whether the 200-year-old building should be demolished. Although rated of special historic and architectural interest, a surveyor's report and public enquiry had found that the property would need expenditure of £167,000 to make it habitable.

So the new shop in the form we see it today was allowed to go ahead and was finished on Patrick's 31st birthday in May 1986 –an appropriate gift, although he had been obliged to part with his Lotus Esprit to help fund the project!

Limmings' redevelopment also took in premises at No. 23 Fleet Street –which had seen service as Fidlers the grocers and the electrical shop once rented by Gordon Woodman from 'Piggy' Taylor –and No. 25, now represented by the concreted entrance to Limming's yard, where stone squirrels, hedgehogs and voluptuous classical statues form an external display when it is not raining –or sometimes when it is, the rows of accompanying wheelbarrows filling up with water. A commemorative tablet to Jack Limming can be seen on the shop's frontage, reflecting the same feeling of reassuring permanency that appeared in the firm's 40th anniversary booklet, when it stated: 'We do not sell you a load of rubbish and then close down a few months later.'

The old campaigners

Johnsons
'Can you put new heels on these?'

'Certainly. Saturday all right?'

'Oh, you are an old darlin'.'

Take heed of this display of personal service to the customer from Colin Johnson. You are witnessing not just the only cobblers at work in Holbeach nowadays, but the carrying on of a business begun by father Harry from as long ago as 1921. In those days he would have had one or two rivals: 'Gandi' Foster, for instance, in St Johns Street, able to complete many shoe repairs in half an hour, Sundays included. But it was Johnsons who stayed the course, though not always trading from the shop opposite Somerfield –old though it is, dating from the early 1800s and taken over from an unprofitable branch of Radio Rentals in 1968. For Johnson Senior, once a familiar sight sitting in his window, clad in a leather apron, began in a hut rented off Rammie Ramsden at the top of Hallgate, before moving to the little cottage still standing

(just) next door to Coubro Chambers in West End. The business then moved across the road into one half of the present oriental takeaway, the other half occupied by Hardys greengrocers. When the time came to move down the road to Fleet Street, all the equipment was shifted by Brian Paul, driving the famous Geoff Parker Engineering breakdown truck.

Laddies
Another long-term survivor –almost a household word around Holbeach, in fact– is Laddies. The decision whether or not to go into ice cream sales was decided on nothing more than the toss of a coin by William Ladbrook, who was just as prepared to become a butcher. The Ladbrook name of course was already well known in Holbeach, for W Ladbrook Senior, the self-styled 'Chocolate King', ran a general grocery business in Barrington Gate and was a regular not only on the market, but also at Holbeach Town Football Club's matches, where he sold fruit and sweets to spectators.

Ices take to the road
William Junior started ice-creaming in 1922 from a shed at 4 Wignal's Gate, operating at first with a horse and cart, then a motor cycle and sidecar combination bought for him by his uncle. Regular business during the 1920s came from supplying the country shows, school and church and chapel feasts held on Thompson's field before the building of East Elloe Avenue. But there was local competition to contend with in the form of Harry Harris and Brock Biggadike. So the acquisition of his first ice cream van, in 1932, enabled William's business to take on a new dimension. It was a First World War ambulance that had been languishing in Eric Lane's garage, bought for £6 and converted to its new task by carpenter, Harry Reddin. All went well with constructing the body until they came to choosing a suitable material for the roof. Eventually the problem was solved by using sailcloth impregnated with linseed oil, with instructions from Harry Reddin to 'drive up and down to get rid of the smell, like'.

Thus equipped, William, accompanied by his young son, Derek, went as far afield as Sutterton, Swineshead, East Heckington and

North Kyme, ringing a handbell to bring out the customers. One of his regulars at North Kyme was a large woman who at the end of the ice cream season would buy 24 packets of cream crackers as part of her stocking-up for the winter. Another at East Heckington was an Alsatian, well trained in the art of proffering tuppence in exchange for his master's cornet!

Rabbits from Norfolk

As a means of obtaining a living during the winter months, William Ladbrook used to bring rabbits back from Norfolk to sell. Derek recalls these excursions well, when at Christmas they would come back from 'over the border' in their big, square Austin, laden with rabbits, turkeys, mistletoe and turnips. He was already playing an important supporting role in the business to the extent that at the age of 14, his father needed him to leave the Board School to help him.

Moving to Church Street

The move to the shop in Church Street took place in 1946 after Mr Sprotberry, a staunch Methodist dealing in boots and shoes, died. William Ladbrook adapted the premises by rebuilding the frontage and when the opportunity presented itself in 1955, pulled down two old cottages at the back to build a warehouse. In terms of facilities, the business has come a long way from the days of primitive refrigeration, when the family relied on blocks of ice delivered from Crowland to keep the ice cream cool. At the height of the summer season, the firm makes over 200 gallons of ice cream a week and supplies other businesses both locally and nationally. In the old days the ice cream was made with butter, but when the wholesalers began to concentrate on yoghurt, double cream took over as the principal ingredient. The rest of the delicious taste is a trade secret, and while the Ice Cream Alliance is on hand to provide standard recipes, Laddies always use their skill to modify these, for just the right taste.

Derek and his wife Nell, a retired nursing sister, still live on the premises, but their son Richard now runs the business on a daily basis. The couple have been married for over 50 years, Nell obviously undaunted by the fact that one of their first dates to the

pictures coincided with the arrival of the Dilly Man, and all that entailed on Derek's part to ensure that the household receptacle was put out for the cart before they could set out for the cinema.

It was not the first time that this unsavoury conveyance had crossed the Ladbrooks' path. Once, when returning from a day's trading at a country show, the ice cream van was barred from passing into Market Hill. A car had collided with the dilly cart, which had deposited its contents all over the street…

Back yard with a view

The view from Mr and Mrs Ladbrook's conservatory takes in not only the pleasant vista of the rolling grounds of the defunct Old Rectory with its huge listed trees, but also, to the north, Back Lane, where a relative, 'Uncle' Eric Ladbrook, once had his scrapyard, distinguished at its entrance by a metal flag inscribed '1644', its origins unknown. Up until the 1960s the lane also featured a row of old cottages on either side, three of which were home to Geoff Capes in his formative years, and a pub, the Carpenters Arms. Langwith Builders were also to be found there in their early days. Now modern town houses grace one side of Back Lane, while the scrapyard, later managed by Eric Ladbrook's son, moved to Fen Road on the first bend out of town.

Jacksons

Meanwhile, Jacksons the Butchers has provided over 50 years' service in West End, in a shop that had already been a butchers for many years previously when owned by the Thompson family, originating with Edward Thompson, who hailed from Stamford. In addition to the shop, the Thompsons owned property and land in various parts of Holbeach, including a field in Boston Road, upon which the East Elloe Avenue development was eventually built.

John Tinsley Thompson (motto: 'There are enough troubles in the world without adding to them') was the last of the line to own the shop. Related to the Tinsleys through his mother, he lived with his family over the butcher's shop, where their first-floor sitting room, with guest Winnie Staley at the piano trilling 'Just A Song At Twilight', was the scene of many an evening's old-style entertainment. In fact, the bell for summoning the maid can still be seen upstairs as a memento from those genteel times.

At one stage, the rear of the premises extended as far as the present Holbeach Tyres, backing onto the foundry where Savages turned out cast-iron pig troughs. After the War, John Thompson retired and Alfred Jackson, newly out of the Forces, just missed out on acquiring the business which was sold to a Mr Smith. However, the new butcher was not entirely successful and Jackson's chance came up again at Christmas 1948, when Smith approached Alfred at his workplace, Binghams in Long Sutton, to see if he would still be interested in buying the shop. A deal was struck and Alfred Jackson began trading on 21st February 1949.

Post-war austerity
At that stage the family were renting the front part of the accommodation upstairs, while Edna Thompson and her sister lived on in the rear half before retiring to Hunstanton, John Thompson having died in 1947. As for appointments, or lack of them, 'It was typical of the sort of Holbeach premises you would find in the early post-war years', recalled Alfred's son, Len Jackson, who was 13 when his father took over. 'There were not many modern conveniences and the old gas light fittings were still installed'. Nor were conditions in the late 1940s and early 50s conducive to brisk business, with food rationing still in force as a legacy of the War. Conditions dictated that the shop only opened for a limited number of hours, and within two weeks Mr Jackson had to let go two of the existing staff. Initially, purchases were restricted to ninepence-worth (4p) of meat per person per week, later rising to 1s 1d (5½p). There were no queues, however, for all customers knew that they would get their entitlement, however meagre. In any case, added Len Jackson, 'They were glad of anything they could get'. A sobering thought today, when half of a finicky child's plateful is often scraped into the bin!

When rationing came off, Jacksons joined the East Elloe Meat Traders. This was run by Charlie Thorpe as an association for buying all the meat required on behalf of the dozen or so members. But after six months or so, Alfred preferred to buy his own meat, obtaining beef from Wisbech market. As trade resumed its normal stride, much of it came from delivery sales. The young Len catered for local requirements such as the Spalding Road houses on his bike, while a van covered areas as diverse as Holbeach Marsh, Holbeach Fen, Long Sutton, Whaplode and the Moultons as a matter of routine. It was still the era of the Sunday joint that justified this activity and which, in Len Jackson's estimation, accounted for 99% of their trade. But buying habits were about to change.

Change in demand
The first indication came when farm workers went onto a five-day week and increased their mobility with cars. This meant that fewer people were at home when the roundsman called, a situation made worse when they or other members of the family went to work for local canneries or food processing factories, where shift patterns further affected weekend habits. Not only that, but it goes without saying that supermarkets have also made their mark on trade and personal preferences.

For the smaller business, it is a very different set of backroom circumstances nowadays. The relatively straightforward process of cutting up a carcass for Sunday joints has been overtaken by the far greater level of preparation required to make meat user-friendly for the modern heat-and-eat consumer, and all that implies in a virtual doubling of labour costs. Accompanying paperwork, meanwhile, proliferates to the point where it almost takes longer to complete than serving the public! Naturally, there are still loyal, Sunday-joint customers who appreciate quality and personal service and Jacksons will always cater for them. But in recent years the shop has taken changing demand very seriously by concentrating on pastry-based meat products such as pasties and sausage rolls –and opening at 6.30 a.m. to sell them to the passing work traffic.

Hawkins

Hawkins, the hardware business in Barrington Gate, has also achieved 50 years' service to the town. Len Hawkins (1913-1998) came to Holbeach after the war from Stamford to manage the hardware side of Bettinson's rapidly-extending empire, starting at what is now the health food shop in the High Street. He soon built up Bettinson's trade, resulting in premises moves, first to the present Dryden's site and then across the road to a new purpose-built shop which Woolworths were later to occupy.

This shop, with a retail area on two floors and ground-floor windows extending to the Park Road side which were later bricked in, displaced both Curtis's and the saddlery next door (leather goods, however, continued to be available from Lewins* in Barrington Gate). It was of considerable size for such a business in a modest market town. But after only a short time, Bettinson wanted to move again to more new premises in Boston Road, at which point Len decided there was more future in running his own business.

Premises in Victoria Street provided him with the opportunity. In years gone by, these had housed Bayston's bakehouse –perhaps a prototype of the Holbeach takeaway– where meat dinners could be cooked for you to carry home– a blacksmiths and an undertakers. Now there was to be a trade of of a different kind.

Len's 1953 move to the former Bayston bakery was well timed as it turned out. For this was the era of post-war kitchen and bathroom grants for old terraced houses, with a big demand from small builders for all the appropriate fittings. Opportunities then arose in the late 60s to clear an old three-storey house –once Fox's jewellers– and the Wesleyan Chapel in Barrington Gate, complete with its lean-to that was formerly Mr Boyce's the cobblers, to allow the present Hawkins shop to go up in 1969, built for old time's sake by Bettinson's building company.

The demolition of the bakery in Victoria Street five years later made way for an extension for cycles and garden machinery.

*George Lewin sponsored an impressive silver football cup for the Holbeach Boys and Holbeach Bank Schools.

Len's wife added china and crockery to the merchandise, and since the departure of Pledgers and Denton & Biggadike in the late 1990s the business, now controlled by Len's son Andrew Hawkins, has offered a wide range of electrical appliances.

Decorating materials in particular have become one of their most popular lines in a shop that has kept up with the times, although usefully, one can still buy small items like hooks and screws individually, without paying for a minimum of, say, 20.

Market Life

'Holbeach has a market on Thursdays, and two fairs, on May 17th and the second Monday in September, for horses,' stated *A Dictionary of the World*, published in 1772. 'It is situated in a flat among dykes, and is but an indifferent town'.

Despite this eighteenth-century slight, the market remains an important part of town life today, is still held on Thursdays and Saturdays, and averages up to ten pitches in normal weather. Regular stalls include those for discounted electrical appliances, footwear, vegetables, matting and carpets, haberdashery, cut-price provisions and watches, clothing, and an occasional takeaway snack van graced with a Tasmanian devil emblem. Another regular, on his Magical Mystery Tour of the markets, proclaims from a board: 'I am the egg man'. Close by, reclining in his familiar caravan, the proprietor of Foysters Transplants might be seen in a moment of relaxation with his Walkman before giving you wise advice on which shrub to buy. And as one inches past on the edge of the pavement, trying to assess those velcro slippers or that £5 watch, most stalls represent meeting places for the town's traditional shoppers, exchanging pleasantries with each other or the traders.

Once open till late

It was a busier place however, in living memory. Pre-war Thursdays featured an auction, as continued today at Long Sutton but more comprehensive, with cages of hens, cockerels, pullets, rabbits and even pigs adding to the usual variety of old furniture and garden tools passing to the highest bidder. Here is a sample from January 1931: ' In Mr Joe G Hix's poultry auction there was a good supply of fowls which met with a good demand. Prices were: Best killing cockerels 4/- to 5/9. Pullets 3/- to 5/, hens 2/6 – 5/3, Rabbits 1/6.' Saturday was more the shopper's market, with a double row or even three ranks of stalls in the High Street selling meat, vegetables, flowers and clothes well into the evening, when naptha flares and pressure lamps were lit. This heralded the market's closing hour, a good time to be around for perishable goods to be sold off cheaply. Joyce Tingle, for instance, recalled being sent as a girl to Harry Harris's fruit stall by the Church wall once it had turned 8.30 p.m., to be rewarded with a large handful of ripe bananas for 6d. Harris's father, who in season would have been the pride of today's marketing tactician, even risked a barrow on the Fishpond when it was frozen over, to attract the skaters.

For many, working a five-and-a-half day week on the land and living in outlying villages, the Saturday market was their only shopping opportunity, arriving by pony and trap or perpendicular Morris Cowley, and parking up in the Ram Inn yard, the father of the family conveniently remaining in the pub environs while the womenfolk went shopping.

'Things didn't get going till about 6-6.30 p.m. and carried on till 10 at night', said Derek Ladbrook. Among the butchers' and drapers' stalls, his grandfather offered confectionery at 6d a pound or four half pounds for a shilling, although there was rivalry in the form of Golder and his famous cough sweets, made on site with boiled sugar and a special roller. Occasionally, if trade was slow,

the Ladbrooks threw in a free bar of chocolate –worth 2d– as an incentive.

Traffic threatens

In the immediate post-war years, traders found their spaces challenged by changing traffic conditions. Even as far back as 1932, Coun. Curtis of the old Holbeach Urban Council had proposed that a line should be painted on the High Street, showing the limit to which stalls could overlap the main roadway.

In those days, the crossroads at Market Hill were manned by an RAC guide to control the traffic. But after the war, this service was only resumed for two years and in the interests of road safety in 1949, there was pressure on stallholders to vacate their High Street pitches and move them around the corner into Church Street. The EERDC was anxious to have traffic lights installed at the crossroads, and they reasoned that it would give their application a better chance if the market was not cluttering up the approaches to the junction, when the Ministry of Transport official visited for a day's feasibility study.

But the stallholders opposed it and, supported by a petition signed by 191 ratepayers, the move had to be abandoned.

Holbeach did not get its traffic lights, but not because of the market. In the Ministry's view, people were able to cross the road in safety, even at peak hours, and nor were they moved by tales of schoolchildren experiencing near misses. 'Youngsters needed more help with their judgement' was their parsimonious reply to that one.

As a result, the best that could be achieved was the provision of a 'traffic warden' on a year's trial –by agreement with the County Education Officer.

ONE NOT FOR SALE. A horse that pulled one of the earlier fire engines in Holbeach.

[Photo Freda Coley.]

It was not enough, and even two years after the inevitable happened, when a child was killed in December 1953, the plea for traffic lights was still waiting to be answered. The only more immediate outcome of this focus on the Market Hill crossroads was the removal of its old central lamppost in favour of a traffic island. The lamp had been there longer than anyone then alive could remember, and in spite of the difficulty experienced in removing its base –much to the delight of the old stagers watching– the pneumatic drill won in the end. Naturally, many were the subjective views that the new lamp installed in its place did not shine as far as the old one!

The Horse Fairs
As mentioned in the chapter dealing with the nineteenth century, the main west-east thoroughfare through Holbeach was also the horsetraders' pitch during the mid-May and mid-September horse fairs.

Up until the 1940s, agricultural use of horses justified such events, a large farm still relying on as many as 30 animals. To those living at the time it was an unforgettable mix of sights, sounds and smells. 'Farm horses of every age, colour and size were trotted up and down the High Street for buyers to make their choice', recalled George Crowson. 'A few with a foal beside them, others which soon would have, and young broken ones ready for work.

'Many hands ran over them, checking hooves and teeth, a bargain struck –sealed over a pint– and grubby notes changed hands. The fish and chip shops and pubs did a roaring trade, the aroma of those temptation to the appetite. Mixed with this, the ammoniac smell of horse urine and dung, and the tang of twist tobacco, from puffing pipes and beery breath of the bargain hunters.'

The Horse Fair of May 1913 as reported on by the *Spalding Free Press* must have been a good example of a typical day's trading: 'Cart horses met with greatest demand, but nags were not required to any extent. Good geldings sold at from £25 to £30, and the better-class five-year-old horses ranged from £55 to £75, whilst one belonging to Mrs T

Thompson, Grove Farm, Holbeach Hurn, fetched about £80.'

As with secondhand car buying, it was the custom of prospective punters to take the horse for a trial run, typically up to the post office and back. Sometimes a mutual unfamiliarity between steed and rider could lead to things getting out of control, as when a large shire horse bolted and ended up wedged in the back doorway of the Tingle household at No. 46 High Street. Fortunately the combined efforts of Messrs Tingle, Sellabanks and a butcher from Bayston's next door succeeded in coaxing the horse out with no harm done.

Up until the 1920s at any rate, tolls were levied at Wignal's Gate, which, as a feeder road to the market, must have benefited considerably from the varied animal traffic. A 1922 tariff charged 8d per horse, reducing to half price for numbers exceeding four. The lower-status ass was 4d, an ox 6d, and live geese and turkeys, 2d each. The cheapest creature to bring into Holbeach by this route was a duck at ½d, and the most expensive, a bull at one shilling.

Of the many horses that came and went in the High Street during the earlier years of the last century, none were of greater importance than the equine residents at the Horse & Groom. In emergencies these pulled the fire engine, which was kept in the yard behind the building opposite, now Dervensure insurance brokers.

Gradual mechanisation in the fields brought an end to the Horse Fairs in 1954, by which time even a large farm's quota of horses could barely be counted on the fingers of one hand. The figures once quoted by Ken Barker for the Proctors' Onslow Farm near Long Sutton say it all: 30 horses in 1925, declining to two or three in 1958, at which stage there were 10 tractors and two lorries, while only one horse was left by 1966.

Licensing hours questioned
Meanwhile, with the demise of the Horse Fair, the extended licensing hours afforded to farmers and former horsetraders were thrown into sharper relief when in February 1962, the police questioned whether enough

162

of a normal market remained on Thursdays to justify the bars of the Crown, Bell and Talbot Hotel staying open longer.

There had been instances of the market 'drying up' before, as in July 1914 when with much of the farming community away at the Boston Show and many more working in the fields, no more than twenty-three people and only a couple of stalls turned up for market day. But such occasions were rare compared with what was happening now. If the constabulary were to be believed, the market had indeed declined on Thursdays, for Sgt J Bullimore had noted that since December 21st 1961, only one stall had been seen on the High Street, while the Retreat and Exchange Inns had been found locked up on a couple of occasions. Supt Charles Johnson was keen to bring a precedent at Bungay to bear, where the High Court ruled that the existence of market stalls and farmers meeting in a public house did not constitute a market.

Fortunately, the objection was overruled by the fact that the Holbeach market had been authorised by royal charter. So if it had not been for Thomas de Multon's successful application to the King in the thirteenth century, the market may not have been able to celebrate its 750th anniversary in 2002. But one aspect of Holbeach marketing which did die out by the First World War, happily for the better, was the custom at the May-Day Statutes of hiring farm servants.

'Like slaves in the markets of Rome', they grouped themselves along the pavements of the High Street –men and plough boys on one side, women on the other– waiting to be hired by a new master, all their belongings wrapped up in handkerchiefs.

The size of the hiring fee depended on the individual's usefulness and experience, waggoners engaged for up to £24 with a ten-shilling-a-week standing wage in 1910, and 'second men' £16-£18 and nine shillings a week.

Farmers Market, 2000
A new dimension to Holbeach pavement trade from August 2000 was the Farmers Market.

Held monthly on Saturdays, it represented both the traditional and the progressive: traditional in the sense that it brought back the old, busier atmosphere of the market, enhanced by traders dressed in boaters and striped aprons; progressive in that it hoped to attract not only the townspeople looking for something different, but those living outside Holbeach who would 'discover' the town and use its other facilities.

Leading figures on the Chamber of Trade such as Richard Ladbrook welcomed the project from the start and fears about unreasonable competition were countered by the fact that the goods on sale were mainly 'niche' and not available widely elsewhere in Holbeach. Products included ostrich meat, venison, specialist and organic poultry and exclusive cheeses, honey and herbs. All the items on sale were grown, reared or prepared by the stallholders who, as members of the Lincolnshire Farmers Market Company, preferred to sell direct rather than through middlemen or supermarkets. In Holbeach however, the venture failed to gather momentum.

OSTRICH MEAT COMES TO HOLBEACH. The first Farmers Market, August 2000.

At the other extreme, Tesco, the largest supermarket to date to arrive in Holbeach, rapidly took shape over 2000/2001 on the former Parkers Fireplaces site.

This unprecedented dimension to Holbeach retail life owed much to a carefully-prepared proposal submitted to Tesco's management by a private resident of Holbeach Clough, Alfred French, who set out a strong case for the food giant's presence in the town, justified by the increasing population and housing development in the area.

As a result, Tesco's self-contained site has provided 180 new jobs, its own bus stop on Boston Road, on-site cash machine, a cafeteria, and a car park laid out with pedestrian crossings and flashing beacons. It was opened on Spring Bank Holiday Monday, May 6th 2001, by Holbeach Paralympian, Sally Reddin.

The departure of established names in Holbeach from the late 1990s onwards has included Denton and Biggadike electrians, when the proprietor Mr Norris retired, Ivor Dowse butchers, Pledgers, as part of a branch rationalisation, the Wool & Fabric Centre, and P & M Fruits.

Lloyds Bank on the corner of Market Hill and West End was also closed after the TSB merger. In the early years of the new millennium, this leaves us with the following as a reflection of the town's current consumerism:

High Street south side, starting from Fleet Street end, to West End

Holbeach Heating – Morriss & Haynes undertakers – Malvern Hair Studio – The Flower Basket (former Ram public house) – Holbeach Fish Bar – Johnsons shoe repairs – Holbeach Video Library – Kan-Ton Chinese takeaway – Barnet Fair hairdressers – The Sewing Centre – Y Beauty fashionwear – BKK Thai Restaurant (the former Café Roma Ristorante) – K9 to Equine pet store– The Hollys (gifts, cards and stationery) – Susan's Shoes – Victoria Crafts – In Style Hair Design – the former Hi-brow Brides – Dervensure insurance brokers – (Chapel St/Barrington Gate junction) – Jocelyn's Fashions – Victoria Wine off licence – To the Point Body Imagery – Cyprus Kebab – Holbeach Whole Foods – Kasha ladies' clothes shop – Swepstones butchers – The Good Earth Chinese takeaway – The Barber Shoppe – (Albert Street junction) – the former Forbuoys newsagents – Brian Foster chemist – Caprice fashions – The Card Gallery – Principal estate agents – Barclays Bank – (Church and churchyard) – Elegance hairdressers – Graham's hairdressers - Dryden & Son jewellers – (Market Hill junction) – Albion Chambers – Nationwide Bank – the Crown Hotel.

High Street north side, starting from West End

West End Garage – Cross Bros Ltd furnishings – One-Stop Convenience Stores – The Picnic Hamper takeaway food – National Westminster Bank – Jacksons butchers – Hairport hairdressers – Mendelec electricians – Stradling opticians - Morriss & Mennie estate agents - A P Sales estate agents – Shanghai oriental takeaway – Longstaff estate agents– (Boston Road/Park Road junction) – Woolworths – Hartleys gents outfitters – Joan's ladies wear — Break Charity Shop (in the old Boots store) Martins newsagents – the Chequers Hotel – Eastern Delight takeaway – the former Y-Beauty – the Bell Inn – Lloyds/TSB Bank – Boots chemists– Galaxy Travel – The Dry Cleaners – Priceless Discounts – East Lea Furnishings, Windows and Conservatories – Lisa's household ware – the Post Office – the Job Centre – Sue Ryder charity shop – HSBC Bank – the Horse & Groom public house – the Central Fish & Chip Bar – Regency Property Services (the former Wool & Fabric Centre) – the former P & M fruits greengrocers (closed March 2003)– B & B in old shop premises run by the String of Horses – (entrance to Somerfield's car park) – Somerfield – East Lea House – Carousel cards, stationery and party novelties – Limmings garden and pet supplies – Face Value hairdressers – Aquapets – Kitchen Plus.

Boston Road west side, from High Street end

P Cassidy booksellers – String of Horses public house – Angelic Nails Tan & Toning – Holbeach Tyres – (The former) Ma Clampit's Country & Western Store – Silverdale Veterinary Surgeons – behind which E G & L B Martin plumbing and heating engineers – Bryan Thompson Windows – Chandlers (formerly Boston Tractors).

Boston Road east side, from Tesco to High Street

Tesco supermarket – Jewson building supplies – Co-op supermarket – Massey O' Brien Cars – Classique Hair Design – Fellaz barbers.

Park Road west side, from High Street end

Video Out-Takes – Kellys flower shop – The Girlie Shop.

Park Road east side, from old Public Hall to High Street

Halstead & Fowler cabinet makers and upholsterers – Holbeach Warehouse antiques – The Strand Hair Salon – Call Right (mobile phone and computer shop) - Lincs Crafts.

Barrington Gate west side, from High street end

Hawkins Hardware – Nick's Plaice fish and chips – Secondhand Land.

Barrington Gate east side, from Post Office to St John Street

Post Office Sorting Office – S & D Bookmakers Ltd (extended into new premises on the old Roys Motors site, March 2001).

St John Street –from the junction with Barrington Gate to High Street

Chameli Tandoori Indian Restaurant – (junction with Fishpond Lane) – the Dragon Pearl Chinese Restaurant.

Market Hill/Church Street west side, from High Street end

Positive Bodies gym and fitness centre – Clubley Funeral Services (both these establishments sharing the old Co-op building) – Oceans Chinese & English Hot Food Takeaway – Butties – Holbeach Angling – Spotty Dog Cat rescue – Salway & Wright Chartered Accountants – Occasions flowers – Hix & Son estate agents – Laddies ice cream and confectionery – Gills Allsorts clothing and general items– Holbeach United Services Club Limited – a unit of three shops comprising a job agency, Holbeach Launderette and E.T.C. hardware – Lynas Vokes Financial Services Ltd.

'Outpost' shops –those serving high-density residential areas out of the town centre– are currently restricted to one: CJ's newsagent off-licence and general store, at the corner of Cranmore Lane.

There are many customers in Holbeach, including senior citizens –who account for approximately 30 per cent of the population in the town– continuing to appreciate the one-to-one customer relationship offered by the surviving local family business, where the opportunity to buy quality goods in a sociable atmosphere will always be valued.

But it would be unrealistic, in an age of high mobility, mail order and the internet, to contemplate a return to the Victorian or earlier twentieth-century years of over-duplicated (from a modern viewpoint) shops and services. Recent years have seen the survival of the fittest for the Holbeach retail trade, as it has adjusted itself by natural wastage to the current needs of the townspeople, many of whom travel out of the town both for work and other shopping needs. Thus with the smaller shop, it seems a question of two or three of each kind as the optimum number for survival, a surplus-to-requirements business tending to disappear in as little as a matter of months. However, convenience in terms of varied merchandise, ease of access and adequate parking facilities will go a long way towards keeping people in the town.

♣♣♣♣♣♣

12 — Observations on Industry

With land reclamation drawing increasing numbers to the area from the early eighteenth century onwards –a process furthered by the needs of several landlords to attract more tenants by subdividing their lands into smaller units– it was the farmer and his colleague, the smallholder, who determined the nature of local trade and industry.

We can read much into Arthur Young's comment in his *View of the Agriculture of the County of Lincoln*, 1813, that, 'The farmers of this County are alive to improvements and ready to adopt any new instruments which promise utility.' The

inventions of the Industrial Revolution had, after all, provided farmers with all manner of new tools and devices to help them make the most of cultivation, and in Holbeach the number of trade suppliers proliferated considerably between 1820 and 1850. The use of seed drills, ploughs, harrows, swath-turners, steam power with threshing equipment, drainage tools and pumping engines –to name but a few vital tools of the local trade– attracted a large service industry, sourced by many small to medium-sized workshops all around Holbeach, from High street to West End, from Littlebury Street to Boston Road, and from the Washway to Fleet Road.

Smithies and Ironfounders
In the key trades of ironfounding and agricultural implement-making, Henry Ellis of Boston Road was one such specialist in the mid-nineteenth century, and in 1882 William Haslam was another. Haslam, noted for his high-quality seed drills, also

advertised himself as a 'millwright ironfounder', thus serving the half a dozen or so corn millers existing in Holbeach at the time. But in spite of

creeping mechanisation, the horse was still essential to most propulsion needs in the nineteenth century. So it is not surprising to find 14 blacksmiths listed in White's Directory for 1856, usefully distributed around Holbeach and as indispensable then as the town's garages are to the car today. Smiths included Richard Collins and Joseph Cocker in the Fen, Joseph Woodward and

MADE IN BOSTON ROAD. An 1890 Haslam seed drill, as demonstrated at the 2003 Holbeach Vintage Rally.

Thomas Wray in the High Street, Amos Hunt and William Kirton in Boston Road and St John Street, Henry Ellis in Boston Road, and Frederick Gapp in Chapel Street. Ellis, Kirton and Woodward also doubled as wheelwrights and 'machine makers'. Beforehand, the young or untried horse would have to be prepared for its working life, a task falling to horse-breakers such as George Germany in the High Street, or William Rose around the corner in Albert Street.

Knowing the ropes
Another local supply industry, not only to horse transport, but also fairground owners and farmers, was ropemaking, carried on first in Edinburgh Walk and then in Hallgate by the Robb family, who brought their craft with them from Outwell in Norfolk in the 1860s. It would have been John Robb who, having bought land on the mound near the station yard, uncovered some of the bones in the ancient burial ground while levelling out the surface as a new site for his business in 1868. Here, in an aroma of melting Stockholm tar, he and his son Wilfred spun ropes for both practical and decorative purposes, examples of which have found their way into museums all over the country.

His supply source was markedly international, hemps arriving from Czarist Russia, henequen (a form of leaf fibre) from Mexico and Cuba, manilla from the Philippines and sisal from Java, Africa and the Bahamas. These exotic connections apart, it was very much an industry of Old England, with nothing but honest, literally homespun methods used for ploughing-ropes, horse-halters, pig ropes, string, haystack and wagon cloths, and ropes for the swings and awnings of travelling fairs when the marts came to Lynn, Wisbech and Boston.

This was doomed to obsolescence, as synthetic substitutes and mechanisation took over. Wilfred Robb carried on until retirement in the early post-war years, by which time he was the only ropemaker left in Lincolnshire. Before his death in 1956 at the age of 76, he was bandmaster of Holbeach Silver Band of which his father, who lived to be 99, had also been a member as a drummer.

Fleet Road Ketchup

Of all the unusual activities credited to Holbeach, none comes more original than ketchup manufacturing. A new departure for local industry in the 1880s was Joseph Farrow's mushroom ketchup factory. Heinz may or may not have had its 57 varieties by that time, but Joseph's father in Whaplode had come up with his own mushroom concoction. Originally a saddler, the son saw the sales potential of his father's recipe as a more profitable alternative to the horseriding trade, and set up the Carlton Works where the present Factory Shop is situated.

He took The Maltings, once a brewer's premises, on the opposite side of the road at the Damgate junction for storing mushrooms –facilities which enabled him to achieve an annual ketchup output of 5,000 gallons. But further expansion led him to new factory premises in South Square, Boston –later

HIGH ST BREWERS in the 1890s were Ridlingtons (top) and J H Carter (below).

occupied by Johnson's Seeds– where he switched to mustard production.

As for the Maltings, it later became the official address of builders John Campion and Son, and ended its active days as a corn storage depot for Tindall's Mill.

These were busy final years for this building, as farmers' tractors, trailers and lorries queued into its yard to unload corn for storage and eventual processing. After a period of dereliction, it was demolished in the early 1970s to make way for housing development.

Milling up to the early twentieth century

Milling at this time was still conducted in the classical tower-and-sail form. The mills themselves were situated in Barrington Gate, the Washway, Penny Hill and Damgate, while another was literally rolled into town, according to the memoirs of William Snarey, the West End ironmonger who first came to Holbeach in 1847. A mill purchased by John Parsons, one-time manager of the eight-sail mill in Barrington Gate, was moved complete from Whaplode to Boston Road on rollers.

The operation could not be accomplished in a day, so it was merely left overnight in the roadway with a few men to guard it! Next day the move was completed with negligible damage to the structure, which continued in use until demolished in the early 1900s. Holbeach cannot have seen the like in monumental manoeuvring again until the installation of the 15-tonne, 65ft-high flour bin towers at Barrington Gate in 1988.

A useful insight into how mills of a century ago were equipped and driven can be gained

NEAREST OLD MILL TO HOLBEACH STILL STANDING is the former Horreys, later C & H Dawson's Penny Hill Mill, where youngsters would often be sent to fetch a bag of bran for the family pig.

from a 1900 advertisement for the auction of Damgate Mill. Power came either from the wind or a 12-horsepower steam engine, and ancillaries included a Cornish boiler fitted with 'Galloway tubes, sieve dickey and an offal stripper'. The existing miller was retiring through ill-health after 28 years,

dwelling house adjoining, with two paddocks covering some four acres.

Unfortunately, all but one of the traditional mill buildings in Holbeach have disappeared. Kilby's Damgate Mill was demolished in 1960, thus disturbing the routine of all the old Holbeachians who used to walk out to it on Sunday mornings, on a circular promenade that took

them along the public footpath from Barrington Gate, round by the mill, and then back again along Damgate and Fishpond Lane. The old mill didn't die without putting up a fight, for it successfully resisted initial attempts to pull it down by two caterpillar tractors! The mill house survives, two doors along from Shearers on the Damgate Road, but the only mill still operating in Holbeach is represented by the modern plant at Barrington Gate, of which more below.

MODERN INDUSTRY

Milling at Barrington Gate

The mill at Barrington Gate has been in continuous use for over 170 years, the former manager's cottage, dating from 1828, and the original proprietor's residence next door, Barrington House, surviving as evidence of its long history.

EARLY SELF-CONTAINMENT. A mid-19th-century engraving of the Barrington Gate mill on a bill-head clearly shows Barrington House – little altered externally to this day– as part of the business premises, although curiously, the manager's cottage has been omitted.

[Courtesy J W Belsham.]

thus presenting a 'Splendid opportunity for an energetic young man, the district being the best in the country for strong wheat.' Other than the mill itself, the new incumbent stood to be a person of some property. Included in the sale was the miller's cottage, corn and flour granaries, stabling, gig-house, 'Waggon hovel, and other convenient Out-buildings'. Prospective bidders were also offered the option to buy a newly-built

In the earlier years of the mill's existence, an eight-sail windmill, also built in 1828, provided the motive power. Steam later took the place of wind to drive it when more equipment was installed, but in 1887 it progressively lost four of its sails. So the mill tower was dismantled, along with all functional ironwork, and became redundant. Louisa, widow of the mill's founder, Frederick Adolphus Harrisson, died in 1892 and after a long period of neglect with little

168

A LAST VIEW IN FULL SAIL. The mill, circa 1884.
[Courtesy David Baker.]

interest shown in the asking price of £1,000, the premises were bought in 1909 by a Moulton miller, A W Tindall. The far-sighted Tindall realised that to take full advantage of a prime wheat-growing area, the old tower and sails method was inadequate for the potential volumes involved, and embarked on a full renovation and modernisation programme. He installed a complete roller plant and silos, created additional storage facilities, built a new warehouse and connected a gas supply. With continuous updatings the mill became a

1920s VIEW. The mill plant before the 1928 fire.
[Courtesy David Baker.]

model plant, where such devices as rinsing worms, whizzers and reduction rolls were all part of the bewildering terminology. Even the old mill tower performed a function, with pipelines leading into and out of it as distribution points for grain, and the whole enterprise was neatly described as 'the embodiment of progress' by a visiting journalist from the milling press.

Rebuilding after the fire
A limited company was formed in 1926, with J W Bennett, hailing from a corn-milling family in Downham, joining as a director.

All went well until the evening of March 21st 1928, when the mill caught fire. The town's firefighting equipment, consisting of a secondhand steam-powered fire engine, about to undergo its first tryout since overhaul, and towed by the brigade's long-wheelbase Model T Ford, may not have had far to come, but the situation looked critical. Captain J C Hardy and his team first drew water from the drain near the mill, and then when that was exhausted, transferred to a pit. Unfortunately, not even the 500 feet of additional fire brigade hose –purchased two years earlier at a cost of £14.7s.6d per 100ft– was enough to avert destruction.

However, the 'trouble at mill ' in Barrington Gate was a valuable turning-point in disguise, for it consolidated the way ahead for local milling if it was to survive competitively. In a further major rebuilding programme, A W Tindall Ltd invested in new buildings and more modern equipment on the Simon system. With the discovery that the ground was waterlogged two feet below the surface this was no mean feat, and the new buildings had to be constructed on a concrete raft resting on 18 inches of poor clay. What remained of the old mill tower after the fire was trimmed down to half its original height, so that it could be retained for storage. With self-generated electricity as its main power source, the mill continued its traditional function of producing all grades of bread flour from locally-grown and imported wheat, and with its distinctive tulip emblems, advertised its wares to bakers both locally and nationally. After a major overhaul of the machinery in 1947, it was business very much as before, dealing directly with local farmers, especially those to the south of the town. Many of them, with no storage facilities of their own, towed in trailers full of grain straight from the combine. It was stored at the Maltings in Damgate, while the mill also had sheds at Fosdyke. As part of its involvement in the community, provision was later made for receiving French children on exchange visits from Mondement and Sézanne, with literature printed in French entitled *La Mouture de Blé en Farine.*

New business

REBUILT ON A CONCRETE RAFT. *The mill as reconstructed after the 1928 fire. The neatly shortened remains of the old mill tower were retained for a time.*
[Courtesy David Baker.]

When old Mr Bennett died, the nature of the business took on a new dimension with the arrival of David Baker in 1972. With a background in a Lincoln family milling concern which had to make way for ring road development, Mr Baker brought with him a new and valuable customer base, among whom were Carrs, McVities, Huntley & Palmers, Cadburys and Jacobs.

However, with costs continuing to rise and with higher output the only way to meet the problem, Tindalls replaced nearly all of their plant with Swiss Buhler machinery in 1980, with the aim of increasing production to 700 tons a week.

From Garretts to Smiths

When G Garrett & Sons Ltd took over in 1988, more investment –worth £1¼ million– followed. The three, 65-ft flour bins mentioned earlier, delivered by road from Scotneys of Hull, were lifted into place by one the world's largest cranes, while a new packing plant and better storage facilities were later installed.

These improvements ensured an output by 1991 of 900 tonnes in a good week, with most of the wheat coming in from farms within a 50-mile radius of Holbeach. But major concerns such as Allied, Spillers and Rank producing the lion's share of British flour for their own bakeries made life tough for smaller independents like Garretts, who felt it advisable to sell out to Smiths Flour Mills in 1993. A screen room of computers now monitors every aspect of the mill's function, banks of unattended Italian Golfetto machines shake and shimmy their way through riddling and sieving routines, and with staff working round-the-clock shifts apart from Good Friday, Easter Sunday and Christmas Day, every day is a busy one for Smiths, often with several incoming lorries waiting outside to use the weighbridge at once, after which the load is tested and transferred to the bins according to moisture, protein and blend. Each customer –sharing in the mill's weekly output of 55 lorry-loads totalling some 1,200 tons– has his own specific requirement as to high or low protein, or strong or low gluten. Yet the premises housing this sophisticated activity are no masterpiece of steel and glass. For the shell of Tindall's main building, as put up in 1929 with its substantial old staircases, ornate fire doors and maple floors, is still more than equal to the task.

Peter Cunnington

Innovators do not come two-a-penny, often to the extent that they remain undiscovered, even by their own community, for some appreciable time.

A last blacksmith

In Peter Cunnington's case, this was probably because he appeared initially to the outside world as a traditionalist rather than a forward-thinker. Traditionalist in that he began at Cranmore Lane near the old

PETER'S SMITHY. *Inside the Nissen hut, 1964. [Photo Peter Cunnington.]*

railway line with what was possibly the last blacksmith's business in Holbeach –an unusual occupation in itself for a young man of 22 in February 1962– but in equal measure, forward-thinking enough to use those facilities to plug gaps in a market that, since the demise of the farmhorse in the 1950s, was accelerating its demand for all types of specialised machinery.

Even had he done nothing in this direction, there would have been no shortage of work in the first few years. He found plenty to do adapting horse ploughs for tractor use, making farm trailers out of old lorry chassis, fashioning domestic wrought-ironwork, and even shoeing the odd die-hard's horse.

But Peter had a creative streak that needed to be satisfied, and that chance came when a farming customer from Whaplode, R A Pocklington, came to him with a brief for a tractor-driven pea elevator.

Over-the-Top and Speedi Spud

The result was the Over-the-Top Elevator, which despite its name was a practical, no-nonsense machine for attaching to a Massey Ferguson tractor, in which form it was capable of green-pea lifting, bale lifting, stationary elevating and beet loading and cleaning. It was revealed to the press in November 1963 retailing at a basic £800, and was demonstrated throughout the following year at various agricultural events.

LITERALLY 'OVER THE TOP'. This early elevator development from 1963 had great potential, hampered only by lack of production facilities at the time. Driver Stan Cliff lets it all pass over his head.
[Photo Peter Cunnington.]

SPEEDI SPUD IN ACTION, 1969. Somewhere up in the 'pulpit', Peter Cousins controls the spud-lifting, while Derek Smith on the conventional tractor collects them in his trailer. This fantastic-looking device could be operated with or without its canopy.

[Photo Peter Cunnington.]

The next Pocklington-Cunnington project followed in late 1968 in the form of the Speedi Spud Lifta, a fantastic-looking device featuring a wheel-less Massey Ferguson 35, perched high on top of a maze of chains, wheels and drivebelts that went to make up a species of combine, which could harvest potatoes to the extent of nearly an acre an hour, at half the normal cost.

At that time, Cunnington's workshop facilities were restricted largely to an ex-wartime Nissen hut purchased and transported from Hethel aerodrome for £101 all in, so series production of the Over-the-Top and the Speedi Spud in Holbeach proved impossible.

It was intended to farm out manufacture to national-status companies, but John King of Leeds –after printing all the sales literature– found themselves unable to proceed with Over-the-Top, while Massey-Ferguson had to drop the Speedi Spud to concentrate on problems they were having with their own combine-harvester range.

In-house elevator range

Undaunted, Cunningtons specialised from 1969 in a range of variable-reach elevators that were to consolidate their future. These Swift Lifts, for use with potatoes, sugar beet, onions, root crops, grain, sacks –in fact anything that needed lifting and could fit onto the adjustable-profile conveyor belt– became the staple products. They were updated as the larger-capacity Euro range from 1980, to which tailored accessories could be added, such as cushioned potato chutes to avoid drop damage when loading into lorries, alternative hoppers, and slewing platforms to enable the machines to swing safely through wide arcs with minimal manoeuvring. This led on to ever more ambitious projects, with elevators adapted in the late 1980s for bulk storage work, shooting vast amounts of grain into warehouses in a fraction of the time taken by tipper trucks.

An early key employee was 'Lin' Secker, who left to start his own welding business when Cunningtons finally had to discontinue their repair side in 1977 to concentrate on manufacture, research and development, the design work remaining the responsibility of Peter Cunnington, who has always enjoyed 'being creative'. This modest self-description of his work resulted in Swift Lift Conveyors becoming European market leaders with an export trade to areas as diverse as Siberia and Nigeria. Where customers were concerned, Peter learned early on not to

THE SKY'S THE LIMIT as the range of Cunnington's Swift Lifts extends ever upwards outside the Cranmore Lane factory, mid-1980s.

[Photo Peter Cunnington.]

judge a book by its cover. In 1969, a young man of casual, hippy appearance came to look round an elevator. Peter doubted if a sale would result, but Mr Cunnington Senior thought otherwise, and he was right. The enquirer turned out to be Lord de Ramsey's son and not only did he buy that elevator, but an order for 11 more followed soon after!

In 1994 Peter retired and sold the business to Terry Johnson Ltd, a firm hitherto located in Boston Road and run by its founder who had originally worked for Bettinsons and its acquiring company, Hestair. So significant elements of home-grown expertise, skilled labour and local manufacturing capacity have been retained and continued in the town, a situation Peter Cunnington regards with much satisfaction whenever he looks across the field to his former enterprise, from the rear of his house in Hallgate.

Other Industry

Plans to introduce a new wave of light industry into Holbeach during the mid-1970s met with a mixed reception. Misgivings were expressed by Robert Side, then Headmaster at The George Farmer School, who felt that 'the town's already overcrowded schools will not be able to cope with the influx of new families the development might bring'. One could sympathise with Mr Side's predicament. He was already faced with beginning another school year with 200 children over the 400 limit for which the school was originally built. But his comment did not acknowledge the employment potential for school-leavers. If faced with the same situation today, it is likely that the Holbeach schools would take a more accommodating view, keen as they are to see pupils' talents and abilities 'ploughed back', wherever appropriate, into the local economy. Coun. John Pearl recognised this at the time, when he commented that too many young people were leaving the town and going to Peterborough.

The South Holland District Council was also keen to further the opportunity and gave the application from the Council for Small Industry in Rural Areas (CoSIRA) their immediate backing.

It took until 1978 to reach the next stage, and out of the five sites earmarked on the eastern side of town, one was chosen on the Fleet Road opposite Geoff Parker's house. Coun. Chris Brewis opposed the choice as a waste of good farmland –in his view there was an equally suitable site elsewhere on poorer quality land– but the SHDC was adamant, as the Fleet site was one of the few readily available for connection to the then-new Long Sutton and Sutton Bridge sewerage scheme. And, said Chief Excutive James Brindley, it is also in an area where new employment opportunities were needed.

From carpets to welding
The initial few units proved a success and by 1988 there were plans to build nine more

NEAT AT FLEET. M & R Glass & Glazing, one of the many neat factory units of all sizes at Fleet Road Industrial Estate, with its wide access roads.

workshops. At the time this drew further concerns from local residents, with a plea from the Holbeach and District Civic Society that the emphasis should be maintained on light industry. But after 20 years' existence, the site remains tidy and acceptably unobtrusive in operation. There are now 22 occupied units of varying sizes,

carrying on activities as diverse as industrial flooring, light engineering and stainless steel fabrication, pine furniture-making, printing, greeting card manufacture, vehicle repairs, tyre and exhaust fitting, carpet warehouse retailing, a veterinary practice, glazing, packaging, welding, aquaria retailing, kitchen and bedroom unit construction, agricultural engineering and the production of 'world class' weighing and packaging machines.

Behind the station

SECKER WELDING
'WELDERS OF DISTINCTION'
Tel 01406 423424
Hours of Business Mon - Fri
8 - 12am 1 - 5pm
ALL VISITORS
REPORT TO RECEPTION
Proprietor Lin Secker

Over a similar period, the former railway station and its surrounding land has also seen some development for light industry. While this is on a much more limited scale than at Fleet Road, the adaptation has been an interesting one, relying largely on former railway buildings or extensions of the same. Freeholders of the site are the Lefley family, whose garage premises have occupied a dominant position on the corner of Fen Road since 1970. Although policy changes in the dealership chain marked an end to the Rover franchise in the late 90s, the motor vehicle side of the business continued as normal, with intriguing changes made to the showroom's contents: for a time, a lone Ferrari became an unlikely exhibit among the sumptuous divans and suites of Susan Lefley's furniture displays.

Across the yard, the main station building survives as an intact example of local railway architecture, and between the old platforms, the former trackbed forms the access to Secker's welding workshops, where the family business has been kept busy for over a quarter of a century, producing and installing tanks for bulb-sterilising purposes and turning out many other jobs involving specialised steel and ironwork. Clifford 'Lin' Secker is a noted figure in the welding business, accepting regular commissions and consulting work from as far afield as Cornwall, the Isles of Scilly, the Channel Islands and Canada and Australia. Even in the days when he first passed out top in the country in the City and Guild Welding examinations, Lin's personal library of books on welding numbered nearly 400 titles!

While wife Doreen looks after the admin side, training courses and consulting sessions are held in the main part of the office building, not only for those learning the trade, but for skilled welders from all over the UK looking to upgrade to a higher level to recognised British and European standards. Lin's sons Stephen and Linden bring their own talents to the business; Stephen assists his father with the training sessions as a highly accomplished welding craftsman, while Linden has built up a reputation for electrical troubleshooting and servicing and repairing domestic and industrial heating appliances. Closing time for customers may be 5 p.m., but the team works much longer behind closed doors than the opening hours suggest.

Other service industries for agriculture have by their very nature been able to diversify and adapt readily for other markets. Hortech Systems Ltd in Hallgate for instance, a young company established in the late 1980s, not only provides tailored glasshouse and irrigation systems for growers –and all that goes with it in the form of ballvalves, solenoids, reservoir liners, misting and fogging systems– but can turn its hand to irrigation systems for golf courses, football pitches, bowling greens and gardens.

DOUBLE DUTY. Units for Holbeach Body & Plastic (left) and Lefleys (right) look modern at the front, but share a back wall with an old goods shed.

In a workshop just opposite 'Lin', a Metro bonnet specially sprayed with the artwork of Rover cars ancient and modern testifies to the award-winning skills of Kevin Broughton, making good the dents and rust of Holbeach's motorists, and helped by his father. Holbeach Body & Plastic's back wall still shows traces of the railway age, with bricked-up arches and doorways to what may have been an unloading bay. Next door to him is another brick railway shed, a more complete one this time, right down to its series of half-moon windows high up in the walls, and the roof space still black from the soot of steam engines long gone.

WILL IT SERVE ANOTHER OCCUPANT? Former railway office behind the goods shed, still standing in 2003.

♣♣♣♣♣♣♣

13 – Sporting Holbeach

Over the years, Holbeach has mustered clubs, teams and individuals who have at best been outstanding, or at the very least made a very worthwhile contribution to sport in general, from football, shot-putting and weight-lifting, through cycling and athletics, to cricket and even paralympic events. Here are a few examples which have done much to put Holbeach on the sporting map.

Bell End Speedway

Whirlwind Watkin on the 350 AJS; Ron Newman piloting the 490 Norton; H Winterton astride the 500 AJS; G R Green from the Hurn with a 500 Douglas. Just a few of the Holbeach men who kept the crowds spellbound at the Bell End Speedway in the 1930s.

From far and wide

In a decade when car and motorcycling events of varying organisational quality proliferated, Bell End stood out as one of the better ones. In a typical season of a dozen or so major fixtures lasting from April through to October, the Holbeach & Spalding Motor Cycle and Light Car Club drew fans from a considerable surrounding area. It was one reason why the Club optimistically aimed to recruit 1,000 members in 1939 and, acknowledging the huge following

SPEEDWAY THRILLER. A competitions bike like this was typical of the machines racing at Bell End.

from places outside Holbeach, occasionally held races as far afield as Wisbech and March. At the home ground, many fans were quite content to make a day of it and travel distance-no-object to Bell End by push-bike. Young Brian Paul, for instance, fortified by flask and sandwiches, pedalling from Shepeau Stow; or Ann Green, a Tip Mills supporter from Star Cross, complete with her eldest son in the handlebar seat, safe in the knowledge that no charge was made for cycles in the car park, provided they were propped 'by the left-hand hedge only'. Special buses were laid on, too, on those Sunday afternoons: Eastern Counties left Wisbech at 1 p.m., while Lincolnshire Road Car Company departed from Holbeach 15 minutes later.

Bell End was situated in a field near the Bell Inn at Weston Hills, with the Club Secretary's office at 29 Fleet Street, Holbeach. The subscription was a reasonable 3/6 (18p) a year, or 2/- (10p) for associate members, for which both categories were entitled to half-price admission to race meetings, use of the clubroom at Holbeach, and participation in 'social outings, trials and competitions'. They could also buy Club regalia, such as badges at 6/- (30p) each, 'stud or brooch' coat badges at 1/- (5p), or one-shilling pennants.

Star riders

Star rider of 1938 was Roy Duke, who in his first ride for Holbeach the previous year on the Carter's Park cinder track had defeated the town's virtuoso, Buster Yeomans. With many of today's sportsmen refusing to 'get out of bed', as the saying goes, for less than several thousand or even millions, Bell End's carrot of £1, payable to any rider who could break the track record for four laps, sounds laughable now. But not only was it sufficient incentive for Bill Kitchen to manage it in 82 seconds in April 1939, but it drew in more formidable opposition from down south, who saw it as easy money. Nevertheless the home team were more often than not victorious and, occasionally joining forces with Spalding, were more than capable of taking on the best that the likes of Birmingham, Bournemouth, Nottingham, Romford and Worcester could muster, as they raced around the track. Coming under the watchful eye of the Clerk of the Course Gordon Woodman, Timekeeper A Bradley and W J Patchett, the Holbeach favourites wore distinctive helmet colours: Ted English, Captain, would be in red, Alan Smith and Tip Mills, blue, and Geoff Godwin and Roy Duke also in red. Whatever the outcome of those distant roaring days of thrills and spills, there would be plenty for spectators to talk about over tea afterwards at one of the Holbeach hostelries mentioned in the programme: the Black Bull or the Station and Talbot Hotels. There were special attractions, too, with the antics of 'Eric Peacock, the One-Armed Wonder', whose 'exhibition of solo and sidecar acrobatics will thrill and amaze you'. He had even performed these manoeuvres on the music-hall stages of London, Paris and Brussels!

While Bell End's activities may have suggested a male preserve, many women attended the events. Wives, girlfriends and families were included in the Holbeach and Spalding Motor Cycle and Light Car Club's summer outings, such as the August Trial of 7th August 1938. This commenced at Long Sutton's Market Place at 10.45 a.m. and finished 72 miles away on the Norfolk coast, with a programme of sports and amusements. 'So fill those back seats and pillions!' commanded the organisers.

Portentously, there was a programme printed for Sunday 3rd September, 1939. But the event was cancelled for obvious reasons. It would have been an important meeting that day, with riders like Crasher Warren as part of the Holbeach and Spalding team ready to take on the Dominions, captained by Eric Chitty from Canada.

Post-war revival
Although the Club's affairs were wound up while the war was on, it resumed activities after 1945. For a while, it remained a successful crowd-puller, as the 1946 season showed. The first post-war meeting on 19 May that year got off to a flying start, when 7,500 people watched Bill Kitchen establish a new record. Thousands came, too, to the Whit-Sunday meeting, where they were brought to their feet by the predicament of Tiger Hart and Don Houghton when their machines locked together, while it fell to Wilf Jay, Bell End Captain, to provide a spectacular finish, winning his heat with a mudguard trailing on the ground and his exhaust pipe twisted around the bike's frame. The crowd swelled to 8,000 when F W 'Freddie' Dixon opened the meeting in early August. Dixon had achieved fame at

Brooklands track in Surrey pre-war, both on motor cycles as one of the first to coax 100 mph out of an eight-valve Harley Davidson, and later in Riley sports cars. In September the 'test match' that could not be staged on the outbreak of war – 'England v. the Dominions'– was run at last. Bill Kitchen could not take part because of injury, but Norman Parker and Tiger Hart provided plenty of excitement and England went on to win by 44 points to 28, the new concrete starting strip having proved its worth.

Decline
All these events were big money-raisers for charity, and the 1946 season alone provided substantial donations towards the Holbeach Forces Commemoration Fund, the Whaplode St Catherine Memorial Hall, and a new car for the Holbeach & District Nursing Association's District Nurse (Miss M J Powell). But all good things come to an end, and interest waned in the early 50s. Not even the introduction of midget racing cars was enough to revive matters, although this development was considered by some to have hastened the closure of Bell End by changing its character too much. But while the glory years lasted in the 30s and 40s, Bell End was a nationally famous venue that gave of its best.

The spirit lives on
After the demise of Bell End, there were others from the town who distinguished themselves on two or four wheels, though not necessarily in or around Holbeach. In the 1970s, the brothers Mike and John Horsepole, for instance, scored several wins in national sidecar meetings and achieved a respectable 6th position in a 1976 Brands Hatch event, after starting from the back of the grid on their Bingham Yamaha. And August 1984 saw 22-year-old Dave Tinn and co-driver Richard Ladbrook lying in the top ten of the Eastern Association of Motor Clubs Championships, driving their 2300cc Vauxhall Chevette HSR which, they claimed, was 'faster than a Porsche 911 Turbo.' While Dave's experience had started with go-karts at the age of 12, George Baines was kart racing for charity at the age of 50 in 1996, having set up a five-man team from Holbeach, Sleaford, Nottingham and Leicestershire to enter the

National Karting Challenge. But years after the closure of Bell End, its spirit was still inspiring one old campaigner: the Revd Wilf 'Kid' Curtis, who had first competed at Bell End at the age of 16 in 1939. In 1993 after suppressing an urge to contact *Jim'll Fix It*, he wrote to the management of Belle Vue Speedway in Manchester. His wish was granted, and in October that year, at the age of 70, he was speeding round the Belle Vue track, reliving those heady days at Holbeach.

Holbeach Cricket Club

Early records of Holbeach Cricket Club are somewhat sketchy, except to say that it was obviously in existence in the late nineteenth century. Expertise flourished in the 1900s with the Harrissons, S S Mossop and W D Curtis, who in June 1905 had the Farmers of the District XI all out for 44. 'It is hoped our farmer friends [numbering among them A H Worth, E and W H Tinsley, A West and H Thompson] will not be down-hearted, but live to fight another day', read a report. Meanwhile history was made on 16th May 1906, when J C Harrisson, in the match against Holbeach Hurn, scored 108 runs in just under two hours before being caught by E Tinsley. This was believed to be the first century ever recorded in Holbeach, a state of euphoria impossible to repeat during this period when facing the dreaded Sutton Bridge, against whom, one Holbeach cricketer remarked, 'We seem fated to defeat'. The Neneside village presented a Bermuda Triangle, where, in July 1913, even three of the Harrissons were dismissed for five runs between them, only G Driffill achieving 13.

In later years many more well-known names in Holbeach helped to bring much promise to the Club, before its sad demise in 2000 due to lack of players. For some enthusiasts, in the Club's heyday, it was often a lifelong involvement, individuals such as Bryan Stamp playing from the age of fourteen, when Walter Derry Curtis was still President in the immediately pre-war years. Secretary at that time –a post he held for several years, interrupted only by war service in the RAF– was fast bowler Dick Kent - Woolsey, well known as a schoolmaster at the Boys School and later The George Farmer. John Pearl eventually took over the secretaryship, and together

with his wife Christine, who was Treasurer and later Social Secretary, was involved with the Club to the very end.

After the Second War, the first Holbeach cricket season was held in 1946. W D Curtis resumed the presidency for a while, to be succeeded in that position by Dr J C Hunter. The Club restarted with almost no equipment and negligible funds. But with the raising of adult and junior subscriptions to 10s (50p) and 5s (25p) respectively, and thanks to the loan of bats from Messrs W L Bentley and R Bowser, the use of John Mossop's offices as the Club's HQ and the restoration of the wicket by park keeper Ralph Emmitt, matters were soon on a workable footing. Occasionally, the bowling may have outshone the batting in those early post-war days, typified by Kent-Woolsey's 107 wickets for 398 runs! But it was an era of good attendances, watching such noted players as C J Harrison, who also played at County level, Alec West junior, schoolmaster Joe Franks, Vern Keeble, Ron Nurse, Ted Ibbott and Danny Ambrose. Ambrose also captained the likes of Ray Jackson, Peter Lown, Bryan Stamp, Dick Megginson, Ron Nurse and Frank Woolley, with John Mossop, a later President of the Club, captaining the Second XI. Mrs Mary (Molly) Mossop, too, was seen to play on occasion, as in the mixed team that took on the Holbeach Youth Centre Boys. She was joined by four other ladies –Miss Crawford, Mrs Palmer, Miss D Bryan and Mrs C Lockwood. But their combined might, which included Dick Kent-Woolsey, John Mossop, W G Hix and the Kent, Storey and Keeble boys, failed to defeat Holbeach Youth Centre!

Mossop's merry 20
Holbeach 'A' cricket team contributed consistently good value to the local press columns in the late 1940s and early 50s, as when they once beat Long Sutton 'A' by 162 runs. 'On a featherbed wicket devoid of life', ran the report, 'D Neale hit 69, including seven fours, and Huyton retired after scoring 50, which included four fours and a six. Mossop retired after a merry 20, which included two sixes and a four. Sutton batsmen had no answer to the attack and were all out for 32 in 25 overs.' John Mossop's penchant for sixes and fours saved the day on another occasion,

when Holbeach faced a tough time against Crowland 'A', with 'alternating phases of dour defence and hard hitting'. The Holbeach solicitor 'signalled his arrival by hitting a six in his first over and followed it by five fours in his second'. The all-out total was 98, but after a careful opening, Crowland collapsed after 'a good spell of bowling by Skate'.

A valued addition to the strength in the late 1950s was Joe Price, recipient of the batting cup, who captained Lincolnshire for two seasons. Nor must one forget those faithful . umpires in Charlie Woolley, Jack Neal, Herbert Wright, Reg Wright, and Eric Kilbon, son of the landlord at the Nelson in St John Street.

VICTORIOUS IN JULY 1989. Holbeach Cricket Club about to trounce Moulton Harrox in a 44-run victory at Carter's Park. Front row, left to right: Shaun Keeble, Frank Kenyon, Brian Overton, John Bowers, Richard Franks and Andy Bills. Back row, left to right: Robin Ambrose, Trevor Tyler, Sam Baxter, Tim Baxter and Stewart Hatton.
[Photo Lincolnshire Free Press/ Spalding Guardian.]

Grand finale in the 90s
Under Peter Worth's captaincy, the Club entered the South Lincolnshire and Border League. Brian Boucher, Brian Morris, Bryan Stamp, Tony Keeble, David Hatton, Robin Ambrose and John Pearl were all sterling team players at this time. But a manpower shortage was already beginning to make an impression, with several members reaching retirement age at the same time.

It was hoped that better facilities at Carter's Park, such as a new pavilion, built through the generosity of Eric Lane and shared with the Bowls Club, would attract new players, but to no avail. Nevertheless, with Shaun Keeble captaining the side in 1990s, Holbeach Cricket Club achieved a grand finale by winning the Guardian Trophy twice and the championship of Division 1 South Lincs Border League.

Although in 1999 Holbeach cricket was able to take its place in the newly-formed Premier Division, the writing was on the wall. Ever-dwindling numbers were rendering the selection of suitable players an impossible task, and an unwelcome blow followed in 2000 when the committee were faced with paying 50% rates for their bar facilities at Carter's Park – restricting the social facilities that were part and parcel of every match.

So it was that the Club, once proudly described by Kent-Woolsey as having 'caught on with Holbeach public' sadly folded.

The Football Club
Holbeach United, alias 'The Tigers', was formed in 1927, but football in Holbeach goes back much further, although, as with cricket, exact dates of origin are not known.

The trouncing Rangers, 1880s and 90s
United's nineteenth-century equivalents were known as the Holbeach Rangers, who certainly attracted an enthusiastic following, as random press reports indicate. Matches were being played in the 1880s, when Holbeach had already built a reputation, attracting such comments, in an away match against Bourne Town, as: 'Holbeach, (who have been winners of the Shield two years in succession) were the best team', having won 3-1. A typical match in the period would see J C Harrisson in goal, H Smith and H Ostler as backs, T Vise, J A Barclay and J Waller half-backs, W C Patterson and J Goodrick on the right wing, R E Patterson and F A Harrisson as left-wingers, and G T Mason, centre forward. Not surprising then, that between five and six hundred spectators

turned up at Holbeach Cricket Ground to watch Rangers trounce Walsoken 4-1 one fine Bank Holiday Monday in April 1893. By the early 1920s the Club was known as Holbeach Town with Park Road as the home ground, and meeting socially and administratively at the String of Horses pub (or 'Hotel', as it was termed then) in Boston Road. Mr F Fletcher was President, over a committee composed of master grocer Walter Derry Curtis, E Bullen, J Towns, F Hardy, S Waltham, C Ibbott, F Poole, H Chenery and W Waltham. Captain was H Pywell and Vice-Captain C T Driffill, heading a list of 50 registered players, some of whose surnames, such as E Capes, H Beeken, A S English, A S Bayston and F H Bowser (goalie) sound familiar to us today. Playing colours were red-and-white vests with 'white knickers', and some of the team were doubtless shod with E Bullen's football boots, from the West End Boot Stores (slogan: 'You will tread the path of life easier').

The Lynn League years

In 1927 the Club was reformed as Holbeach United, and up to the war years competed in the Lynn League. Typical of the team's successes in this League was their match against Upwell in April 1936. 'It was an excellent game', remarked the press article, 'and Holbeach deserved their 5-3 win. In the early stages, G Elston gave Holbeach the lead with a fine shot after a solo run...After Upwell had reduced the lead, Holbeach netted with a terrific shot from Johnson, who played a great game at centre-half...Holbeach made the game safe with goals by Curtis and G Elston.'

With attendances continuing to rise, spectator comfort became a priority. So between them, Secretary Les Stephenson and Chairman Gordon Woodman developed the idea of a fund to build a grandstand, eventually installed at a cost of £400 in the spring of 1940. This venerable structure is still with us, if not a little overdue for replacement.

The crowd-pulling 40s

In 1946 Holbeach joined the United Counties League and the succession of player-managers began. First of them all was G Simmonds, in an era that packed in the crowds.

'We used to get about 2,000 people coming to watch games against Wisbech and Spalding just after the War,' said Les Stephenson. And no wonder, for the Club had a new phenomenon to show off.

'Who is this Wally French?' asked a journalist in the *Boston & Free Press's* Sporting Chatter column in December 1946. 'Week after week Wally French, the Holbeach County amateur centre-forward, comes into the news as a goal-scorer. Spalding United and their supporters learned something of his abilities a week ago, when he led the defence a merry dance and found the net four times.'

Wally, a master baker who until 1965 was a partner in French & Hargraves in Fleet Street (now the Kan-Ton) had originally impressed spectators in Home Guard matches, having arrived in Holbeach just after war broke out, and married Betty Fox. Dad's Army had never seen the like, for he came with a pedigree honed

HOLBEACH'S BECKHAM. Wally French with Betty Fox on their wartime wedding day.
[Photo Bruce French.]

since the early 1930s playing for Margate (then the 'nursery' for Arsenal), Ramsgate, the Spartan and Southern Counties Leagues, and Newmarket Town. His strengths lay in positioning abilities, ball control, and a neat tactic of 'roving out to the wings, making him a nightmare to the opposition', and where 'it often took more than one to hold him'.

In his first full season for Holbeach, French scored 18 goals. So it was not surprising that he was soon selected by the Lincolnshire Football Association to play as centre-forward in the Lincs team to meet Derbyshire, and later Nottinghamshire.

In these matches he was one of only two players from the south of the County, which explains the convoluted travelling arrangements that seemed little better than in J C Harrisson's day, involving providing his own transport ('Can you borrow a car?' asked the LFA) before joining a Lincolnshire Road Car bus at some point along its route via Grimsby, Lincoln and Newark.

The accolades continued: 'French completed the hat-trick'...'they scored a couple of goals –that good man French obtaining both of them'...'French gave the home team the lead and two more goals were added through French'...'French made a quick recovery after being floored in a tackle, and scored'.

All good things come to an end however, even though Wally did not retire from the game until he was 50. A potential Beckham of his time, opportunities had presented themselves along the way, including a chance to play for Cambridge. But he said he would not play for money, although after taking up squash very successfully from the age of 60, he once wagered £1,000 that his son Bruce could not beat him at his new pastime. On that rare occasion Bruce won, but is still awaiting the cash!

Rallying the crowds –with Shakespeare, 1950s
Did Holbeach and District really appreciate the efforts the Tigers were making in this period? A letter in the *Spalding Guardian* for 18th January 1952 suggested otherwise. Rather in the spirit of Laurence Olivier as Henry V addressing his troops before Agincourt and mysteriously signed 'Old Gold', it tried hard to stir up more enthusiasm:

'There is a tide in the affairs of men, said Shakespeare, which if taken at the flood leads to fortune…We have a team we can be proud of, young, fast virile –and above all, local... Of the 22 players in our colours today, no less than 18 reside in East Elloe, and 13 of these are products of local football…Do your friends and neighbours realise the standard of football they are now missing?…Let us show the lads that we are with them in the fight –all 500 of us –AND 500 MORE'.

Over 1954-55 Len Ritchie took over as manager, coinciding with the Club's admittance to the Eastern Counties League (later to become the Town & Country League). There was also a brief and unsuccessful spell in the Midland League which saw Holbeach returned to the UCL after only a year, but followed by a happier period with the late Freddie Watkin as player-manager, during which Holbeach won the United Counties League Cup and also achieved runner-up position on another occasion. Freddie contributed 28 years of his loyal talents to Holbeach Utd, playing until he was 48 and continuing as manager to 1978. A bench in his honour was donated by Mrs Watkin in 1999.

A HOME WIN OVER SPALDING, AUGUST 1953.
Back row, left to right: Wells, P R Wright, Cole, Hargrave, Watkins, Tootill. Front row, left to right: Price, Bett, Skidmore, Fox, and Stamp. The Tigers were United Counties League Runners Up in 1953-1954.

[Photo courtesy John Hall.]

Fighting back
In the mid-to-late 1970s, the Club went through a difficult financial period. But thanks to the efforts of Chairman Brian Paul, Kip Kierman, Bob Merchant, Russ Delahoy, Registration Secretary Bryan Stamp (like Freddie Watkin, another long-term player and subsequently, reserve team manager), fundraiser Hubert Thain, Treasurer Brian Peachman and builder Derek Brown, who built the social club backing onto the stand in Park Road,

Holbeach rose again for one of its finest hours: the first round of the F A Cup in 1982. Unfortunately, the Tigers lost 4-0 to Wrexham at Peterborough that November, but it was still a great achievement for a team composed largely of local men, while their Under-18 team was consistently strong at that time.

Cash continued to be a problem as United entered the 1990s. The old changing rooms had been condemned back in 1986 and although the team was able to share the Cricket Club's facilities, economies could not prevent the Club slipping £30,000 into the red by 1992, thus delaying replacement of the old 1940 stand and restricting the amount of finance available for new players.

At the time of writing, the Club still enjoys the loyalty of long-service members like Bill Ladbrook, Bill Shortland, and Peter Cousins, while Bryan Stamp's involvement with United has passed the 50-year mark. If gatekeeper Bill Ladbrook won the Lottery, he would sponsor the Tigers, which would certainly have paid for the proposed new grandstand. But like everyone else who supports and plays for the Club, his real ambition is to see Holbeach United win the coveted FA Vase.

Bowls at Carter's Park

The original deeds to Carter's Park stipulated that a part of it was to be set aside for football, cricket and bowls. Of the two main surviving sports played there, football may draw the more obvious crowd, but bowls are no less active. In fact, from the last Thursday in April to the second week in September, there is something going on almost continuously in one league or another.

Familiar names, established awards
Well-known Holbeach names of old are immortalised on the sides of trophies. Still awarded is the W D Curtis Cup for mixed doubles matches; the S S Mossop Cup for triples, and the Stukeley Challenge Bowl for mixed singles, not to mention the Carter Cup for men's forward singles.

These have been joined in more recent years by the F Aubin Cup, and the Arnold Shield, donated by David and Val Arnold, who are respectively the Club's Secretary

and C Team Captain. The Shielagh Steel Cup is awarded in the Ladies' section. Holbeach 'household' names have occupied the President's chair, too: John Mossop in 1969, and Len Hawkins in 1985, for example.

The clubhouse, formerly shared with the Cricket Club, is the venue for committee meetings now. But back in the 1930s and 40s they were held in various places, such as the String of Horses pub in Boston Road, the Park pavilion, or Mr G Stanberry's house at 70 Church Street.

Sawdust, slag and fertiliser
In 1937, rental of the green was £15 annually from the Parish Council, who also maintained it. It was to them, for instance, that Mr L Weatherhogg applied when it was decided that the Club should add 3 cwt of fertiliser to the turf that October, to be supplemented by wormkiller the following spring. Sometimes members helped out in these matters: in 1950, Mr Stanberry supplied basic slag for the green when sawdust was unobtainable.

Membership revisions
Also unobtainable at that time was full playing membership for ladies, although 19 of them had added £4.15s (£4.75) to the Club's coffers in 1937 with their associate subscriptions of 5/- (25p) each. One hoped that their involvement amounted to more than the predictable wielding of teapots and breadknives, but at any rate all that changed with their final admission as playing members during the 1970s, with the result that 21st-century Carter's Park bowls feature Team Captains Lesley Dunham, Maxine Rawet, Val Arnold, Doreen Horner, Banks Captain Janet Ashton and committee members Edna Gray and Linda Price as essential contributors to Club life.

Bowls continued uninterrupted through the War and were game for anything thereafter: friendly matches with Spalding Police and the Moulton Chequers, County matches played triumphantly on the home green, winning Holbeach the title of County Champions on occasion, and national competitions at Worthing. Nowadays there are 56 members making up four teams, with a 19-strong committee under President Roy Griffiths and

Chairman Dick Dunham. And it is not just a mature person's sport, either. The Club is determined to attract the younger element: one member who joined them in recent years at the age of 12 became proficient enough for England trials and County matches within a decade!

Les Fensom and the Holbeach Wheelers

'Top Dog' – 'No Stopping Les Fensom'– 'Outstanding County Road Rider'– 'Fensom Makes Fast Time' – 'County's Best Road Rider' – 'Breaks More Records' – 'Fenland's Fastest Cyclist'. The superlatives, however, are the journalists', entirely unprompted by the central character. For anyone less a self-publicist than Les Fensom, especially in this age of victorious sportsmen directing champagne bottles at each other like water cannons, could hardly be imagined.

Following in brothers' wheeltracks, 1940
While still a pupil of Holbeach Boys School, Les already had two proficient elder brothers –T W and L G Fensom– reaping the local cycling honours before the war. They expected him to follow their example,

WHEELER AT SPEED. Les Fensom flat out in one of his trials.

[Photo courtesy the late Leslie Fensom.]

having emphasised the point by assembling a racing bike for him with the words: 'You have got to get started'.

They need not have worried. Les won his first race, a Spalding Cycling Club 10-mile event for under-18s, at the age of 14. This was in 1940 and although war, the ATC and the Forces intervened, he went on gaining experience whenever he could, such as the occasional 25-mile trial, and was placed in the 1944 Fenland Longmarker's Ride.

After demobilisation, he returned to his job at Cheers outfitters on the corner of Boston Road and West End, eager to resume competitive cycling. This coincided in April 1946 with the return of the Holbeach Wheelers Cycling Club, which had been in the doldrums since the early 1930s and was now resurrected to promote 'better friendship between cyclists in and around Holbeach', under the presidency of Mr Field, and later P H Ellis. Les became an early member and soon after, Club Secretary, the Wheelers eventually settling on a hut behind Whaplode's Lamb & Flag as its clubroom.

In the King's Lynn Open 25-mile race on Easter Monday 1949, he won ahead of 120 riders with a new record of 1 hour, 3 minutes, 59 seconds. It wasn't long however, before he had beaten his own record in the Fenland Championship '25', from where he went from strength to strength, in 50, 100-mile and 24-hour races. By this time Les also belonged to the Spalding Cycle Club which, thanks to his input, only failed once during 1949 to scoop the fastest team award. Out of 14 open events in which Les competed that year, he won eight.

Fenland Champion, 1951
After becoming Fenland Champion again in 1951, followed by a series of other prizes, his triumphs became so much of a talking point that many people in Holbeach came into Cheers' shop during working hours to see how he had fared the previous weekend.

Meanwhile, the Wheelers provided plenty of activity between competitions. Weekly runs were staged to places of interest on Sundays, generally averaging 40 miles, but sometimes extending to resorts such as the South Coast or the Peak District. Touring Captain was Ray Savage, the Club's sole tricyclist, who preferred the stability of three wheels in wintry conditions. Where such outings did not impose a time limit, it was a pleasant way of passing the day, although on the single-carriageway roads of the period, especially in coastal areas, riders had to be prepared for the back-draught created by the many excursion coaches rushing past. Although new members were not expected to better 10 mph, 10-100-mile events were organised for the more experienced. On most of these outings Les was accompanied by his wife Jean, herself an able cyclist, riding with distinction in the 17-mile Sealed Handicap and the Ladies 10 Miles, achieving '10 Best' in 1955.

Excelling in time trials

Meanwhile, Les's speciality –time trials– won him seven trophies in this category over a period of 10 years. But in 1954 he donned the Wheelers' red-and-yellow colours for the ultimate event: the North Road Club's 24-hour time trial. This had a long tradition going back to 1885, with a tortuous route that followed the old A1 Great North Road for certain stretches, but with the aid of hundreds of marshals from local cycling clubs to guide the way, went off at all sorts of tangents through Bedfordshire, Hertfordshire, Cambridgeshire, Northamptonshire and Lincolnshire, involving the competitors in phenomenal mileages. The course began at 12 noon at places such as Cross Halls near Eaton Socon in Cambridgeshire, and before wending its way back through the aforementioned counties to end at the Black Cat Corner near Biggleswade, led competitors through Holbeach during the night. Here, on Fleet Road, Mr and Mrs Field provided a 'fuelling' station, passing soup and drinks in aluminium bottles to the riders to quaff as they passed. As soon as the bottles were jettisoned, they were picked up by other bystanding members of the Wheelers and immediately refilled for the following competitors, with little time for a wipe-over. 'No worries about hygiene in those days!' laughed Les. More important, though, was the value of this trackside support. To quote from the *North Road Gazette* of that 1954 race: 'What about Holbeach? Here Mr and Mrs Field keep open house all night. He is President of the Holbeach Club and their hospitality knows no bounds.'

Unexpected victory, 1955

In his first '24', Les came in a distinguished 6th, immediately behind his brother, T W, who was riding for Spalding Cycle Club. On that occasion he covered 435 miles, 1,360 yards, in an initial placing that would have delighted most amateurs. But Les astounded everyone in his own quiet way when the following year, he won the North Road '24' outright. This time his mileage was 463.047 miles, and 'I did not expect to win it', was his only recorded remark. Tom Fensom came in third, making it an even prouder occasion for the family than in 1954.

For several more years, Les was to do consistently well in this event: 5th in 1956, 3rd in 1957, and 2nd in 1959. But he was most satisfied with his achievement in 1960 when he came 3rd, for this was the year in which the race became more of a cut-and-thrust battle in his estimation, attracting a greater number of top national riders. His success brought him into contact with many famous names of the time, such as Beryl Burton, whom he met at prestigious award ceremonies, dinners and gala evenings held specially for members of the sport at London hotels and the Albert Hall.

Unfortunately the Holbeach Wheelers disbanded during the 1960s and there is no local equivalent to the Club at the time of writing. As for Les, a pushbike remained in his garage at Edinburgh Walk, but the emphasis shifted to gardening and propagating. In which activity, it went without saying that Les tended his soil with the same meticulous attention that he once applied to cycling.

Sally Reddin

Some people say that 'Life begins at 40'. And in Sally Reddin's case, golden achievements certainly followed after the same age.

Yet to begin with, it looked as if all the cards were stacked against her, when at the age of only 33 in 1980, this former supermarket worker from East Elloe Avenue was faced with an operation to remove a tumour of the spine that left her wheelchair-bound.

RECORD ACHIEVEMENT! Sally with her gold medal in 2000.
[Photo Lincs Free Press/ Spalding Guardian.]

Determined to turn this into a positive situation, Sally joined a sporting club for the disabled in Spalding, where she tried various activities, such as table tennis and bowls. But a 'have a go' day at a Wellingborough meeting in 1989 confirmed a talent for putting the shot, and from this point, she never looked back.

A School of Sport course at Nottingham university followed, and an opportunity to train with the British Wheelchair Athletic Association, the benefits of which really paid off. As a result, she was good enough to travel around the world with the British squad, and her athletic career culminated in selection for the 2000 Paralympics in Sydney.

Her achievement here was outstanding to say the least. For after contracting an unlucky virus which affected her breathing and landed her in hospital for 10 days as soon as she arrived at Brisbane airport, Sally not only won the gold in the F52/F54-classification shot putt, but established a new world record throw of 6m 28m –and this from the oldest member of the team!

'That last throw' –her best– 'was just heaven', she said afterwards.

As BBC TV's *Look North* Sports Personality of the Year in 2000, Sally feels that if she can do it, many more disabled people could get involved in sport; the younger people suggest themselves as the most obvious age group here, but those in their 30s and 40s, who seem to her the most indifferent, should also be motivated to have a go.

Geoff Capes

The World's Strongest Man in 1983 and 1985 –the first Briton to achieve that title– was born in Holbeach on 23rd August 1949, and was raised as one of a family of

IMPRESSING THE LOCALS. Geoff Capes putting the shot in Carter's Park.
[Photo: Lincolnshire Free Press/Spalding Gdn.]

nine in three converted cottages in Back Lane. He owes his size to his mother who, standing six feet tall and weighing 18 stone, took no nonsense from anybody, particularly when trying to exonerate Geoff the lad from various scrapes. His comparatively diminutive father (5ft 5in) was a ganger relying on seasonal agricultural work, and times were often hard.

It created a strong survival instinct in Geoff, whose efforts to assert and prove himself often landed him in trouble with authority, both in and out of school. This reputation preceded him to The George Farmer where on his first day at secondary school, Head Joe Fathers asked him: 'Right-o. I've four years to make or break you. What's it going to be?'

From wellington boots to AAA

School certainly wasn't going to 'make' him in academic subjects. But from the day he won a sprint in wellington boots at the age of six in Carter's Park, it was clear where his positive abilities lay. During his time at George Farmer between 1959 and 1964 he represented the school in nearly all sports, particularly athletics, where he received every encouragement from the PE teacher, Gary Cooke, and Holbeach's 'Mr Athletics', Tommy Clay, whose ground-breaking combination of athletics-with-field events at Carter's Park provided the ideal training conditions for Geoff.

By the age of 11 he had established himself as the school shot-putter after a victory over a formidable Donington schoolboy nicknamed 'The Tank', and within the next five years he would be good enough to compete in the AAA Junior Championships at Crystal Palace, as a run-up to his Commonwealth Games and Olympic career.

Weightlifting scrap metal

Stung into action by the remark of a sweetshop owner, who likened his bare torso to a Belsen victim, Geoff took up weightlifting as a teenager, and began training with a 100-lb iron bar he found in Ladbrook's scrapyard at the end of his street.

He and a few others formed the Holbeach Weightlifting Club, whose robust activities proved a little too much for the stage at the Youth Club in Park Road, but eventually found a permanent home in Alison Avenue, in former pre-fab buildings. In those early days, his record for a bench press was 575 pounds.

It was all part of a potential waiting to be realised, hampered as it was by lack of sponsorship, little help with travelling arrangements, and a pair of Woolworths plimsolls that were hardly adequate for shot-putting. Unless Tommy Clay was on hand to give him a lift, it was a question of buses and trains if he could afford it, but more likely hitch-hiking if he couldn't.

Association with Stuart Storey

Meanwhile another slightly older Holbeach athlete of distinction, Stuart Storey, had, after going into the teaching profession, given Geoff his first taste of foreign competition by including him in his Buckinghamshire school's athletics tour of Germany. This saw Capes scattering the onlookers by throwing a 14lb shot right over their heads!

Storey later used his contacts to provide Geoff with coaching from Les Mitchell in Peterborough, and the late 60s became a turning point in the Capes career, bringing eligibility for the Commonwealth and Olympic Games as the next step. In the following few years, his shot-putt successes won him two Commonwealth gold medals, two European indoor medals, various British titles and selection for three Olympic Games.

'Training' on the job

For a while, one of Geoff''s many 'day jobs' was helping his father, and even this provided training opportunities. Lifting a bag of potatoes, for instance, enabled him to do ten presses with it before stacking, and he could load a lorry faster than five men, having once placed 20 tons of potatoes on a cart in as many minutes.

It was all part of a training mix that, combined with all the many other sports he had practised as a teenager, equipped him with what is known as 'a tremendous cardiovascular base'.

Later he joined the police, on the understanding that amateur athletics were to take precedence over any career advancement. Although not a presence to be trifled with, especially in uniform, his power of arrest occasionally took on a rather unique charm.

Once, when arriving to serve a warrant, Geoff digressed into conversation for an hour and a half with the offender over the latter's collection of parakeets before he remembered the purpose of his visit; after which the wrongdoer, considering it more than a fair cop, presented Geoff with three pairs of parakeets, and thus launched him on a lifelong interest in the bird, to the extent that he is now a world champion breeder and a Class One judge.

Meanwhile, where a different breed of bird –the eagle– soared, Geoff proved himself a great Highland Games competitor, winning the Scottish Games seven times and the World Games on five occasions.

Turning professional

The political undercurrents that were beginning to taint Olympic events, typically the boycott of Moscow in 1980 by the USA, West Germany and Kenya, had prompted Geoff to turn professional, and thus be eligible for the Strongest Man competitions.

He had already won the 1979 British event. Europe's Strongest Man he won straight away (in 1980), and he was to repeat this success in 1982 and 1984. In his first World Strongest championships in New Jersey, he finished a creditable third behind Bill Kazmaier and Lars Hedlund, came second in '81, 4th in '82 (injury intervened), but won in 1983 –a first-time-ever achievement for Britain in an event hitherto monopolised by America! He was to win again at Cascais, Portugal in 1985.

With increasing fame came many public appearances, local as well as national, for he switched on the Millennium lights in Holbeach High Street in 1999, among many other 'sightings' in the town.

Naturally he was good value for TV commercials, and Gordon's Gin and Volkswagen obliged. In the making of the VW ad., which set out to prove that their car could be flipped over by Capes without denting, Geoff recalls damaging 10 cars before a satisfactory take was achieved!

A lasting legend

Geoff's last competition appearance was in 1994. But the money earned from strength athletics has funded a very active business career that now revolves chiefly around a security firm called Capes UK, employing 1,200 people, and also involvement in Live Promotions, a company organising outside events, and the Britain's Strongest Man Competitions, televised on Sky. He is a JP and has even exhorted you, from stickers on fish-and-chip shop windows, to 'Support your local takeaway'.

Not bad for a rough-and-tumble member of a class in Holbeach Junior School, who were told that there were limits to what they could do in life. Suppression rather than encouragement has never had any place in his philosophy: 'If you do something, you should always do well to succeed –or don't do it', he says.

Tommy Clay –'Mr Athletics' 1916-1996

'There was never a more generous man. Never a more sincere man. Never a more dedicated man…A mentor to the many whose lives he touched.'

Ex-hurdler, BBC commentator and Holbeachian Stuart Storey, who paid this tribute to him in 1996, and many others, Geoff Capes among them, would readily acknowledge the significant encouragement given to the launching of their athletic careers by Tommy Clay, whose talents, so easily marketable at national level, were devoted selflessly to the benefit of Holbeach and Lincolnshire sport.

A man of firsts

Tommy (real first names, Richard Edward Sadler) Clay was a man of firsts. He helped to found the first athletics club at Carter's Park, Holbeach, remaining its secretary for 46 years, and was involved in setting up one of the earliest athletic leagues in Britain: the Fenland League, which did much to transform the way these sports were perceived and organised in Britain, composed of teams from Holbeach, Boston, Crowland, Sleaford and Wisbech, in the 1950s. Holbeach United FC also called on him to run their first post-war Under-18 and U-16 teams –the Colts– in 1946 (a position he held for 20 years) and later produce their club programme: commitments which in fact began his involvement in Holbeach sport, and earned him the Lincolnshire Football Association Long Service Medal in 1962.

Local athletics however remained a priority, in which Tommy made his mark by employing his tireless organisational skills.

The athletics side began when Tommy organised the first Holbeach Show and Sports for the football club at Carter's Park in 1948.

It was all rather a gamble at first: 'I committed them to all sorts of money–they hadn't a clue what it was going to cost', laughed Tommy, whose hire of a motor cycle display team came to £160 alone –a small fortune then. But his confidence was justified, because people were starved of entertainment after the war, turning up at the Park in their thousands, and this came to be remembered as the grand period of Holbeach shows, featuring events for all ages. Even the achievements of seven-year-olds running in wellingtons were taken seriously, as a young Stuart Storey discovered. He fell over twice and came in second –and there were only two boys in that race. 'But I still got my silver medal –that was how Tommy was', said Stuart years later.

Starting from nothing

The success of the Holbeach Show pointed the way ahead, and led to Tommy becoming Founding Secretary of Holbeach Athletic Club on 27th May 1949. Only Boston had preceded Holbeach with an athletics club after the war, and Geoff Capes had yet to be born, some three months later in fact. But in the meantime much hard work lay ahead in promoting athletics to a credible level. With the benefit of hindsight, Tommy looked back on that first programme as almost 'pathetic', with few entrants and even fewer actually turning up. But a vital start had been made, for better or worse, with the quaint handicapping system then employed. 'All the events in those days were handicapped', explained Tommy. 'It was assumed that the English champion was running among the competitors. He never did, but it was imagined that he was running off a notional scratch mark.' So it meant that, in the 100 yards for instance, which the winner was announced as having achieved in, say, 9.8 seconds, he would in fact have only run about 88 yards! It was a system that brought its disadvantages. Many of the girls in the 100 yards were positioned even nearer to the front and ran only 86 yards, which meant that when someone really good came along, like Janet Pearson from Sutton St James in the early 1950s, she was repeatedly penalised!

Developing field events

The other situation Tommy set out to conquer in those early post-war years was the lack of field events, hitherto out of sight and out of mind, and something the Clay determination was to bring to the fore. His aim was to shift away from athletics meetings concentrating merely on running events, and make a start by introducing the high jump, long jump and later the shot putt into the sports at Carter's Park.

But he wanted to take things further. It was all part of his plan to develop a combined sport that attracted 'all shapes and sizes' and all levels of ability, adding other field events in the process, such as the javelin, triple jump and discus.

The Fenland League and Fenland Road Race, 1952-53

The result came in 1952, when he formed the Fenland League, representing Holbeach, Boston, Sleaford, Peterborough, Crowland and Wisbech. Again it was a pioneering effort. At the beginning, 'What sort of standards people were achieving, I wouldn't really know. We were running on grass, jumping onto heaps of sand –we didn't have anything fancy to land on'.

Nevertheless it was an important advance. The appeal of athletics had not only been broadened, but inter-club events had been born and with them came a welcome move away from the outmoded handicapped track competitions. Fixtures, too, were now more rationally planned –over four to five events in a season instead of crammed into one day. History was also being made elsewhere at this time, with Tommy's organisation of the first Fenland Road Race in 1953. This attracted entrants who were later to turn 'international', such as Brian Kilby, Bill Adcocks, and Mike Tagg (who went on to the 1968 Olympic

DESERVING RECIPIENT. Tommy Clay (far right) receiving the East Elloe Rotary Club's Paul Harris Award in 1995 from local Rotary President Andrew Hawkins (left), with Rotary District Governor David Green (centre).
[Photo Lincolnshire Free Press/Spalding Guardian.]

187

Games), and the Race, run for over 40 years, became well known.

The nature of these events tended to reflect the characteristics of local sporting talent, for Tommy once remarked that this area always produced good long distance runners and throwers, yet with some exceptions, few outstanding sprinters. But Tommy ensured any available strengths were maximised, by devoting all his organisational skills, time, and often his own money to develop raw talent. He would transport competitors to and from coaching activities and championships, carefully assessing when an individual was ready for the next stage, to say, County or National level, and always encouraging them, on a one-to-one basis, to better their existing best against the stopwatch or tape measure.

Working with Storey and Capes

Two of Clay's most outstanding protegés were Stuart Storey and Geoff Capes, who came to regard him as their mentor. Both were to achieve Commonwealth Games and Olympic standard in the 60s, Storey as a hurdler and Capes as a shot-putter. Afterwards, both were soon to go their independent ways at a relatively early age, Stuart Storey embarking on a career as a PE specialist in Britain and America and a lectureship at North Thames Polytechnic, which saw him later becoming a BBC sports commentator, and Capes to intensify his field-eventing, taking in successive Olympics along the way, as a prelude to turning professional. But while Capes was under Tommy's wing between the ages of 12 and 18, there was predictably never a dull moment. 'We managed to keep him occupied. He was a bit of a rebel, of course,' recalled Tommy.

With Geoff, triumphs and tribulations seemed to go hand in hand, as when he once informed Tommy, from a phone box in central Holbeach, that he had won the Three As Junior Championship at Crystal Palace, but incidentally, he had just broken someone's window. It made a change one supposes from the stinkbombs he let off at the cinema. But the teenage powerhouse was also the despair of a park groundsman at Scunthorpe, who complained to Tommy that 'this great big guy' was ruining his turf by heaving the shot far past the neat landing area he had cut out for ordinary mortals. 'He was a one-off', said Tommy succinctly.

The Dewhurst Games, 1977-83

Their working relationship was not a one-off however, for Geoff and Tommy were to collaborate again in the late 70s. By this time, much water had flown under the bridge. Holbeach Athletic Club had moved its base to Castle Fields, Spalding, when a cinder track was laid there in 1970. From 1977 it became the venue for an important national event, arising out of links Geoff Capes had previously forged with the Dewhurst master butchers group.

By harnessing this connection to the resources of Spalding Round Table and the skills of Tommy Clay, the Dewhurst Games became a key athletic event, attracting crowds of 7-8,000 people. And no wonder, for all the big names competed, Daley Thompson, Brendan Foster, Sebastian Coe and David Moorcroft featuring among the many who came to Spalding in the years 1977, 1979, 1981 and 1983.

It was one thing producing the stars –that was where Geoff Capes came in. But it was another finding good enough individuals for the celebrities to compete against, and here was where Tommy pulled the stops out, using all his contacts in various athletic clubs around the country to come up with some suitable talent.

It was about this time that Tommy sensed a change in the sport's atmosphere. As someone who had always involved himself for the love of it rather than personal gain, he probably regretted the mercenary aspect that was developing in the sporting scene generally. Not for him were the inordinate expense claims, the wheeling and dealing, the cashing-in of international air tickets. Nevertheless his dedication remained undimmed, remaining a driving force in County track and field matches and championships. Even the loss of his left leg in 1981 did not deter him, for within a month after leaving hospital he was there in a wheelchair at a cross-country event, shouting words of encouragement and continuing afterwards as field judge, timekeeper and organiser.

Tommy was unique in that he was able to bring to his grass-roots approach an education and life experience that had equipped him in several other apparently unrelated directions. Originally from Gosberton Risegate, he studied at Nottingham University after Spalding Grammar School, graduating in 1937 with a BA in English, French and Latin, to become a Civil Servant. Called up for war service in the Royal Corps of Signals in 1940, he survived five years in India and Burma and was awarded the Burma Star. Demobbed in 1946, he secured a management position at Levertons in Spalding. But then 14 years later, resorting to writing skills honed by a classical education, he made a sea change by joining the editorial staff of the *Lincolnshire Free Press*, where he soon progressed to Chief Reporter. In 1964 he made another unusual change, but for which he was again more than well qualified, by becoming a teacher at Spalding High School for the next 15 years, where he was described by a colleague as 'the only member of the English department who knew any grammar!' Meanwhile, his journalistic days were far from over, for he continued to turn in a weekly athletics column for the local papers until his death in 1996, his contributions recorded in 45 personal scrapbooks dating back to 1948.

Honours

Three years earlier, a fitting tribute had been paid to him by East Elloe Rotary Club, who awarded him their Paul Harris Fellowship, 'in appreciation of tangible and significant assistance given for the furtherance of better understanding and friendly relations among peoples of the world'. The accolades on that day continued, with the words: 'Many young people owe a lot to Tommy for his organising abilities and vision to encourage our youth into competitive sport.'

It was one of several richly-deserved honours made over the years, preceded during the 1980s by the National Playing Fields Association Torch Trophy for services to athletics, and the British Empire Medal for services to sport in Lincolnshire.

But there was more to come, for although Holbeach Athletic Club's activities were wound up in 2000 and absorbed into Boston and District Athletic Club, the Boston Borough Council's athletic stadium project has since provided for a Tommy Clay Track.

Tommy's last sporting engagement was assisting at the Holbeach 10-mile Road Race in September 1996, some two weeks before his death. He had only just given up the Athletic Club secretaryship, although it was continued by his wife, Beryl.

Holbeach and all the circles he moved in are the poorer for the passing of individuals like him, whose reassuring and capable motivation of talent, while seeking no glory or financial gain for themselves, added that vital sense of proportion and humility so often lacking in today's impetuous sporting world.

Other Sports

Karate has been successfully introduced to the town in recent years, with Black Belt John Gill beginning his activities for a wide age range in 1991, based at both George Farmer and the Holbeach Youth Centre. Membership soon picked up and the Club joined the Traditional Association of Shotokan Karate in 1993.

But as with swimming, other sports have come and gone. Even the conker championships

***STILL GOING STRONG** —literally! Holbeach Weightlifting Club in Alison Avenue has gone from strength to strength. Here Steve Merrison trains for the junior championship title in 1987.* *[Photo Lincs Free Press/Spalding Guardian.]*

in Carter's Park became a casualty of poor attendance in the 1970s, despite the attraction of witnessing 67 - year - old florist Lynden Pape's triumph over the Red Lion's Keith Richardson. Pape's re-flowering of skills unexercised for 50 years is now just a pleasant memory –as was his shop which used to form part of the Park Hall frontage.

Relatively speaking, football has been the lucky one in Holbeach, with extra space made available to play on in fields off Wignal's Gate in 1996. Otherwise, the problem dogging certain other sports and activities, from the 1980s onwards, was one of finding or remaining on or in suitable land, premises or facilities.

No more golf...

In a modestly-sized town with the need to make the most of any building land available, golf became an early casualty after a promising start in 1983 on the field opposite the Community Centre in Damgate. The Club, with its nine-hole course and affiliation to the Lincolnshire Union of Golf Clubs (LUGC) offered great potential. It brought the game more within the means of young beginners and others who could not otherwise have afforded it, for joining and subscription fees were less than a third of those in Spalding.

With unsatisfactory compromise the only alternative, involving the reduction of the course to eight holes and therefore loss of LUGC affiliation, not to mention recognition of handicaps gained, the Club folded early in 1987.

Or squash...?

A similar fate attended Holbeach Squash Club, having lost its rented Fishpond Lane premises in the early 1990s. Searching for alternative facilities, which included approaching The George Farmer School, United Services Club and the Community Centre, proved fruitless and the unfortunate Club, which in 1987 proudly achieved 2nd Division Championship status in the Lincolnshire and South Humberside League, faced disbandment by 1994, their plans for new sauna and jacuzzi-equipped courts remaining unrealised.

Youth Club expansion

But it was not all doom and gloom. One project, having proved abortive in its original objective, changed direction to achieve a positive result. The unsuccessful initiative to build a swimming pool in the 1970s was a case of *déja vu*, as a similar plan that had originated way back in 1945 was also called off because of the expense. However, in this instance, the trustees were able to re-focus their activities into providing proper premises for the Youth Club. The first fund-raising event could not have carried a better pedigree, for in addition to the proceeds of a boxing match, Mrs Hunter persuaded the Queen Mother to donate a tea service which raised £800 at an accompanying bazaar! Starting life in the Public Hall in Park Road, the Club was able to move into the present premises, the former Junior School, in 1983, after the new Holbeach County Primary School opened. Phase two, a sports hall costing nearly £85,000 and built at the rear of the Club, was achieved in 1987, a proud moment for the original trustees of 1945, who included Mr Pat Tinsley, Mr Eric Lane –after whom the hall was named– Mrs Nora Lane, Mrs Alison Hunter, Mr Alec West and Mr and Mrs William Worth. The Chairman of the Trustees at that time was Mrs Christine Carter, who appropriately had been a member of the Youth Club herself and had remained on the committee since the age of 20.

Youth Leader Jim Brogan paid tribute to the many sources from which the money had come: the Sports Council, The George Farmer Trust, Holbeach Parish Council, South Holland District Council and the Lincolnshire Council for Voluntary Youth Services, not forgetting the Youth Club members themselves –who had needed no prompting to help demolish two old classroom buildings to make way for the new block– and senior citizens.

The new building enabled all sports to be played indoors and over the years has proved well up to the impacts of footballs kicked over-enthusiastically in all directions! A final stage ·in the development, connecting this new building with the old one at the front, was completed in June 1994 at a cost of £70,000.

Gymnastics

Gymnastics were another story of survival against the odds, accumulating an impressive reputation along the way. Begun in 1983 by Colin Christensen, Holbeach and Fenland Gymnastic Club scratched together finance and sponsorship from wherever it could.

With the help of dedicated parents and volunteers, it made the best of sharing the newly-opened Community Centre with other users. Originally it was hoped that the Club could take up a designated area of its own at the Centre, thus keeping its equipment permanently in position. But by 1990 the pressure of other bookings for the building, such as weddings and dances, moved the all-girl gymnasts on.

Other premises were subsequently used, including a short spell in a paint shop behind a Whaplode Garage and the Holbeach Youth Centre, until they settled at their current base at Root Farm, Washway Road.

All this upheaval could have had its effect on morale. But as Senior Gymnast Jenny Christensen says, the Club is no stranger to success. A combination of perseverance and home-grown talent over the years has resulted in competition successes over better-funded teams. Prominent placings in the County and Junior under-10 squads, County golds in four-piece competitions; early upgradings to intermediate level and other regular high placings in County Junior Championships have all followed.

The Club ended the 1990s on a high note, with an Awards for All grant enabling both the acquisition of more equipment for Root Farm, and a greater number of places to be offered to younger children between four and seven years old.

If only...

The inconsistencies and shortcomings obtaining with existing sports and arts facilities have not gone unexamined. In 1997 an ambitious plan on a 'what-if' basis involving Lottery money was discussed, featuring a multi-functional sports hall and performing arts centre at The George Farmer School. It was the stuff dreams were made of for the likes of athletes Geoff Capes, Stuart Storey ('We were chased off Carter's Park for making too many dents in the pitch'), Holbeach Youth Club Leader, Jim Brogan, and Director of the Holbeach Young Players, Terry Harrington.

But all were agreed that with facilities so fragmented in Holbeach, such an ideal would only succeed if everyone pulled together. For instance, a young athlete, Alan Rudkin, had different ideas on spending Lottery funds: 'I have nowhere to train locally and have to go to King's Lynn or Peterborough. The money would be better spent on an all-weather track, although a sports hall would be useful'. And so it goes on.

♣ ♣ ♣ ♣ ♣

14 —It Happened Like This...

-Holbeach events and yarns happy, sad or indifferent

The Holbeach Card Players

Legend has it that All Saints Church was once desecrated by the antics of the Holbeach Card Players, also referred to as the Holbeach Rangers, or Holbeach Revellers. Sources differ as to the date: one says 1783, another believes about 1800 to be more likely. But consistent to nearly all the stories is the fact that the Revellers followed up a drinking session at the Chequers by breaking into the Church and playing whist on the altar, in the company of a corpse awaiting burial.

Which version to believe?

Four persons were reputed to be involved. One story gives the names as L Slator, J Barker, T Codling and a local doctor, Jonathan Watson. Macdonald's late nineteenth-century account, based on 'careful inquiry of one or two octogenarians', agrees on Watson's and Slator's names (the latter was also known as 'Lord' Slator). But the others, he states with equal certainty, were called Wheldale and John Key, while the year was 'about 1783' –the date he saw inscribed on a poem of the event which had passed into the hands of Canon Hemmans. Macdonald also claims that only three of the men went over to the church, damaging tombstones on the way, for which they subsequently paid.

In another version of the event, a man saw a light in the Church late one night, shining nearest the altar. Propping a ladder against the nearest window, he scaled it just in time to see and hear a game finishing and the question being asked, 'Dummy, can you one?' This 'Dummy' turned out to be the corpse, which had been positioned in a chair beside the Communion table, with cards placed in its hand for a last rubber.

Poetic licence

The poetess Eliza Cook composed some verses on the subject, having been inspired by information from a work entitled *Sketches of a Seaport Town*. She describes the body being specifically disinterred from the churchyard for the occasion:

And away they strode to the old church wall,
Treading o'er skull and tomb;
And dragg'd him out triumphantly
In the midnight murky gloom.

They carry him down the chancel porch,
And through the fretted aisle;
And many a heartless, fiendish laugh
Is heard to ring the while.

However, it is more likely that the corpse was already inside the church when the gamesters entered, for, following contemporary practice, the body of a

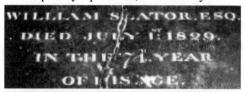

MORE THAN HE DESERVED? *Memorial set in the floor of the south aisle to William 'Lord' Slator, a name allegedly associated both with the Revellers and the wagon on the church roof incident.*

person who had died in the marshland was brought to the church on the eve of the funeral. This ensured that it was ready for the service in plenty of time, in view of the then unreliable state of the country roads. Other poetic licences taken by Eliza Cook are commented on by Macdonald, (Curate at Holbeach 1871-79), who says that the offenders' lips could not have reeked of 'sacramental wine', as this would not have been consecrated until it was time for Communion.

As to the gamesters' fate, stories again differ. Cook has one of the players struck dead with remorse when the church clock chimes one. But a Mr Rawnsley's verses ('The Three Revellers; or Impiety Punished') add 'fiends and spectres', who carry off the men 'Midst scenes which the senses annoy and appal', while:

Sad and silent old Holbeach appears,
As if doom'd to lament her hard fate from the Fall,
Like a Niobe* wash'd with her tears.

*From Greek mythology, a daughter of Tantalus, turned into stone as she wept for her children after they had been killed by Artemis and Apollo.

Bragging Jemmy

Then again, Richard Harris, described as a visiting barrister, penned a poem that contrasted strongly with the rest. He has one of the four, referred to as 'bragging Jemmy', dying before the church scandal, less than a week after resolving to give up gambling, leaving one of the surviving three to die during the church game. But no mention is made of this final game being played with a corpse as the dummy. It was all part of the mix of gossip, fact and exaggeration which has surrounded this story over the years. Some say all the perpetrators were forced to leave town, but others that two of the men eventually became churchwardens, one of whom ended up a bankrupt. However, 'S E', contributing item 1359 to Volume 7 of Fenland Notes and Queries (1907-1909), declared that the last survivor of this group (Slator) died in 1829. Also more certain was the fate of Doctor Watson, who later committed suicide by cutting his wrists and by doing so, denied himself a Christian funeral and was buried one mile north-west of the church, at a crossroads on Spalding Road in 1803. As for John Key, Macdonald says that he died at Holbeach in 1810, aged 47.

The wagon on the Church roof

This incident, supposed to have taken place sometime at the beginning of the 19th century, was attributed along with other individuals to William 'Lord' Slator, a farmer from Penny Hill. This name also comes up in connection with the Holbeach Card Players. So if the same man *had* been involved in both incidents, it was surprising that he had not only been a churchwarden of All Saints since 1794, but also earned the privilege of a stone to his memory, set into the south aisle floor after his death in July 1829, aged 74.

Slator was reputed to be one of a party who dismantled a friend's wagon laden with wool and reassembled it, complete with its load, on the north aisle roof of the Church. At least that was one version of the story. Another was that the wagon was reassembled and left in the churchyard – but not placed on the roof– by a group returning home somewhat the worse for wear from an inn.

Either way, a critic later said, when writing to the editor of *Fenland Notes and*

Queries in the late 1900s, the feat would have been a 'supernatural' one, even for a group of robust 'Holbeach roysterers' to accomplish. 'This would have been a great labour', continued the correspondent, referred to as 'WEF', 'owing to the churchyard wall then being a high one, and no wide gates as now. It would have been impossible for a few young men to have placed the wagon on the church and reloaded it *in a night'*.

A 'ghost' in the Churchyard, 1889

In 1889, railwayman Martin Meadows was walking home through the churchyard, slightly uneasily as he did so.   He had

SHADOWY GRAVES. But the ghost was really a resentful husband, 1889.

heard stories recently of strange movements and noises in the graveyard. So he was all the more relieved when the footsteps he heard behind him turned out to be those of two harmless women returning from an evening out.

Suddenly however, a terrifying wail broke out from behind some tombstones, accompanied by shadowy movements. The ladies panicked and Meadows chased after the perpetrator, eventually running him to earth after the 'ghost', far from being capable of passing through matter, had stumbled across railings and fallen over a tombstone.

The 'spirit' turned out to be a vengeful husband staging an elaborate protest over his wife going out to visit friends. The newspaper report, while not mentioning any names, talked of a ghost at large in Holbeach with a black eye. As the individual was well-known in the town, his identity was not too difficult to guess!

Non-stop dance music on cups of Oxo, 1931

'Bye Bye Blues', 'Falling in Love Again', 'Happy Days Are Here Again', 'Tip-Toe Through the Tulips', Body and Soul', 'On a Little Balcony in Spain': all these popular tunes of the period and many more must have formed the repertoire of an unemployed Holbeach warehouseman when he set out to break the world record for non-stop playing at the Park Hall one Saturday in January 1931.

Trained on toast

The inter-war years, particularly the 20s and early 30s, were dance-crazy, and up until 1931, the record for non-stop playing stood at 11 hours, established by Harry Thorlby's band at the Strand Café, Edinburgh. In common with many others during the Depression, thirty-one-year-old Len Hall was out of work during the day. But in the leisure hours he ran a dance band which fulfilled many local engagements. Only the night before his record attempt, the band had been playing at Whaplode from 7 p.m. until midnight, while the following week they were booked up every evening for six hours a night. But Len was more than ready to meet the challenge, having 'trained' on nothing but toast for three days before the event!

Eileen tangoes with the RAC Scout

The band, with Len at the piano, carpenter W Tatam on banjo, Long Sutton veg grower H Howes playing drums and chauffeur H Cook wielding the violin, assembled at Park Hall on the Saturday morning, and with sweet shop owner C Blackbourn officiating as timekeeper, the ensemble began playing at 11 a.m. First on the floor were 14-year-old Eileen Keight, daughter of the landlord and landlady of the Talbot Hotel, and her partner Mary Hall, Len's younger sister. They danced together until 5.20 p.m., when Mary had to go to work at the Hippodrome (where incidentally, they were showing *Loose Ends*, starring Owen Nares –'a down-and-out, embittered man who is rescued from the depths'– and Edna Best), and Eileen changed partners to Arthur Hallam, the RAC Scout. This duo tangoed, foxtrotted and waltzed until 8 p.m., when Eileen retired after nine hours. Another couple, Miss L Cox and Mr F Larrington, managed a creditable six hours.

600 on the floor

Meanwhile, the band played on, fortified by cups of Oxo passed to them by friends, while Len himself survived on a mere cup of water. During the afternoon his left wrist had started to give out, so for a short spell he changed places with Howes and beat the drums with his right hand while his left wrist was being bandaged. As word got around the town, more and more people came in to watch progress. Park Hall must have had its best day ever, for with admission at 1/6 for dancers and 6d for spectators, the 800 who visited the dance floor throughout the day must have certainly set the till ringing. After the 10.05 p.m. deadline for breaking Thorlby's record had been successfully passed, excitement became intense, and there were still 600 on the floor (one wonders what present-day fire regulations would have made of this), making it 'almost impossible to dance', when Len and his band retired to rousing cheers at 11 p.m.

'World records are not broken very easily in these days,' enthused the *Spalding Guardian* afterwards, 'and Holbeach, go-ahead little Fenland town as it is, seems one of the last places where one would expect to find a world record breaker.'

But Holbeach has been surprising the world fairly regularly ever since. And as for Eileen Keight, she went for a three-mile walk the next day!

Climbing the steeple for a bet, 1932

It must be a rare occasion indeed when the Church itself was responsible for leading two souls into temptation. But this was exactly what happened one Saturday in May 1932, when George 'Ned' Hall and his friend Fred 'Sonny' Fox were passing All Saints and came across some ladders left in position by steeplejacks, who had been conducting an inspection during the week on the state of the weather vane and the lightning conductor. Showing the same family determination that his brother had revealed a year earlier when breaking the record for non-stop dance music (although a sip or two of ale had probably helped things along), Ned bet Sonny that if he (Ned) climbed the steeple and placed his hat upon the weather vane, Sonny would not be able to climb up and fetch it down. As a large crowd gathered, Ned, without any safety precautions whatsoever, picked his way upwards. 'I climbed onto the first roof ', he said later, and a little door opened onto the leads. This door was only fastened with a small catch, and I unhooked it with a piece of wire.'

CLIMBED FOR A BET, with no safety precautions, 1932.

Froze halfway up

Once Fox learned that Ned had reached a certain stage, he followed. Ned went on to place his cap on the weathercock as arranged, but its retrieval proved too much for Fox and he froze halfway up. So Hall retrieved his own headgear and when both men got down to terra firma, the *Spalding Guardian* laconically stated that Canon Hutchinson and PC Macdonald 'were present to receive the climbers'. No further action was taken, although it is known that the Constable reprimanded both men for their prank.

Ned, incidentally, went on to form his own hardware and builder's merchants in Fleet Street, where his house and shop were built in 1937 by Campion and Penney as one unit on the corner of Edinburgh Walk, formerly a field where fairs were held. It was also next to Mr Templeman's greenhouses, once burgeoning with grapes. In later years the business became Hooks of Holbeach, where the original house and shop front –filled with a long-term display for Dulux paints– remains largely unaltered, complementing the 1930s Black Bull frontage across the road.

Tunnels

The creation in Victorian times of an underground conduit for the Holbeach River has added to the fund of stories already abounding of subterranean passages under the town centre, be they the fabled secret tunnel from the Chequers to the Church, the bottomless well at the end of Church Walk, or the cellars reputed to extend under the street from houses and shops in West End. Then there was the wooden conduit which Frank Bradley unearthed when digging a pit for an 800-gallon fuel tank for motor cycle dealer Gordon Woodman's Fleet Street premises in the 1950s (now Morriss & Haynes undertakers), in which, it has to be said, little interest was shown at the time.

The last man to walk the Tunnel

Unfortunately, road and sewer works over the years have obliterated any significant evidence of extensive cellars or passageways under the High Street. More certain however, was that several individuals had walked through the tunnel for the Holbeach River during its existence and in 1965 a Mr G Simpson, of Edinburgh Walk, claimed to have been the last man alive to have done so in the 1920s, when the tunnel was being cleaned out. He remembered it as being some 5ft 8in in diameter for most of its length, but under Market Hill, the tunnel assumed more the form of a chamber, with vertical walls and an arched roof extending to a height of over 7ft. At that time the brickwork, then some 70 years old, was in generally good condition, apart from an area under the old Reading Room near the present library. And a little further along, in October 1968, excavations under Market Hill confirmed traces of an ancient bridge, its stonework reputedly resembling that used for the Parish Church, while there was also talk of iron rings still in evidence, to which boats may once have been tied. Nearby, an alarm bell used to ring in the underground room of the old Lloyds Bank on Market Hill if water levels threatened...

Mr Simpson related how a bull belonging to one of the Patchett brothers had to be cajoled through the tunnel by a drover after the animal inadvertently found its way in at one end while being led to a show. There was another story, too, of a 'Jammy' Smith, who successfully led a donkey through the tunnel for a bet, emerging in Station Road. In later years, the tunnel at this end of town was piped through to Bowsers farm in Fen Road.

The Odours of Sanitation

While the river tunnel had been a source of humorous stories, it was also part of a sewerage system that by the early 1960s could no longer be taken as a joke. In 1962 it prompted the appearance of an anonymous poem in the *Lincolnshire Free Press* which read:

'But there is another picture
Of our little town of Holbeach.
What comes rumbling down our roadways
On a sunny summer evening,
With those monstrous buckets swinging
And those monstrous buckets clanging;
Stopping at those luckless houses
In the name of Sanitation?
And the odour that surrounds it
Mingles with the scent of lilacs
And the fragrance of the beanflowers.

'But the councillors who guide us,
Sitting round their council table,
Ruminate on facts and figures,
Look at sites and then dismiss them;
Say, "We'll think of sanitation
When the costs have risen higher,
And the sites have become scarcer."
Then the fairest one among them,
Ponders on the ills and dangers
Of our unique sanitation. '

Was the 'fairest one' Mrs Alison Hunter?

Drainage smells, of course, had been an accepted fact in Holbeach beyond living memory. It was probably the real reason why people often kept their windows closed at night, and not, as Dr Evans, Medical Officer of Health for the town had supposed back in 1913, that Holbeachians were 'Molly-Coddles'.

WASHDAY BATTLEGROUND, 1900s. The Tenters washhouses recently, the left chimney since removed.

Until the sewerage system was properly overhauled in 1970, the only temporary remedy was an occasional flushing out of the main tunnel under the town – a ritual that, according to the November 1933 Parish Council Minutes, involved an application to the Ruritanian-sounding Surveyor to the Court of Sewers, who would then promise to flush as soon 'as sufficient water was available'.

An inevitable result of the Grand Flush, however, was that it merely shifted most of the offending matter into the open drain in Park Road.

Washday Blues in The Tenters, 1900s

The row of cottages that lines one side of The Tenters as you enter it from the police station end of Edinburgh Walk remains as a complete example of traditional terraced dwellings, with a communal yard and wash-house, the shell of which survives with one of its pair of chimneys intact.

'Wordy warfare'

In the late 1900s it was the scene of a skirmish between two women which had been on the boil for two and a half years. Annie Wright, wife of mail cart driver Charles Wright, and Harriet Crowson, married to railway signalman Harry Crowson, had been neighbours for five years, but for most of that time had never seen eye to eye, indulging in what was described as 'wordy warfare'.

One February however, actions spoke louder than words when Mrs Wright entered the wash-house where Mrs Crowson was attending to her linen and winded her, exclaiming, 'I will kill you. I will do for you!'

A struggle followed between the two women and other neighbours and lodgers rallied round to help Mrs Crowson, who claimed to have a weak heart.

On that occasion Mrs Wright was fined 2s 6d and costs, and bound over to keep the peace for six months in the sum of £5 and a surety of £5. But this was not the end of the matter.

Tit for tat

After an uneasy silence, the situation was rekindled two weeks later on a Monday morning, when Mrs Wright was watching over a copper full of clothes in the wash-house at 6.30 a.m. Mrs Crowson entered, removed Annie's washing from the copper and threw it on the floor. This began a charade –of Annie replacing the clothes and Harriet ejecting them– that continued for some time before another fight developed, during which Mrs Crowson struck Mrs Wright on the face and threw some buckets at her, bruising her legs. The dispute then took a more lurid turn, with accounts of Mrs Wright's arm being scalded, and claims that, in return, she had dumped water and cinders outside Mrs Crowson's door.

It appeared very much as if Mrs Crowson had tried to incite Mrs Wright to cause further trouble while she was bound over, allegedly threatening, 'Before you shall be master, you shall pay that £10'. But the bench dismissed the case. They may have felt that the sting had by now gone out of the argument, as it transpired that Mrs Wright had since moved elsewhere in Holbeach, to the relief of all the neighbours concerned.

A Dog in Court, 1909

The Dogs Act of 1906 broke new ground in making an owner liable for any injury caused by his dog to sheep and cattle. Roland and Stanley Hix were both minors (under 21) in 1909, but they kept a flock of sheep on a piece of land known as the Cricket Field in Barrington Gate, owned by their father, the auctioneer George Hix. On the morning of 25th June, labourers William Wignall of Battlefields Lane and Thomas Anderson from Woolbarn Yard observed three dogs worrying sheep in the field. In the course of trying to drive the hounds out, the labourers came across a dead lamb by the hedge. One of the dogs got away completely, but the second dog was recognised as a Mr Templeman's, while the other was thought to belong to David Jackson, a baker in West End. Templeman later admitted liability, but Jackson denied his dog's involvement, despite supplying conflicting stories of the animal's whereabouts to different members of the Hix family. Mrs Jackson claimed the dog had never been off their premises all morning. But the baker's apprentice Tom Thurston let the cat out of the bag, so to speak, by admitting that the dog sometimes slipped out on its own, and may well have done for at least a quarter of an hour that morning.

His Honour Judge Mulligan brought matters to a head by asking for the dog to be brought into the Holbeach County courtroom and placed on the solicitor's table. Its identity thus established, Jackson was fined 10s (50p) with costs, a fairly lenient penalty considering the lamb was worth between 28 and 30 shillings (£1.40 - £1.50).

An African Chief attends a Holbeach Sale

An interesting example of the varied events that took place at the Market House appears in the family cuttings book of Emma Jane Harrisson (née Carter), who lived from 1845 to 1915. It is a poem about an African chief who visited what appears to be a bailiff's sale in Holbeach. The date is not recorded, but it is most likely to be the Edwardian period, as it makes reference to 'statutes sealed and sanctioned by our King'. Nor can one be certain that the account is fiction or fact; except that, if true, the arrival of such a character in the town at that time must have aroused great curiosity. The African, too, was absorbed by what he saw, in these verses penned under the *nom de plume* of 'Another Fellow':

A Tale of a Wayside Market House (Another Lay from Holbeach)

*A modern traveller, from an Afric shore,
Had journeyed far across this land of our.
Amazed, at home, by England's civic power,
This chief would learn our methods. O'er and o'er
The country he had wandered, wondering yet
How we grew wise with weather ever wet.
Flound'ring thro' Fens, which bleached his studious feet,
He came to Holbeach, when a bell did greet
His ear with invitation to a Sale. 'O yez! O yez!'*

'Their goods we sell –ratepayers who will not pay.'
Along he trekked to where were laid on view
A commandeered assortment: goods old and new.
A new phrase met his ear: 'We passively resist
The statutes sealed and sanctioned by our King,
And here are seizures for your bargaining.
For justice on our payment will insist.'
A bachelor was mulct his sewing instrument;
The crowd thought this a Merry sentiment;
A man of aspect studious bought some gears;
Another skates –which moved the Chief to tears.
He saw how helpless in these things they'd be!
And barrels went to bidders who should know
That barrels do not grace a staunch tee-to!
It quite upset the Afric's gravity.

Then, from the gossip of the throng he learned
These 'loyal' sons of England law had spurned.
Yet- with a paradox unusual to his mind-
They gladly paid these rates when costs were fined:
Thus adding to their country's revenue,
Giving to Law more than to Law was due.
'Ah, this is wisdom!' cried the dusky chief,
And now my journey homeward shall be brief.
John Bull is wise tho' always wet and cold,
He will Resist, to swell his nation's gold!
To mine own tribe this rule shall be proposed–
To pay me double, when to pay opposed!

The pot of gold that never was, 1890

An agricultural worker who shouted too loudly soon had Holbeach and district gossiping and speculating about a valuable find that had appeared out of the earth near the town, one December afternoon in 1890.

What in fact happened was that two men ploughing Mr F Howard's 'twenty-six acre' on the Washway had uncovered and inadvertently smashed an earthenware pot containing silver coins dating back to Tudor times. When Hubbard, one of the farmhands, shouted ahead to his mate to stop ploughing, his cry was heard a quarter of a mile away. Word spread rapidly that a pot of gold had been found, and it was the talk of the town and district for several days.

Opportunists lost no time. A local publican offered the labourers £10 for the entire find, while another individual enticed them with a sovereign in exchange for a single coin. But resisting temptation, the farmworkers handed over the treasure to their Long Sutton employer. The find totalled 29 coins described by expert Justin Simpson of Stamford as crowns, half-crowns, shillings, testoons, sixpences, groats, threepences, twopences and pence. All were from the consecutive reigns of Edward VI, Mary, and Elizabeth I. Although rather worn, the general condition was described by contemporary observation as 'splendid', with the regret that there was 'no museum in the district where such treasures might be inspected by the public if not claimed by the Crown'.

When the horse called it a day, 1920s

Until 1940 when a mechanised scheme was introduced by the local council, refuse collection was sub-contracted to farmers who could supply both the necessary labour and a horse and cart. For these individuals it was a useful way of supplementing income at 6s 6d a day for daytime collections and 7s 6d for the night-time sanitary rounds, in an era when many houses still had no flush toilets.

However for someone performing this unsavoury task single-handed the hours were very long, and would not have been allowed today. When Jack Tyler, of Low Lane, Holbeach retired in 1965 after over 40 years' service with the cleansing departments of both the Holbeach Urban and East Elloe Rural District Councils, he recalled his own incredible daily schedule of the 1920s. It ran from 7 a.m. to 6 p.m., followed only by sufficient time for a meal and a rest before working the night shift from 9.30 p.m. to 4 a.m., when the ghostly sound of the horse's hooves echoed through the town.

Tyler's horse was well versed in this routine, except that in old age, she became increasingly intolerant of bad weather. One night, when conditions were particularly rough, the animal ran out on the job, and was well on her way home before Tyler caught up with her!

The Gunpowder plotters: it wasn't our Holbeach —1605

In *A Concise History of Great Britain and Ireland* (abridged from Hume, Smollet and Others in four parts by John Murphy, 1828) we read that 'Catesby, Percy and others of their accomplices, on hearing of the arrest of Fawkes, hurried down to Warwickshire, where Sir Everard Digby, thinking himself assured of the success of his confederates, was already in arms, in order to seize the Princess Elizabeth. Having joined Digby, they next proceeded to Holbeache, being the residence of one of their associates in the name of Littlejohn.' Once at 'Holbeache', the conspirators' luck ran out on November 8th. Their personal supply of gunpowder ignited after a foolhardy attempt to dry it out in front of a fire, killing Percy and Catesby, and the survivors were captured by the Sheriff of Worcester and his men who had surrounded the house. Within a week, everyone connected with the plot had been rounded up and later executed.

Certainly an exciting sequel to the Plot. But in case any confusion should be created by reading this or any similar account, it can be confirmed that 'Holbeache' refers to a house situated in a small hamlet in Worcestershire, and not the Lincolnshire town. This is proved by Macdonald's 19th-century researching of a narrative held at the British Museum entitled, *Relation of the apprehension of Henrie Garnet, Provinciall of the Jesuites, and of the escape of Robert Wintoon and Stephen Littlejohn, when the other Traytors were taken at Holbeache.*

Arthur Thistlewood and the Cato Street Conspiracy, 1820

However, Holbeach *was* connected with a political plot through a certain Arthur Thistlewood. According to Grant Macdonald, he once lived near 'the Bridge' or central crossroads in Holbeach, although from the *Lincolnshire Herald* report of 2nd November 1858 on a property sale, it also appeared that Thistlewood built and occupied the White House Lodge farm near Holbeach (now part of the Worth estate), which is where he may well have held his secret meetings.

Soldier, farmer, and enemy of the state

Born the illegitimate son of a prosperous Tupholme farmer, he was educated at Horncastle Grammar School, but afterwards gave up land surveying to join the army. Thistlewood's first wife died in 1806 and on his second marriage, he left the army and took up farming – unsuccessfully as it turned out, for he then moved to London. By this stage his previous travels in France and America had inspired him with revolutionary ideas, and as a member of the Spencean Philanthropists he was viewed as

ARREST IMMINENT. A contemporary cartoon captures the moment when Thistlewood (far left) is about to be apprehended after stabbing a law officer, in the skirmish that occurred when the plotters were cornered in their hayloft in Cato Street, near Grosvenor Square, London on 23rd February, 1820.

[Courtesy John Simkin, Spartacus.schoolnet.co.uk.]

potentially dangerous, especially after John Castle, a police spy, had infiltrated the Spencean committee. From late 1816 onwards Thistlewood and his Spenceans were prime suspects in a plot to overthrow the Government. His arrest after a riotous meeting at Spa Fields thwarted his emigration plans to America with his wife and child, so Thistlewood continued to cause trouble on his release, using his wasted passage money to the States as an excuse for challenging the Home Secretary, Lord Sidmouth, to a duel –an action which landed him in jail again for breach of the peace.

Assassination plan foiled
Freed in 1819, he concentrated on a plan to assassinate members of the Cabinet, but the plot went wrong after another infiltrator fed Thistlewood with false information on the time and place of the next Cabinet dinner. On 23rd February 1820, the police raided the Spenceans' hayloft in Cato Street, near to Grosvenor Square in London, and arrested everyone involved, including Thistlewood, who had tried to escape after killing a police officer in the skirmish. As a result, the former resident of Holbeach was charged with high treason and hanged at Newgate prison in May 1820. One of his last remarks hinted at metal instability when he declared: ' My genius is so great just now, I don't think there is any man alive [who] has so great a genius as mine at the moment.'

Interestingly, there is a note in the front of William Burges' Hurdletree Farm account book to the effect that on 6th January 1878, 'Mrs Martha Thistlewood Departed this Life, in her 74th year', and one wonders if there was some connection with the plotter of nearly 60 years earlier.

Advertising for a wife, 1797

 The theory behind Dateline and Lonely Hearts columns is nothing new, but even this Holbeach resident, hiding behind the pen-name of 'Omicron' (meaning, 'the fifteenth letter of the Greek alphabet'), must have been treading new ground when he placed the following lines in the *Stamford Mercury* in the Valentine month of 1797:

A Wife wanted immediately for a sober steady healthful man in a little Way of Business:
No objection if a Dissenter,

Or to a little Money in Business to enter,
A healthful middle-aged Woman, if neat,
With an indulgent Husband she will meet;
If she dare venture to send a Line,
She will get in return a Valentine,
To save Imposition and Mistakes being made,
There will be only be Answers to Letters post paid.
Direct to Omicron, at Mr Mason's, Holbeach, Lincolnshire.

Having introduced a mercenary element into his plea, one can only ponder on Omicron's chances of success, for any lady of means would have wondered whether she was being courted merely for her money!

When a council house site 'invoked' Magna Carta, 1949-55

The problem began in 1940 when the East Elloe Rural District Council (EERDC) requisitioned the Hall Hill Farm house and grounds belonging to Mrs Kathleen Rose Smith, of The Crescent, Chapelfield, Norwich, for wartime evacuees. During this requisition period, which did not officially end until 1951, the Council took the opportunity to make a compulsory purchase order of the land at a cost of £3,000 for council housing.

Not everyone in the EERDC agreed with this decision when it was made in 1948. Protests came from traditionalists like Councillor C I Patchett, who in airing his view was accused of leaking information before it had been properly discussed by the EERDC. Quite happy to be censured for his action, Patchett considered the acquisition of this land unnecessary, deploring both the implied destruction of trees and despoilment of the view from Stukeley Hall. He had a certain partiality of course as part-owner of the Stukeley estate, and was accused by Alison Hunter of deliberately 'sabotaging' the housing plans.

However it almost seemed as if Patchett would enjoy the last laugh, for what began as a joke for the EERDC reappeared at intervals like a bad penny to become a source of great frustration.

'A special provision for widows'
First, although the Ministry of Housing

and Local Government had approved the purchase order, the district valuer's negotiations with the landowner over the course of 1948-50 got nowhere. Meanwhile, the Council received a quaint letter in January 1949 from an obscure body called the Preston Common Law Council, who pointed out that the EERDC's compulsory purchase of land owned by Mrs Smith was 'in gross defiance' of Clause 70 of the Magna Carta. This document King John had been obliged to sign in 1215, in the interests of respecting the rights of his subjects against tyranny and arbitrary power. The Magna Carta, reminded the Preston Common Law Council, made 'a special provision for widows and their inheritance, whereby any man shall lay hands on it at his peril.'

Laughter at the 'five and twenty barons'
Hall Hill farm and grounds had been a source of humour before when, in its uncultivated state, it had provided Ethel Foreman with the means to create a grass skirt for a fancy dress competition at Barrington Gate Schoolroom –a costume that had prevented her from sitting down all evening in case it disintegrated.

Now it was to excite more mirth. Amid laughter, Cecil Pywell, the Clerk to the EERDC, advised everyone to ignore the Common Law Council's letter. He said the same two months later, when the Preston Common Law Council wrote again. Admittedly the second letter invited ridicule, notably in the way it signed off with, 'You have the honour to be my obedient servant'.

But this time, the Preston group were threatening to petition the King, asking him to refer the matter to the 'five and twenty barons for redress in 40 days', as provided for in the old Clause 70. And in April, the story had reached the national press who lost no time in quoting Mrs Smith as saying: 'I want my land to start a business. The Council have stopped me going into my own home.'

'Tantamount to trespass'
Eventually the matter was brought to Court, with Mrs Smith suing both the EERDC and the building contractors for damages in October 1952. It was contended that the wartime requisition had been made in 'bad faith' after April 1941

and that after January 1951, the defendants had 'entered on the land to build houses' which was tantamount to trespassing. Mr Richard Elwes, QC, appearing for Mrs Smith, accused the EERDC of keeping Mrs Smith out of the land until they had been able to use all their powers of compulsory purchase. And 'as a free-born Englishwoman, she was entitled to be obstinate in defending her rights.'

In suggesting to the jury that Cecil Pywell, Clerk to the EERDC, had exceeded his authority in persisting with the requisitioning of the land, Mr Justice Devlin stated that although the Council should be held fully responsible as a body, no councillor had been guilty of bad faith. The EERDC was ordered to pay damages of £850 to Mrs Smith, but it was finally agreed that the Ministry of Housing and Local Government were ultimately to blame. So the bill for damages, plus £1,500 legal costs, was passed to them. Mr Pywell's solicitor, John Mossop, still viewed it as a victory for the Council, as they had retained possession of the site. But it was not quite the end of the matter, for even as late as July 1955, after 12 houses had been built on the Hall Hill site, Mrs Smith was still trying to appeal against the compulsory purchase order.

All on a budget of £45: June 1953
A 20-foot flagpole tower for Market Hill painted pale blue, surmounted by a golden crown and radiating lines of banners to various rooftops. Two baskets of flowers hung from every lamppost and at the High Street/Park Road junction, a large flowerbed of geraniums, lobelias and marguerites. Eleven-foot banners in blue and white and superimposed with 'E R' in gold along the Church wall, hung from 14-foot poles topped with golden balls. These were just some of the features of the Holbeach Coronation decorations of June 1953.

It sounded as if no expense had been spared, and as the Coronation Souvenir Programme hoped, 'residents, visitors and passers-by may be agreeably surprised by the decoration'. Indeed they were. But no one would have guessed that it had all been done on a budget of £45.

At first, it seemed as if it would be a recycling affair, with members of the Parish Council wondering if they could re-use decorations left over from George VI's coronation in 1937. However nothing serviceable was left and fortunately, this was yet another occasion when the first ladies of Holbeach possessed the flair, sophistication –and the right contacts– to go one better. Mrs Nora Lane went straight to the top and consulted Sir Hugh Casson, whose directorship of architecture for the Festival of Britain in 1951 had just earned him a knighthood and a commission to design the London Coronation decorations.

Casson, also Professor of Interior Design at the Royal College of Art (a position he held until 1975) recommended a pale blue-and-white theme. Not only would it strike a dainty and feminine note in keeping with the young Queen's image, but it was also unlikely to be duplicated by other towns and villages, who would opt for the more predictable red, white and blue. The Decorations Sub-Committee, led by Mrs Hunter, Mrs Lane and Miss E H Patchett 'endeavoured to act upon Sir Hugh's advice within the limits of their slender resources', and set to

CHILDREN'S CORONATION PARTY, 1953,
at the Red Lion –and not a burger and chips to be seen.

work at Serpentine House to produce the necessary. The banners were all Miss Patchett's own work, while Percy Bettinson both donated and erected the 20-foot flagpole on Market Hill.

Coronation Day carnival, June 2nd
Needless to say, the overall effect was a great success and formed an impressive backdrop to a day packed with events. It began with a united thanksgiving service

at 9.30 a.m. –an early start to allow the townspeople to return home for the TV and radio coverage of the ceremony in London. After lunch, at 1.30 p.m., it was time for the carnival procession to assemble in front of the main grandstand in Carter's Park. Miss Ransom, the soon-to-retire Junior School head, was one of its organisers. It was composed of every concept you could think of: decorated cars, cycles, dolls' prams, hoops, fancy dress characters, tableaux –individuals portraying scenes from history, for which there were 1st, 2nd and 3rd prizes of £3, £2 and £1– plus members of all the local clubs and societies. Headed by the band of the 4th (Boston) Cadet Battalion, Royal Lincs Regiment, this formidable convoy set off on a route that took in Park Road, High Street, Barrington Gate, Station Street, Church Street and then back into the Park.

This was followed by children's and adults' sports, children's and older folks' teas, more fancy dress parades, and open-air dancing, culminating in a torchlight and fancy dress procession marshalled by Mr Tubbs the butcher, and starting at 9.15 p.m. This time the parade started on the eastern side of town, progressed through Park Lane, Edinburgh Walk, then up the High Street to West End, Northons Lane, East Elloe Avenue, Boston Road, and returning to Carter's Park.

Even then there was more to come, with a grand display of fireworks at 10 p.m., ending with dancing until 2 a.m. at the British Legion's dance in the W I Hall. Meanwhile, Carter's Park had provided its own attractions throughout the day, in the form of British Legion side-shows, Punch and Judy, a model camp created by the

Boy Scouts, and TV programmes for the senior citizens set up in the Youth Centre.

All in all a great deal of organisation, dedication and talented improvisation on the part of the 40-odd people involved on the Celebrations Committee. By comparison, the 2002 Golden Jubilee in Holbeach seemed a quieter affair. Relatively few shops and houses indulged in much decoration, although Peter and Clarice Clements could be relied on to have many flags flapping from East Lea House, Mr and Mrs Maurice Lown's frontage in Edinburgh Walk was well pennanted, and an estimated 2,000 people attended the Community Centre gala –an all-day affair on June 3rd of jive-dancing, disco, charity stalls and displays by the Holbeach and Fenland Gymnastics Club and Holbeach Model Car Club. Meanwhile, the street party and games in East Elloe Avenue organised by Sally Reddin, Barbara Bailey and Sue Young recalled the pleasant celebratory style of earlier days.

'Drat the lino', 1947

The War may have ended, but the British were still pulling together, this time in a climate of austerity and shortages. And in many parochial circles, a suspicious eye was being kept open for any hint of extravagance.

LINO CONTROVERSY. Mattimore House, Fleet Road, when in use as the East Elloe Rural District Council Offices.
[Photo from the EERDC Tenant's Handbook.]

Holbeach was no exception, where attention was focusing on the appointments at Mattimore House. Built in the mid-Victorian era at the corner of Damgate, this large, four-square house belonged in its early days to Joseph Chamberlain Barker (1809-1876) JP, Lord of the Manor of Blanches, and a Deputy Lieutenant of Lincolnshire. It then became for many years the seat of the Harrisson family, who had been millers, landowners

and members of the legal profession, and had even served as a private girls' school, run by one of the Harrisson ladies, before occupation in the 1930s by the Wright family. During the Second World War, it was the HQ of the 3rd Holland (East Elloe) Battalion Home Guard.

In 1947 the house was being made ready for the East Elloe Rural District Council's new offices, to replace the old ones in Spalding Road on the corner of Northons Lane. But if the EERDC was looking forward to some decent flooring when they moved in, the Parish Council was having none of it. J L Bayston proposed that a letter be sent to the EERDC, protesting about the 'sheer waste of public money in fitting the "palatial" new Council offices with linoleum', which was going to cost £600.

Councillor Fred Bowd, a plain-speaking smallholder, retorted that the Parish Council should 'get on with their own business' –at least that was the official version– while, 'We all say, drat the lino!' was Alison Hunter's response.

And 'Drat' it had to be, for Cecil Pywell revealed that no new lino was available in any case. So they would have to transfer the partly worn-out floor covering from the old offices in Spalding Road. It was in this slightly dishevelled state that the staff moved in on 12th January 1948, but one assumes that it was eventually replaced, as Mattimore House went on to serve as the council offices for a quarter of a century more until, as a result of the 1972 Local Government Act, East Elloe Rural District Council, Spalding Urban District Council and Spalding Rural District Council were amalgamated to form South Holland District Council and based in Spalding, from 1974.

'You say "Mondemont" - I say "Mondement"...' 1996

'Mondemont', as in 'Mondemont Close', takes its name from one of the two French towns, Mondement and Sézanne, linked with Holbeach under a twinning arrangement forged in 1958 by Mrs Nora Lane, Mrs Alison Hunter, and Mme Christine de Roche Noblecourt, a friend of Mrs Lane's from her earlier days in France.

In May 1959, a party of French dignitaries cemented the initiative by making an official visit to Holbeach, led by M. Desroches, Mayor of Sézanne, and M.Blouin, the Deputy Mayor of Mondement. They were received at Mattimore House, then the offices of the East Elloe Rural District Council, and during a three-day visit saw the sights of Holbeach where they were most impressed with Stukeley Hall Old People's Home, as it was then termed, the new George Farmer School –where members of the party seemed particularly interested in the modern staircases– and the high standard of land cultivation generally.

Their itinerary included bulb growers Jacques Amand on the Washway, and on the way to Tindalls Mill, they stopped at Laddies where they were each presented with an ice cream, a stick of Holbeach rock and a pencil. On the Saturday, they were entertained to a roast beef and Yorkshire Pudding lunch by Mossop & Bowser at the Bridge Hotel, Sutton Bridge. Whether the novelty value of this meal to the French overcame its lack of inventiveness –compared with sophisticated French cuisine– is not known!

Maintaining the link
Over the years the link was maintained by exchange visits between respective schools and private individuals. For Fenland visitors, Sézanne is a typically French delight. With a population of 6,600, the town is situated some 70 miles south-east of Paris, and offers an interesting comparison to Holbeach, sharing an agricultural background and a history traceable to Roman times. The Place de la République town square is all one expects of a traditional French setting, complete with ornate fountain, pavement cafés, and many charming walks through a champagne-producing countryside.

After the 1974 local government reorganisation, South Holland District Council assumed responsibility for the exchanges with a twinning committee, and in October 1982 an official visit of 67 people from Holbeach and Spalding was staged, 17 of them schoolchildren. Heading the delegation was Councillor Dewsbury, described in the French local newspaper as 'vice-cherman du district

«Shouth Holland» ', who presented a ceremonial cloth bearing the Holbeach coat of arms.

Boulevard Holbeach
The spelling in the newspaper report may have been quaint, but it was spot-on in 1984 when Sézanne created a 'Boulevard Holbeach'. So it was slightly disappointing when the opportunity arose for the Fenland town to return the compliment, and spelled the name of a new road 'Mondemont' instead of 'Mondement' Close.

Unfortunately the mistake was not discovered until after the street sign had been made up and all the housing literature and documentation printed. The error was explained away before the housing development's opening ceremony in April 1996 by informing the visiting French dignitaries, including the Mayor of Mondement, Mme Anne-Marie Desroches, that this was the English way of spelling it. Plausible enough, except that the French didn't have the corresponding luxury of a French spelling for Holbeach!

♣ ♣ ♣ ♣ ♣ ♣

15 –Still Making History

'It's a Lovely Day Tomorrow'.

At least that's what the wartime song hoped for after 1945. How well has the town fared in the quest for continuous improvement?

It has taken time for Holbeach to catch up with its own shadow; one that began to be cast with the demand for post-war council housing. Eighteen houses had been built before 1914 (in Fishpond Lane), and 275

FISHPOND FIRSTS. These dwellings in Fishpond Lane were originally the earliest examples of Holbeach council housing.
[Photo EERDC Tenants' Handbook.]

between 1919 and 1939. But a further 315 were needed after the Second War –nearly 100 more than in Long Sutton or Sutton Bridge. Both during and after hostilities, it had been a story of building council houses against the clock, often hampered by sub-standard or scarce materials to meet a lengthening housing list that by the end of 1951 had grown to the longest anywhere in the district. Such a shortage allowed no favours: when an incoming policeman attempted to take over his predecessor's prefab at 25 Alison Avenue in 1950, he had to join the housing queue like everyone else. 'We're not trying to be awkward,' said Alison Hunter, after whom the road had been named, 'we just don't have the houses.'

Power connects slowly
Even as the 1950s dawned, mains electricity had yet to reach council-house dwellers in outlying villages such as St Marks, who had already waited a decade for the extension of a supply that ended 300 yards from the village boundary. It was feared that agricultural workers would be lost to the land if they could not live in adequately-equipped houses near their jobs. Even when power was connected, the story went that Marsh housewives on washday had to avoid running their new

washing machines simultaneously, in case it overloaded the system!

New council houses a priority, 1940s
Terms such as Airey, Gregory, Traditional and Trusteel crept into the post-war Holbeach housing vocabulary as examples of different methods of council house construction, all designed to be put up as economically and cheaply as possible. Forty-four 'traditional-style' council houses had been occupied on the Northons Lane site by August 1948. But with provision on that same piece of land for another 34 dwellings and faced with 276 tenancy applications, Councillor Alison Hunter was pressing hard for further development. Corner-cutting however was not allowed for in her book. She toured building sites and picked up critically on instances of shoddy paintwork and skimped surfaces, against the architect's protests that paint supplies had not yet returned to pre-war standards.

TOO SMALL FOR A MOUSE? The pantries in some of the Battlefields Lane houses.

Councillor C I Patchett also had his say on design shortcomings. The pantries in the 30 Gregory-type houses being built in Battlefields Lane during 1954 were 'too small for a mouse'. At 2 by 5½ ft, he had a point, but the architect was not prepared to alter the design, nor entertain Coun. Parker's suggestion of transferring the pantry to a larger cupboard under the stairs and adding a window. Eventually the Council offered the compromise of installing kitchen dressers at an extra £15 per house. A little more latitude was allowed later on however when in 1973, Battlefields Lane residents were offered £30 in cash to decorate their own homes if they did not care for the Council's standard colour schemes. At least it made up for the plight of the householder at No. 59, whose back garden during the previous autumn had been used as a tip for rubble while work was going on.

Prefab problems

Meanwhile back in the earlier post-war years, occupants of the new 'temporary bungalows' on the Mattimore Lane site had noticed that all was not white with their washing. When the water reached boiling point, the jointing plaster around the boiler melted and soiled their clothes. This was later solved by substituting an asbestos compound.

The prefabs also developed acute condensation problems, aggravated by the aluminium outer skin originally used for the roofing. But despite their implied sketchiness, these bungalows –40 on the Mattimore site and 14 in Farrow Avenue– not only outlasted their 'shelf life', but were effectively converted into the pensioners' bungalows still in use today, having proved themselves well worth spending money on in terms of continuous improvements and updatings.

EFFECTIVELY MODERNISED. The Alison Avenue bungalows, originally prefabs, viewed from Fishpond Lane.

On the other hand progress with the larger developments was not always straightforward. The decision to purchase the Hallgate site in 1948 promised much, with its potential for 72 three-bedroomed council houses and 12 'aged persons' ' bungalows. But as Chapter 14 shows, what began as a comic-opera protest from the landowner turned into years of legal wrangling, preventing full development of the site until well into the 1950s.

Adjusting attitudes

It took a while, too, for attitudes to catch up with this expansion of council house living. Scant provision had been made for

car owners on these sites and their protests were met with little sympathy. In September 1948, five East Elloe Avenue residents petitioned the EERDC after one of them had been summoned for parking his car on the verge overnight without lights, because there was nowhere else to put it. A proposal to provide temporary parking on an undeveloped strip of land was opposed by several councillors. Coun. Wells thought it, 'The silliest decision I have ever heard,' while Coun. Cragg voiced greater disapproval. 'Now we are asked to provide amenities so that tenants can ride about in something. If they can afford a car, they should be able to afford somewhere to put it.' The official reason for not providing garages was one of cost. But the tenants were not going to let anyone stop them watching their TVs, which obliged the EERDC to take out cover in 1950 against the H-pattern aerials damaging roofs and chimneys.

Senior citizens' accommodation

The several senior citizens' bungalow developments that followed also attracted their fair share of frustrations, objections and animated discussion, but were a positive achievement nevertheless. One of the first of these in Arthurs Avenue broke new ground and was the pride and joy of Mrs Alison Hunter, who had done so much for local welfare services. With 26 pensioner-applicants for bungalows by 1954, some of whom had already been waiting 8 years, she was very anxious to get building in motion and Arthurs Avenue was finished in 1959. The Dorset Scheme as it was known featured 18 bungalows wired by bell system to a warden's house, and the concept of Arthurs Avenue as a peaceful, self-contained area for pensioners was further enhanced by the opening of the neighbouring Patchett Lodge –then a trendsetting design– by the Earl of Ancaster in October 1960. The Lodge, constructed by Langwith builders at a cost of £40,000 was named after Alderman Charles Ingamells Patchett to commemorate his long association with welfare matters, which had begun with the old Board of Guardians and Public Assistance Board. It was a fitting tribute towards the end of his long life, for after living many years at Holly Lodge, Princes Street, he died at Bishop's Stortford in 1964.

Originally the Patchett Lodge home was administered by Holland County Council, but the Order of St John Care Trust took over in 1992, whose ultimate objective was to redevelop the Lodge to double its existing accommodation.

Similar in concept to Arthurs Avenue was the Cecil Pywell and Willders Garth housing of the 1960s and 70s. The only drawback of these developments was that they were some distance from the town's shops. And ever since Mr G W Hunt had his application turned down to sell tobacco, sweets and soft drinks from his Alison Avenue prefab in 1950, that situation has remained largely unchanged.

House building accelerates, 1950s on
'There are not enough houses for private enterprise', said Coun. C I Patchett in December 1951. 'So now let these people have a chance'. And indeed from that decade on private residential areas have expanded, particularly to the west and south of the town in areas leading off Spalding Road to provide homes in Langwith Drive, Langwith Gardens, Harwood Avenue and associated closes and crescents. After Machins haulage company's departure from its controversial site in the late 1980s, more houses were built in a varied town-house format in the area beyond North Parade and Park Lane. Since 1998 the most significant developments have been at Beechers Brook on ground opposite The George Farmer Technology College in Park Road, on land adjoining Foxes Low Road, and at points leading off Hallgate and Wignal's Gate.

More houses brought with them more young people seeking better sporting and recreational facilities. As early as 1975, pupils from The George Farmer, asked for their views on Holbeach, wanted more shops and entertainment, including a sports complex for swimming, tennis, squash and ten-pin bowling. A few of the more environmentally-conscious also mentioned a nature reserve, and a general tidying of the town, to include a 'scrub-up' for the churchyard.

Pursuing the ideals
Since then, a nature reserve *has* become a reality in Fishpond Lane, while it, the Spalding Road roundabout and grass in front of the Reading Room benefit from the voluntary maintenance activities of the Holbeach & District Civic Society. Meanwhile in 2003 a skateboard and BMX track took shape as part of a plan to bring Carter's Park facilities into the 21st century.

But other wishes have yet to be fulfilled. The Youth Club, open three nights a week, is well attended. But as for swimming, Holbeach is still worse off than well over a century ago, when a club founded in 1894 at Mr R P Mossop's pond in Fishpond Lane, equipped with changing huts and diving boards, flourished until the 1920s. It was unfortunate that in the late 1970s plans to build a new swimming pool for the town were eventually defeated by inflation.

After a subsequent proposal to convert Mattimore House, the former District Council offices on Fleet Road, into a community centre and sports hall was abandoned in 1980 on discovering terminal dry rot, much momentum went out of the project, aggravated by grants that were difficult to obtain. But at least the town got a community centre in Fishpond Lane, which has seen extensive use since it opened in 1983.

Meanwhile local schools and the local police Crime Prevention Unit have provided moral support for those wishing to open a restaurant and entertainment centre for young people, equipped with PCs, PlayStation, snooker and other facilities. However the problem lies in finding suitable premises.

Holbeach Hospital –back from the brink
It has been something of an achievement in an era of ever-reducing services that the town has managed to retain its own hospital, although the situation could not have been achieved without the considerable efforts of a charitable trust to keep it open.

From tramps' hostel to emergency hospital, 1937-39
Apart from an isolation unit that once existed on the Washway, to which patients with infectious diseases were taken from the doctors' surgeries in a sinister, black,

207

horse-drawn brougham during the early years of the last century, the town had been without a hospital for centuries.

But in 1937 the old Workhouse in Fleet Road was redefined as a psychiatric institution, admitting its first intake of patients from Caistor Hospital. To

THE TAXI NOBODY WANTED. Many years ago this carriage used to take patients with infectious diseases to the Isolation Hospital in Washway Road. George Edward Hall of West End was its driver and groom, whose own son, Ned (later the hardware merchant), was taken in it to the hospital with scarlet fever around 1912.

[Photo courtesy John Hall.]

accommodate some of the former occupants of Fleet Road –travelling people or 'men of the road'– a new building was completed that year in Boston Road as their hospital or overnight stop. But the new facility was soon to take on a more significant function, for on the outbreak of war it became an emergency unit with three wards, 46 beds for general medical use, and a 12-bed maternity ward, all in the charge of Matron Miss Coxon, before her transfer to Boston General after the War. In 1948 under the new National Health Service, it was classified as a General Practitioner Unit, with additional medical cover and visiting consultants from other hospitals at Boston and Grantham. It was all part of a post-war heyday that included the development of an X-ray unit, operating theatre and outpatients services, the nurse management presided over during this period by Miss Franks, who retired in 1966.

Reducing facilities, 1960s
All went well until the 1960s, when the first rationalisations marked the beginning of a long decline. Talk of total closure

even rang in the air as the medical cover from other hospitals was withdrawn in 1964, and with it went the X-ray and operating theatre. Resources were being concentrated on the building of the new Pilgrim Hospital in Boston. So things did not look good for Holbeach, especially after the closing of the maternity unit in 1976, although the physio and occupational therapy departments were at least upgraded and there was certainly sufficient demand to retain the outpatient clinics, with a casualty department manned by rota coverage from six GPs and trained ward staff. Even with fewer facilities the hospital treated 240 patients in 1980, accommodating them from between one to 366 days, with heart disease, stroke and general nursing or 'social' cases predominating.

To the brink of closure –and back
After Ethel Whitehurst retired in the 1980s, even the nurse management became shared with the Johnson Hospital in Spalding. But when in March 1988 the final blow came with the local health authority's announcement that it would close Holbeach Hospital the following year, the local community resolutely refused to take no for an answer, and formed a charitable trust to fund and run a re-launched hospital service. Within five months from April 1989, the Holbeach and East Elloe Hospital Trust exceeded its target of £150,000 by £30,000! It seemed that the old British wartime spirit had reawakened as, to the delight of Trust Chairman John Taylor and Treasurer Peter Coupland, money rolled in from every possible source: from the East Elloe Lions, garden open days, home-made cakestalls and dances, to sponsored and sporting events, pub collections, private donations and those from butchers' and growers' associations. It all reduced the official closure on March 31st 1989 to a mere formality as behind closed doors re-equipping took place and members of the fundraising committee such as Julia Taylor and Joyce Tingle involved themselves in the new décor, while the manager-elect and former night sister Joyce Fines attended personally to a multitude of matters, from clerical details to scrubbing down bedside fitments.

The big day came on September 4th, 1989, with Bill Sleaford reversing the Last In,

First Out principle by being the first patient to be readmitted among the initial dozen installed during opening week. To begin with there were 26 beds available, but thanks to a large legacy from Mrs Ann Waltham's estate, a £400,000 extension later brought this figure up to 40. With the premises on a 25-year lease from the area health authority, and income largely

COLLECTOR'S ITEM. The special plate commissioned to celebrate the re-launch of Holbeach Hospital, 1989.
[Courtesy Peter Coupland.]

sourced by nursing home beds and GP funding, self-sufficiency continues into the Millennium* with, since Joyce Fines' retirement in July 2002, Jean Garner as Manager.

This successful fight to save a hospital which even 20 years before its re-opening had a catchment area of 16,000 people to serve, reminds us that Holbeach's increasing population and property development presents a situation that has severely challenged existing commercial and medical services, and all this has to be considered against a background of what should or should not be conserved to create a satisfactory balance between the town's economic progress, and the preservation of its traditional atmosphere.

The Conservation Area
In June 1970 it was decided by a resolution of the then Holland County Council to designate a Conservation Area in Holbeach. Bounded to the west by the extremities of the old Stukeley Hall grounds (adjacent to Stukeley Hall Drive) and in the east by St John Street, its extremities follow a complex pattern

around the limits of the town centre, and

encompass an area that includes 35 listed buildings, 27 buildings of local heritage interest, and preservation orders on seven trees. Put in more detail it is sectionalised, at the time of writing, as in the map overleaf.

There are therefore many properties full of character in this modestly-sized town, not to mention the wide pedigree of trees that include examples of apple, ash, beech, birch, sweet buckeye, cherry, cypress, elder, elm, holly, hornbeam, horse chestnut, lime, maple. oak, evergreen oak, turkey oak, plane, spruce, sycamore, wellingtonia, willow and yew.

'Cherish your house' was the message in a leaflet reissued in 2002 by the Holbeach & District Civic Society. It encouraged house-owners to consider the original features of their dwellings before altering the appearance, with this advice: 'If you have to replace, aim to have a **faithful reproduction of the original.** There are plenty of good firms locally who can do good reproduction work.'

Mixed reception
But the principle has not always met with total approval. In 1997, a survey conducted by South Holland District Council resulted in a petition signed by over 200

ELEGANCE. Aptly-named High Street premises in the Conservation Area.

people, asking for the Conservation Area to be abolished.

This view was largely endorsed by traders in the town centre. It was unfair, one of

The Conservation Area

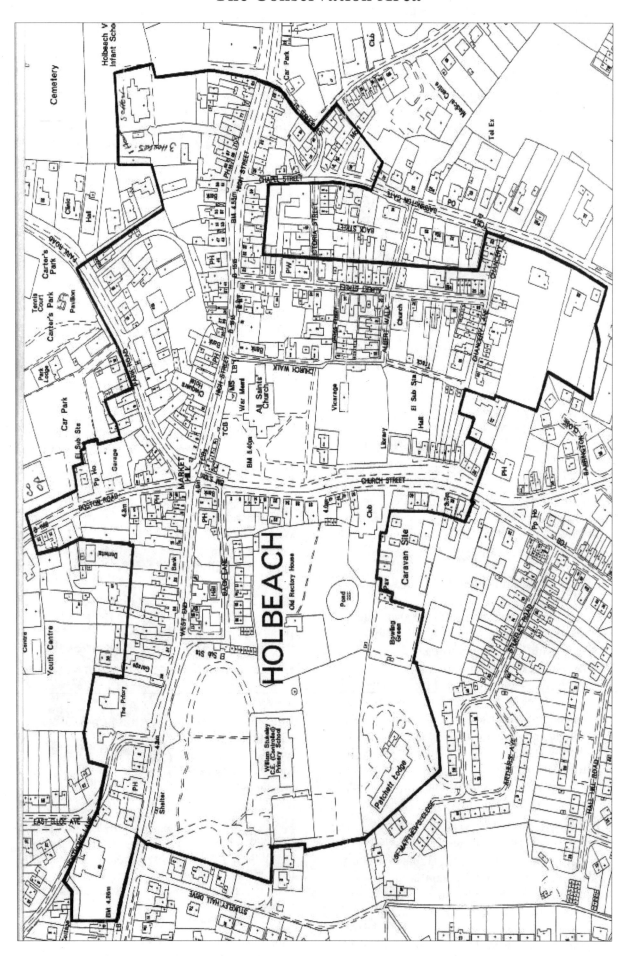

them pointed out, that a business within the Conservation Area should be restricted as to signage and shop front styles when traders only a short distance away, outside the area's boundary, were not. Another felt that there was some justification for conservation where a large enough pedigree prevailed, such as in Lynn or Stamford, but not in Holbeach where there was comparatively little left to preserve. Not oblivious to keeping up appearances however, he had enough faith in the prevailing attitude of the District Council's planning officers to predict that any further development would be tasteful, and not an eyesore.

'Conservation is practical'

In this respect, the appearance of the extended S & D Bookmakers at the beginning of Barrington Gate, completed in April 2001, is a reassuring example of this view.

INTRIGUING PASSAGEWAY. West End House.

But, says the Holbeach & District Civic Society, there are many elements to a conservation area that are more practical than many people realise. Preserving open spaces as more land is built on, ensuring new shop fronts are attractively presented and even installing the right kind of lamp standards, plant tubs and litter bins –all of which has been done over recent years– help to weave a fabric that can only benefit the town, because 'Local people and visitors want a pleasant place to visit and when they do so, businesses flourish'.

GOOD ENOUGH FOR SERENADING. Balcony detail adds to preserved character of the Chequers' yard.

Reservations and achievements

A visit paid by South Holland District Council's Strategic Planning Committee in October 1997 was not a happy affair, resulting in a refusal to extend the Conservation Area to include Carter's Park, the Cemetery, the Youth Centre, the extended garden of the Priory, Victoria Street, Back Street and Chancery Lane. The Committee's general reaction was that too much damage had been done already, particularly over the past 40 years, and local residents were blamed for destroying and devaluing their buildings with unsympathetic modernisation. While this may be true in certain instances, it also brings us back to the Lynn and Stamford comparison, where higher property values and incomes make it easier and more justifiable to carry out maintenance and improvements in keeping with the surroundings. This said, what cannot always be controlled in one area, such as a lurid colour scheme or unsuitable window frame, is made up for in another. Over 2001, for instance, the Civic Society planted two black walnut trees in Stukeley Gardens, and a fern leaf beech tree in the churchyard to replace one blown down in the autumn 2000 storms. New railings were installed at the Fishpond Lane Nature Reserve, and the Society donated £1,500 to the Reading Room refurbishment project in Church Street.

Against all the odds with which the average small town has to contend nowadays –litter, vandalism and destructive, speeding traffic– such efforts do bear fruit. For in 2002 Holbeach won the East Midlands in Bloom First Best Small Town title, thanks to the dedicated efforts of a Bloom committee which ensures that the town looks consistently good enough during spring and summer for a high placing, as distinct from just an instant planting offensive in time for judging day.

Full circle

As South Holland's second largest town, the planners currently feel that the only way for Holbeach to grow is westwards, to the line defined by the

A151 where it links the A17 with the Spalding Road roundabout. If proposals become a reality, attracting a broader range of industry large and small, stimulating the job market, and encouraging agricultural diversification, then better support services and recreational facilities should follow. It is a plan that recaptures the self-reliance and status of medieval times. In which case, we will have come full circle.

♣♣♣♣♣♣

As at early 2004, Holbeach Hospital, with reserves of £911,000, had 46 beds (39 nursing home and 7 doctors' beds), and in the year immediately preceding had attended 5,009 outpatients, accommodated 12,483 nursing-home bed nights and 1,794 doctors' bed nights

Holbeach History at a glance.

AD 54-68: Possible Roman settlement in Holbeach on old railway station site.

AD 650?: Anglo-Saxons first settle on dry land area, naming their village 'Holobech' ('deep brook' or 'stream').

AD 833: Holbeach mentioned in King Wiglaf's charter.

1085: Domesday survey includes Holbeach.

1100s: First church built.

1142-1175: Beginnings of serious land reclamation.

1252: Henry III grants permission to hold a market.

1338-1361: All Saints built on site of previous church.

1536-1540: Dissolution of the monasteries; Church treasures melted down or sold and walls whitewashed.

1687: William Stukeley, famous antiquary, born in Holbeach.

1783: Chequers rebuilt to present external form.

1808: First Methodist Church built in Chapel Street.

1820: Arthur Thistlewood of Holbeach Hurn arrested in the Cato St Conspiracy.

1828: Harrisson's mill in Barrington Gate begins 175 years of milling to date.

1837: Workhouse opens on Fleet Road.

1844: Market House and Assembly Rooms opened on the corner of High Street and Market Hill. All Saints National Girls and Infants School opens in Albert Street.

1845: First Baptist Church built in newly-created Albert St.

1853: Holbeach River in Church Street covered over by a roadway.

1855: New Cemetery opened between present Park Rd and Edinburgh Walk.

1858: Railway reaches Holbeach from Spalding.

1868: Ancient burial ground unearthed between railway station and Hallgate. Bones reburied in Cemetery, 1899.

1872: Sir Norman Angell (real name, Ralph Norman Angell Lane), Nobel Prize Winner 1933 for his book *The Great Illusion*, born at the Mansion House in Holbeach High Street.

1870: Reading Room built (next to present Library)

1877: Boys Board School opens in Church Street.

1894: New Infants School (forerunner of Holbeach County Primary) opens in Boston Road.

1900: First car in Holbeach, owned by Tom Lane.

1906: Kathleen Major, distinguished medieval scholar and Principal of St Hilda's College, Oxford, born in Holbeach.

1929: Hippodrome Cinema opens on present Somerfield site.

1929: Herbert Parkinson Carter donates Carter's Park to the town.

1937: Holbeach Hospital opened on Boston Road.

1949: Tommy Clay founds athletics in Holbeach. Public Library opens in what is now the Pop-In, Market Hill; moves to new premises, 1973.

1949-55: Controversy over East Elloe Rural District Council's right to build council houses on Hallgate. Claims that it invoked a clause in Magna Carta!

1955: Sporting cyclist Les Fensom of Holbeach Wheelers wins North Road Club 24-hour time trial, travelling a distance of 463 miles.

1958: The George Farmer School opens, absorbing pupils from the Boys Board School and the Girls School in the High Street.

1959: Railway passenger services end after 100 years.

1965: Railway closed for good.

1966: New Roman Catholic Church opens on the corner of Foxes Low Road and Fleet Road.

1969: Talbot Hotel closes; demolished 1974.

1970: Sewerage system overhauled. Cinema closes.

1980: Mattimore House on Fleet Road demolished.

1982: New Holbeach County Primary School opened on Boston Road.

1983: Community Centre opened, Fishpond Lane/Damgate

1983 & 1985: Geoff Capes wins World's Strongest Man championships.

1986: New Methodist Church opened in Albert Street.

1993: Stukeley Hall demolished.

1994: New William Stukeley Primary School (founded 1992) opened on site of former Stukeley Hall.

2000: Sally Reddin wins gold medal at the Sydney Paralympics. The George Farmer School uprated to Technology College status.